DEMISE OF THE SOVIET UNION: A Bibliographic Survey of English Writings on the Soviet Legal System 1990-1991

Sequel to *SOVIET LAW IN ENGLISH* and *GORBACHEV'S LAW*

Igor I. Kavass
Vanderbilt University

William S. Hein & Co.
Buffalo, New York
1992

Library Of Congress Cataloging-in-publication Data

Kavass, Igor I.

Demise of the Soviet Union : a bibliographic survey of English writings on the Soviet legal system, 1990-1991 / Igor I. Kavass.

p. cm.

Includes bibliographical references and index.

ISBN 0-89941-804-X

1. Law--Soviet Union--Bibliography. 2. Soviet Union--Politics and government--1985-1991--Bibliography. 3. Soviet Union--Economic policy--1986-1991--Bibliography. I. Title.

KL3.K38 1992

016.34947--dc20

[016.3447009]

92-24865

CIP

Printed in the United States of America.

This volume is printed on acid free paper by

William S. Hein & Co., Inc.

ABSTRACT AND INSTRUCTIONS

This bibliography lists and describes books, articles, papers, and other publications in the English language about law and related subjects in the Soviet Union. It covers works published mainly during the 1990-1991 period.

The arrangement of the book follows the traditional lines of similar bibliographic works. It consists of two types of inter-connected bibliographies:

(1) Author Bibliography
Arranged alphabetically by the authors' names (or by main titles where there are no authors), this bibliography is extensively annotated and cross-referenced. It is preceded by an alphabetical check-list of authors.

(2) Subject Bibliography
Arranged alphabetically by main subjects and, where applicable, by sub-subjects. Within each subject or sub-subject category, the entries are listed alphabetically by authors' names (or by main titles where there are no authors). The entries are not annotated in the Subject Bibliography. Users should turn to the relevant entry in the Author Bibliography if more information is desired. The Subject Bibliography is preceded by an extensively cross-referenced check-list of subject headings.

For the convenience of readers, works written by Soviet authors (i.e., authors living in the Soviet Union) or published in the Soviet Union are indicated in both bibliographies by a star (☆).

The two bibliographies are preceded by a few notes on the current resources for legal research, entitled "Legal Research in the New Age".

Additional notes about subjects:

While many of the subjects used in the Subject Bibliography refer to the standard topics or subject areas of law, there are some subject headings of a more general character. They are intended to aid the user of this book in gaining quick access to writings not strictly on law which might be directly or indirectly relevant to legal research. These particular subject headings are—

Economic System
Foreign Trade
General Studies
Government System
Individual and the Law
and
Political System.

Some of these subject categories are subdivided into more detailed sub-categories. For example, writings on joint ventures in the Soviet Union are listed within the sub-category of that name in the general category on Foreign Trade.

In an effort to highlight the political and economic changes in the Soviet Union and the increased volume of writings thereon, the Subject Bibliography also contains several subject headings such as—

Future of the USSR
Glasnost
Nationalities and Nationalism (there are also separate subject headings for the Baltic and Jews)
Perestroika
and
Private Economic Activity

Other subject headings are more standard. Users are advised to peruse the checklist of subject categories preceding the Subject Bibliography.

Table of Contents

INTRODUCTION

August - December, 1991

The Soviet Union officially ceased to exist at the end of 1991. In August of that year Gorbachev was making his bid for continued leadership of the Soviet Union through the proposed "All-Union Treaty", a declaration hopefully to be signed by the country's republics which would pledge continued support for Gorbachev's reforms and promote continued unity under a centralized government. It was assumed by most Western observers that the treaty would be signed, though it was found to be unsatisfactory in one way or another by almost all of the Soviet Union's diverse factions. It should not be surprising that the Communist Party hard-liners chose this time to attempt a coup, because if the All-Union Treaty came into effect, the Party would lose most of the power it had so far retained throughout the Gorbachev reform era. The August coup failed. The Communist Party was discredited and vilified. And to the astonishment of the Western world, Gorbachev was unable to ressert his leadership when the coup was over.

Boris Yeltsin, the first popularly elected President of the Russian Republic, had already been established as the most prominent of Gorbachev's non-Communist opponents. During the coup he gained widespread popularity and was seen as the primary force in defeating the coup's leaders. It was evident when Gorbachev returned to Moscow that Yeltsin was unwilling to accede to a return to the status quo. In an atmosphere of mixed loyalties and considerable confusion, the central government rapidly lost control.

The disintegration of the Soviet Union took place very quickly. The Baltic republics of Estonia, Latvia, and Lithuania reasserted their independence and won support both internationally (with some reluctance by the United States), and from Yeltsin. As the leaders of the Soviet Union's other republics quickly followed suit in recognizing the Baltic States' independence, Gorbachev was forced to abandon his policy of negotiating a gradual autonomy for the Baltic republics and admit that they had effectively seceded from the Soviet Union. The central government had obviously lost its control over the country. One by one the Soviet republics began to declare their own independence from the Soviet Union—again led by Yeltsin's Russian Republic.

In December, probably in order to preserve some semblance of federation, but more so to put an absolute end to Gorbachev's rule, Yeltsin persuaded most of the non-Baltic republics to establish a Commonwealth of Independent States. The Commonwealth issued the Minsk

Accord, which outlined the loose and rather vague arrangement for continued economic and political cooperation among the republics.

By the end of December Gorbachev resigned as head of the Soviet Union. His resignation marked not only the final days of the Gorbachev Era, but that the Soviet Union itself had ceased to exist.

The Years before the End

The last two years of Gorbachev's rule (1990-1991) were turbulent and uncertain. A large variety of legislation was passed by the Supreme Soviet of the USSR as well as by the larger Congress of People's Deputies, which Gorbachev had created as a broader representative forum for shaping and developing the policies of the Soviet Union. A number of different—and conflicting—economic programs were introduced, but none of them were undertaken consistently or successfully. Gorbachev expressed a wish to improve the economy, but he was neither emotionally nor politically prepared to embrace a complete free market approach. The absence of clear direction from the country's leader, who insisted upon reform, and the opposition of the country's traditional leaders—the Communist Party—led to a rapid deterioration of the country's economy.

Political difficulties, largely ignored during that period by most Western analysts, were even more serious. The extensive and cumbersome government system, centripetally focused on Moscow, was becoming unravelled. Doubts began to appear in the middle echelons of administration and bureaucracy as the leading figures started to abandon the Communist Party ship and leap onto the reform bandwagon. Unfortunately, the reform movement was never unified—there was no clear-cut, well-defined policy which could be implemented. Rather, there was a mix of factions—some idealistic, some power-oriented solely—with no definite winners or losers. Gradually at first, then more rapidly as the former leadership lost force, the government's administrators throughout the Soviet Union began to give their loyalties not to the Moscow center but to the locally emerging "winners"—those political organizations and individuals who were able to step into the power void and maintain control. Many of these local organizations were ethnic in character, or appealed to non-Russian nationalistic populations.

It is impossible to determine at this stage whether Gorbachev was truly unaware of the new dynamic forces which he himself helped to unleash through his liberal policies of *glasnost* and *perestroika*. It is not unlikely, given the history of the Soviet Union, that he assumed in the beginning years that the traditional attitudes of absolute respect for central government authority at every level in the Soviet Union, backed by implicit threat of military force, would preclude the development of any widespread popular movements directly opposed by the government. Throughout his reform program, he was explicit in one respect—he expected the Soviet Union to remain intact. The very fact that various national groups began to agitate for recognition, followed quickly by even stronger demands for autonomy by the republics themselves, indicates that Gorbachev had seriously underestimated the ways in which even limited freedom of speech and openness would undermine totalitarian authority. He made minor concessions towards the independence factions, entered into negotiations (but without any evidence of good faith), at the same time demanding loyalty to the Soviet Union and its central government. Local *nomenklaturas* quickly changed their political ideologies from centralized communism to local nationalism, and established their own government structures.

In the Western world few governments, or even experts in studying the Soviet Union, conceived that it would be possible for this powerful country to break apart. There were a few who speculated upon the viability of the individual republics as independent countries—almost universally the verdict was that they were too intertwined economically and politically to survive as sovereign entities. For every government in the West, it was taken as a given that Gorbachev would be supported in his efforts to maintain unity. Throughout its history Western perceptions of the Soviet Union have been filtered by opinion and censored by government. During the Gorbachev era, though access to information was somewhat broadened, the Western world had no "presence" in the Soviet Union outside Moscow, and had not developed reliable methods to gauge the importance of political developments. Both through inclination and lack of reliable information, governments in the West were blind to the significance of the difficulties facing Gorbachev. It is highly likely that the support Gorbachev received outside his own country led him to make some of the miscalculations which resulted in his failure to retain power.

Despite the political and economic unrest of the early 1990's, the opening of the Soviet Union brought about a tremendous interest in that country among Western businesspeople and investors. The Soviet Union was viewed as a vast untapped marked which would not only bring great riches but also serve as the panacea for the incipient economic ills of the West. This enthusiasm inevitably waned when Western businesses encountered the intractable Soviet red tape and when they became aware of the vacillations in Gorbachev's economic plans. In the event, while there was much publicity for joint ventures and a great deal of visiting to and fro, the number of contracts actually signed was small, and the number of businesses which entered the Soviet Union from the West was even smaller.

Notwithstanding the initial enthusiasm, during Gorbachev's regime the foreign trade of the Soviet Union actually declined, and foreign investment in that country had not appreciably increased by the end. Naturally, a number of other factors were at work—the Soviet Union lost a great deal of its foreign market when it lost its monopoly over the markets of Eastern Europe. "Reform" in the Soviet banking system and controls over foreign investment led to confusion and a break-down in confidence on the part of foreign investors.

Gorbachev's economic legacy was difficulty and hardship. The old systems which worked in fits and starts were undermined and no effective mechanisms were put in their place.

Publishing in the West, 1990-1991

The continuing and rapid changes in the Soviet Union did not deter Western analysts from writing about the Soviet Union at an increasing rate. In fact, publications in the West about the Soviet Union in general as well as its economy, legal system, politics, and society was a growth industry in the early 1990's. Generally writings were brief and very obviously focussed on the business and public-interest markets. Proportionately, there was very little substantive analysis of the Soviet political or legal systems. Publications which attempted to make sense of the rapid changes taking place in the economic system were frequently outdated by the time they were printed and distributed. It became obvious to most Western observers that the spate of new laws emerging from the central government were not to be taken seriously—there was therefore a slowdown in translation of the new laws and analysis of their content. Gradually, a "wait and see" attitude developed among many of the hitherto most prolific Western Sovietologists. That the Soviet Union was in turmoil was evident, and Western writers described some of its most obvious elements well. The Western literature failed almost universally, however, to analyze the depth and the significance of the events in the Soviet Union. It could not do otherwise. The transformation was too profound, and in its details frequently unpredictable; many developments were not even rational.

Soviet legislative activity was both extensive and turbulent. Much of it was also conflicting. During this period, Gorbachev succeeded in acquiring the power to make laws by decree, so that his pronouncements frequently were intended to have the force of law. On the local level, even before independence, the republics began to legislate in earnest. This law-making rarely proceeded systematically. One of the main uses of the law in the Soviet Union had traditionally been to set policy guidelines. The laws created during the 1990-1991 period failed even in this respect—they were frequently contradictory and incomplete. In contrast to the early Gorbachev years, when, for example, a new family law was examined by the Western experts in detail and analyzed for its similarities and differences to pre-Gorbachev Soviet law and other civil law codes, the laws passed by the Soviet legislatures during 1990-1991 were largely ignored in the West. Records were kept of their existence, but comparatively few were translated into English or analyzed. The new legislation of most interest to the Western world dealt with business matters—joint ventures, corporate formation, trade, investment, and taxation. Many of the republics had considerable legislation in these areas in place at the end of 1991.

Much of the English-language legal writing of this period consists of papers presented at hastily organized conferences and symposiums where, in addition to the usual bevy of Western Soviet experts, it was now also possible to invite scholars, publicists, and officials from the Soviet Union itself. Collections of papers covered a wide variety of topics, but a large majority of them focussed on issues of interest to businesses and investors in the West. The quality of the conference papers, as indeed the quality of most of the writing of this period, varies considerably.

An interesting exception to the often superficial publications were the historical books and articles based on information made available with the opening of the Soviet archives and access to previously secret data. Even here, however, Western publishers were looking for something which could be marketed quickly. Therefore the tendency was to popularize rather than produce serious, analytical works. Nevertheless, several authoritative and excellent biographies of Stalin were published by American historians during the early 1990's.

English translations of autobiographical works originally written in Russian by the leading Soviet political figures—including Gorbachev, Yeltsin, Sobchak, and Shevardnadze—were also popular. Whatever their intrinsic literary and historical quality, these books enabled the public in the West to glimpse the personalities, mentalities, and characters of those who played major roles in shaping the destiny of the Soviet Union and its dissolution.

Demise of the Soviet Union: A Bibliographic Survey of English Writings on the Soviet Legal System 1990-1991

This work is an annotated bibliography of books, articles, papers, and other publications on the Soviet law and related subjects published in the English language from 1990 through 1991. It may be used as a sequel to the author's previous volumes — *Soviet Law in English: Research Guide and Bibliography, 1970-1987*, and *Gorbachev's Law: A Bibliographic Survey of English Writings on Soviet Legal Developments 1987-1990.*

The *Demise of the Soviet Union* consists of two parts: a detailed annotated bibliography arranged in alphabetical order by author, and a subject bibliography without annotations arranged in the form of a topical index. Works by Soviet authors or representing primarily the official Soviet viewpoint are preceded by a "☆".

The subject coverage of this work is generally broad. Since the Soviet Union's governmental controls extended into every area of human life, including economic and political activity, works on the political structure and the regulation of economy can be directly relevant to law-oriented research.

The dates of the bibliography refer to dates of publication. The bibliography is not limited to publications relevant to events taking place in the Soviet Union during 1990-1991. Historical studies and analyses which were published during this time-frame are included.

Annotations in the bibliography vary in length. Some titles are not annotated at all because they are self-explanatory and further descriptions of the respective works do not seem to be necessary. To enable researchers to wade through the bulk of material, some works are described and commented on at length. There are also notations of reviews relating to works listed in the bibliography.

Preceding the bibliography is a section entitled "Legal Research in the New Age", which briefly describes some of the information sources—primarily databases and periodicals—useful for current research on law and economics in the new republics of the former Soviet Union.

Unfortunately, the author cannot claim that there are no errors or omissions. The bibliography includes all publications from 1990-1991 personally reviewed by the author or verified by him from publishing records. Please note, however, that there is some overlap for 1990 publications with the previous volume, *Gorbachev's Law*. Publications from 1990 listed in the previous volume are not listed herein.

It is not possible to produce a bibliography of this type alone. Numerous Vanderbilt University law students assisted me in locating and surveying the publications. Peter Garland and William Walker of the Vanderbilt Law Library helped immensely in the bibliographic survey. Marietta LaBauve typed the bits and pieces and assembled a workable manuscript. Ellen Toplon edited and verified the final product. As ever, I am grateful to all those who worked diligently on this project, with attention to detail and willingness to follow through on hints of information to locate frequently obscure sources.

Conclusion

All of the writings included in this bibliography deal with the Soviet Union as it existed until December, 1991. There is no doubt that this bibliography can serve as a useful background, providing a chronology of the events leading up to the disappearance of the Soviet Union, or assisting historians to gain perspective on how the Soviet Union was viewed during this period. It might also be natural to conclude also that the writings of the period 1990-1991 have little relevance to current events in the new countries which formerly constituted the Soviet Union.

The break-up of the Soviet Union was not a revolution in the traditional sense. Politically and economically, the central government ceased to function effectively. The August coup tipped the scales against the Communist Party, and therefore the central government, making it feasible for local leaders to seize the opportunity to push for complete autonomy. In many ways, this was the "least likely" scenario.

In any event, this break-up of a once powerful country was not undertaken by a group of concerted individuals with definite plans for replacing the existing government systems with something new. The new countries quite extensively continue to apply the laws which were made during the Soviet regime. The official thinking on the purposes of law and government, institutions, and particularly on how things should be conducted, has not changed all that much. There has not been a drastic and abrupt termination of the institutions and procedures of the past, not even in the Baltic countries or other fiercely nationalistic republics. The scholarly as well as the popular works which appeared in the West during the *glasnost* period of Gorbachev will have both informational and intellectual value for many years to come. They track not only the collapse of the Soviet regime, but they offer glimpses of changes of thoughts and procedures as well.

The attitudes of those in power and their values have not, as yet, altered significantly. It will take many years for substantial variations to evolve. Some experts say that it may take several generations. It is perhaps appropriate to remember that Lenin predicted it would take four generations to develop a Communist society. With the wisdom of hindsight, it can be said that it took almost four generations for the Communist system to crumble. It is possible that, in future years, the 1990-1991 period may be considered as an important precursor to the formative and transitional stages of the people of the former Soviet Union. At least for some of the former republics, however, this may be an optimistic forecast. There is an equal possibility that some of the new countries will not develop towards more democratic governments or adopt free market economic systems, but rather embrace the former Communist Party's hard-liner approach and re-instate governments along the lines of the pre-Gorbachev Soviet Union. All roads no longer lead to Moscow (despite Boris Yeltsin's efforts to maintain Russia—and himself—as the predominant authority). Only a few months after the dissolution of the Soviet Union, it is too early to predict what new roads will be built and where they will lead.

Igor I. Kavass
May, 1992

Legal Research in the New Age

This volume on the *Demise of the Soviet Union* contains considerable information on materials for conducting research on the Soviet Union as it existed until December, 1991. Indeed, some of the materials are equally useful for researching legal, economic and general events in that part of the world after 1991 as well.

In previous bibliographic surveys, the author offered some preliminary advice to researchers about general reference sources, periodicals, and other information services which might provide background on the Soviet legal system and useful additional information for current research. However, with the break-up of the Soviet Union, many of the customary sources of information have disappeared. Others have become less reliable, or have experienced transformations which are clearly transitional in nature. Information on the former Soviet republics, never easily obtained, is both harder and easier to access now than before. It is harder because communications are imperfect, and the distribution system for official publications has crumbled. For all practical purposes, there is no systemized government distribution at this time. On the other hand, access to some information is easier because many private news and publishing entities have come into existence in Russia and the other new republics. As long as they can make a living, they are keen to publish and distribute information in every shape and form.

If the conditions in the Russian Federation and the other new republics were orderly, this section would consist of a clear and coherent guide for researchers to new materials and sources of information for each country. Unfortunately, the new republics do not have efficient means for disseminating information—and when it comes to "official" publications (e.g., laws, decrees, reports, etc.), the old habit of secrecy keeps raising its ugly head on multiple fronts. Until new research methodologies are developed, the most that can be offered at this moment for those interested in facing the challenge of researching the law as it develops in the new republics are a few sources which the author has found useful in the "new age" for Russia, the Baltics, and the other countries formed from the Soviet Union.

Information Services

Frequently, non-traditional sources can be quite productive for information on legal developments in the new countries which emerged from the Soviet Union.

For example, English translations of laws of the Russian Federation and other new republics are available from:

ASET Consultants, Inc.
Suite 260
2020 North 14th St.
Arlington, VA 22201
Telephone: 703-516-9266
Telefax: 703-516-9269
Prices of the translated items vary.

Even more valuable for researchers are the various electronic databases (usually on-line) containing information on the political, economic and legal developments of the former Soviet Union. A variety of databases are offered in English. Both the scope as well as the geographic reach of these sources is expanding, and for the most part their costs, due to growing competition, are becoming reasonable.

The following is just a sampling of what is available by means of databases. It is by no means complete, and is oriented towards what is available in the United States. There are other resources available in Europe, no doubt.

RUSSIAN LAW DATABASE

A service of English translations of laws, decrees and regulations governing business in Russia and the other countries of the Commonwealth of Independent States. Translations are sold individually. Standing orders are also available. The supplier of this service is—

Business Information International, Ltd.
Suite 224, 5201 Great American Pkwy.
Santa Clara, CA 95056-4180
USA
Telephone: 408-986-1406
Telefax: 408-988-0150

ST. PETERSBURG BUSINESS NEWS

The original *St. Petersburg Business News* is a daily Russian-language newspaper distributed electronically. A digest version of this newspaper is prepared in English and also distributed electronically twice every week (usually Mondays and Thursdays). Each issue of the English version consists of short notes on news events and developments relevant to business, finance, investment, and trade.

The publisher's address—

St. Petersburg Business News Agency
P.O. Box 589
190000 St. Petersburg
Russia
Telephone: 812-278-19-04 *or* 812-278-18-12
Telefax: 812-278-16-33
Telex: 121465 LSWS SU

In the United States the *St. Petersburg Business News* can also be accessed over INTERNET, a computer network which is connected to networks in Europe, which in their turn have direct links with Russian networks.

The cost of this English-language news service is surprisingly reasonable. In early 1992 it was only US$15/month.

OFFICIALS AND BUSINESSMEN OF RUSSIA

This is a newly advertised electronic publication, which supposedly will serve as a "Who's Who" for today's Russian governments and businesses. It is intended to include telephone numbers for 70-odd Russian regions, information on banks, joint ventures, and other commercial enterprises. The database will be updated quarterly, and is available in multi-language formats. It is a database which is intended to be transferred to one's microcomputer—requiring at least 6 megabytes of available hard-disk space.

Electronic mail addresses for more information:

korsa@zooid.guild.org *or*
book@korsa.uukorsa.canrem.com

LEXIS

The Mead Corporation produces a number of databases in conjunction with its massive legal information service—LEXIS.

The LEXIS database is divided into a number of sub-sections called "libraries", each of which contains "files". It is sometimes impossible to determine the sources of information in each individual library/file, and researchers will need to exercise patience in retrieving useful materials. When known, titles of source publications used for the database files are included in parentheses. Please note, however, that this does not mean that full-text reproductions of each title appear in the respective databases. Frequently the material from the printed publication is edited and excerpted for the database.

- INTLAW Library
  - USSR file
- World Library
  - Mosnws file (*Moscow News*)
  - SBE file (*Soviet Business and Economic News*)
  - SBLaw file (*Soviet Business Law Report*)
  - SPD file (*Soviet Press Digest*)
  - Sovleg file (Soviet legal texts)
- ASIAPE Library
  - Sovnws (*Kremlin International News Broadcast*)
- Europe Library
  - USSR file
  - CDSP file (*Current Digest of the Soviet Press*)
  - DISUSEV file (*Business Eastern Europe* and *Doing Business with Eastern Europe*)
- NEXIS Library
  - ITAR-TASS file (news agency reports)

DIALOG

DIALOG databases are subscribed to either independently or through the WESTLAW legal database system.

The DIALOG database is not law-oriented, but contains some information which may be of interest to legal research in its SOVIETPR database, which contains excerpts from the *Current Digest of the Soviet Press*. DIALOG makes the BIS-Intl database available to its subscribers, but not WESTLAW subscribers. BIS-Intl contains excerpts from *Business Eastern Europe* and *Doing Business with Eastern Europe*.

Periodicals

The whole world of periodical literature on the Soviet Union is in even more turmoil than the Soviet Union was before its collapse. A comprehensive survey is not only impractical, but impossible at this stage. The following is a summary of the author's notes on when and where to look, including what titles have changed and which of the previously recommended publications have ceased to exist.

Baltfax.

A combined news bulletin of *Interfax*, the leading non-government news agency in Russia, and the *Baltic News Service*. Bulletins are issued at least four times a day. Subscribers include most major world news agencies.

Annual subscription rates, early 1992: US$200/month.

Baltic Business Bulletin. West Newton, MA: Baltic Ventures, Inc.

A monthly 8-10 page newsletter focussing on economic and business news.

Subscription price, 1992: US$ 260.

Baltic Observer.

A weekly newspaper in English on political, economic and business developments in the Baltic states. Includes legislative reviews and government actions.

Available in the United States from Copyland/Baltic Observer, 558 Pilgrim Dr., Foster City, CA 94404. Telephone 415-341-2679; Telefax 415-345-5116. Annual subscription for 1992: US$85.

BNA'S Eastern Europe Reporter. Washington, D.C.: The Bureau of National Affairs, Inc., Oct. 1991-

The most timely and comprehensive of the wide range of newsletters on developments of interest to business in Eastern Europe, including the former Soviet Union. Published every two weeks since October, 1991, it has been very prompt and exceptionally reliable in reporting the latest changes and developments. Occasionally includes English translations of new laws.

The subscription price for 1992 is US$795 (overseas airmail additional).

Business Eastern Europe. London: Business International Ltd.

A weekly newsletter which includes information about the former Soviet Union.

Annual subscription 1992—US$1060 or £660. United States subscriptions—Telephone 312-704-0381; Telefax 312-704-0388. United Kingdom subscriptions—Telephone 441-493-6711; Telefax 441-491-2107.

Butterworth's Central and East European Business Law Bulletin. London: Butterworth's, 1990-

FORMER TITLE: *Butterworth's Soviet and East European Business Law Bulletin*.

A quarterly newsletter edited by the law firm of Cole, Corette and Abrutyn. It consists of short articles and notes on new legal developments.

Subscription in 1992: £200 or US$425.

Commersant.

Founded in 1990 as the publication of the USSR Union of Cooperatives, this weekly newspaper reports in an interesting and generally reliable manner news from throughout the former Soviet Union (but mainly Russia) which may be of interest to businesspeople. Some reports tend to be on the sensational side. The paper is published simultaneously in Russian and English.

Subscriptions outside Russia are available through a wide range of agencies. Costs in 1992 range between US$160 to US$200 a year.

Doing Business in Eastern Europe. Bicester, Oxfordshire, UK: CCU Editions Ltd., 1991-

A monthly newsletter about legal and administrative developments in Central and Eastern Europe, including the former Soviet Union, which may be of interest to foreign businesses and investors. Each issue, some 20-30 pages long, consists of short articles, notes, and tables. The information is surprisingly current. The contributors are predominantly attorneys, members of large law firms, who specialize in the legal systems of Central and Eastern Europe.

The subscription in early 1992 was US$230 (with additional start-up and airmail charges). The publisher's telephone number is 0869-253-300; Telefax 0869-245-814.

Doing Business with the USSR. London: Business International Ltd.

Business International Ltd. publishes a multi-volume looseleaf service entitled *Doing Business with Eastern Europe*. One volume in the series, called *Doing Business with the USSR*, is particularly relevant for legal research into Soviet law. Updates for the series are monthly; updates for the individual volumes are quarterly. This is a highly reliable and authoritative source of information.

Eastern Europe Business Bulletin. Washington, D.C.: Eastern Business Information Center, International Trade Administration, U.S. Department of Commerce.

A monthly newsletter that includes short articles about developments in Eastern Europe and the former Soviet Union of interest to American businesses. Also has information about programs and policies of the United States which relate to the conduct of trade and business with the Central and East European countries.

Available free.

East European Business Law. London: Financial Times.

One of a series of specialized newsletters published by the *Financial Times* in London. It comes out on a monthly basis and contains short articles or notes on legal developments in all of Eastern Europe, including the former Soviet Union, of interest to businesspeople.

1991 subscription: £375 annually.

East-West Executive Guide. Concord, MA: World Trade Executives, Inc., 1991-

This well-written and competently edited newsletter reports on business-related developments in politics, laws, economics, and government throughout all of the countries which have emerged from the former Soviet Union, as well as other Central and Eastern European countries. Each issue has about 30 pages. The information is presented in a clear and concise manner.

This publication incorporates the previous *East/West Business Report*. Subscription in 1992 is US$576. Publisher's telephone: 401-454-2000.

Environmental Policy Review. Jerusalem: Marjorie Mayrock Center for Soviet and East European Research, Faculty of Social Sciences, The Hebrew University, 1987-

This journal contains short papers and reports on environmental problems in Eastern Europe and the former Soviet Union. Most of the papers either report factually on the incidence of pollution in specific regions or are scientific in character. Some papers discuss legal and policy issues.

In early 1992 the subscription was US$15 annually.

Most-Pravo Newsletter (Legislation, Practice and Commentary: The Commonwealth of Independent States and the Republics). London: Interlist, 1991-

This monthly newsletter is prepared by the Moscow law firm of Most-Pravo. Each issue, about 12 pages in length, consists of short summaries of news legislation and presidential decrees on matters of interest to foreign businesses and investors. Despite the broad geographic subtitle, the summaries deal predominantly with the laws of the Russian Federation.

The publisher advises that in addition to the monthly newsletters, there are also four special issues a year as well as additional supplements. *Most-Provo Newsletter* is expensive. As of mid-1992, the annual subscription is £395.

The Parker School Bulletin on Soviet and East European Law. Ardsley-on-Hudson, NY: Transnational Juris Publications, 1990-.
NAME CHANGED TO *Parker School Survey of East European Law (SEEL)*.
Published ten times a year, it consists of short articles on new laws and other current legal developments.

Problems of Communism. Washington, D.C.: Documentary Studies Section, United States Information Agency, 1952-1992.
This venerable and scholarly journal ceased publication with the May issue of 1992.

Review of Central and East European Law. The Hague: Martinus Nijhoff.
FORMER TITLE: *Review of Socialist Law*.
This successor to the *Review of Socialist Law* continues to be edited by the Documentation Office for East European Law at the University of Leiden in the Netherlands, and should continue to be a mainstay for substantive information on legal developments in Central and Eastern Europe.

RFE/RL Research Report. Radio Free Europe/Radio Liberty.
A MERGER OF *Report on the USSR* and *Report on Eastern Europe*, also published by Radio Free Europe/Radio Liberty.
The new publication, like its predecessors, is issued weekly. In its new format, this publication is one of the best and most timely information sources on the countries which have emerged from the former Soviet Union.
1992 subscription rate: US$150.

Russia and Commonwealth Business Law Report. Washington, D.C.: Buroff Publications, 1991-
TITLE CHANGED FROM: *Soviet Business Law Report*.
This newsletter tracks the latest legal developments in the former Soviet Union. Each issue has about 12 pages.
Subscription cost 1992: US$970.

Russian Far East Update. Seattle, WA: RFEV.
FORMER TITLE: *Soviet Far East Update*.
A monthly newsletter on trade, business and economic developments in the Russian Far East.
Subscription costs, 1991: US$190 (US$220 outside the United States and Canada). Publisher's telefax 206-583-8345.

Russian Politics: A Journal of Translations. Armonk, NY: M.E. Sharpe, Inc., Summer 1992-
FORMER TITLE: *Soviet Law and Government*.
The new publication, intended to begin in summer, 1992, will be published biweekly.

Soviet Journal of International Law.
Publication of this journal was announced in 1991. Its founders were supposed to be the State Institute of International Relations of the USSR Ministry of Foreign Affairs and the Union of Jurists of the USSR. One issue appeared in early 1991 with articles originally written in Russian and translated into English.
It is not certain whether this journal is still being published.

Soviet Law and Government. Armonk, NY: M.E. Sharpe, Inc.
TITLE CHANGING TO: *Russian Politics: A Journal of Translations*.
The subscription in 1992 is US$390 (US$423 outside the United States.

Soviet Statutes and Decisions. Armonk, NY: M.E. Sharpe, Inc., 1964-
TITLE CHANGING TO: *Statutes and Decisions: Laws of the USSR and Its Successor States*.
Continuing the tradition of the original publication, this bimonthly service is intended to contain translations of laws and other important documents.
The subscription in 1992 is US$441 (US$474 outside the United States). Publisher's telephone 914-273-1800; Telefax 914-273-2106.

Ukrainian Business Digest.
A monthly publication containing information of interest to foreign businesses and investors, including current legislation and government actions, joint venture and foreign trade practices, and economic trends.
Available in the United States from Ukrainian Business Digest, P.O. Box 3127, Westport, CT 06880; Telephone 203-221-7450; Telefax 203-221-7414.

USSR Legal Materials. Ardsley-on-Hudson, NY: Transnational Juris Publications, 1990-1991.

CEASED PUBLICATION. REPLACED BY:

English translations of laws enacted in the Baltic countries (Estonia, Latvia, and Lithuania) are included in the publisher's *Central and Eastern European Legal Materials*.

English translations of the laws enacted by the non-Baltic republics of the former Soviet Union are published in a new Transnational Juris looseleaf volume entitled *Legal Materials: Russian Federation, Ukraine, Belarus*, etc.

Work Papers on Soviet Law. London: Interlist, 1991-

An irregular series of laws and documents in English translation published since mid-1991. Each issue is devoted to a particular topic, and consists of Russian texts and English translations. The publisher advises that translations into other languages may be arranged. As of mid-1992 the following issues have been published:

The Sakhalin Free Economic Zone, July 1991 (legislation and other documents);

The Limited Responsibility Society, December 1991 (model documentation, compiled by V.V. Mukhacheva).

FOREIGN BROADCAST INFORMATION SERVICE (FBIS)

The United States Foreign Broadcast Information Service (FBIS) formerly published a number of useful series of newsletters, bulletins, etc., on the Soviet Union and Eastern Europe. William Walker of the Vanderbilt Law Library has prepared the following summary of his research on what has happened to these publications and what new titles have emerged:

Daily Report: Soviet Union

(Alternate title: *FBIS Daily Report: Soviet Union*)

The name was changed as of January, 1992 to *Daily Report: Central Eurasia* (or *FBIS Daily Report: Central Eurasia*). Prior to the name change, at some point in 1991, some material on the Soviet republics was transferred from the *Daily Report* to a new publication, *FBIS Report: Soviet Union, Republic Affairs*.

FBIS Report: Soviet Union, Republic Affairs.

Incorporates some materials from the *Daily Report* (see above). Also contains coverage of material on Soviet republics which was previously included in the following series: *JPRS Report: Soviet Union, Economic Affairs*; and *JPRS Report: Soviet Union, Political Affairs*.

The *FBIS Report: Soviet Union, Republic Affairs* split sometime in 1991 into two new publications: *FBIS Report: Soviet Union, Russian Affairs*; and *FBIS Report: Soviet Union, Baltic States and Republic Affairs*.

FBIS Report: Soviet Union, Baltic States and Republic Affairs.
For origin, see above entry.
At some point in late 1991 or early 1992 the title was changed to: *FBIS Report: Central Eurasia, Baltic and Eurasian States.*

As a result of all the title changes, combinations of contents, etc., the current (as of May, 1992) FBIS publications on the Soviet Union and its former republics appear to be—

DAILY REPORT: CENTRAL EURASIA (also known as *FBIS DAILY REPORT: CENTRAL EURASIA*)
FBIS REPORT: SOVIET UNION, RUSSIAN AFFAIRS
FBIS REPORT: CENTRAL EURASIA, BALTIC AND EURASIAN STATES

As its name indicates, the "Daily Report" is issued daily, Monday through Friday. The frequency of the other FBIS publications is unknown—most of the old FBIS series were issued on an irregular basis.

Reference Books

Not surprisingly, there are no new long, detailed surveys of the legal systems of the new republics, with helpful charts delineating governmental authority and explaining how things work. When traditional publication and information systems break down, it is helpful to know who is doing what and where. More than ever before effective research will depend on personal contacts to provide reliable information.

Archie Brown's *THE SOVIET UNION: A BIOGRAPHICAL DICTIONARY* (London: George Weidenfeld and Nicolson Ltd., 1990; New York: Macmillan, 1991) provides good information on individuals. While it is concerned with officials of the former Soviet Union, it must be remembered that many of these same persons hold similar positions of authority under the new regimes.

Another handy reference work published in 1990, *POLITICAL AND ECONOMIC ENCYCLOPEDIA OF THE SOVIET UNION AND EASTERN EUROPE*, edited by Stephen White (Harlow, Essex, England: Longman Group UK Ltd.), contains information about government, politics, economics, religion, nationality issues, etc., as well as short descriptions of countries, biographies of leading personalities, and a chronology of events. Unfortunately, much of the information has been made obsolete or inaccurate by the extensive and rapid changes in the Soviet Union. However, it can still be useful as a general guide to spotting what exactly has changed and what hasn't when looking at the systems of government in the new republics.

DEMISE OF THE SOVIET UNION: Annotated Bibliography by Author

CHECK LIST OF AUTHORS

ANNOTATED AUTHOR BIBLIOGRAPHY: CHECKLIST OF AUTHORS

NOTE: A "☆" indicates that the author is Soviet and the author's writings present the official Soviet perspective.

☆Afanasyeva, Larisa
☆Agayev, Ednan T.
Ajani, Gianmaria
☆Alexeyev, Sergei
☆Aliyev, Rafik
Allison, William C., V
Allworth, Edward
Anderson, Edgar
Andrew, Christopher
Apostolakis, Bobby E.
Arbess, Daniel J.
☆Artemova, Tatyana M.
Artz, Donna E.
Åslund, Anders
Atkinson, Scott
Augustyn, Francene M.
Aulin, Lisen
Aurbach, Laurenc J.
Avner, Michael

Bagley, T.M.
Baker, John H.
☆Balkina, M.A.
Barale, Lucille A.
Barbanel, Jack A.
☆Bardina, Marina P.
Barry, Donald B.
Barschevsky, Mikhail
☆Baturin, Yuri[y] M.
Bazyler, Michael J.
Beichman, Arnold
Belkindas, Misha
Berg, Ger P. van den
Beissinger, Mark
Berkowitz, Julie S.
Berliner, Rochelle S.
Berman, Harold J.
Beyme, Klaus von
Birenbaum, David E.
Black, J.L.
Blase, John C.
Blaustein, Albert P.
Block, Kevin P.
Blueger, Valentin
Bociurkiw, Bohdan R.
Boczek, Boleslaw Adam
☆Bogomolov, Oleg T.
☆Boguslavskii[y], Mark M.
Bohn, John A., Jr.
☆Bondarenko, V.S.
Bonnell, Victoria E.
Bonnie, Richard J.
Borcke, Astrid von
☆Borodin, Stanislav
Bova, Russell
Brabant, Jozef M. van
Brada, Josef C.
Bradley, A.P.M.
☆Braginskii[y], Mikhail I.
Branson, Louise
Breslauer, George W.
☆Brinchuk, M.M.
Brown, Archie
Brunner, Georg
Bryner, Cyril
Brzezinski, Zbigniew
Buchsweiler, Meir
Bulsys, Joseph A.
Burt, Jeffrey A.
Butler, William E.
Butterfield, Jim
Buxbaum, Richard M.
☆Bykov, Aleksandr N.

Calingaert, Daniel
Carey, Sarah C.

Carlisle, Donald S.
Carpenter, Russell H., Jr.
Carr, Josephine
Carter, Stephen K.
Carty, Anthony
Chandler, Andrea
☆Chistiakov, Nikolai F.
Clark, David S.
Claudon, Michael P.
Clingan, Thomas A., Jr.
Connor, Walter D.
Conquest, Robert
Cook, Linda J.
Cooper, Julian
Copeland, Emily A.
Critchlow, James
☆Czaplinski, W.

☆Danilenko, Gennady M.
☆Danilenko, Viktor
Davis, Nathaniel
Dean, Richard N.
DeBenedictis, Don J.
Deriabin, Peter
Desai, Padma
Diuk, Nadia
Dobson, Richard B.
Doder, Dusko
☆Doronin, Igor G.
☆Drugueva, Olga
D'Zurilla, William T.

Elferink, Alex Oude
☆Emelyanov, Alexei.
English, Richard D.
☆Entin, Vladimir L.
☆Eventov, Zinoviy M.

☆Faminsky, Igor P.
☆Fedorenko, Sergei
☆Fedorov, Vladimir N.
☆Fedotov, Mikhail A.
Feige, Edgar L.
Feldbrugge, F.J.M.
Felker, Timothy L.
☆Feofanov, Iurii.
Fitch, Stephen D.
Fitzmaurice, M.
Flanz, Gisbert H.
Floroff, Olga
Fogelkou, Anders
Franckx, Eric
Fraser, Niall M.
Freeman, M.D.A.
French, Hillary F.
Frenkel, William G.
Friedlander, Michael
Furtado, Charles F., Jr.

☆Gamaiunov, Igor
Garbrisch, Hubert
Gardner, Richard N.
George, Arthur L.
Georgopoulos, Zach
Geron, Leonard
Getty, J. Arch
Gifford, Donald C.
Ginsburgs, George
Girnius, Kestutis
Gitelman, Zvi
Giuliani, Federico
Gleason, Gregory
Glick, Steven M.
Goble, Paul A.
Gödan, Jürgen Christoph
Goldberg, Stephanie B.
Goldman, Marshall I.
Goldman, Stuart
Goldstein, Gordon
Goldstein, Irving
☆Gorbachev, Mikhail
Gordievsky, Oleg
☆Gorin, Alexander
Gotbaum, Noah E.
☆Gradov, Yuri
Grancelli, Bruno
Grazin, Igor
Griffin, Andrew T.
Grzybowski, Kazimierz
Gureckas, Algimantas P.
☆Gureyev, S.
Gutner, Tamar L.
☆Gutsenko, Konstantin

Hajda, Lubomyr
Halbach, Uwe
Hanke, Steve H.
Hanson, Philip

Harwin, Judith
Havlik, Peter
Hazard, John N.
Heitman, Sidney
Henderson, Jane
Hendley, Kathryn
Herlach, Mark D.
Hertzfeld, Jeffrey M.
Hines, Jonathan H.
Hipel, Keith W.
Hobér, Kaj
Hogan, James E.
Holland, William W.
Hosking, Geoffrey
Houri, Nicole M.
Hoya, Thomas W.
Huber, Robert T.
Huskey, Eugene
Huttenbach, Henry R.

☆Ikonitskaya, I.A.
Iliukhin, Viktor
Ilves, Toomas Hendrik
Irwin, Zachary
☆Ivanov, S.A.

Jaworsky, John
Jones, Anthony
Jorgensen-Dahl, Arnfinn
Juviler, Peter

Kalicki, Jan H.
☆Kamenetskaya, Elena P.
Kampelman, Max M.
Karatnycky, Adrian
Karklins, Rasma
☆Karpetz, Igor I.
☆Kartashkin, Vladimir A.
Kaser, Michael
☆Katkov, Alexander L.
Kavass, Igor I.
☆Kazimirchuk, V.P.
Kelley, Donald R.
Kellman, Barry
Kennedy, R. Cameron
Khazanov, Anatoly
☆Khazova, O.
☆Khlestov, O.N.
☆Khudyakova, Lyudmila S.
☆Kiselev, Sergei N.
Kitchin, William
Kitching, Laurence P.A.
☆Klimenko, Boris M.
☆Klishin, Alexei A.
Knight, Amy W.
Knudsen, Holger
☆Koldacva, N.P.
Kolkey, Daniel M.
☆Kolodkin, Anatoly L.
☆Kondrashov, Stanislav
☆Korolev, Ivan S.
☆Kortunov, Sergei V.
Kramer, John M.
☆Krans, Maksim
☆Krasnov, Mikhail
☆Krupnik, Igor
☆Krylov, Boris S.
☆Kudryavtsev, Vladimir
Kuhlman, James A.
Kuiper, W.G.
☆Kumanin, E.V.
☆Kurashvili, Boris.
Kuromiya, Hiroaki
Kux, Stephen
☆Kuznetsov, Valerii I.
☆Kvint, Vladimir
Kwiatkowska, Barbara

LaFollette, Karen
Lampert, Nick
Landfried, Christine
Langer, Robert E.
Langrind, Peter M.
Lapidus, Gail W.
☆Larin, Aleksander M.
Lawrence, Paul R.
☆Lazarev, B.M.
☆Lazarev, M.I.
☆Lediakh, Irina A.
LeDonne, G.P.
Lee, Janet
Lefeber, R.
☆Lemeshev, Mikhail
Leonard, Edward S.
☆Leont'eva, A.V.
Levey, David H.
Levin, Martin P.

Lewenz, Susan M.H.
Lisitsyn, Eugene N.
☆Litavrin, Petr. G.
Litman, Gary V.
☆Livshits, R.Z.
Loeber, Dietrich André
Lowe, Vaughan
Ludwikowski, Rett R.
☆Lukasheva, Yelena
☆Lukashuk, Igor I.
Lukic, Reneo

MacDonald, Bruce A.
Madara, Eugene E.
Maggs, Peter B.
Maillet, Lynda L.
Maisto, G.
Makay, John J.
☆Mamiofa, Iosif E.
☆Mamoot, Leonid
☆Mamutov, V.K.
Markovits, Inga
Marples, David R.
☆Maslov, Alexander
☆Maslov, Vyacheslav O.
Mason, David S.
Matthews, Mervyn
☆Matyukhin, Georgy
Maurins, A.
Mayer, Carl J.
McAuley, Alastair
McCauley, Martin
McLure, Charles E., Jr.
McNeill, John H.
McWhinney, Edward
Mears, H. Michael
Melville, Andrei
Meri, Lennart
Meron, Theodor
☆Meshkov, Aleksei Yu.
Mihalisko, Kathleen
☆Milchakova, Natalia G.
Millar, James R.
Mishchenko, P.
Misiunas, Romuald J.
Moody, James E.
Moon, David
Morgan, John
Morrison, John
Morton, John
Motyl, Alexander J.
☆Movchan, A.P.
☆Mozolin, Viktor P.
☆Muchlinski, P.T.
Muller, Peter-Michael
☆Mullerson, Ray
☆Mullerson, Rein A.
Muravina, E
☆Musatov, Vladimir

Nahaylo, Bohdan
☆Naumov, Alexander
☆Nersesyants, Vladik
Newburg, Andre W.G.
Newcity, Michael
Nigh, Douglas
Nightingale, Christopher
☆Nikitinsky, Leonid

Obláth, Gábor
Oda, Hiroshi
Odom, William E.
O'Donnell, Thomas A.
Olcott, Martha Brill
☆Orlov, Lev N.
Osakwe, Christopher
Ostreng, Willy
Owen, Thomas C.
Oxenstierna, Susanne

Palmer, Matthew S.R.
Paul, Allen
Pearson, Raymond
Pearson, Thomas S.
Perkins, Roswell B.
Pete, Peter
Pettibone, Peter J.
Phillips, Jeremy
☆Piasheva, Larissa
☆Pichugin, Boris M.
☆Platonova, Natalya L.
Plender, Richard
Plotnieks, Andris
Pockney, B.P.
☆Podlesnyi, Pavel T.
☆Polenina, S.V.
☆Polubinskaya, Svetlana

☆Popov, Vladimir
☆Portnoy, Mikhail A
Pospielovsky, Dimitry V.
Potichnyi, Peter J.
Powell, David E.
Pravda, Alex
Prins, Corien
Pryde, Philip R.

Quigley, John

Racklin, Dimitri P.
Rácz, Margit
Radon, Jenik
Rakowska-Harmstone, Teresa
Ramans, Miervaldis
☆Ranenko, Lyudmila A.
☆Ranenko, V.
Razvigorova, Evka
Redway, A. James
Remington, Thomas F.
☆Reshetov, Lurii A.
Richter, Sándor
Rigby, T.H.
Rittersporn, Gabor T.
Roberts, Geoffrey R.
Roberts, Paul Craig
Robinson, Nicholas A.
☆Rodina, Lyudmila A.
Ro'i, Yaacov
☆Romanova, O.B.
Rosencranz, Armin
Rossi, Jacques
Rosten, Keith A.
Roth, Stephan J.
☆Roulko, Eugeniy T.
☆Rozenberg, Mikhail
☆Rubanov, A.A.
☆Rubanov, Vladimir
Rubin, Gary E.
Rush, Myron

☆Sadovoy, Eugene
☆Saguirion, Artemy A.
Saliman, S. Gerald
Salter, Leonard M.
☆Samorodov, A.
Samuelian, Thomas J.
Sanjian, Andrea Stevenson
☆Savinkin, Alexander
☆Savitskii, Valerii
Schmid, Karin
Schmidt, Gustav
Schmitt, Michael N.
Schneider, Eberhard
Schneider, Richard C., Jr.
Schroeder, Gertrude E.
Schuler, Kurt
Schwartz, Eric J.
Schweisfurth, Theodor
Scotland, Francis A.
Scott, Antony
Sedaitis, Judith B.
Selianovsky, Sergo
☆Semeyko, Aleksei L.
☆Semilutina, Natalya G.
Shadbolt, R.A.
☆Shakhnazarov, Georgy
Shanks, Robert B.
☆Sharafetdinov, Nuriman
Sharlet, Robert
☆Shcherbak, Iurii
☆Shcherbakov, V.I.
Sheedy, John F.
Sheehy, Ann
☆Sheinis, Zinovy
Shelley, Louise I.
☆Sheremet, Konstantin
Sherr, Alan B.
☆Shevardnadze, Eduard
Shillinglaw, Thomas J.
☆Shinkaretskaya, Galina G.
Silliman, Emily
Simes, Dimitry
☆Simkin, Lev
Simmons, David M.
Simon, Gerhard
Simons, William B.
Skolnick, Joanne
☆Slavin, M.M.
Slider, Darrell
☆Smagin, Mikhail
☆Smidovich, Nikita P.
Smith, Cynthia M.
Smith, Gordan B.
Smith, Graham
Smith, Hedrick

Sneider, Carolyn M.
Snowe, Olympia J.
☆Sobchak, Anatoly A.
Soderquist, Larry D.
Solchanyk, Roman
Solomon, Peter H., Jr.
☆Soloviev, A.
Solzhenitzyn, Aleksandr
Soros, George
Speekhard, Rebecca A.
Sperber, Jeffrey
Spring, D.W.
Sprudzs, Adolf
Standing, Guy
Starr, S. Frederick
Steckelman, Peter D.
Stephan, Paul B., III
Strautmanis, J.
Stubbs, Eric A.
Sunstein, Cass R.
Suny, Ronald G.
☆Sviridenko, Oleg
Swaford, Michael
☆Sydorenko, Svetlana

Tanzman, Edward A.
Tatu, Michael
Theroux, Eugene
Thompson, Kenneth W.
Thompson, Lorri M.
Tiefenbrun, Susan W.
Timmermans, Wim A.
☆Timoshenko, Alexandre S.
Tolz, Vera
Toop, R. Scott
Torbert, Preston M.
Trapans, Andris
Trapans, Jan Arveds
Treml, Vladimir G.
☆Trofimov, Vladimir
Tucker, Robert C.
☆Tumanov, Vladimir
☆Tunkin, Grigory I.
Tupper, Stephen
Turro, John
☆Tuzmukhamedov, Bakhtiar R.

☆Uljanov, Eugene
☆Ul'yanov, Mikhail I.

Vacic, Aleksandar M.
Vaksberg, Arkady
Vardys, V. Stanley
☆Vasil'ev, Andrei
Vause, W. Gary
Vecchio, Mark S.
☆Vereshchetin, Vladlen S.
Vierdag, E.W.
☆Vilegjanina, Elena E.
☆Vinogradov, Sergei V.
Vizulis, Izidors Joseph
Vlachoutsicos, Charalambos
☆Volkogonov, D
☆Volkov, F.M.
☆Vorobyova, Olga V.

Wädekin, Karl-Eugen
Walker, Edward
Waller, Robert L.
Walters, Peter
Watts, Ronald
Wcisclo, Francis W.
Webb, William T.
Welt, Leo G.B.
White, Stephen
White, Walter H.
Whitman, Sylvia
Winiecki, Jan
Winter, David
Wolf-Laudon, Gottfried
Wyman, Lowry

☆Yablokov, A.V.
☆Yakovlev, Alexander M.
☆Yakovleva, Evgeniya L.
☆Yakushev, L.P.
☆Yegorov, Sergei A.
Yuan, Cheng
☆Yudin, Alexei

Zanft, Oksanna
Zeidman, Philip F.
Ziegler, Charles E.
Zile, Zigurds L.
Zimbler, Brian L.
Zisk, Kimberly Marten
☆Zmeyevskii, Aleksandr V.
Zuljan, Ralph

DEMISE OF THE SOVIET UNION:

ANNOTATED BIBLIOGRAPHY BY AUTHOR

A

☆Afanasyeva, Larisa. "Insurance and Risk Management of Joint Ventures in the USSR", *22 NEW YORK UNIVERSITY JOURNAL OF INTERNATIONAL LAW AND POLITICS* 447-459 (1990).

Insurance and other methods of risk reduction are generally not discussed in works on joint ventures. In this article a Soviet law expert examines this important and academically much neglected subject.

☆Agayev, Ednan T.
See Stephan, Paul B. III., and Boris M. Klimenko.

Ajani, Gianmaria. "The Soviet Experience with Codification: Theoretical and Comparative Perspectives", in *THE SOVIET SOBRANIE OF LAWS*, edited by Richard M. Buxbaum and Kathryn Hendley (Berkeley, CA: University of California at Berkeley, 1991), pp. 184-196.

☆Alexeyev, Sergei. *LAW AND LEGAL CULTURE IN SOVIET SOCIETY*. Moscow: Progress Publishers, 1991. 214 pp.

A somewhat confusing (and confused) explanation of the function of law in the Soviet Union during the Perestroika era. Even though this is one of the first full-length books to come out of the Soviet Union critical of the past, the explanation nevertheless tends to be heavily "dialectic" in that it deals with the law in a predominantly abstract manner. In this respect the book is reminiscent of pre-Perestroika legal writings

The author is a Soviet legal scholar and a correspondent member of the USSR Academy of Sciences. The book, originally published in Russian under the title *Pravo i Pravovaia Kultura v Sovetskom Obshchestve*, was translated into English by Jane Sayer.

☆Aliyev, Rafik.
See THE HEARTBEAT OF REFORM; SOVIET JURISTS AND POLITICAL SCIENTISTS DISCUSS THE PROGRESS OF PERESTROIKA.

Allison, William C., V. "Self-Determination and Recent Developments in the Baltic States" (Comment), 19 *DENVER JOURNAL OF INTERNATIONAL LAW AND POLICY* 625-640 (1991).

A summary of the different arguments relating to the illegality of the annexation of the Baltic countries by the Soviet Union in 1940, and a brief account of recent political developments in Estonia, Latvia, and Lithuania.

Allworth, Edward. "A Theory of Soviet Nationality Policies", in *SOVIET NATIONALITY POLICIES: RULING ETHNIC GROUPS IN THE USSR*, edited by Henry R. Huttenbach (London: Mansell Publishing Ltd., 1990), pp. 24-46.

Amnesty International.
See USSR: FIRST STEPS TOWARDS REFORM OF THE CRIMINAL JUSTICE SYSTEM.

Anderson, Edgar. "How Narva, Petersi, and Abrene Came to Be in the RSFSR", 19 *JOURNAL OF BALTIC STUDIES* 197-214 (1988).

An interesting overview of the history of the process by which land formerly belonging to Estonia and Latvia was incorporated within the Russian Federation. The author examines this case in the context of Russia's history of annexing land from other countries.

Andrew, Christopher, and Oleg Gordievsky. *KGB: THE INSIDE STORY OF ITS FOREIGN OPERATIONS FROM LENIN TO GORBACHEV*. London: Hodder & Stoughton, 1990. xxxii, 704 pp.

An entertaining and exceptionally detailed history of the KGB with a focus on its foreign intelligence and other covert activities. One of the authors is a former KGB operative who defected to the West in the 1960s. The book is based on previously inaccessible archival materials. Its overall conclusion is that the KGB was a state within the state, and that its influence may continue for many years despite its formal dissolution in late 1991.

Apostolakis, Bobby E. "Technology Transfer to USSR: Exaggerations, Myths, or Utopia?", 37 *RIVISTA INTERNAZIONALE DI SCIENZE ECONOMICHE E COMMERCIALI* 289-306 (1990).

This analysis of technology acquisitions by the Soviet Union from an economist's standpoint concentrates predominantly on the assessment of the econometric benefits of such acquisitions. Nevertheless, the article also contains an interesting historical summary of technology transfers to the Soviet Union, as well as what this reviewer believes to be a useful table of Soviet imports of Western machinery from 1955 through 1985 (reproduced below because the journal where the information is published may not easily be accessible to many readers).

TABLE 1

Soviet Imports of Western Machinery 1955-1985

YEAR	1	2	3	4	5
1955	104	1.0	38.0		48
1956	139	1.2	30.3		54
1957	128	0.9	27.0		61
1958	123	0.8	24.0		68
1959	177	1.1	33.8		76
1960	310	1.7	38.3	1.39	80
1961	390	1.8	32.2	1.64	89
1962	436	1.8	41.8	1.92	100
1963	402	1.4	37.2	2.22	111
1964	489	1.6	35.8	2.47	124
1965	366	1.1	33.4	2.65	137
1966	395	1.1	31.2	2.78	150
1967	457	1.2	33.7	2.93	163
1968	639	1.6	38.3	3.21	176
1969	889	1.9	39.0	3.66	190
1970	905	1.7	35.0	4.18	208
1971	840	1.4	32.5	4.56	227
1972	1113	1.5	30.0	4.84	246
1973	1566	1.6	27.1	5.24	266
1974	2100	1.7	26.9	5.63	289
1975	4000	2.4	25.4		313
1976	4759	2.3	25.0		
1977	5070	2.1	24.1		
1978	6375	1.9	23.7		
1979	6927	1.7	23.1		
1980	8058	1.6	22.5		
1981	8219	1.5	21.4		
1982	8411	1.7	20.6		
1983	8111	1.4	20.0		
1984	7644	1.2	19.2		
1985	6116	1.1	18.4		

Column 1: Imports of western machinery in US $m, f.o.b., current prices.

Column 2: Machinery imports as per cent of domestic machinery investment of the following year.

Column 3: Column 1 as % of all imports (f.o.b) from the West.

Column 4: Estimated stock of foreign machinery, 1960-1974, in billion of 1966 Rubles. Stock in place on January 1 of the year.

Column 5: Total Soviet capital stock, 1955-75, in billion of 1966 Rubles.

SOURCES: Columns 1, 2: 1955-75 in HANSON (1977-78); 1976-85 from our calculations from U.N., *Statistical Yearbook* and *IMF, Direction of Trade Statistics*. Column 3: 1955-73 in HANSON (1975); 1974-85 from our calculations. Column 4: GREEN and LEVINE (1977-78). Column 5: 1955-59 from our calculations; 1955-59 from our calculations; 1955-75 in WEITZMAN (1979).

Arbess, Daniel J. "A Few Things U.S. Businesspeople Should Know about Joint Ventures in the Soviet Union: A Lawyer's View", *22 NEW YORK JOURNAL OF INTERNATIONAL LAW AND POLITICS* 411-434 (1990).

An exceptionally informative article about practical issues facing United States lawyers involved in the process of negotiating and establishing joint ventures in the Soviet Union.

☆Artemova, Tatyana M.
See Sherr, Alan B., et al.

Arthur Anderson & Company.
See Barbanel, Jack A., and Lynda L. Maillet.

Artz, Donna E. "Soviet Anti-Semitism: Legal Responses in an Age of Glasnost", 4 *TEMPLE INTERNATIONAL AND COMPARATIVE LAW JOURNAL* 163-183 (1990).

This article discusses anti-semitic conduct in the Soviet Union and legal responses thereto.

Åslund, Anders. "Gorbachev, Perestroyka, and Economic Crisis", *40 PROBLEMS OF COMMUNISM* No. 1-2, 18-41 (January-April, 1991).

A careful and detailed analysis of Gorbachev's economic programs and the reasons for their failures. The author, who is Director of the Stockholm Institute of Soviet and East European Economics, contends that whilst the Soviet economy has been stagnant for some time, it was not so bad in terms of its major indicators as to precipitate the crisis which became evident in 1990. It was Gorbachev's wavering between conservative and radical reform plans and his reluctance to move decisively towards an open market which brought about serious imbalances in production and fiscal matters. In this respect Gorbachev's behavior resembles the economic failures of the last communist government in Poland.

Åslund, Anders. *GORBACHEV'S STRUGGLE FOR ECONOMIC REFORM*. 2d ed. Ithaca, NY: Cornell University Press, 1991. x, 219 pp.

The first edition of this book is listed in *Gorbachev's Law: A Bibliographic Survey of English Writings on Soviet Legal Developments 1987-1990*. According to the publisher's synopsis, the author has added two new chapters, rewritten the concluding chapter, "and made extensive revisions throughout the book to take into account the current situation in the USSR. He maintains that *perestroika* has proved to be an utter economic failure, and explores the formidable economic and political obstacles now confronting Soviet leaders as they attempt to forge an alternative to the discredited 'command-administrative system.' Aslund states that 1991 marks the beginning of a new and dangerous period in Soviet history—one that will powerfully influence world events well into the 21st century." Recent events may prove him to be right.

Atkinson, Scott. "The USSR and the Pacific Century", 30 *ASIAN SURVEY* 629-642 (1990).

This article suggests that in the late 1980's the Soviet Union changed its policies in the Pacific by opening free economic zones in theretofore restricted areas of the Far East and by forging closer trading and investment links with Japan, South Korea and other economically successful countries of that region. The development of these new policies is described in some detail by the author.

Augustyn, Francene M. "Foreign Investment in the Soviet Union: The Dawning of a New Era", 2 *TAX NOTES INTERNATIONAL* 1115-1120 (November 1990).

The author describes the formation of a more favorable climate in the USSR towards foreign investment. She maintains that various laws enacted by the Soviet legislature encourage such investment as well as changes in attitudes among Soviet functionaries. Finally she looks at tax provisions which may affect foreign investors.

Aulin, Lisen. *ESTABLISHING JOINT VENTURES IN THE USSR*. Deventer, The Netherlands; Boston: Kluwer Law and Taxation Publishers, 1990. ix, 149 pp.

In general, this book deals with the formation and management of joint ventures in the Soviet Union. What sets it apart from other works on the same subject is that it also examines the impact of the 1988 Law on State Enterprises and the 1990 Law on Enterprises (which entered into force on January 1, 1991) on the operation of the joint venture law. There are also brief references to the 1988 Law on Cooperatives, the 1990 USSR Council of Ministers Decree on Joint-Stock Companies, and recent USSR laws on foreign and domestic investments.

On the whole, the book is too brief to be of any meaningful use. About one-third of it is taken up by texts of various forms and documents (which are not explained well in the text) and by the BBC English translation of the 1990 USSR Law on Ownership.

Originally the book was published in Swedish. This English edition was revised and updated.

Aurbach, Laurence J., ed. *BEYOND PERESTROIKA: OPTIONS FOR A NEW SOVIET UNION*. Chicago: American Bar Association, Section of Urban, State, and Local Government Law, 1991. iv, 40 pp.

A compilation of papers and remarks presented at the fall 1990 annual meeting of the ABA Section of Urban, State, and Local Government Law. Includes the following papers of note:

"Prospects for a New Type of Federation" by John N. Hazard.

"Perestroika—Restructuring the Soviet Union" by Boris S. Krylov.

The appendix contains an English translation of the November, 1990 draft of Gorbachev's Union Treaty.

Avner, Michael. "Franchising in Eastern Europe and the Soviet Union".
See Zeidman, Philip F., and Michael Avner.

B

Bagley, T.M. *KGB: MASTERS OF THE SOVIET UNION.*
See Deriabin, Peter, and T.M. Bagley.

Baker, John H., ed. *JUDICIAL RECORDS, LAW REPORTS, AND THE GROWTH OF CASE LAW.* Berlin: Duncker & Humblot, 1989. 353 pp.

Includes a paper on "The Role of Case-Law in the Russian Legal System" by William E. Butler.

☆Balkina, M.A., ed. *NEW POLITICAL PARTIES AND MOVEMENTS IN THE SOVIET UNION.* Commack, N.Y.: Nova Science Publishers, Inc., 1991. 156 pp.

A joint effort of many contributors from the Soviet Union, this book discusses the emergence of political consciousness and the development of a multiparty environment in the Soviet Union. It includes extensive descriptions of new political parties in Moscow and other parts of Russia, as well as Ukraine and Kazakhstan.

Barale, Lucille A. *JOINT VENTURES IN EASTERN EUROPE.*
See Herlach, Mark D., and Lucille A. Barale.

Barbanel, Jack A., and Lynda L. Maillet. *BUSINESS IN THE SOVIET UNION: A PRIMER AND OVERVIEW.* Ardsley-on-Hudson, NY: Transnational Juris Publications, Inc., 1991. xxiv, 287 pp.

A guide on the Soviet Union for business people, prepared by two members of the international accounting firm of Arthur Andersen & Co. Unfortunately, due to the extensive and rapid changes in the political and economic structure of the Soviet Union, much of the information was outdated by the time this work was published. More useful are the brief summaries and checklists on the conduct of business, the formation and operation of business organizations, and other business-related issues.

☆Bardina, Marina P. "The New Shape in International Economic Relations and the Foreign Trade Reforms in the USSR", in *FROM COEXISTENCE TO COOPERATION: INTERNATIONAL LAW AND ORGANIZATION IN THE POST-COLD WAR ERA*, edited by Edward McWhinney, et al. (Dordrecht, The Netherlands: Martinus Nijhoff Publishers, 1991), pp. 211-240.

Barry, Donald B. "State and Social Structure: Part I of the Sobranie", in *THE SOVIET SOBRANIE OF LAWS*, edited by Richard M. Buxbaum and Kathryn Hendley (Berkeley, CA: University of California at Berkeley, 1991), pp. 26-44.

Barschevsky, Mikhail, Sergo Selianovsky, and Bruce A. MacDonald. "An Introduction to Soviet Intellectual Property Law," 1 *INTELLECTUAL PROPERTY LAW* 227-238 (1990).

☆Baturin, Yuri[y] M.
See also THE HEARTBEAT OF REFORM: SOVIET JURISTS AND POLITICAL SCIENTISTS DISCUSS THE PROGRESS OF PERESTROIKA.

☆Baturin, Yuriy M., Vladimir L. Entin, and Mikhail A. Fedotov. "The Road to Freedom for the Soviet Press", 12 *JOURNAL OF MEDIA LAW AND PRACTICE* 43-47 (1991).

A discussion of the legislative history and the practical implications of the new Soviet legislation on the freedom of press and other mass media.

Bazyler, Michael J. "The Gorbachev Revolution", 12 *WHITTIER LAW REVIEW* 147-150 (1991).

A brief speech about the changes taking place in the Soviet Union through early 1990, presented at the 1990 International Law Symposium at Whittier College School of Law.

Bazyler, Michael J. "Soviet Family Law", 39 *UNIVERSITY OF KANSAS LAW REVIEW* 125-174 (1990).

A truly encyclopedic survey of Soviet family law. The author concludes that this is a branch of Soviet law "closest to Western law", and he adds that it is alike not only in theory, but also in practice. One of the few major differences is the intrusion of the state into family matters. This is explored in the article, which describes the development of Soviet family law as well as its sources and modern application.

Bazyler, Michael J., and Eugene Sadovoy. "Television and the Law in the Soviet Union", 11 *LOYOLA ENTERTAINMENT JOURNAL* 293-351 (1991).

The editorial abstract preceding this article offers the following description of its content:

> The television industry in the Soviet Union has been a good indicator of that nation's political evolution. Soviet television has served as a useful tool for the government—first as a vehicle for Communist Party ideas, then as a catalyst for democracy, and now as a means of once again disbursing government propaganda. This article examines television and the law in the Soviet Union and concludes that the two must work together to achieve the democratic goals of the Soviet people.

Includes an English translation of the USSR Law on the Press and Other Information Media of August 2, 1990, as well as several decrees of President Gorbachev on freedom of television.

Beichman, Arnold. *THE LONG PRETENSE: SOVIET TREATY DIPLOMACY FROM LENIN TO GORBACHEV*. New Brunswick, NJ and London, England: Transaction Publishers, 1991. xiv, 303 pp.

A historical survey of the Soviet record of compliance with the treaties they made from 1933, when relations were established with the United States, to the time of Gorbachev's disarmament and trade negotiations in the late 1980's. Beichman, a former foreign correspondent and a research fellow at the Hoover Institution on War, raises important questions about the degree to which the Soviet Union can be relied upon to honor its treaty commitments. Its track record in this respect is poor. In the name of the Marxist-Leninist ideology it has frequently disregarded or broken its promises. This ideology, as Beichman points out, continues to guide the Soviet Union under Gorbachev.

Belkindas, Misha. *PRIVATIZATION OF THE SOVIET ECONOMY UNDER GORBACHEV II: 1. THE CAMPAIGN AGAINST UNEARNED INCOME. 2. THE DEVELOPMENT OF PRIVATE COOPERATIVES*. Durham, NC: Department of Economics, Duke University, 1989. ii, 97 pp. (Berkeley-Duke Occasional Papers on the Second Economy in the USSR, 14).

The first part of this paper examines the fuzzy distinction the Soviet government makes between legal and illegal private economic activity. The second part discusses cooperatives as the first step in Gorbachev's effort to "privatize" the Soviet economy, and the difficulties they face.

Berg, Ger P. van den. "Soviet Labor Law in the Collection of USSR Laws", in *THE SOVIET SOBRANIE OF LAWS,* edited by Richard M. Buxbaum and Kathryn Hendley (Berkeley, CA: University of California at Berkeley, 1991), pp. 68-101.

Beissinger, Mark. *THE NATIONALITIES FACTOR IN SOVIET POLITICS AND SOCIETY.*
See Lubomyr, Hajda, and Mark Beissinger.

Berkowitz, Julie S. "A Look into Glasnost's Impact on the Soviet Art World" (Student Note), 11 *LOYOLA ENTERTAINMENT LAW JOURNAL* 453-477 (1991).

From the editorial abstract to this article:

> Glasnost has had a tremendous effect on the Soviet art world. The Soviet government has reduced censorship of the creative process of art as well as the exhibition or performance of various art forms. This comment examines Soviet film, music, theater and painting, which have become more accessible to Western audiences resulting in an interchange of ideas and money crossing the line drawn between the East and West.

Berliner, Rochelle S. "The Disappearance of Raoul Wallenberg: A Resolution Is Possible" (Note), 11 *NEW YORK LAW SCHOOL JOURNAL OF INTERNATIONAL AND COMPARATIVE LAW* 381-432 (1990).

Raoul Wallenberg, a Swedish diplomat, is known throughout the world for attempting to save Hungarian Jews from Nazi extermination in 1944. In 1945 he was arrested by Soviet agents and disappeared. This note tells the story of Wallenberg's disappearance and subsequent international attempts to discover his whereabouts in the Soviet Union. Only in the late 1980's did the Soviet authorities begin to disclose information about Wallenberg's fate.

In addition to the Wallenberg story, this note discusses in general terms the Stalinist attitude towards law and human rights, how this attitude changed after Gorbachev came to power, and Soviet legal obligations under Soviet and international diplomatic laws as they pertain to the seizure and incarceration of foreign diplomats. The note is interesting and timely. Since its publication, the Soviet authorities have made more files available which explain Wallenberg's fate.

Berman, Harold J. "Counter-Revolution or Transition: A Response to Human Rights and the Emergence of the State of the Rule of Law in the USSR", 40 *EMORY LAW JOURNAL* 903-909 (1991).

A brief and general comment about the changing character of the Soviet law, made in response to the paper by Professor Vladimir

Kartashkin on "Human Rights and the Emergence of the State of the Rule of Law in the USSR" (40 *EMORY LAW JOURNAL* 889-902 (1991)).

Berman, Harold J. "Doing Business in the Soviet Union: The Legal Environment", in *LEGAL ASPECTS OF TRADE AND INVESTMENT IN THE SOVIET UNION AND EASTERN EUROPE* (New York: Practising Law Institute, 1990), pp. 39-49.

Berman, Harold J. "The Rule of Law and the Law-Based State (Rechtstaat) (with Special Reference to the Developments in the Soviet Union)", 4 *HARRIMAN INSTITUTE FORUM* No. 5, 1-12 (May 1991).

In the wake of Gorbachev's reform efforts during the late 1980's Soviet officials and scholars, as well as the Soviet press, began to make frequent references to "pravovoe gosudarstvo" (the "law-based state"), which was erroneously mis-translated into English as "rule of law". In this paper Professor Berman explores the expressions "rule of law" and "law-based state" in the context of their historical origins and as the terms are understood in modern Soviet legal thought. Interesting observations are made about the inclusion of protective "rule of law" provisions in the 1990 Russian Federation Draft Constitution (published in Russian, according to Professor Berman, in the newspaper *Sovetskaia Rossia*, November 24, 1990, pp. 1-8).

Berman, Harold J. "Some Jurisprudential Implications of the Codification of Soviet Laws", in *THE SOVIET SOBRANIE OF LAWS,* edited by Richard M. Buxbaum and Kathryn Hendley (Berkeley, CA: University of California at Berkeley, 1991), pp. 172-183.

Beyme, Klaus von. "Social and Economic Conditions for Ethnic Strife in the Soviet Union", in *SOVIET FEDERALISM: NATIONALISM AND ECONOMIC DECENTRALISATION,* edited by Alastair McAuley (Leicester and London: Leicester University Press, 1991), pp. 89-109.

A perceptive analysis of the geographic locations and historical or other causes of ethnic conflict in the Soviet Union. Includes useful statistics about internal migration patterns among the republics.

Birenbaum, David E., and Dimitri P. Racklin. *BUSINESS VENTURES IN EASTERN EUROPE AND THE SOVIET UNION: THE EMERGING LEGAL FRAMEWORK FOR FOREIGN INVESTMENT*. Englewood Cliffs, NJ: Prentice Hall, 1990- . 2 volumes, looseleaf.

This expensive looseleaf reference work includes a chapter on the emerging commercial and investment laws in the Soviet Union. Regular supplementation is intended. Unless such updates take place, the information in the chapter will become quickly obsolete (and incorrect).

Appendices include English translations of relevant Soviet laws as well as other documents, some quite interesting, relating to the sharing of economic information, investment procedures, etc. The two main authors are associated with the law firm of Fried, Frank, Harris, Shriver & Jacobson. The international accounting firm of Arthur Anderson is also participating in the publication of this material.

Black, J.L., ed. *USSR DOCUMENTS ANNUAL 1989. THE GORBACHEV REFORMS CONTINUE. THE END OF THE EMPIRE?* Gulf Breeze, FL: Academic International Press, 1990. xii, 435 pp.

In addition to English translations of selected laws and decrees enacted in 1989, this volume includes translations of newspaper articles, speeches, reports and other documents on the nationalities problem, environment, foreign policy, media and freedom of the press, and of course *perestroika*.

Black, J.L., ed. *USSR DOCUMENTS ANNUAL 1990. RESTRUCTURING PERESTROIKA*. Gulf Breeze, FL: Academic International Press, 1991. 2 Vols. (ix, 335 and vii, 379 pp. respectively).

Includes translations of some twenty-five laws enacted by the USSR Supreme Soviet in 1990.

Blase, John C., and Cynthia M. Smith. "Soviet Republics' Demand for Autonomy: The Need for Constitutional Reform and the Institution of Canadian-Style Judicial Review" (Note), 17 *JOURNAL OF LEGISLATION* 237-260 (1991).

A student note about the excessively centralized federal system of the Soviet Union. Estonia is used as a case study in point to illustrate the heavy hand of Moscow centralization. The Soviet system is compared with that of Canada to show how federalism can work in a multinational setting with a balance satisfactorily maintained between the center and its component parts.

Blaustein, Albert P., ed. *CONSTITUTIONS OF DEPENDENCIES AND SPECIAL SOVEREIGNTIES.* Dobbs Ferry, NY: Oceana Publications, 1977- .

Recent supplementary pamphlets in Blaustein's monumental collection of constitutional texts contain translations of declarations of independence, draft constitutions, and other relevant documents relating to sovereignty and independence published in the various republics of the former Soviet Union, including the Baltic states, Armenia, Azerbaizhan, Belorussia, Moldavia, Ukraine, etc. There is also a selection of former Soviet legislation pertaining to the status and independence of the republics.

Blaustein, Albert P., and Gisbert H. Flanz, eds. *CONSTITUTIONS OF THE COUNTRIES OF THE WORLD.* Dobbs Ferry, NY: Oceana Publications, 1970- .

Recent supplementary pamphlets of this encyclopedic work contain translations of important 1990-1991 constitutional drafts of the Russian Federation and related documents.

Block, Kevin P. "The Disciplining and Dismissal of Employees by Joint Ventures in the USSR", 23 *GEORGE WASHINGTON JOURNAL OF INTERNATIONAL LAW AND ECONOMICS* 619-667 (1990).

A detailed examination of the Soviet labor law and its application to joint ventures. The author warns foreign investors that bad working habits of the Soviet workers and provisions of Soviet labor legislation favoring workers may create problems for many joint ventures.

Blueger, Valentin. "Observations of a Latvian Practitioner", 24 *VANDERBILT JOURNAL OF TRANSNATIONAL LAW* 389-393 (1991).

Brief remarks about the effect of political and economic changes on foreign trade and investment in the Baltic and Russia. Blueger practices international trade law in Riga, Latvia.

Bociurkiw, Bohdan R. "Nationalities and Soviet Religious Policies", in *THE NATIONALITIES FACTOR IN SOVIET POLITICS AND SOCIETY*, edited by Lubomyr Hajda and Mark Beissinger (Boulder, CO: Westview Press, 1990), pp. 148-174.

Bociurkiw, R. Bohdan. "The Ukrainian Catholic Church in the USSR under Gorbachev", 39 *PROBLEMS OF COMMUNISM* No. 6, 1-19 (November-December, 1990).

This article is described as follows in the editorial abstract:

> An unintended consequence of Mikhail Gorbachev's policies of *glasnost'* and democratization in the USSR has been the emergence from the underground of the banned Ukrainian Greek Catholic Church. In their drive to realize a fully legal status for their Church, Ukrainian Catholics have been hampered by Gorbachev's vacillating nationality and religious policies and by the strong opposition of the Moscow Patriarchate, which had absorbed the Ukrainian Catholic Church in 1946. Frustrated by the center's policy of offering "too little too late," the believers have begun to reclaim their former churches on their own and have turned for help to the newly elected local organs of people's power to complete the "half-way" legalization conceded to the Ukrainian Catholic

Church under the October 1990 USSR law on freedom of conscience.

Boczek, Boleslaw Adam. "The Baltic Sea: An International Legal Profile", 38 *OSTEUROPA RECHT* 25-51 (1992).

☆Bogomolov, Oleg T. "Integration of the Soviet Union and Eastern Europe into the World Economy", in *REFORMS IN FOREIGN ECONOMIC RELATIONS OF EASTERN EUROPE AND THE SOVIET UNION*, edited by Michael Kaser and Aleksandar M. Vacic (New York: United Nations, 1991), pp. 162-166.

☆Boguslavskii, Mark M. *JOINT VENTURES IN THE USSR: A GUIDE TO SOVIET LAW.* London: W.H. Everett and Son Ltd, 1991. 192 pp.

For an author of his calibre this is a surprisingly superficial work on the Soviet joint venture legislation of 1987.

☆Boguslavskii, Mark M. "The Legal Status of Free Economic Zones in the USSR", 29 *SOVIET LAW AND GOVERNMENT* 78-91 (1991).

A discussion of the Soviet laws regulating free economic zones. The author asserts that the regulations are highly restrictive.

The original Russian version of this article was published in *Sovetskoe Gosudarstvo i Pravo*, 1989, No. 12 (December 1989).

☆Boguslavskii[y], Mark M., and Olga V. Vorobyova. "Transfer of Technology: Recent Developments", in *PERESTROIKA AND INTERNATIONAL LAW: CURRENT ANGLO-SOVIET APPROACHES TO INTERNATIONAL LAW,* edited by Anthony Carty and Gennady Danilenko (Edinburgh: Edinburg University Press, 1990), pp. 147-157.

Bohn, John A., Jr., and David H. Levey. "Models of Capital Market Development", in *THE EMERGING RUSSIAN BEAR: INTEGRATING THE SOVIET UNION INTO THE WORLD ECONOMY*, edited by Josef C. Brada and Michael P. Claudon (New York: New York University Press, 1991), pp. 73-85.

According to the authors, this paper examines "whether credit risk, that is, the risk of default or delayed payment by a borrower, will exist in the Soviet financial system as it is further transformed, and, if so, within what institutional structure and by what procedures the required credit analysis will be performed." More specifically it looks at the formation of a securities market and the creation of rating agency services.

☆Bondarenko, V.S. "Coastal Management in the USSR: Perestroika on the Coast", 18 *COASTAL MANAGEMENT* 337-363 (1990).

The author, who is a Soviet scientist, outlines region by region the system of government agencies empowered to manage and control the coastal areas and rivers of the Soviet Union. The article is surprisingly informative and revealing in its descriptions of the problems and conflicts which occur in Soviet coastal and river management. It describes quite openly the critical ecological condition of many of the Soviet coastal areas and rivers. The article includes several tables and maps.

Bonnell, Victoria E. "Voluntary Associations in Gorbachev's Reform Program", in *CAN GORBACHEV'S REFORMS SUCCEED?*, edited by George W. Breslauer (Berkeley, CA: Center for Slavic and East European Studies and the Berkeley-Stanford Program in Soviet Studies, University of California at Berkeley, 1990), pp. 63-76.

A survey of the emergence of cooperatives, professional and labor organizations, and other types of voluntary associations in Gorbachev's Soviet Union.

Reprinted in *The Soviet System in Crisis: A Reader of Western and Soviet Views*, edited by Alexander Dollin and Paul W. Lapidus (Boulder, CO: Westview Press, 1991).

Bonnie, Richard J. "Coercive Psychiatry and Human Rights: An Assessment of Recent Changes in the Soviet Union", 1 *CRIMINAL LAW FORUM* 319-346 (1990).

Borcke, Astrid von. "The KGB and Perestroika", in *THE SOVIET UNION, 1988-1989: PERESTROIKA IN CRISIS?*, edited by The Federal Institute for Soviet and International Studies (Boulder, CO: Westview Press, 1990), pp. 61-66.

☆Borodin, Stanislav.

See THE HEARTBEAT OF REFORM: SOVIET JURISTS AND POLITICAL SCIENTISTS DISCUSS THE PROGRESS OF PERESTROIKA.

Bova, Russell. "Worker Activism: The Role of the State", in *PERESTROIKA FROM BELOW: SOCIAL MOVEMENTS IN THE SOVIET UNION*, edited by Judith B. Sedaitis and Jim Butterfield (Boulder, CO: Westview Press, 1991), pp. 29-42.

Brabant, Jozef M. van, ed. *ECONOMIC REFORMS IN CENTRALLY PLANNED ECONOMIES AND THEIR IMPACT ON THE GLOBAL ECONOMY.* New York: United Nations, 1990 (Published by the United Nations Department of International Economic and Social Affairs as *JOURNAL OF DEVELOPMENT PLANNING* No. 20. UN Classification No. ST/ESA/216; UN Sales No. e. 90. II. A.9).

Contains an article by George Matyukhin entitled "The Union of Soviet Socialist Republics and Other Socialist Countries in the International Monetary and Financial System".

Brada, Josef C., and Michael P. Claudon, eds. *THE EMERGING RUSSIAN BEAR: INTEGRATING THE SOVIET UNION INTO THE WORLD ECONOMY.* New York: New York University Press, 1991. xiii, 228 pp. (Geonomics Institute for International Economic Advancement Series).

A collection of papers and documents presented at a Geonomics Institute seminar on "Financial Markets, Joint Ventures, and Business Opportunities in the Soviet Union", held in May 1990. The seminar dealt with such topics as business law, money and banking, capital markets, credit risk analysis, and joint ventures.

The volume includes the following papers specifically dealing with the development of Soviet law, practices arising therefrom, and the expansion of trade relations between the Soviet Union and the United States:

"Can Joint Ventures Help to Create a Market Economy in the Soviet Union" by Alexander L. Katkov.

"Facilitating U.S.-Soviet Joint Ventures through Legislative Reform" by Peter B. Maggs.

"Major Financial Obstacles to the Formation and Operation of Joint Ventures" by Mikhail A. Portnoy.

"Models of Capital Market Development" by John A. Bohn, Jr., and David H. Levey.

"The Positive Influence of Legal Reform on Soviet-U.S. Joint Ventures" by Viktor P. Mozolin.

"Soviet Financial Reform: Money and Credit" by Francis A. Scotland.

"Soviet-U.S. Joint Ventures: Problems, Challenges, and Opportunities" by Keith A. Rosten.

"What Congress and the Administration Can Do to Improve Soviet-U.S. Trade Relations" by Peter J. Pettibone.

The volume begins with the proposals of three working groups established at the seminar, recommending improvements in the business law, the money and banking system, and the capital markets of the Soviet Union. English translations of several draft laws for foreign investments and joint ventures are also included.

Brada, Josef C., and Michael P. Claudon, eds. *REFORMING THE RUBLE: MONETARY ASPECTS OF PERESTROIKA*. New York: New York University Press, 1990. x, 228 pp.

A collection of papers edited by the Geonomics Institute for International Economic Advancement.

A paper of interest to law-related research is "The Soviet Credit and Enterprise Structure System under Reform", by Vladimir Musatov.

Bradley, A.P.M.
See Tatu, Michael.

☆Braginskii[y], Mikhail I. *JOINT VENTURES: BENEFIT FOR ALL.* Moscow: Novosti Press Agency Publishing House, 1988. 15 pp.

A short pamphlet containing practical advice on joint ventures in the Soviet Union. Intended for the general public, it is rather superficial and uninformative.

☆Braginskii, Mikhail I.
See also Butler, William E., *FUNDAMENTAL PRINCIPLES OF LEGISLATION ON INVESTMENT ACTIVITY IN THE USSR AND REPUBLICS*; and
Butler, William E. *THE LAW OF OWNERSHIP IN THE USSR.*

Branson, Louise. *GORBACHEV: HERETIC IN THE KREMLIN.*
See Doder, Dusko, and Louise Branson.

Breslauer, George W., ed. *CAN GORBACHEV'S REFORMS SUCCEED*? Berkeley, CA: Center for Slavic and East European Studies and the Berkeley-Stanford Program in Soviet Studies, University of California at Berkeley, 1990. vii, 135 pp.

A collection of articles on the various aspects of the changes taking place in the Soviet Union during the first five years of Gorbachev's rule (1985-1990).

The following two articles may be of interest to students of the Soviet legal system:

"Voluntary Associations in Gorbachev's Reform Program" by Victoria E. Bonnell.

"Can Gorbachev Manage the Nationalities Crisis?" by Gail W. Lapidus.

☆Brinchuk, M.M. "Ecological and Legal Problems of Agro-Chemicalization", 7 *PACE ENVIRONMENTAL LAW REVIEW* 171-177 (1989).

Brown, Archie, ed. *THE SOVIET UNION: A BIOGRAPHICAL DICTIONARY.* London: George Weidenfeld and Nicolson Ltd., 1990; New York: Macmillan Publishing Co., 1991. xiv, 489 pp.

An alphabetically-arranged biographical dictionary of some 1400 Soviet luminaries. Though already dated, it is still useful as a reference work on personages in the Soviet Union who, prior to 1990, had acquired fame in politics, government, arts, science, the military, religion, media, etc.

Brunner, Georg. "State Structure, Part 2: Organizational Matters", in *THE SOVIET SOBRANIE OF LAWS*, edited by Richard M. Buxbaum and Kathryn Hendley (Berkeley, CA: University of California at Berkeley, 1991), pp. 45-54.

Bryner, Cyril. "The Issue of Capital Punishment in the Reign of Elizabeth Petrovka", 49 *RUSSIAN REVIEW* 389-416 (1990).

A historical overview and analysis of the abolition of the death penalty during the reign of Empress Elizabeth in the mid-1700's.

Brzezinski, Zbigniew.
See Commission on Security and Cooperation in Europe, *THE USSR IN CRISIS: STATE OF THE UNION.*

Buchsweiler, Meir. *A COLLECTION OF SOVIET DOCUMENTS CONCERNING GERMANS IN THE USSR.* Jerusalem: The Hebrew University of Jerusalem, The Marjorie Mayrock Center for Soviet and East European Research, 1991. 26 pp. (Research Paper No. 73).

Close to two million ethnic Germans are supposedly living in the Soviet Union. The changing policies of the Soviet government towards them are briefly discussed in the introduction to this collection of documents dealing with the Soviet government's handling of the Germans. The documents themselves are published in German and Russian. They date from 1961 through 1990.

Bulsys, Joseph A., and John J. Makay. "Gorbachev's Rhetoric of Glasnost: How Openness Intersects with Freedom of Expression", 27 *FREE SPEECH YEARBOOK* 55-67 (1989).

A contextual analysis of Gorbachev's discourse seeking to determine the status of freedom of expression in the Soviet Union and the effect of Gorbachev's rhetoric on the American public.

Burt, Jeffrey A. "Joint Venture Experience: Observations on the Business and Legal Challenges", *22 NEW YORK UNIVERSITY JOURNAL OF INTERNATIONAL LAW AND POLITICS* 435-445 (1990).

An interesting paper on joint ventures in the Soviet Union. It contains many practical tips as well as descriptions of successful joint ventures which involve United States participants (Pepsi Cola, McDonald's, Honeywell, etc.).

Butler, William E. "The 1867 Russo-American Convention: Some Textual Issues", 40 *INTERNATIONAL AND COMPARATIVE LAW QUARTERLY* 457-463 (1991).

Butler, William E. *BASIC DOCUMENTS ON THE SOVIET LEGAL SYSTEM*, 2nd ed. New York: Oceana Publications, Inc., 1991. v, 492 pp.

A collection of some major laws enacted in the USSR up to August 15, 1990. All translations were made by the author of the book.

Butler, William E., ed. *CONTROL OVER COMPLIANCE WITH INTERNATIONAL LAW.* Dordrecht, The Netherlands: Martinus Nijhoff Publishers, 1991. vi, 209 pp.

Papers presented at the 4th Anglo-Soviet Symposium on Public International Law, held in Moscow at the Institute of State and Law, USSR Academy of Sciences, May 14-16, 1990. Includes several papers by Soviet specialists and on subjects of Soviet international law policies and practices:

"Control in Contemporary International Law" by I.I. Lukashuk.

"Control Machinery in the Ecological Security System" by A.S. Timoshenko.

"Dispute Settlement under the Washington Convention on the Settlement of Investment Disputes" by P.T. Muchlinski.

"The International Labour Organisation: Control over Application of the Conventions and Recommendations on Labour" by S.A. Ivanov.

"Monitoring Compliance with International Human Rights Standards" by R.A. Mullerson.

"On a Theoretical Concept of Control over the Fulfilment of International Obligations of States" by M.I. Lazarev.

"'Open Skies'—The Metamorphoses of One Concept" by V.S. Vereshchetin.

"The Origin and Prospects for Development of Control over Compliance with International Obligations of States" by O.N. Khlestov.

"Verification Machinery in the Antarctic Treaty System" by Sergei V. Vinogradov.

Butler, William E. *THE CUSTOMS CODE OF THE USSR AND THE LAW ON THE CUSTOMS TARIFF OF THE USSR.* London: Interlist, 1991. xxvi, 210 pp.

On March 26, 1991, the USSR Supreme Soviet enacted a new USSR Customs Code and a new USSR Law on the Customs Tariff. They replace earlier customs legislation, including the 1964 USSR Customs Code. However, the existence of both of these legislative measures may be very short. With the breakup of the Soviet Union, the individual republics are introducing their own customs regimes.

This book contains English translations of both legislative measures by Professor Butler.

Butler, William E. *FUNDAMENTAL PRINCIPLES OF LEGISLATION ON INVESTMENT ACTIVITY IN THE USSR AND REPUBLICS.* London: Interlist, 1991. viii, 302 pp. (The Butler Commentaries on Soviet Law).

On December 10, 1990, the USSR Supreme Soviet enacted *Fundamental Principles of Legislation on Investment Activity in the USSR.* This law was preceded on October 26, 1990, by an edict of the USSR President on Foreign Investments in the USSR. On July 5, 1991, the USSR Supreme Soviet also enacted *Fundamental Principles of Legislation on Foreign Investments in the USSR.*

These three measures relating to investment, as well as their enabling decrees, have been translated by Professor Butler. The translations are included in this book together with lengthy commentaries by Professors M.I. Braginskii, William E. Butler, and A.A. Rubanov.

Butler, William E., ed. *THE LAW OF OWNERSHIP IN THE USSR.* London: Intershelf, Ltd., 1991. viii, 392 pp. (The Butler Commentaries on Soviet Law).

English-language translation of the Law on Ownership adopted by the USSR Supreme Soviet on March 6, 1990 together with explanatory commentaries by Professors M.I. Braginskii, William E. Butler, and A.A. Rubanov.

Butler, William E. "Perestroika and the Rule of Law", in *PERESTROIKA AND THE RULE OF LAW: ANGLO-AMERICAN AND SOVIET PERSPECTIVES,* edited by William E. Butler (London: I.B. Tauris & Co., Ltd., 1991), pp. 7-21.

Butler, William E., ed. *PERESTROIKA AND THE RULE OF LAW: ANGLO-AMERICAN AND SOVIET PERSPECTIVES.* London: I.B. Tauris & Co., Ltd., 1991. 199 pp.

In addition to some contributions on more general topics of law, this collection of papers by English and Soviet scholars deals with the introduction of a rule of law in the Soviet Union.

Papers on the Soviet Union or by Soviet scholars are as follows:

"Inviolability of the Individual in a Rule-of-Law State" by M.M. Slavin.
"Jus and Lex: Evolution of Views" by R.Z. Livshits.
"Law and Glasnost" by V.L. Entin.
"On Constitutional Supervision in the USSR" by V.P. Kazimirchuk.
"Perestroika and the Rule of Law" by William E. Butler.
"Political Pluralism and Law" by E.V. Kumanin.
"The Rule of Law—Conservative, Liberal, Marxist and Neo-Marxist. Wherein Lies the Attraction?" by M.D.A. Freeman.
"Separation of Powers in the USSR: Emerging Theory" by N.P. Koldaeva.
"The Supremacy of Lex and Legal Reform in the USSR" by S.V. Polenina.

Butler, William E. "The Role of Case-Law in the Russian Legal System", in *JUDICIAL RECORDS, LAW REPORTS, AND THE GROWTH OF CASE LAW*, edited by John H. Baker (Berlin: Duncker & Humblot, 1989), pp. 337-352.

In this interesting paper, based predominantly on the works of Soviet scholars, Professor Butler describes the court systems in pre-Communist Russia and the importance of judicial opinions in the decision-making process of imperial Russian courts.

Butler, William E. "The Rule of Law and the Legal System", in *DEVELOPMENTS IN SOVIET POLITICS*, edited by Stephen White, Alex Pravda and Zvi Gitelman (Durham, NC: Duke University Press, 1990), pp. 104-119.

A concise description of the Soviet legal system as it existed in 1990.

Butler, William E. "Soviet Business Law: Training the Rising Generation", 2 *EUROPEAN BUSINESS LAW REVIEW* 79-80 (1991).

Butler, William E. "Soviet Foreign Trade Reform and Technology Transfer", in *LAW AND POLITICS OF WEST-EAST TECHNOLOGY TRANSFER*, edited by Hiroshi Oda (Dordrecht/Boston/London: Martinus Nijhoff/Graham & Trotman, 1991), pp. 211-231.

A good analysis of Soviet legislation of the 1987-88 period on foreign investments, technology transfers, and foreign trade in general.

Butler, William E.
See also Sherr, Alan B., et al.

Butterfield, Jim. *PERESTROIKA FROM BELOW: SOCIAL MOVEMENTS IN THE SOVIET UNION.*
See Sedaitis, Judith B., and Jim Butterfield.

Buxbaum, Richard M. "The Sobranie: A Postscript", in *THE SOVIET SOBRANIE OF LAWS,* edited by Richard M. Buxbaum and Kathryn Hendley (Berkeley, CA: University of California at Berkeley, 1991), pp. 211-226.

Buxbaum, Richard M., and Kathryn Hendley, eds. *THE SOVIET SOBRANIE OF LAWS.* Berkeley, CA: University of California at Berkeley, 1991. xii, 226 pp. (Research Series No. 78).

Papers presented at the Conference on the Codification of Soviet Law, held at Berkeley on August 3-5, 1989.

In early 1987, the University of California at Berkeley received a microfiche set of the "Sobranie deistvuiushchego zakonodatel'stva SSSR" (Collection of Laws in Force of the USSR) which included more than 10,000 individual pieces of legislation operative in the Soviet Union at the time of the Collection's compilation in the 1970's and arranged in sixty volumes. The conference was convened to discuss the collection. The conference papers, published in this volume, are—

"Agriculture" by Karl-Eugen Wädekin.
"Earlier Publication Practice: The Case of the 1959 Sbornik" by George Ginsburgs.
"Law Enforcement Agencies" by Hiroshi Oda.
"Legislation on the Soviet National Economy in the Sobranie" by Peter B. Maggs.
"Of Laws, Secrecy, and Environmental Quality in the USSR" by Zigurds L. Zile.
"Secret Justice and Personal Rights" by Peter Juviler.
"The Sobranie—A Challenge to Glasnost" by Dietrich André Loeber.
"The Sobranie: A Postscript" by Richard M. Buxbaum.
"Some Jurisprudential Implications of the Codification of Soviet Laws" by Harold J. Berman.
"Soviet Criminal Law and Justice: Are There or Were There Secrets?" by Louise I. Shelley.
"The Soviet Experience with Codification: Theoretical and Comparative Perspectives" by Gianmaria Ajani.
"Soviet Labor Law in the Collection of USSR Laws" by Ger P. van den Berg.
"State and Social Structure: Part I of the Sobranie" by Donald B. Barry.
"State Structure, Part 2: Organizational Matters" by Georg Brunner.

☆Bykov, Aleksandr N. "Institutional Framework of Foreign Trade Relations of the Soviet Union", in *REFORMS IN FOREIGN ECONOMIC RELATIONS OF EASTERN EUROPE AND THE SOVIET UNION*, edited by Michael Kaser and Aleksandar M. Vacic (New York: United Nations, 1991), pp. 37-44.

C

Calingaert, Daniel. *SOVIET NUCLEAR POLICY UNDER GORBACHEV: A POLICY OF DISARMAMENT.* New York: Praeger, 1991. x, 180 pp.

This book surveys the policy changes and negotiation methods of the Soviet Union in nuclear disarmament talks from 1985 through 1990.

Carey, Sarah C. "Five Years Later: Evaluating Foreign Investment Experience in the 'Former USSR'", in *LEGAL AND PRACTICAL ASPECTS OF DOING BUSINESS IN THE SOVIET REPUBLICS* (New York: Practising Law Institute, 1992), pp. 51-68.

An excellent summary of the investment climate in the Soviet Union, including comments on the problems foreign investors may expect to encounter and their chances of success.

Carey, Sarah C. "The Process of Negotiating a Joint Venture in the USSR: Questions Resolved and Unresolved", *10 INTERNATIONAL QUARTERLY* 42-52 (1989).

A brief description of the 1987 joint venture legislation.

Carlisle, Donald S. "Uzbekistan and the Uzbeks", 40 *PROBLEMS OF COMMUNISM* No. 5, 23-44 (Sept.-Oct. 1991).

According to the editorial abstract on this article:

> The Soviet republic of Uzbekistan is an artifact of Moscow's policy: in 1924-25, Moscow carved out state formations named for historically well-known ethnic groups that were not yet consolidated as distinct peoples, let alone modern nations. An Uzbek national identity remained largely latent, unconsolidated, and unfocused until the "Uzbek Affair," which tarred the whole republic with the stigma of

corruption. Moscow's inept handling of this situation appears to have triggered a reactive nationalism that just might turn the republic's diverse groups into an Uzbek nation. Another possible development is *uzbek* participation in some sort of Turkic league or confederation. However, the intentions and allegiances of Uzbekistan's masses—urban and rural—are still unannounced.

Carpenter, Russell H., Jr. "Soviet Joint Enterprises with Capitalist Firms and Other Joint Ventures between East and West: The Western Point of View", 222 *RECUEIL DES COURS. HAGUE ACADEMY OF INTERNATIONAL LAW* 365-421 (1990 III).

A detailed analysis of the Soviet joint venture legislation of January 3, 1987, as amended, and other legal issues relevant to the establishment of joint ventures and the making of investments in the Soviet Union. The author is a partner in the Washington law firm of Covington & Burling.

Carr, Josephine. "The Decline and Fall of the Soviet Empire", 10 *INTERNATIONAL FINANCIAL LAW REVEIW* No. 12, 14-20 (December 1991).

A very brief report on the declining foreign trade and investment prospects in the Soviet Union.

Includes a useful list of international law firms in Moscow.

Carter, Stephen K. *RUSSIAN NATIONALISM: YESTERDAY, TODAY, TOMORROW.* London: Pinter Publishers, 1990. 175 pp.

An excellent historical survey of the Russian nationalist thoughts and trends from its beginnings in Czarist Russia to 1990. The scope of the book can be seen best from its chapter titles:

1. Origins
2. Russian Nationalism 1900-17
3. Stalinist Realities
4. Krushchev's 'revisionism'
5. Alexander Solzhenitzn and the New Right
6. The Brezhnev Years, I: Russian Nationalist Thought
7. The Brezhnev Years, II: 'The Countryside Writers'
8. The Road to Pamyat
9. Theories of Russian Nationalism
10. Gorbachev and the Politics of Russian Nationalism
11. Conclusion
12. Postscript

The book also includes an excellent list of further reading.

Carty, Anthony, and Gennady Danilenko, eds. *PERESTROIKA AND INTERNATIONAL LAW: CURRENT ANGLO-SOVIET AP-*

PROACHES TO INTERNATIONAL LAW. Edinburgh: Edinburg University Press, 1990. ix, 231 pp.

A collection of essays by British and Soviet international law experts on selected topics of international law. Some of the essays by Soviet contributors discuss changes and developments in Soviet international law practice.

The following essays are Soviet contributions or deal with Soviet attitudes on international law:

"International Arbitration in the External Policy of the Soviet Union" by Galina G. Shinkaretskaya.

"International Environmental Security: The Concept and its Implementation" by Sergei V. Vinogradov.

"International Law-Making: Issues of Law and Policy" by Gennady M. Danilenko.

"The International Protection of Human Rights and the Domestic Jurisdiction of States" by Rein A. Mullerson.

"International Space Law: New Institutional Opportunities" by Elena P. Kamenetskaya.

"The Primacy of International Law in World Politics" by Vladlen S. Vereshchetin and Rein A. Mullerson.

"The Principle of Peaceful Settlement of Disputes: A New Soviet Approach" by Elena E. Vilegjanina.

"Transfer of Technology: Recent Developments" by Mark M. Boguslavskii[y] and Olga V. Vorobyova.

"Verification of Disarmament" by Bakhtiar R. Tuzmukhamedov.

Reviewed by Peter B. Maggs in 85 *American Journal of International Law* 723-724 (1991), and by William E. Butler in 50 *Slavic Review* 1026 (1991).

Chandler, Andrea. *PERESTROIKA IN THE SOVIET REPUBLICS: DOCUMENTS ON THE NATIONAL QUESTION.*
See Furtado, Charles F., Jr., and Andrea Chandler.

☆Chistiakov, Nikolai F.
See Ginsburgs, George, and Vladimir Kudryavtsev, eds. *THE NUREMBERG TRIAL AND INTERNATIONAL LAW.*

Clark, David S., ed. *COMPARATIVE AND PRIVATE INTERNATIONAL LAW: ESSAYS IN HONOR OF JOHN HENRY MERRYMAN ON HIS SEVENTIETH BIRTHDAY.* Berlin: Duncker & Humblot, 1990. xxii, 450 pp.

Includes the following papers of interest to legal research:

"Latvia's 1937 Civil Code: A Quest for Cultural Identity" by Dietrich André Loeber.

"Socialism and the Rule of Law: Some Speculations and Predictions" by Inga Markovits.

Claudon, Michael P. *THE EMERGING RUSSIAN BEAR: INTEGRATING THE SOVIET UNION INTO THE WORLD ECONOMY.*
See Brada, Josef C., and Michael P. Claudon.

Claudon, Michael P. *REFORMING THE RUBLE: MONETARY ASPECTS OF PERESTROIKA.*
See Brada, Josef C., and Michael P. Claudon.

Claudon, Michael P., and Tamar L. Gutner, eds. *INVESTING IN REFORM: DOING BUSINESS IN A CHANGING SOVIET UNION.* New York: New York University Press, 1991. xix, 279 pp.

As the Soviet Union began to disintegrate in 1991 the question of making all or some of its republics into viable economies became a much-discussed issue. This book consists of papers first presented at a seminar organized by the Geonomics Institute for International Economic Advancement in May, 1991. Many of the papers are of interest to law related research:

"The Baltics: The Premier European Gateway to the Soviet Union" by Jenik Radon.

"The Latest Developments in the Foreign Currency Practices and Regulations of the Soviet Union" by Eugene Uljanov.

"Local Government: Structure and Economic Regulation" by Emily Silliman.

"Ownership Rights" by Peter B. Maggs.

"Recent Trends in Foreign Trade and Investment" by Kaj Hobér.

Clingan, Thomas A., Jr., and Anatoly L. Kolodkin, eds. *MOSCOW SYMPOSIUM ON THE LAW OF THE SEA: PROCEEDINGS OF A WORKSHIP CO-SPONSORED BY THE LAW OF THE SEA INSTITUTE, THE SOVIET MARITIME LAW ASSOCIATION, THE SOVIET PEACE FUND*, November 28-December 2, 1988 in Moscow. Honolulu: The Law of the Sea Institute, William S. Richardson School of Law, University of Hawaii, 1991. xi, 394 pp.

This is a collection of papers and commentaries presented at a workshop in Moscow on November 28-December 2, 1988. The papers are very brief and all of them deal with the international aspects of the law of the sea. Some of the papers were presented by Soviet scholars.

Cole Corette & Arbutyn. "Legal and Practical Aspects of Doing Business in the Soviet Republics", in *LEGAL AND PRACTICAL ASPECTS OF DOING BUSINESS IN THE SOVIET REPUBLICS* (New York: Practising Law Institute, 1992), pp. 71-102.

A useful summary, previously published elsewhere, of the governmental and economic changes that took place in the former Soviet Union after the collapse of the August, 1991 coup.

Commission on Security and Cooperation in Europe. *ELECTIONS IN THE BALTIC STATES AND SOVIET REPUBLICS: A COMPENDIUM OF REPORTS ON PARLIAMENTARY ELECTIONS HELD IN 1990.* Compiled by the Staff of the Commission on Security and Cooperation in Europe. Washington: U.S. Government Printing Office, 1990. x, 188 pp.

Staff members of the Commission on Security and Cooperation in Europe travelled to the Soviet Union in early 1990 to observe the elections held at that time in the different Soviet republics. This volume contains reports of their observations for eight of the republics: Azerbaijan, Estonia, Georgia, Latvia, Lithuania, Moldavia, Russia, and Ukraine. The report for each of these republics begins with a description of the contemporary political environment and the various party alignments. This is followed by summaries of the respective election laws, funding, campaigning, balloting, and the election results. Each report concludes with an analysis of the political implications of the election results. All in all, this volume is not only a useful reference source for the first "free" elections in the Soviet Union, but also a good summary of the political developments in the eight republics during the first part of 1990.

Commission on Security and Cooperation in Europe. *REFERENDUM IN THE SOVIET UNION. A COMPENDIUM OF REPORTS ON THE MARCH 17, 1991 REFERENDUM ON THE FUTURE OF THE USSR.* Compiled by the Staff of the Commission on Security and Cooperation in Europe. Washington: U.S. Government Printing Office, 1991. viii, 46 pp.

On March 17, 1991 a referendum was held in the Soviet Union at the behest of Gorbachev for the purpose of determining whether the country should remain united in its present form or adopt some other structure. The referendum results were reported as an overwhelming vote in favor of Gorbachev's idea of a union. However, the referendum was boycotted in six republics, which asserted that they had either been illegally annexed by the Soviet Union (i.e., the Baltic countries) or that they were independent.

The referendum was monitored by staff members of the U.S. Commission on Security and Cooperation in Europe. This publication contains the Commission's reports.

Commission on Security and Cooperation in Europe. *THE USSR IN CRISIS: STATE OF THE UNION.* Hearing before the Commission on Security, Feb. 6, 1991. Washington: U.S. Government Printing Office, 1991. iii, 77 pp. (Sudoc No. Y4.Sc.2:102-1-3.)

Presentations by Zbigniew Brzezinski, Marshall I. Goldman, and Lt. Gen. William E. Odom on the political and economic situation in the Soviet Union in early 1991.

Connor, Walter D. "Equality of Opportunity", in *SOVIET SOCIAL PROBLEMS*, edited by Anthony Jones, et al. (Boulder, CO; San Francisco; Oxford: Westview Press, 1991), pp. 137-153.

Connor, Walter D. *SOVIET SOCIAL PROBLEMS*.
See Jones, Anthony, Walter D. Connor, and David E. Powell.

Conquest, Robert. *STALIN: BREAKER OF NATIONS*. New York: Viking, 1991. 346 pp.

According to Richard Pipes, who reviewed the book in the *New York Times Book Review* (November 10, 1991, p. 14):

> This biography is about a mean-spirited little man with 'cockroach whiskers' (the phrase is the poet Osip Mandelstam's) whose ambitions far outran his capacity: to realize them, he used the machinery of total power set in place by Lenin and Trotsky to destroy all who stood in his way. They numbered in the tens of millions.... [The book] provides a superb portrait of the man who terrorized his country for 30 years and inflicted the cold war on the rest of the world. It is the third major study of the tyrant to appear in a year (the other two are by Robert Tucker and Dmitri Volkogonov, a Soviet general turned historian). Briskly written, authoritative yet not pedantic, filled with interesting incidents and anecdotes, [it] makes for fascinating reading.

Cook, Linda J. "Lessons of Soviet Coal Miners' Strike of Summer 1989", 4 *HARRIMAN INSTITUTE FORUM* No. 3, 1-10 (March 1991).

A detailed description of the first large labor unrest in Gorbachev's Soviet Union. The author, a political science professor at Brown University, explains the economic and political causes of the strike, as well as the generally unsuccessful government approaches to the settlement of the miners' grievances.

CONSTITUTION (FUNDAMENTAL LAW) OF THE UNION OF SOVIET SOCIALIST REPUBLICS: ADOPTED AT THE SEVENTH (SPECIAL) SESSION OF THE SUPREME SOVIET OF THE USSR, NINTH CONVOCATION, ON OCTOBER 7, 1977. London: Novosti Press Agency, 1990. 58 pp.

This edition of the text of the USSR Constitution includes amendments of December 1988, December 1989, and March 1990.

Cooper, Julian.
See Sherr, Alan B., et al.

Copeland, Emily A. "Perestroika and Human Rights: Steps in the Right Direction", 15 *FLETCHER FORUM OF WORLD AFFAIRS* No. 2, 101-119 (Summer 1991).

This article is described as follows in the editorial abstract:

> Soviet human rights policies have long played a major role in influencing foreign perceptions of the Soviet Union. However, human rights, or the rights of individuals, have not always received the same attention and respect from the Soviet leadership. Instead, Soviet leaders traditionally have insisted that all rights are derived from the state, and that in fact, Communist societies have eliminated the social foundations of civil and political injustice. Since 1985, however, Mikhail S. Gorbachev has implemented significant and highly visible reform measures acknowledging that problems remain in the Soviet system and protecting the rights of the individual. Emily Copeland examines the evolution of Soviet human rights policy, focusing on the changes implemented under Gorbachev. She argues that Gorbachev's reforms represent more than political expediencies—that they are a key component of a revised conceptual framework and practical approach that affect and are affected by both foreign and domestic policy.

COPYRIGHT LAWS OF EASTERN EUROPE AND THE U.S.S.R. A Report from the International Intellectual Property Alliance by Proskauer, Rose, Goetz and Mendelsohn. Washington, D.C.: November, 1990. 60 and 4 pp.

Includes a brief summary of the Soviet copyright legislation.

Coudert Brothers. *JOINT VENTURES IN EASTERN EUROPE.* *See* Herlach, Mark D., and Lucille A. Barale.

Critchlow, James. "'Corruption', Nationalism, and the Native Elites in Soviet Central Asia", 4 *JOURNAL OF COMMUNIST STUDIES* 142-159 (1988).

Numerous purges of the local Communist elite took place in Uzbekistan and other Central Asian republics during the 1980's. The ostensible reasons for these purges were to root out "corruption" and create efficient governments. In reality, as the author of this article asserts, the Moscow leadership was intent upon preventing the emergence of nationalism and "particularism" among the elites. Moscow was not very successful. The disparity between the stagnant economy of Central Asia and its rapidly growing population made Moscow dependent on the elites to help it ensure stability in the region.

Critchlow, James. "Islam in Soviet Central Asia: Renaissance or Revolution?", 18 *RELIGION IN COMMUNIST LANDS* 196-211 (1990).

An interesting account of the reemergence of Islamic influence in Soviet Central Asia in recent times.

THE CUSTOMS CODE OF THE USSR AND THE LAW ON THE CUSTOMS TARIFF OF THE USSR: IN FORCE AS OF 1 JULY, 1991. Staines, England: Intershelf Ltd., 1991. xxvi, 210 pp.

Translated by William E. Butler. Also a short introduction by the translator.

☆Czaplinski, W. and Danilenko, G. "Conflicts of Norms in International Law", 21 *NETHERLANDS YEARBOOK OF INTERNATIONAL LAW* 3-42 (1990).

A proposal by two Soviet international law scholars to establish a hierarchy of different norms of international law to resolve different kinds of problems. They assert that such different sets of norms can coexist within the framework of international law.

D

☆Danilenko, Gennady M. "The Changing Structure of the International Community: Constitutional Implications", 32 *HARVARD INTERNATIONAL LAW JOURNAL* 353-361 (1991).

The "constitutional implications" in this article refer to new international realignments as a consequence of ideological and policy changes in Eastern Europe and in the former "socialist" camp in general.

☆Danilenko, Gennady M. "Conflicts of Norms in International Law". *See* Czaplinski, W., and Danilenko, Gennady.

☆Danilenko, Gennady M. "International Jus Cogens: Issues of Law-Making", 2 *EUROPEAN JOURNAL OF INTERNATIONAL LAW* 42-65 (1991).

A discussion of an important topic of international law by a leading Soviet international law expert of the "new" generation.

☆Danilenko, Gennady M. "International Law-Making: Issues of Law and Policy", in *PERESTROIKA AND INTERNATIONAL LAW: CURRENT ANGLO-SOVIET APPROACHES TO INTERNATIONAL LAW,* edited by Anthony Carty and Gennady Danilenko (Edinburgh: Edinburg University Press, 1990), pp. 15-26.

☆Danilenko, Gennady M. *PERESTROIKA AND INTERNATIONAL LAW: CURRENT ANGLO-SAXON APPROACHES TO INTERNATIONAL LAW.*
See Carty, Anthony, and Gennady Danilenko.

☆Danilenko, Viktor. "Electoral Reform", in *PERESTROIKA-ERA POLITICS: THE NEW SOVIET LEGISLATURE AND GORBACHEV'S POLITICAL REFORMS,* edited by Robert Huber and Donald R. Kelley (Armonk, NY: M.E. Sharpe, Inc., 1991), pp. 33-49.

Davis, Nathaniel. "The Number of Churches before and after the Khrushchev Antireligious Drive", 50 *SLAVIC REVIEW* 612-620 (1991).

In the wake of *glasnost*, the Soviet Council for Religious Affairs opened its files to the public by depositing them in the Central Government Archives in Moscow. The author of this article has been able to examine these files.

The article reports on the number of Russian Orthodox and the Ukrainian Catholic (Uniate) churches and religious communities functioning in the Soviet Union between 1945 and 1961. It also includes numerous references to church statistics in subsequent years, especially in the 1980's. The author notes that the number of churches was reduced by some 40 percent in the early 1960's (not two-thirds, as has been commonly believed). Furthermore the largest closings took place in the Ukraine, where also many Ukrainian Catholic churches were transferred to the Russian Orthodox jurisdiction.

Dean, Richard N. "Considering Business Opportunities in the Soviet Union in the 1990s", in *LEGAL ASPECTS OF TRADE AND INVESTMENT IN THE SOVIET UNION AND EASTERN EUROPE.* Commercial Law and Practice Course Handbook Series No. 549. (New York: Practising Law Institute, 1990), pp. 95-116.

An incisive and helpful overview of the incentives and obstacles foreign business people and investors may expect to encounter in the Soviet Union. The author, who has extensive experience of the Soviet Union, describes the general attitude of the country towards foreign trade and investment, as well as the many problems it faces in its efforts to become a fully-fledged partner in international trade.

Dean, Richard N. "Considering Business Opportunities in the Soviet Union in the 1990s", 26 *VANDERBILT JOURNAL OF TRANSNATIONAL LAW* 325-343 (1991). Reprinted in *PRIVATE INVESTMENTS ABROAD—PROBLEMS AND SOLUTIONS IN INTERNATIONAL BUSINESS IN 1991* (The Southwestern Legal Foundation) (New York: Matthew Bender, 1992), Chapter 11 (24 pp.).

An update of Dean's presentation at the Practising Law Institute's program on legal aspects of trade and development in the Soviet Union of July, 1990 (*see above*).

Dean, Richard N. "Gaining a Foothold in the Soviet Market: How to Establish a Representative Office".
See Sheedy, John F., and Richard N. Dean.

Dean, Richard N. "Practicing Law and Doing Business in the Soviet Union", 11 *NEW YORK LAW SCHOOL JOURNAL OF INTERNATIONAL AND COMPARATIVE LAW* No. 3, 439-446 (1990).

A brief overview of the role of lawyers in foreign trade and investment transactions in the Soviet Union. Presented at the Third Annual Ernst C. Stiefel Symposium: Practicing Law and Doing Business in the Soviet Union.

DeBenedictis, Don J. "The Coup's Legal Aftermath", 77 *ABA JOURNAL* No. 11, 22 (November 1991).

A very brief article about the extensive changes in the government structure of the Soviet Union brought about by the failure of the August, 1991 coup.

Deriabin, Peter, and T.M. Bagley. *KGB: MASTERS OF THE SOVIET UNION*. New York: Hippocrane Books, Inc., 1990. xxiv, 466 pp.

As the authorities in the former Soviet Union open up more and more files to the public, books on the sinister Soviet Committee of State Security (KGB) grow in numbers. This is one such book. It is detailed and appears to be thoroughly researched. One of its authors is a former member of the KGB who defected to the West in the 1960's.

The book examines the emergence of a security police during the 1917 Revolution and its subsequent development during the Civil War. It traces the growth and eventual transformation of the organization into the KGB. The emphasis throughout the book is on a thesis, shared by some other experts, that the Soviet Union was in effect governed by the KGB.

Reviewed by Amy Knight in 50 *Slavic Review* 228-29 (1991).

Desai, Padma. "Soviet Economic Reform", 3 *HARRIMAN INSTITUTE FORUM* No. 12, 1-12 (Dec. 1990).

Three different plans for the economic salvation of the Soviet Union were debated in 1990. The plan of Prime Minister Ryzhkov was rejected and presumably also led to Ryzhkov's resignation. The more widely publicized plan was Professor Stanislav Shatalin's "500 Day Plan". It was prepared at Boris Yeltsin's instigation and enjoyed his support. However, Gorbachev found it unacceptable for a variety of reasons, most probably because he was pressured to reject it by the reorganized hardliners and conservatives in the Soviet ruling hierarchy. Gorbachev submitted his own plan which combined elements of both the Ryzhkov and Shatalin plans. However, his plan was shortlived too, and the Sovet Union continued to search for a way out of its economic problems. This short paper offers an excellent comparative explanation of the respective plans.

Diuk, Nadia, and Adrian Karatnycky. *THE HIDDEN NATIONS: THE PEOPLE CHALLENGE THE SOVIET UNION*. New York: William Morrow and Co., 1990. 286 pp.

A description of the nationality tensions and conflicts in the Soviet Union. Intended for a general readership, the book tells the histories of the major Soviet nationalities and explains their aspirations for independence.

Dobson, Richard B. "Youth Problems in the Soviet Union", in *SOVIET SOCIAL PROBLEMS*, edited by Anthony Jones, et al. (Boulder, CO; San Francisco; Oxford: Westview Press, 1991), pp. 227-251.

A thorough examination of juvenile delinquency and crime in Gorbachev's Soviet Union.

Doder, Dusko, and Louise Branson. *GORBACHEV: HERETIC IN THE KREMLIN*. New York: Viking, 1990. x, 450 pp.

Doder, a newspaper correspondent, has written several books about life and society in the Soviet Union. In this book, together with Louise Branson, another correspondent, he attempts to explain the enigma of Gorbachev. There are many interesting insights into Gorbachev's personality and politics (e.g., "the more he sought to disperse power, the more he found it necessary to concentrate power in his own hands"), but in general the authors do not bring any new information about the Soviet Union not described already in other books of the same genre. Nevertheless, this book contains one of the better accounts of the modern Soviet Union.

DOING BUSINESS IN EASTERN EUROPE AND THE SOVIET UNION: COURSE MANUAL. Washington, DC: Federal Publications, 1990. 1 vol., looseleaf.

One more of the many rather superficial descriptions of Soviet and Eastern European laws relating to foreign trade and investment operating in early 1990.

DOING BUSINESS IN THE UNION OF SOVIET SOCIALIST REPUBLICS. New York, Moscow, London: Price Waterhouse, 1991. xii, 134 pp.

In addition to general information about the Soviet Union, this guide includes brief explanations of the main legal, accounting and tax provisions of the Soviet law relating to foreign trade and investment. There is also valuable banking and business information. Unfortunately, many of the details in this publication refer to the situation as it existed prior to the extensive changes which occured in the Soviet Union after the abortive anti-Gorbachev coup of August, 1991.

DOING BUSINESS IN THE USSR. London: Ernst & Whinney (Ernst and Young), 1988. 67 pp.

A brief, business-oriented information booklet about the Soviet Union. Due to the extensive and rapid changes in that country, much of the information is outdated.

DOING BUSINESS WITH THE SOVIET UNION. St. Paul, MN: Advanced Legal Education, Hamline University School of Law, 1991. 369 pp.

Contributions on miscellaneous topics by a variety of lecturers.

☆Doronin, Igor G.
See Sherr, Alan B., et al.

☆Drugueva, Olga. "Legal Education in the USSR", 17 *CORNELL LAW FORUM* 10-11 (July 1990).

A very brief explanation of the most salient features of legal education in the Russian part of the Soviet Union.

D'Zurilla, William T. "Farewell to Lenin: The Story of Russia's New, Non-Communist Constitution", 38 *FEDERAL BAR NEWS AND JOURNAL* 410-412 (1991).

A short account of the Russian Federation's efforts to draft a new Constitution.

EASTERN EUROPE AND THE USSR: A GUIDE TO FOREIGN INVESTMENT LEGISLATION, 3d. ed. KPMG, March 1991. 32 pp.

Several pages of this short brochure published by the international accounting firm of KPMG (place of publication not indicated) contain a convenient summary of the USSR legislation on foreign investments and joint ventures as of the end of 1990.

THE ECONOMY OF THE USSR: A STUDY UNDERTAKEN IN RESPONSE TO A REQUEST BY THE HOUSTON SUMMIT: SUMMARY AND RECOMMENDATIONS. Washington, DC: The World Bank, 1990. iv, 51 pp.

A study of the Soviet economic situation as of 1990, prepared by the staff of the International Monetary Fund, The World Bank, the Organization for Economic Cooperation and Development, and by consultants of the European Bank for Reconstruction and Development. The findings and conclusions are not overly optimistic. One of the main findings is that the Soviet economy is in deep distress, and its reforms during the first five years of Gorbachev's rule have been aimless and inconsistent. The study also deplores the absence of meaningful legal reform. In this respect it comments (at p. 34):

> The most serious legal problem facing the Soviet economic reform effort is the lack of a general accord concerning the location of authority to legislate, the nature and extent of the legislative and executive powers, and the appropriate bodies and methods for implementation of the law.... Some resolution of this conflict, even if temporary and subject to gradual evolution, is clearly required before an economic reform program can be successfully implemented.

On the reform of Soviet economy the study unequivocally recommends an almost total decentralization, the establishment of a market economy and meaningful competition, and private ownership as the first steps in a process which it believes "will be extraordinarily complex and will take many years to complete".

E

Elferink, Alex Oude. "The 1990 USSR-USA Maritime Boundary Agreement", 6 *INTERNATIONAL JOURNAL OF ESTUARINE AND COASTAL LAW* 41-52 (1991).

☆Emelyanov, Alexei. "Agrarian Reform and the Village Today", 22 *SOCIAL SCIENCES* No. 3, 85-97 (1991).

The author, a Soviet agrarian expert, argues that the restructuring of agrarian economy in the Soviet Union is dependent on fair distribution of land. According to the author, this is best achieved through the establishment of cooperatives and the restoration of the old Russian village structure.

English, Richard D. "Privatization by General Fund: Economic Empowerment for Central and Eastern Europe", 24 *GEORGE WASHINGTON JOURNAL OF INTERNATIONAL LAW AND ECONOMICS* 527-586 (1991).

This interesting article discusses the various methods of privatization in Central and Eastern Europe, including the Soviet Union. It explains the problems which the various methods may encounter in their implementations, and the inequities they may create. The author advocates privatization by means of a General Fund. He explains that the essentials of this process or method of privatization can be divided into three phases. These are described as follows (at pp. 535-538):

> In the first phase, ownership of all government-owned enterprises scheduled for privatization would be transferred to a single government agency. Second, the enterprises would be divided into the smallest economically feasible units and organized into corporations. The governmental agency would then allocate assets and liabilities to these units. The single government agency would organize a General Fund, as a corporation, modeled after the closed-end investment company. As the newly organized units are incorporated, each firm would issue its shares to the General Fund, in effect, transferring the agency's direct ownership interest to the General Fund. The General Fund would as a result own shares in all the enterprises to be privatized. The Fund would be

> organized as a closed-end investment company. Since shares would not be redeemable by the issuing General Fund but could be bought and sold by investors, valuation of the shares of the underlying companies would be unnecessary at the time those shares are transferred into the General Fund.
>
> The distribution of shares in the General Fund would be facilitated through issuance of certificates of entitlement to every citizen of the country. Each certificate would entitle a citizen to receive an equal number of shares of the agency's General Fund free of cost or for a nominal sum....
>
> The General Fund would also make a series of public offerings or large sales of shares in its portfolio in order to establish market values for those shares....
>
> Third, the General Fund would eventually dissolve either by sale of underlying shares and distributions to shareholders or by General Fund shareholders converting their General Fund shares into shares in privately organized mutual funds, or a combination of both.

The author believes the General Fund approach to be the fairest and most efficient method of privatization. Other methods, in his opinion, will lead to a concentration of assets in foreign hands or the former *nomenklatura*, which would create more political and economic problems than it would solve.

☆Entin, Vladimir L. "Law and Glasnost", in *PERESTROIKA AND THE RULE OF LAW: ANGLO-AMERICAN AND SOVIET PERSPECTIVES,* edited by William E. Butler (London: I.B. Tauris & Co., Ltd., 1991), pp. 101-116.

☆Entin, Vladimir L. "The Road to Freedom for the Soviet Press."
See Baturin, Yuriy M., Vladimir L. Entin, and Mikhail A. Fedotov.

☆Entin, Vladimir L.
See also THE HEARTBEAT OF REFORM: SOVIET JURISTS AND POLITICAL SCIENTISTS DISCUSS THE PROGRESS OF PERESTROIKA.

Ernst & Whinney.
See DOING BUSINESS IN THE USSR.

☆Eventov, Zinoviy M.
See Sherr, Alan B., et al.

F

☆Faminsky, Igor P.
See also Sherr, Alan B., et al.

☆Faminsky, Igor P., and Alexander Naumov. "A Description of Soviet Laws and Policies on Joint Ventures", in *BEHIND THE FACTORY WALLS: DECISION MAKING IN SOVIET AND US ENTERPRISES,* edited by Paul R. Lawrence and Charalambos A. Vlachoutsicos (Boston: Harvard Business School Press, 1990), pp. 301-306.

☆"Fear: Confessions of a Well-Known Legal Expert Who Has Criticized the Draft Law on the KGB", 30 *SOVIET LAW AND GOVERNMENT* No. 2, 88-96 (Fall 1991).

Interview with Professor Valerii Savitskii of the Institute of State and Law of the USSR Academy of Sciences, originally published in the *Literaturnaia Gazeta* No. 46, 1990 (November 14, 1990).

The Federal Institute for Soviet and International Studies. *THE SOVIET UNION, 1988-1989: PERESTROIKA IN CRISIS?* Boulder, CO: Westview Press, 1990. xv, 410 pp.

Since 1973 the Federal Institute for Soviet and International Studies (das Bundesinstitut für Ostwissenschaftliche und Internationale Studien) in Cologne, the Federal Republic of Germany, has periodically published extensive surveys of political and economic events and developments in the Soviet Union. This volume is the tenth in the series. The contents of several chapters may be of direct interest to legal researchers:

"Anatomy of an Escalation: The Nationality Question" by Uwe Halbach.

"Church-State Relations in the USSR in 1988: The Local Sobor of the Russian Orthodox Church" by Dimitry V. Pospielovsky.

"The KGB and Perestroika" by Astrid von Borcke.

"Legal Reform as a Means of Perestroika" by Karin Schmid.

"The Nineteenth Party Conference: Reform of the Political System" by Eberhard Schneider.

☆Fedorenko, Sergei. "Options for Future Strategic Arms Reduction", in *FROM COEXISTENCE TO COOPERATION: INTERNATIONAL LAW AND ORGANIZATION IN THE POST-COLD WAR ERA,* edited by Edward McWhinney, et al. (Dordrecht, The Netherlands: Martinus Nijhoff Publishers, 1991), pp. 79-93.

☆Fedorov, Vladimir N.
See Stephan, Paul B. III, and Boris M. Klimenko.

☆Fedotov, Mikhail A. "The Road to Freedom for the Soviet Press."
See Baturin, Yuriy M., Vladimir L. Entin and Mikhail A. Fedotov.

☆Fedotov, Mikhail A.
See also THE HEARTBEAT OF REFORM: SOVIET JURISTS AND POLITICAL SCIENTISTS DISCUSS THE PROGRESS OF PERESTROIKA.

Feige, Edgar L. "Perestroika and Ruble Convertibility", 10 *CATO JOURNAL* 631-653 (1991).

An economist examines the institutional and structural prerequisites to a meaningful improvement of the Soviet economy. One of these prerequisites is the stabilization of the ruble currency. But ruble convertibility is predicated upon the Soviet Union choosing the correct reform path and succeeeding in its implementation.

Feldbrugge, F.J.M. "West-East Technology Transfer in the Context of Perestroika", in *LAW AND POLITICS OF WEST-EAST TECHNOLOGY TRANSFER,* edited by Hiroshi Oda (Dordrecht/Boston/London: Martinus Nijhoff/Graham & Trotman, 1991), pp. 265-269.

Observations about changing attitudes towards technology transfers in the Soviet Union as well as in the West.

Felker, Timothy L. "Perestroyka and Western Direct Investment: The Task of Integrating a Western Company into the Changing Soviet Economy", 12 *UNIVERSITY OF PENNSYLVANIA JOURNAL OF INTERNATIONAL BUSINESS LAW* 219-244 (1991).

A thorough analysis of the legal and economic problems foreign investors face in the Soviet Union. The article discusses the Soviet economic and monetary systems, as well as the inefficiences and obstacles emerging from the Soviet attempts to change these systems from centrally controlled bureaucracies into more open market models. The author does not favor foreign investment. He concludes that there are still too many restrictions and barriers, as well as uncertainties about the consequences of any changes that may be introduced by the Soviet governing bodies.

☆Feofanov, Iurii. "A Return to Origins: Reflections on Power and Law", 29 *SOVIET LAW AND GOVERNMENT* No. 3, 15-52 (Winter 1990-91).

Originally published in the Russian language in the February, 1989 issue of *Znamia*, a publication of the USSR Writers' Union, this article underscores (like some other recent writings originating in the Soviet Union) the inability of the Soviet people to understand the proper purpose of the law as a means for the protection of their rights. Even after several years of liberalizing legal reforms, the Soviet public continues to be oblivious of the meaning of civil liberties, and its attitude to law is submissive and distrustful. Feofanov calls for a more extensive rule of law, as well as a stronger sense of justice in the activities of the government.

Interesting are Feofanov's remarks covering Lenin's attitudes toward the rule of law. On the one hand, Lenin recognized the need for a state governed by law. On the other, it was Lenin who used ruthless and brutal force to hold on to personal power. The author asserts that Lenin's deceptive approach set the style for Stalin and subsequent leaders of the USSR. While many of the author's specific comments are made obsolete by subsequent events, his main thesis about the use of the rule of law in the Soviet Union remains valid.

Fitch, Stephen D. "The Harriman Manganese Concession in the Soviet Union: Lessons for Today", 9 *INTERNATIONAL TAX AND BUSINESS LAWYER* 209-271 (1991).

In 1925 W. Averell Harriman, an American industrialist and subsequently one of President Roosevelt's close advisers, signed an agreement with the Soviet Union for a concession to mine manganese deposits at Tchiatouri, Georgia. The agreement was to remain in force until 1945, but was terminated by the Soviet government in 1928. This article describes in some detail the history of the negotiations leading up to the making of the agreement as well as the subsequent events leading to its termination. The text of the agreement is included in an appendix. It makes a good precedent for any concessionary arrangements being negotiated in the Soviet Union today.

Fitzmaurice, M. *THE CHANGING POLITICAL STRUCTURE OF EUROPE: ASPECTS OF INTERNATIONAL LAW.*
See Lefeber, R., Malgosia Fitzmaurice, and E.W. Vierdag.

Fitzmaurice, M. *INTERNATIONAL LEGAL PROBLEMS OF THE ENVIRONMENTAL PROTECTION OF THE BALTIC SEA.* Dordrecht, The Netherlands: Martinus Nijhoff/Graham & Trotman, 1992. xxix, 328 pp.

Perhaps the definitive work on the subject, this book also discusses Soviet policies and attitudes as well as the regional and local Soviet arrangements prior to its fragmentation in late 1991.

Flanz, Gisbert H. *CONSTITUTIONS OF THE COUNTRIES OF THE WORLD.*
See Blaustein, Albert P., and Gisbert H. Flanz.

Floroff, Olga, and Susan W. Tiefenbrun. "A Legal Framework for Soviet Privatization", 18 *PEPPERDINE LAW REVIEW* No. 4, 849-892 (1991).

On July 1, 1991, the USSR Supreme Soviet enacted the Fundamental Principles of Destatization and Privatization of Enterprises, and on July 3, 1991 the RSFSR introduced the Law on Privatization of State and Municipal Enterprises. Both of these laws were intended to pave the way towards the creation of a market economy. The authors, both specialists in Soviet law, examine the adequacy of the Soviet legal framework to ensure a successful implementation of this 1991 privatization legislation. They devote considerable attention to the laws enacted in the Soviet Union during 1989-1991 on cooperatives, joint stock and limited liability companies, property, land use, small enterprises, leasing, and foreign investment.

Floroff, Olga, and Susan W. Tiefenbrun. "New Soviet Fundamentals of Law on Land Ownership", 4 *NEW YORK INTERNATIONAL LAW REVIEW* 92-106 (1991).

The authors discuss the 1990 Soviet legislation.

Fogelklou, Anders. *SOVIET FEDERALISM AND BALTIC CLAIMS FOR SOVEREIGNTY.* Uppsala, Sweden: Uppsala University, Department of Soviet and East European Studies, 1990. 21 pp. (Working Papers, 3).

A thoroughly documented study of the legitimacy of the claims for independence by the three Baltic republics. The author carefully examines the relevant provisions of the Soviet Constitution and laws, as well as the constitutional and legislative measures of the three Baltic republics. His conclusion is that prospects for independence or autonomy are dependent upon the forging of a treaty between the Soviet Union and the republics. He does not believe that within the existing legal structure and political climate of the Soviet Union independence can be achieved unilaterally. Though published in early 1990, the paper foresees subsequent efforts of the

Soviet government to squash attempts toward freedom in the Baltic throughout 1990 and early 1991.

FOREIGN INVESTMENT IN THE USSR. KEY 1990 LEGISLATION. *See* International Chamber of Commerce.

Franckx, Erik. "First Trijunction Point Agreed upon in the Baltic between Poland, Sweden, and the USSR", 5 *INTERNATIONAL JOURNAL OF ESTUARINE AND COASTAL LAW* 394-397 (1990).

Franckx, Erik. "Further Steps in the Clarification of the Soviet Position on the Innocent Passage of Foreign Warships through Its Territorial Waters", 19 *GEORGIA JOURNAL OF INTERNATIONAL AND COMPARATIVE LAW* 535-563 (1989).

Franckx, Erik. "International Cooperation in Respect of the Baltic Sea", in *THE CHANGING POLITICAL STRUCTURE OF EUROPE: ASPECTS OF INTERNATIONAL LAW,* edited by R. Lefeber, M. Fitzmaurice, and E.W. Vierdag (Dordrecht, The Netherlands: Martinus Nijhoff Publishers, 1991), pp. 245-277.

A comprehensive examination of the boundary, fishing, and ecological issues in the Baltic Sea. Includes discussions of policy interests and attitudes of the Soviet Union and the Baltic states on maritime issues in the Baltic.

Fraser, Niall M., Keith W. Hipel, John Jaworsky, and Ralph Zuljan. "A Conflict Analysis of the Armenian-Azerbaijan Dispute", 34 *JOURNAL OF CONFLICT RESOLUTION* 652-677 (1990).

This article by four political scientists may be of some relevance to legal research because it contains a chronology as well as considerable factual information about the ongoing hostilities between Armenia and Azerbaijan which commenced with the disturbances in Nagorno-Karabakh in 1988.

FREE MARKET TAKEOVER: A LEGAL GUIDE TO INVESTING IN EASTERN EUROPE, USSR, CHINA AND VIETNAM, a Special Supplement to the July 1981 issue of *INTERNATIONAL FINANCIAL LAW REVIEW.*

Includes a useful report on Soviet laws relating to investments, formation of business organizations, and conduct of business by foreigners as of mid-1991, written by William E. Holland, Mikhail Rozenberg, and Robert E. Langer.

Freeman, M.D.A. "The Rule of Law—Conservative, Liberal, Marxist and Neo-Marxist: Wherein Lies the Attraction?", in *PERESTROIKA AND THE RULE OF LAW: ANGLO-AMERICAN AND SOVIET PERSPECTIVES,* edited by William E. Butler (London: I.B. Tauris & Co., Ltd., 1991), pp. 37-59.

French, Hillary F. "Green Revolution: Environmental Reconstruction in Eastern Europe and the Soviet Union", 26 *THE COLUMBIA JOURNAL OF WORLD BUSINESS* 28-52 (1991).

A thorough documentation of environmental damage in Eastern Europe and the Soviet Union. There is also a valuable discussion of the relevant political issues influencing or affecting environmental reform.

Frenkel, William G. "Growth of Commercial Banking in the USSR", 9 *INTERNATIONAL FINANCIAL LAW REVIEW* No. 8, 27-28 (August 1990).

A brief introduction to the 1990 Soviet banking reforms.

Frenkel, William G. "Soviet Bank Legislation Enacted", 5 *JOURNAL OF INTERNATIONAL BANKING LAW* 507-510 (1991).

A brief look at the 1991 reorganization of the Soviet banking system and the introduction of commercial banks.

Frenkel, William G. "Soviet Company Law: An Overview", 1 *INTERNATIONAL COMPANY AND COMMERCIAL LAW REVIEW* 153-157 (1990).

Frenkel, William G. "Soviet Insurance Market Open to New Business", 9 *INTERNATIONAL FINANCIAL LAW REVIEW* No. 11, 36-38 (November 1990).

A brief description of the insurance industry and its regulation in the USSR.

Frenkel, William G. "U.S.S.R. Legislation: Proposed Amendments to Soviet Civil Law Concerning Property, Legal Personality, and Commerce", 2 *INTERNATIONAL COMPANY AND COMMERCIAL LAW REVIEW* 46-48 (1991).

Frenkel, William G., and R. Cameron Kennedy. "The Soviet Ruble: How Convertible is Convertible?" 10 *INTERNATIONAL FINANCIAL LAW REVIEW* No. 3, 29-31 (March 1991).

Frenkel, William G., and Jeffrey Sperber. "From Borscht to Bits: Transfer of Technology and Industrial Property in the Soviet Union", 4 *DE PAUL BUSINESS LAW JOURNAL* 3-48 (1991).

The authors begin this comprehensive and excellently organized survey of the relevant Soviet law and practice with a statement that "[t]ransfers of technology and industrial property have probably accounted for the majority of all United States-Soviet trade and investment transactions in the last two decades." The article then describes the legal structures required for transfers of technology, takes a brief look at COCOM and other United States transfer of technology restrictions, and then discusses international and Soviet legal provisions relating to such transfers. The article concludes with a surprisingly informed discussion, given the difficulty of obtaining reliable information, of technology transfer practices.

Friedlaender, Michael, ed. *FOREIGN TRADE IN EASTERN EUROPE AND THE SOVIET UNION.* Boulder, CO; San Francisco; London: Westview Press, 1990. xiii, 241 pp. (Published in cooperation with the Vienna Institute for Comparative Economic Studies as its "Yearbook II").

The title of this collection of papers is self-explanatory. The focus is directed predominantly at economic issues. Papers relevant to the Soviet Union include:

"Finnish-Soviet Economic Relations" by Hubert Garbrisch.
"Four Small Countries' Relations with the Soviet Union" by Sándor Richter.
"Mechanism and Institutional System of the Finnish-Soviet Economic Relations" by Gábor Obláth and Peter Pete.
"The Mechanism of Hungarian-Soviet Economic Relations" by Margit Rácz and Sándor Richter.
"Soviet Perestroika and Foreign Trade" by Peter Havlik.

Furtado, Charles F., Jr., and Andrea Chandler. *PERESTROIKA IN THE SOVIET REPUBLICS: DOCUMENTS ON THE NATIONAL QUESTION.* Boulder, CO: Westview Press, 1992. xxvi, 646 pp.

A collection of official and unofficial documents on nationality issues in the Soviet Union, the quest for independence by the individual republics, and the problems of ethnic conflicts. The documents cover the period from 1986 to early 1991. They are grouped into several sections based on their geographic relationship. The first group consists of documents emanating from the Communist Party and the central government in Moscow. This is followed by documents originating respectively in the Baltic republics, Ukraine, Byelorussia, Moldavia, the Russian Federation, the republics and regions of the Caucasus, and then the republics of Central Asia. The volume concludes with a remarkably detailed and thorough chronology of nationality-related events in the Soviet Union during the 1985-1991 period, prepared by Edward Walker.

G

☆Gamaiunov, Igor. "Without Hypnosis: Supervising the KGB—Myth or Reality?", 30 *SOVIET LAW AND GOVERNMENT* No. 2, 76-87 (Fall 1991).

An interview with Viktor Iliukhin, Chief of the USSR Procuracy's Administration for Supervision of Observance of the Laws on State Security, translated from *Literaturnaia Gazeta*, 1990, No. 42 (October 17, 1990).

Garbrisch, Hubert. "Finnish-Soviet Economic Relations", in *FOREIGN TRADE IN EASTERN EUROPE AND THE SOVIET UNION*, edited by Michael Friedlaender (Boulder, CO; San Francisco; London: Westview Press, 1990), pp. 117-126.

Gardner, Richard N. "The Triple Crisis of the Soviet Union Today", 11 *NEW YORK LAW SCHOOL JOURNAL OF INTERNATIONAL AND COMPARATIVE LAW* 435-437 (1990).

A short address on the struggle taking place in the Soviet Union. The author identifies four main groups of protagonists: Russian nationalists, old Communists, reformed Communists, and liberals. He concludes that the future is unpredictable.

George, Arthur L. *JOINT VENTURES IN THE SOVIET UNION: LAW AND PRACTICE.*
See Theroux, Eugene, and Arthur L. George.

George, Arthur L., and Thomas A. O'Donnell. *BUSINESS OPERATIONS IN THE U.S.S.R.* Washington, DC: Tax Management, Inc., 1991. (Tax Management, Foreign Income Portfolios, 990).

An excellent summary of legislation in the Soviet Union prior to its breakup dealing with business operations by foreigners. It includes a detailed description of the pertinent taxation laws as well as English translations of a number of Soviet laws.

George, Arthur L., and Thomas A. O'Donnell. "The New Soviet Tax System: Moving into the Modern Age, with Growing Pains", 3 *TAX NOTES INTERNATIONAL* 499-502 (May 1991).

George, Arthur L., and Thomas A. O'Donnell. "Russian Republic Joint-Stock Decree: Tidings of Great Joy?", 18 *TAX PLANNING INTERNATIONAL REVIEW* No. 8, 14-16 (August, 1991).

A brief description of the Joint-Stock Company Decree of December, 1990.

George, Arthur L., and Thomas A. O'Donnell. "United States-Soviet Joint Ventures", 20 *TAX MANAGEMENT INTERNATIONAL JOURNAL* 73-85 and 99-114 (1991).

Georgopoulos, Zach. "Soviet and Chinese Dissent Laws: Glasnost v. Tienanmen" (Note), 14 *HASTINGS INTERNATIONAL AND COMPARATIVE LAW REVIEW* 475-503 (1991).

A comparative examination of Soviet and Chinese trends in defining crimes against the state.

Geron, Leonard. *JOINT VENTURES IN THE USSR: DATA BASE 1991 EDITION,* 2d ed. Oxford: D.G. Oxford Consultants, 1991. 432 pp.

First published in 1989 by the Royal Institute of International Affairs in London under the title "Joint Ventures in the USSR: The State of Play", this book surveys the formation and operation of joint ventures in the USSR. It does not specifically discuss or analyze the relevant legislation, but there is much useful information of an economic and practical nature.

Geron, Leonard. *SOVIET FOREIGN ECONOMIC POLICY UNDER PERESTROIKA*. London: The Royal Institute of International Affairs; New York: Council on Foreign Relations Press, 1990. x, 126 pp. (Chatham House Papers).

But for the endless changes in the Soviet Union, this book could well serve as a convenient reference source for Soviet policies and practices in foreign trade and investment. It includes chapters on institutional and legal bases of foreign economic activities, joint ventures, and Soviet participation in international economic organizations. Useful summaries of Soviet legislation on foreign economic matters appear in the appendices.

Getty, J. Arch. "State and Society under Stalin: Constitutions and Elections in the 1930s", 50 *Slavic Review* 18-35 (1991).

It has been generally held among historians that the Stalin Constitution of 1936 was created entirely for propaganda purposes. In this thoroughly researched article, based on newly surfaced materials, Getty attempts to disprove this point of view. This is one of the first detailed studies in English of the drafting history of the 1936 USSR Constitution.

Gifford, Donald C. "Glasnost and Perestroika at West Virginia University: The College of Law's Soviet Exchange Program", 94 *WEST VIRGINIA LAW REVIEW* 165-177 (1991).

In the context of an exchange program between the West Virginia College of Law and the Donetsk University Faculty of Law and Economics, the author comments on the nature and content of legal education in the Soviet Union.

Ginsburgs, George. "The Citizenship of the Baltic States", 21 *JOURNAL OF BALTIC STUDIES* 3-26 (1990).

An excellent article on the struggle of the Baltic States for independence. Ginsburgs takes an in-depth look at the historical factors, the political and ideological factors, and other relevant issues. He also examines the legal aspects of citizenship in the three Baltic republics.

Ginsburgs, George. "Earlier Publication Practice: The Case of the 1959 Sbornik", in *THE SOVIET SOBRANIE OF LAWS,* edited by Richard M. Buxbaum and Kathryn Hendley (Berkeley, CA: University of California at Berkeley, 1991), pp. 197-210.

Ginsburgs, George. "Perestroika in the Soviet Union and the Common Law of Mankind", 17 *REVIEW OF SOCIALIST LAW* 1-49 (1991).

An insightful and penetrating analysis of the forces and motives which shape the attitudes of Soviet leadership on questions of international law and policy. The article examines these issues in the context of the changing Soviet attitudes in international discussions on human rights. The author concludes that in general the Soviet progress toward real implementation of human rights principles and a rule of law is a modest one.

Ginsburgs, George. "Soviet Citizenship Law: Recent Practices and Proposed Reforms", 36 *OSTEURAPA RECHT* 251-275 (1990).

In this article Professor Ginsburgs updates his definitive treatise on Soviet citizenship law. He also comments on the new Soviet law on citizenship enacted on May 23, 1990.

Ginsburgs, George. "Soviet International Law and Baltic Environmental Protection", 38 *OSTEUROPA RECHT* 52-64 (1992).

Ginsburgs, George. *THE SOVIET UNION AND INTERNATIONAL COOPERATION IN LEGAL MATTERS—PART II: CIVIL LAW.* (Law in Eastern Europe No. 43). Dordrecht, The Netherlands: Martinus Nijhoff Publishers, 1991. xiv, 393 pp.

According to the publisher's abstract, this second volume of a three-volume set "concentrates essentially on the post-World War II experience, with some reference to pre-1945 antecedents in order to put the picture in a clearer perspective.... The author analyzes the ensemble of rules observed between states whereby legal organs of one will procure for the legal organs of the other procedural services designed to facilitate performance by the recipient party of its mission to 'administer justice.'"

Ginsburgs, George. "The Soviet Union and International Co-operation in Penal Matters", 41 *INTERNATIONAL AND COMPARATIVE LAW QUARTERLY* 85-116 (1992).

In this exceptionally well-organized article, Professor Ginsburgs explains the operation of the convention which entered into force among the former socialist countries on August 26, 1979. It provided for the transfer of prisoners between the member-states to serve their sentences at home. The convention was signed on May 19, 1978.

It is not certain whether this convention remains in force after the late 1980 political changes in Eastern Europe and the 1991 breakup of the Soviet Union.

Ginsburgs, George. "The USSR and the Socialist Model of International Cooperation in Criminal Matters", 17 *REVIEW OF SOCIALIST LAW* 199-278 (1991).

In this detailed article (really a short monograph), Professor Ginsburgs summarizes all aspects of cooperation in criminal matters among the countries of the former Soviet Bloc. How much of this cooperation remains after the breakup of the Soviet Union is not certain. Nevertheless the article remains useful as historical background for any cooperation which the respective countries may develop in the future.

Ginsburgs, George, and Vladimir Kudryavtsev, eds. *THE NUREMBERG TRIAL AND INTERNATIONAL LAW.* Dordrecht, The Netherlands: Martinus Nijhoff, 1990. xvi, 288 pp. (Law in Eastern Europe No. 42).

Includes contributions by the following Soviet scholars: Nikolai F. Chistiakov, Vladimir N. Kudriavtsev, Aleksander M. Larin, Irina A. Lediakh, Igor I. Lukashuk, and Iurii A. Reshetov.

Girnius, Kestutis. "Baltic States Opt for Independence", in *SOVIET FEDERALISM: NATIONALISM AND ECONOMIC DECENTRALISATION,* edited by Alastair McAuley (Leicester and London: Leicester University Press, 1991), pp. 160-177.

The author of this paper analyzes the various arguments in favor of the independence of the Baltic states.

Girnius, Kestutis. "The Party and Popular Movements in the Baltic", in *TOWARD INDEPENDENCE: THE BALTIC POPULAR MOVEMENTS*, edited by Jan Arveds Trapans (Boulder, CO; San Francisco; Oxford: Westview Press, 1991), pp. 57-69.

Gitelman, Zvi. *DEVELOPMENTS IN SOVIET POLITICS.* *See* White, Stephen, Alex Pravda and Zvi Gitelman.

Gitelman, Zvi. "Glasnost, Perestroika and Antisemitism", 70 *FOREIGN AFFAIRS* No. 2, 141-159 (Spring 1991).

A study of Soviet attitudes towards the Jews, Jewish living conditions in the Soviet Union, appearance of antisemitic manifestations among some groups of the Soviet society, and Jewish emigration. The author points out that there is much less antisemitism in the Soviet Union than is generally reported in the West and that the government's attitude towards the Jews ranges from favorable to neutral. According to Gitelman, the extensive emigration of the Jews is due mainly to the feeling of uncertainty they have about the future of the Soviet Union.

Giuliani, Federico. "Recent Trends in Soviet Legislation: Joint Ventures, Ownership, and Leasing", 2 *INTERNATIONAL COMPANY AND COMMERCIAL LAW REVIEW* 202-206 (1991).

Gleason, Gregory. *FEDERALISM AND NATIONALISM: THE STRUGGLE FOR REPUBLICAN RIGHTS IN THE USSR.* Boulder, CO: Westview Press, Inc., 1990. xiii, 170 pp.

The author of this book takes a careful look at the character of federalism in the Soviet Union. He discusses the inherent weaknesses of the system as well as the different ethnic and social forces emerging in opposition to the intensively centralist nature of the Soviet government system.

Though now predominantly historical in its content, this is an interesting and valuable book which students of the nationality problems of the former Soviet Union should not ignore.

Reviewed by Richard H. Rowland in 51 *Russian Review* 282-283 (1992).

Glick, Steven M., and Alexei A. Klishin. "Doing Business in the U.S.S.R.: Welcome to the 'New Antipodes'", 9 *INTERNATIONAL FINANCIAL LAW REVIEW* No. 12, 28-31 (December 1990).

Two attorneys, one American and one Soviet, both practicing in Moscow, describe in a general way the different options foreign businesspeople have for the conduct of trade or for investment in the Soviet Union in 1990.

This is the first of several short articles by the two authors. Despite the brevity of their presentation, the authors offer much useful information.

Glick, Steven M., and Alexei A. Klishin. "Federalist Fever: Economic and Banking Reform in the USSR", 10 *INTERNATIONAL FINANCIAL LAW REVIEW* No. 1, 32-34 (January 1991).

A short description of the 1990 reorganization of the Soviet banking system.

Goble, Paul A. "Nationalism, Movement Groups, and Party Formation", in *PERESTROIKA FROM BELOW: SOCIAL MOVEMENTS IN THE SOVIET UNION,* edited by Judith Sedaitis and Jim Butterfield (Boulder, CO: Westview Press, 1991), pp. 165-174.

Gödan, Jürgen Christoph, and Holger Knudsen. *BIBLIOTHEK UND RECHT INTERNATIONAL/LIBRARIES AND LAW—INTERNATIONAL, FESTSCHRIFT RALPH LANSKY.* Hamburg and Augsburg: Arbeitgemeinschaft für juristisches Bibliotheks- und Dokumentationswesen, 1991.

Includes an article by Adolf Sprudzs entitled "The Rule of Law and the Baltic States".

Goldberg, Stephanie B. "The Soviet Union Retreats from Reform: Danger on the Right", 77 *ABA JOURNAL* No. 5, 71-73 (May 1991).

Brief interviews with American scholars and a group of Soviet judges during their visit to the United States about the future developments in the Soviet Union: whether liberalism will eventually prevail or the rigid conservatism of the past may get the upper hand again. The responses are highly mixed (and not supported by subsequent events).

Goldman, Marshall I. "Pollution in the Soviet Union: The Growth of Environmentalism and Its Consequences", in *SOVIET SOCIAL PROBLEMS*, edited by Anthony Jones, et al. (Boulder, CO; San Francisco; Oxford: Westview Press, 1991), pp. 39-56.

Goldman, Marshall I. *WHAT WENT WRONG WITH PERESTROIKA.* New York: W.W. Norton & Company, 1991. 258 pp.

Though this book does not focus on law, it will undoubtedly become compulsory reading for some time in the future for anyone who wishes to study the breakdown of the communist regime in the Soviet Union as well as the eventual collapse of the country itself. It is a book about Gorbachev and his main economists—Abel Aganbegyan, Leonid Abalkin, Nikolai Petrakov, Grigory Yavlinsky, and Stanislav Shatalin.

The author, who is the Associate Director of the Russian Research Center of Harvard University and Professor of Economics of Wellesley College, describes how, with the help of these economists—mostly academics and with little practical experience or none—Gorbachev attempted to turn around the Soviet economy.

Reviewing this book for the *New York Times Book Review* (February 2, 1992), Melor Sturua writes that Professor Goldman offers splendid descriptions of the economists, most of whom he knows personally. The same cannot be said about Goldman's description of Gorbachev which, according to Sturua, is based on wrong premises and assumptions. Despite these shortcomings Sturua believes the book to be useful and "even successful". He concludes:

> Reading this book, with its vivid portraits, its stark pictures of incompetence, ignorance and frustration, one comes to sense not why but how perestroika rotted, how the regime that Mr. Gorbachev unsuccessfully tried to save with his invention ultimately decomposed.

Goldman, Marshall I.
See also Commission on Security and Cooperation in Europe, *THE USSR IN CRISIS: STATE OF THE UNION.*

Goldman, Stuart. "The New Soviet Legislative Branch", in *PERESTROIKA-ERA POLITICS: THE NEW SOVIET LEGISLATURE AND GORBACHEV'S POLITICAL REFORMS,* edited by Robert Huber and Donald R. Kelley (Armonk, NY: M.E. Sharpe, Inc., 1991), pp. 51-75.

Goldstein, Gordon. "Anti-Satellite Weapons and U.S. National Security", 22 *NEW YORK UNIVERSITY JOURNAL OF INTERNATIONAL LAW AND POLITICS* 519-555 (1990).

This article examines Soviet and American satellite activities, anti-satellite weapons ("Star War" developments), and the arrangements between the two countries with regard to such activities.

Goldstein, Irving. "Telecommunications in the Soviet Union", 5 *JOURNAL OF LAW AND TECHNOLOGY* 21-23 (Winter 1990).

An adaptation of an address given by the author to the Second Annual Symposium on the Law and Outer Space, discussing the needs and opportunities for telecommunications in the Soviet Union.

☆Gorbachev, Mikhail. *THE AUGUST COUP: THE TRUTH AND THE LESSONS.* New York: Harper Collins, 1991. 127 pp.

A strange and unsuccessful coup against Gorbachev by some of his closest colleagues took place in August, 1991. Gorbachev and his family were kept prisoners at their vacation home in the Crimea for a few days. When the coup failed and Gorbachev could return to Moscow, mainly due to the resistance movement organized by Boris Yeltsin, the structure of government and the balance of power in the Soviet Union became totally different, and Gorbachev was forced to surrender many of his powers to the leaderships of the individual republics. The Baltics became independent. Subsequent events led to a complete geopolitical reorganization of the Soviet Union.

In this hurriedly written book Gorbachev attempts to present his explanation of the coup. Unfortunately, it is not a good work and not even very readable. The Soviet political figures (see also references in this book to Shevardnadze, Sobchak, and Yeltsin) do not seem to understand that they must be frank and honest in their accounts of current events for their books to be meaningful.

Reviewed by Vladimir Bukovsky, *New Republic,* Jan. 6 & 13, 1992, pp. 41-44 (scathing, critical).

Gordievsky, Oleg.
See Andrew, Christopher, and Oleg Gordievsky.

☆Gorin, Alexander, and Piotr Mishchenko. "New Political Thinking as a Tool of Soviet Foreign Policy", 17 *JOURNAL OF LEGISLATION* 13-21 (1990).

Two Soviet scholars reexamine their countries' attitudes towards the character of international relations.

Gotbaum, Noah E.
See Sherr, Alan B. et al.

☆Gradov, Yuri.
See THE HEARTBEAT OF REFORM: SOVIET JURISTS AND POLITICAL SCIENTISTS DISCUSS THE PROGRESS OF PERESTROIKA.

Grancelli, Bruno. *SOVIET MANAGEMENT AND LABOR RELATIONS.* Boston: Allen and Unwin, 1988. xvi, 248 pp.

This is a revised and updated version of a book previously published in Italian. According to a review by Karl W. Ryavec in 40 *Problems of Communism* (No. 1-2, 150-154 (January-April 1991), at p. 150):

> The first of three major sections of this book concentrates on the main characteristics of labor relations during the three major industrialization drives in Russian history: that promoted by Peter the Great, the second and partly capitalist one of the late imperial period, and the one imposed by Stalin. The second section describes labor legislation and the main features of social planning at enterprise and territorial levels. The final section contains chapters on the present and long-standing relationship between factory administrations and higher authorities, particularly "webs of mutual involvement" or "family circles," and their economic effects; on industrial

relations in the workplace and the dualistic functioning of trade-union committees; on the personal characteristics and the strategic behavior of three types of workers—the "vanguard of production," the "individualists," and the "backwards"; and on strikes and attempts to set up new, independent trade unions.

Grazin, Igor. "The International Recognition of National Rights: The Baltic States' Case", 66 *NOTRE DAME LAW REVIEW* 1385-1419 (1991).

A lengthy discussion of ethnic relations in the Baltic states and the claims of the Baltic people for independence. The author, who is a professor of law in Estonia, examines the international legitimacy of these claims.

Grazin, Igor. "The Problems of Federalism in the Former Soviet Union: The Parallels with Pre-Civil War America", 18 *JOURNAL OF LEGISLATION* 69-85 (1991).

The author, a former Soviet legislator and now a professor of law in Estonia, offers interesting parallels between the federal system in the pre-Civil War United States and the former Soviet Union. After examining the secession issue in both countries, he concludes that justifications for the preservation of a federal system in the United States were based on solid grounds, whereas:

> [The] only real justification for the preservation of the Soviet Union was to create a more effective economic system and a system which better protects human liberties... Unfortunately, this had not been the case. By rejecting any kind of economic reform, and by strengthening the system of authoritarian and administrative power, the federal authorities of the Soviet Union managed to sharpen their political conflict with the republics.

Griffin, Andrew T. "Joint Ventures in the Soviet Union: A Review of Current Literature in English".
See Kavass, Igor I., and Andrew T. Griffin

Griffin, Andrew T., and Larry D. Soderquist. "Private Companies in the Soviet Union: Cooperatives in the Era of Perestroika", 32 *HARVARD INTERNATIONAL LAW JOURNAL* 201-225 (1991).

A detailed discussion of Soviet legislation on cooperatives with a particular emphasis on the Law on Cooperatives of May 26, 1988 and its October 16, 1989 and June 6, 1990 amendments.

Griffin, Andrew T., and Larry D. Soderquist. "The Soviet Cooperative before Perestroika: The Leninist versus the Stalinist Concept", 39 *AMERICAN JOURNAL OF COMPARATIVE LAW* 599-609 (1991).

A brief historical account of the emergence of cooperatives in the Lenin period and their subsequent fate during the early period of Stalin's rule. The authors do not see cooperatives having a successful future.

Grzybowski, Kazimierz. "Soviet Theory of International Law for the Perestroika", 36 *OSTEUROPA-RECHT* 276-282 (1990).

In a clear and concise manner Professor Grzybowski explains the changes taking place in the Soviet policies on international law. He comments on the writings of V.S. Vereschchetin and R.A. Mullerson, both of the Institute of State and Law at the USSR Academy of Sciences, who were among the first of the Soviet scholars to develop new directions in Soviet international law.

Gureckas, Algimantas P. "Lithuania's Boundaries and Territorial Claims between Lithuania and Neighboring States", 12 *NEW YORK LAW SCHOOL JOURNAL OF INTERNATIONAL AND COMPARATIVE LAW* 107-150 (1991).

A historical account of Lithuania's boundaries and boundary rights. The author discusses in great detail Lithuania's boundary adjustments during the Soviet period of annexation. He concludes that recent Soviet claims to some of the Lithuanian territory are without legal merit.

☆Gureyev, S. *THE ECONOMIC ZONE: AN INTERNATIONAL LEGAL ASPECT.* Moscow: Progress Publishers, 1990. 164 pp.

An examination from the Soviet perspective of the legal regimes applicable to waters, sea-bed, and ocean subsoil contiguous to land. The author explains the emergence of territorial waters, and the subsequent expansion of government controls over maritime areas by the creation of such concepts as the "continental shelf", "economic zone", etc.

A translation of the author's work originally published in Russian as *Ekonomicheskaia Zona.*

Gutner, Tamar L. *INVESTING IN REFORM: DOING BUSINESS IN A CHANGING SOVIET UNION.*
See Claudon, Michael P., and Tamar L. Gutman.

☆Gutsenko, Konstantin. "The Right to a Defense", 30 *SOVIET LAW AND GOVERNMENT* No. 3, 78-95 (Winter, 1991-92).

A general and rather emotional plea for the rights of accused in criminal investigations and trials.

H

Hajda, Lubomyr, and Mark Beissinger. *THE NATIONALITIES FACTOR IN SOVIET POLITICS AND SOCIETY.* Boulder, CO: Westview Press, 1990. vii, 331 pp.

An important collection of papers on the problems of nationalities in the Soviet Union. All of the papers discuss, from different angles, the differences of attitudes and conflicts which prevail between the nationalities, the role of Russian as a dominant language and culture, unification and "russification" attempts, as well as the attitudes of the nationalities themselves. The efforts of the nationalities to achieve freedom and independence are examined in detail.

The following papers may be of particular interest to legal researchers:

"The Baltic Republics: Stagnation and Strivings for Sovereignty" by Romuald J. Misiunas.

"Central Asia: The Reformers Challenge a Traditional Society" by Martha Brill Olcott.

"Nationalities and the Soviet Economy" by Gertrude E. Schroeder.

"Nationalities and the Soviet Military" by Teresa Rakowska-Harmstone.

"Nationalities and Soviet Religious Policies" by R. Bohdan Bociurkiw.

"Transcaucasia: Cultural Cohesion and Ethnic Revival in a Multinational Society" by Ronald G. Suny.

"Ukraine, Belorussia, and Moldavia: Imperial Integration, Russification, and the Struggle for National Survival" by Roman Solchanyk.

Reviewed by Judy Batt in 67 *International Affairs* 616 (1991).

Halbach, Uwe. "Anatomy of an Escalation: The Nationality Question", in *THE SOVIET UNION, 1988-1989: PERESTROIKA IN CRISIS?,* compiled by The Federal Institute for Soviet and International Studies (Boulder, CO: Westview Press, 1990), pp. 73-82.

Hanke, Steve H., and Kurt Schuler. "Ruble Reform: A Lesson from Keynes", 10 *CATO JOURNAL* 655-666 (1991).

Two economists examine the problems of the Soviet monetary situation from historical and comparative perspectives. They suggest as a possible solution the setting up of a currency board system in the Soviet Union, which has worked successfully in similar situations elsewhere.

Hanson, Philip. "Property Rights in the New Phase of Reforms", 6 *SOVIET ECONOMY* 95-124 (1990).

A review of proposals put forward in 1991 for the division of property and its privatization. These proposals are contrasted with the "Shatalin Plan".

Hanson, Philip.
See also Sherr, Alan B., et al.

Harriman, Averell W.
See Fitch, Stephen D. "The Harriman Manganese Concession in the Soviet Union: Lessons for Today".

Harwin, Judith. "Union of Soviet Socialist Republics: Child Care in the Soviet Union—Law, Policy and Practice", 28 *JOURNAL OF FAMILY LAW* 627-635 (1990).

An analysis of Soviet laws for the protection of children who cannot be cared for by their natural parents and the effect of these laws.

Havlik, Peter. "Soviet Perestroika and Foreign Trade", in *FOREIGN TRADE IN EASTERN EUROPE AND THE SOVIET UNION*, edited by Michael Friedlaender (Boulder, CO; San Francisco; London: Westview Press, 1990), pp. 7-18.

Hazard, John N. "Codification of Soviet Nationality Policies", in *SOVIET NATIONALITY POLICIES: RULING ETHNIC GROUPS IN THE USSR*, edited by Henry R. Huttenbach (London: Mansell Publishing Limited, 1990), pp. 47-61.

Hazard, John N. "Opportunities and Problems for Joint Ventures in Soviet Law", 22 *NEW YORK UNIVERSITY JOURNAL OF INTERNATIONAL LAW AND POLITICS* 407-410 (1990).

A brief look at the changes in Soviet economic policy and attitudes toward foreign investors.

Hazard, John N. "Prospects for a New Type of Federation", in *BEYOND PERESTROIKA: OPTIONS FOR A NEW SOVIET UNION*, edited by Laurence J. Aurbach (Chicago: American Bar Association, Section of Urban, State, and Local Government Law, 1991), pp. 5-14.

Hazard, John N. "Risks in Investing in the USSR: Can There Be Protection against Them?", 11 *NEW YORK LAW SCHOOL JOURNAL*

OF INTERNATIONAL AND COMPARATIVE LAW No. 3, 457-461 (1990).

A brief survey of Soviet attitudes towards foreign investment. Presented at the Third Annual Ernst C. Stiefel Symposium: Practicing Law and Doing Business in the Soviet Union.

Hazard, John N. "Soviet Law Takes a Fresh Breath", 5 *HARRIMAN INSTITUTE FORUM* No. 6 (February 1992). 13 pp.

A brief review of the changes in the Soviet legal system during the late 1980s. The author concludes his survey with a comment on the emergence of the Commonwealth of Sovereign States on December 9, 1991, and the retirement of Gorbachev as well as the demise of the Soviet Union at the end of 1991.

☆*THE HEARTBEAT OF REFORM: SOVIET JURISTS AND POLITICAL SCIENTISTS DISCUSS THE PROGRESS OF PERESTROIKA*. Compiled by Juri Baturin. Moscow: Progress Publishers, 1990. 368 pp.

A new trend emerged in the Soviet political and scholarly writing in 1988 with the publication of the first volume in a series aptly named "Perestroika: Glasnost, Democracy, Socialism". Each volume consists of papers by eminent Soviet politicans, scholars, and journalists. Some of these papers are refreshingly candid about conditions in the Soviet Union. Many are critical of the Soviet past and even of Gorbachev, though they were written at the time of his rule. All of the papers are committed to a reform of some kind or another, though some advocate a return to the Stalinist period of order and discipline. All in all, about ten volumes were published in the series by the end of 1990. The volumes are numbered, and each has a different editor or compiler. *The Heartbeat of Reform* is the first volume in the series to be translated into the English language (its Russian title is *Pul's Reform*).

On the whole, *The Heartbeat of Reform* is rather disappointing. Most of the writing follows the traditional Soviet genre of slogans, lofty phrases, and even nostalgic references to the Communist past. The majority of footnotes refer to the writings of Marx, Engels, and Lenin. While Stalin and Brezhnev are generally condemned, Lenin is glorified. A number of papers allude to him as the architect of "socialist justice" and a builder of a true and "good" Communism. Several papers go so far as to find positive elements in Stalin's rule. For example, Boris Kurashvili writes (p. 58):

> These days, Stalinism is most often depicted as a bloodstained tyranny. And that it certainly was. But it was not only a bloodstained tyranny. It was a by and large brilliant organization, albeit abounding in mistakes, of the greatest labor and military exploit in the history of the country and in all world history,

> prepared and carried out in order to save the Soviet people from enslavement and destruction, to a net socialism, and to secure humanity's further progressive development....

Of course, not all of the papers in this volume praise the Soviet past. Some are openly critical in their condemnation of former Soviet rulers. But with few exceptions, they are all written in the same style as the excerpt quoted above. As for the present ills of the Soviet Union, all papers blame the inefficient bureaucracy and the excessive red tape it has created. They all seem to suggest that everything would change for the better if these two problems could be alleviated, and the bureaucracy as well as the people become more "humanized". Indeed, moral revival seems to be the theme of the volume. There are more suggestions for people to become better in their hearts — more honest, conscientious, and considerate — than for structural or institutional changes of the society itself. The overall impression of the volume is a desire for an idyllic recreation of the "socialist past" which the contributors, most of them members of the former "nomenklatura", could continue to enjoy. The real value of the book is in this rather subconscious revelation of the mentality of the Soviet elite. On the surface it may advocate democracy, free markets, and whatever else may be deemed politically fashionable at a particular time, but deep down there is a yearning for the system which brought privilege, power, and fame to loyal adherents of the system which prevailed in the Soviet Union until its recent collapse.

The volume consists of twenty-one relatively short papers. Since the papers are more in the form of political essays rather than scholarly articles, listing them separately would serve no useful purpose. The contributors to the volume are—

Rafik Aliyev
Yuri Baturin
Stanislav Borodin
Vladimir Entin
Mikhail Fedotov
Yuri Gradov
Mikhail Krasnov
Vladimir Kudryavtsev
Boris Kurashvili
Yelena Lukasheva
Leonid Mamoot
Ray Mullerson
Vladik Nersesyants
Leonid Nikitinsky
Svetlana Polubinskaya
Vladimir Rubanov
Alexander Savinkin
Georgy Shakhnazarov
Nuriman Sharafetdinov
Lev Simkin
Mikhail Smagin
Vladimir Tumanov
Vladlen Vereshchetin
Alexander Yakovlev
Alexei Yudin

Heitman, Sidney. *THE RIGHT TO LEAVE: THE NEW SOVIET DRAFT LAW ON EMIGRATION.* Cologne: Bundesinstitut für ostwissenschaftliche und internationale Studien, 1990. iii, 53 pp. (Report 26-1990).

A detailed analysis of the draft law on emigration which, extensively modified, was enacted on May 20, 1991.

Heitman, Sidney. *SOVIET EMIGRATION IN 1990.* Cologne: Bundesinstitut für ostwissenschaftliche und internationale Studien, 1991. iii, 45 pp. (Report 33-1991).

In addition to a general description of the Soviet Jewish emigration patterns, this report analyzes the draft law on emigration which in a modified form was eventually enacted on May 20, 1991.

Heitman, Sidney. "Soviet Emigration Policies toward Germans and Armenians", in *SOVIET NATIONALITY POLICIES: RULING ETHNIC GROUPS IN THE USSR*, edited by Henry R. Huttenbach (London: Mansell Publishing Limited, 1990), pp. 235-259.

Henderson, Jane. "The 1988 Soviet Constitutional Reforms and Sources of Law", 1 *KINGS COLLEGE LAW JOURNAL* 59-77 (1990).

Henderson, Jane. "Law of the USSR: On the Status of Judges in the USSR", 16 *REVIEW OF SOCIALIST LAW* 305-338 (1990).

A lengthy and very useful analysis of the first law ever enacted in the Soviet Union dealing with the status of judges and people's assessors. The law was enacted on August 4, 1989 and came into force on December 1 of that year. A full English translation of the law follows the analysis.

Henderson, Jane. "Legal Aspects of the Soviet Federal Structure", in *SOVIET FEDERALISM: NATIONALISM AND ECONOMIC DECENTRALISATION*, edited by Alastair McAuley (Leicester and London: Leicester University Press, 1991), pp. 33-55.

A solid legal analysis of the federal system in the Soviet Union. There is also a brief discussion of the 1990 draft Union Treaty which became obsolete by reason of the political developments in 1991.

Henderson, Jane. "The Soviet Constitutional Reforms of December 1, 1988: An Analysis of the Changes from Draft to Law", in *LEGAL HISTORY AND COMPARATIVE LAW: ESSAYS IN HONOR OF ALBERT KIRALFY*, edited by Richard Plender (London: Frank Cass and Co. Ltd., 1990), pp. 73-97.

A carefully documented account of the reasons which led to the reform of the 1977 Soviet Constitution in 1988 and of the political maneuvers which enabled the reforms to take place. A brief endnote refers to the 1989 constitutional changes.

Hendley, Kathryn. *THE SOVIET SOBRANIE OF LAWS.*
See Buxbaum, Richard M., and Kathryn Hendley.

Herlach, Mark D., and Lucille A. Barale, eds. *JOINT VENTURES IN EASTERN EUROPE.* London: Euromoney Publications PLC, 1990. xi, 183 pp.

Includes a chapter on joint ventures in the Soviet Union. The chapter consists of a short introductory note, English translations of the relevant laws, and some tables. The publication itself is incredibly expensive (close to US $1.20 a page). The editors are associates of the international law firm of Coudert Brothers.

Hertzfeld, Jeffrey M. "Joint Ventures: Saving the Soviets from Perestroika", 69 *HARVARD BUSINESS REVIEW* No. 1, 80-91 (January-February 1991).

The author of this exceptionally interesting article is a partner at Selans, Hertzfeld & Heilbronn, a Paris-based international law firm. He has represented many United States corporations in their dealings in the USSR. In this article he argues that the success of joint ventures in the Soviet Union is dependent on the willingness of the foreign partners to make a long-term investment plan for the growth of their joint ventures, and to allow for vertical integration. He does not look favorably upon short-term investments or deals. They may be successful on rare occasions in special circumstances, but in general they are doomed to failure. The article examines those aspects of the Soviet economy which are relevant to joint ventures. It also touches upon different legal and political considerations. The article includes many practical examples of the strategies and experiences encountered by such successful United States investors in Soviet joint ventures as McDonald's and others. Easy to read, this article should not to be missed by anyone interested in joint venture activities in the Soviet Union.

Hines, Jonathan H. "Dispute Resolution and Choice of Law in United States-Soviet Trade", in *LEGAL ASPECTS OF TRADE AND INVESTMENT IN THE SOVIET UNION AND EASTERN EUROPE 1990* (New York: Practising Law Institute, 1990), pp. 117-187.

Hines, Jonathan H. "Soviets Chance Currency Rules".
See Perkins, Roswell B., and Jonathan H. Hines.

Hipel, Keith W. "A Conflict Analysis of the Armenian-Azerbaijan Dispute".
See Fraser, Niall M., Keith W. Hipel, John Jaworsky, and Ralph Zuljan.

Hobér, Kaj. "Joint Ventures with the Soviet Union", 6 *INTERNATIONAL FINANCIAL LAW REVIEW* 15-18 (1987). Reprinted in *INVESTING IN REFORM: DOING BUSINESS IN A CHANGING SOVIET UNION,* edited by Michael P. Claudon and Tamar L. Gutner, eds. (New York: New York University Press, 1991), pp. 99-137.

This is one of the first of the many practice-oriented analyses of joint ventures in the Soviet Union. Some of the later writing by the same author is more detailed and comprehensive.

Hobér, Kaj. "Recent Trends in Foreign Trade and Investment". A paper presented at the Geonomics Institute Seminar, Middlebury, Vermont, May 10-13, 1991. 43 + 5 pp. Also published in *INVESTING IN REFORM: DOING BUSINESS IN A CHANGING SOVIET UNION,* edited by Michael P. Claudon and Tamar L. Gutner (New York: New York University Press, 1991).

A brief survey of the Soviet economic situation and foreign trade investment developments as of Spring, 1991. Hobér coins the term "katastroika" to describe the choatic conditions of the country, the breakdown of central government, and the conflict between Gorbachev's all-Union government and the republics. The paper ranges over a wide variety of topics. It demonstrates the author's extraordinary knowledge and understanding of the Soviet Union.

Hogan, James E. "New Tax and Companies Legislation in the USSR", 16 *REVIEW OF SOCIALIST LAW* 351-362 (1990).

A brief description of the USSR Law on the Taxation of Enterprises, Associations and Organizations, enacted June 14, 1990, and the USSR Council of Ministers Regulations on Joint Stock Companies and Limited Liability Companies, adopted June 19, 1990.

English translations of the above law and regulations, as well as their enabling resolutions, appear in 16 *Review of Socialist Law* 363-423 (1990).

Holland, William E., Mikhail Rozenberg, and Robert E. Langer. "USSR", in *FREE MARKET TAKEOVER: A LEGAL GUIDE TO INVESTING IN EASTERN EUROPE, USSR, CHINA AND VIETNAM*, a Special Supplement to the July 1991 issue of *INTERNATIONAL FINANCIAL LAW REVIEW*, pp. 55-61.

A succinctly presented and very useful report on Soviet laws relating to investments, formation of business organizations, and conduct of business by foreigners as of mid-1991. The report was prepared by three members of the New York law firm of Chadbourne & Parke.

Hosking, Geoffrey. *THE AWAKENING OF THE SOVIET UNION.* Cambridge: Harvard University Press, 1990. ix, 182 pp.

An incisive study of the changes taking place in the Soviet Union during the first five years of the Gorbachev regime. Like most Western experts on the Soviet Union, the author is cautious about the future. He notes a number of advances in the political arena as well as the emergence of a more pluralistic and outspoken society. Nevertheless, he believes that the powers of the intransigent former power elite and bureaucracy remain extensive, and Gorbachev's own position in the apparent contest between the "conservatives" and the "liberals" is not clear. This is a book which should not be missed by anyone who wants to understand the problems which faced the Soviet Union in 1990.

Houri, Nicole M. "Joint Venture Law in the Soviet Union" (Note), 11 *NEW YORK LAW SCHOOL JOURNAL OF INTERNATIONAL AND COMPARATIVE LAW* 499-518 (1990).

A concise description of the Soviet joint ventures legislation through 1990.

Hoya, Thomas W. "U.S. Governmental Controls over Technology Exports with Particular Reference to the Soviet Union", in *LAW AND POLITICS OF WEST-EAST TECHNOLOGY TRANSFER,* edited by Hiroshi Oda (Dordrecht/Boston/London: Martinus Nijhoff/Graham & Trotman, 1991), pp. 65-89.

The emphasis of this paper is on the law of the United States, but there are some valuable observations concerning past Soviet practices to acquire Western technology.

Huber, Robert T., and Donald R. Kelley. *PERESTROIKA-ERA POLITICS: THE NEW SOVIET LEGISLATURE AND GORBACHEV'S POLITICAL REFORMS.* Armonk, NY: M.E. Sharpe, Inc., 1991. viii, 246 pp.

A collection of very interesting papers on constitutional, legal and political changes that took place in the Soviet Union during the period of Gorbachev's rule.

The following papers bear the greatest likelihood of being relevant to legal research:

- "Electoral Reform" by Viktor Danilenko.
- "Legislative-Executive Relations in the New Soviet Political Order" by Eugene Huskey.
- "The New Soviet Legislative Branch" by Stuart Goldman.
- "Parliamentary Government in the USSR" by Thomas F. Remington.
- "The Path of Constitutional Reform in the USSR" by Robert Sharlet.

Huskey, Eugene. "A Framework for the Analysis of Soviet Law", 50 *RUSSIAN REVIEW* 53-70 (1991).

The author contends that legal thought in the Soviet Union was shaped predominantly by three distinct attitudes: nihilism, statism, and legalism. At different times the formulation of laws and the development of policies were influenced by these respective frames of thought. Study of Soviet law is predicated upon understanding their influences.

Huskey, Eugene. "Legislative-Executive Relations in the New Soviet Political Order", in *PERESTROIKA-ERA POLITICS: THE NEW SOVIET LEGISLATURE AND GORBACHEV'S POLITICAL REFORMS,* edited by Robert Huber and Donald R. Kelley (Armonk, NY: M.E. Sharpe, Inc., 1991), pp. 53-173.

Huttenbach, Henry R., ed. *SOVIET NATIONALITY POLICIES: RULING ETHNIC GROUPS IN THE USSR*. London: Mansell Publishing Ltd., 1990. xvi, 302 pp.

A collection of papers published under the auspices of Columbia University's Seminar of Soviet Nationality Problems. They focus on the major or more visible nationalities of the Soviet Union. Though the papers were written prior to the breakdown of the Soviet Union, they discuss issues of continuing importance in the complex and frequently volatile web of nationality conflicts in Russia and other parts of the former Soviet Union.

Several papers have a direct bearing for legal and law-related research:

"Baltic Nationalism and Soviet Language Policy: From Russification to Constitutional Amendment" by Romuald J. Misiunas.

"Codification of Soviet Nationality Policies" by John N. Hazard.

"Soviet Emigration Policies toward Germans and Armenians" by Sidney Heitman.

"Soviet-Jewish Emigration Policy: Anti-Zionism and Philo-Semitism" by Zachary Irwin.

"A Theory of Soviet Nationality Policies" by Edward Allworth.

Reviewed by John A. Armstrong in 51 *Russian Review* 291-293 (1992). Also reviewed by Marjorie Mandelstom Badzer in 50 *Slavic Review* 1037-38 (1991).

I

☆Ikonitskaya, I.A. "Legal Protection of Land in the USSR", 7 *PACE ENVIRONMENTAL LAW REVIEW* 161-170 (1989).

A brief description of legal provisions relating to the use of land in the Soviet Union.

Iliukhin, Viktor.
See Gamaiunov, Igor.

Ilves, Toomas Hendrik. "Reaction: The Intermovements in Estonia", in *TOWARD INDEPENDENCE: THE BALTIC POPULAR MOVEMENTS*, edited by Jan Arveds Trapans (Boulder, CO; San Francisco; Oxford: Westview Press, 1991), pp. 71-83.

International Chamber of Commerce. *FOREIGN INVESTMENT IN THE USSR. KEY 1990 LEGISLATION*. Paris: ICC Publications, 1991.

A collection of English translations of 1990 Soviet laws, decrees and regulations relevant to foreign trade and investment. Includes the following:

Decree of the President of the USSR on Foreign Investment (26 October 1990).

Law of the Union of Soviet Socialist Republics on Enterprises in the USSR Decree No. 1524 (4 June 1990).

Decree No. 1530 of the Supreme Soviet of the USSR on the Procedure for entry into effect of the law of the USSR on "Enterprises in the USSR".

USSR Council of Minister Resolution No. 776 on Measures to form the All-Union Foreign Currency Market (4 August 1990).

Decree of the President of the USSR on the introduction of a Commercial Exchange Rate for the Ruble and the creation of a whole-Soviet currency market (26 October 1990).

Decree of the President of the USSR on the Use of Hard Currency Resources (2 November 1990).

Law of the USSR concerning Taxes on Enterprises, Associations and Organizations (14 June 1990).

Decree of the Supreme Soviet of the USSR on the procedure for putting into effect the USSR law concerning Taxes on Enterprises, Associations and Organizations (14 June 1990).

Law on Property in the USSR adopted by the Supreme Soviet of the USSR (March 6, 1990).

☆*INTERNATIONAL LAW*. Moscow: Progress Publishers, 1990. 285 pp. (Student's Library).

A student textbook on international law. The interesting aspect of this book is its attempt to present the structure and principles of international law in a new and non-communist way. It does not begin with references to Marx or Lenin, and its listings of sources include many Western European and American scholarly writings.

"International Law Symposium '90", 12 *WHITTIER LAW REVIEW* 143-267 (1991).

Includes articles relevant to Soviet law and economics as follows:

"The Gorbachev Revolution" by Michael J. Bazyler.

"The Harmonization of Soviet and EEC Trade Law in Anticipation of 1992" by Christopher Osakwe.

"International Arbitration in East-West Trade" by Daniel M. Kolkey.

"Political, Economic and Legal Reform in the Soviet Union" by Vladimir Kvint.

International Monetary Fund.
See "A Study of the Soviet Economy".

Irwin, Zachary. "Soviet-Jewish Emigration Policy: Anti-Zionism and Philo-Semitism", in *SOVIET NATIONALITY POLICIES: RULING ETHNIC GROUPS IN THE USSR*, edited by Henry R. Huttenbach (London: Mansell Publishing Limited, 1990), pp. 260-285.

☆Ivanov, S.A. "The International Labour Organisation: Control over Application of the Conventions and Recommendations on Labour", in *CONTROL OVER COMPLIANCE WITH INTERNATIONAL LAW*, edited by William E. Butler (Dordrecht, The Netherlands: Martinus Nijhoff Publishers, 1991), pp. 153-163.

J

Jaworsky, John. "A Conflict Analysis of the Armenian-Azerbaijan Dispute".
See Fraser, Niall M., Keith W. Hipel, John Jaworsky and Ralph Zuljan.

JOINT VENTURE ACCOUNTING IN THE USSR: DIRECTION FOR CHANGE. New York: United Nations, 1990. v, 46 pp. (United Nations Centre on Transnational Corporations Advisory Studies, Series B, No. 7; UN Classification No. St/CTC/SER.B/7; UN Sales No. E.90.II.A.26).

In 1990 the USSR Ministry of Finance and the United Nations Centre on Transnational Corporations created a task force for the modernization of accounting regulations in the USSR. The present report, prepared specifically for the first meeting of the task force in June, 1990, describes Soviet accounting rules as currently applied to joint ventures, enumerates the problems emerging from the application of such rules, and offers suggestions for change.

Jones, Anthony, and David E. Powell, eds. *SOVIET UPDATE, 1989-1990*. Boulder, CO: Westview Press, 1991. vii, 152 pp.

The first volume in a series, intended to be published biannually, on current developments in the Soviet Union. The present volume covers the 1989-1990 period.

Chapters of possible interest to legal and law-related research include:

"Nationalities and Ethnic Issues" by Rasma Karklins.
"Soviet Society" by David E. Powell.
"Voluntary Groups and Initiatives" by S. Frederick Starr.

Jones, Anthony, Walter D. Connor, and David E. Powell, eds. *SOVIET SOCIAL PROBLEMS*. Boulder, CO; San Franciso; Oxford: Westview Press, 1991. ix, 337 pp.

A collection of papers on different aspects of Soviet social and political conditions during the 1980's. Several papers may be of interest to persons involved in research of law and related topics. These include:

"Crime in the Soviet Union" by Louise I. Shelley.
"Drinking and Alcohol Abuse in the USSR in the 1980's" by Vladimir G. Treml.

"Drug Abuse in the USSR" by John M. Kramer.
"Equality of Opportunity" by Walter D. Connor.
"No End of a Problem: Perestroika for the Family?" by Peter H. Juviler.
"Pollution in the Soviet Union: The Growth of Environmentalism and Its Consequences" by Marshall I. Goldman.
"Prostitution, the Press, and Agenda-Building in the Soviet Policy Process" by Andrea Stevenson Sanjian.
"Youth Problems in the Soviet Union" by Richard B. Dobson.

This book is reviewed by Katrina van den Heuvel in *New York Times Book Review*, Feb. 17, 1991, p.10.

Jorgensen-Dahl, Arnfinn. "The Soviet-Norwegian Maritime Disputes in the Arctic: Law and Politics", 21 *OCEAN DEVELOPMENT AND INTERNATIONAL LAW* 411-429 (1990).

According to the author's abstract:

> Norway is involved in two maritime boundary disputes with the Soviet Union. In relation to Svalbard, the Soviet Union argues that the archipelago has a continental shelf and an exclusive economic zone (EEZ) of its own to which all parties to the Svalbard Treaty have equal access. This is disputed by Norway, which maintains that such a view of the matter implies an expansive interpretation of the Svalbard Treaty for which there is no support in international legal practice. In the Barents Sea there is a continuing dispute between Norway and the Soviet Union over the proper location of the continental shelf and EEZ boundaries. This article sets out some of the reasons behind the different arguments on which the two base their respective cases, and the reasons why Norway in the absence of a delineated boundary has refused to accept Soviet proposals for economic cooperation in the disputed ocean area. Major emphasis is placed on the confluence of several circumstances inter alia, geopolitical and historical factors, a strongly asymmetrical power relationship, and legal ambiguity.

Juviler, Peter. "Human Rights after Perestroika: Progress and Perils", 4 *HARRIMAN INSTITUTE FORUM* No. 6, 1-10 (June 1991).

The author admits to some progress having been made in liberalizing the society in the Soviet Union during Gorbachev's reign of power. However, looking at the realities of the situation in general, enjoyment of freedom by individuals as well as distinct social or national groups remains restrictive, and the dangers of the Soviet

Union reverting to dictatorship are quite strong. The author concludes his paper with a list of twelve postulates which he believes to be necessary for the achievement of a satisfactory state of human rights in the Soviet Union.

Juviler, Peter. "No End of a Problem: Perestroika for the Family?" in *SOVIET SOCIAL PROBLEMS*, edited by Anthony Jones, et al. (Boulder, CO; San Francisco; Oxford: Westview Press, 1991), pp. 194-212.

Juviler, Peter. "Presidential Power and Presidential Character", 16 *SOVIET UNION/UNION SOVIETIQUE* 245-256 (1989).

In this short article Juviler examines the role of Gorbachev as the President of the USSR. He concludes that the Soviet President may have many powers bestowed upon him by reason of his office. However, he cannot effectively exercise complete power by reason of political constraints and ideological commitments. Of course, despite an excessive amount of writing about the present-day Soviet Union and the numerous "revelations" emanating from that country, very little is still known about Gorbachev, his suppporters, or his opponents. The Soviet Union continues to keep its secrets.

Juviler, Peter. "Secret Justice and Personal Rights", in *THE SOVIET SOBRANIE OF LAWS*, edited by Richard M. Buxbaum and Kathryn Hendley (Berkeley, CA: University of California at Berkeley, 1991), pp. 156-172.

K

Kalicki, Jan H.
See Sherr, Alan B., et al.

☆Kamenetskaya, Elena P. "International Space Law: New Institutional Opportunities", in *PERESTROIKA AND INTERNATIONAL LAW: CURRENT ANGLO-SOVIET APPROACHES TO INTERNATIONAL LAW,* edited by Anthony Carty and Gennady Danilenko (Edinburgh: Edinburg University Press, 1990), pp. 172-183.

Kampelman, Max M. "Negotiating with the Soviets", in *NEGOTIATING ARMS CONTROL: MISSED OPPORTUNITIES AND LIMITED SUCCESSES*, edited by Kenneth W. Thompson (Lanham, MD: University Press of America, Inc. 1991), pp. 3-26.

An address by the American negotiator Max M. Kampelman about his experience in negotiating disarmament treaties with the Soviet Union at the time of the Reagan Presidency.

Karatnycky, Adrian.
See Diuk, Nadia, and Adrian Karatnycky.

Karklins, Rasma. "Nationalities and Ethnic Issues", in *SOVIET UPDATE, 1989-1990,* edited by Anthony Jones and David E. Powell (Boulder, CO: Westview Press, 1991), pp. 75-96.

A concise and remarkably comprehensive overview of the national issues in the Soviet Union during the 1989-90 period.

Karklins, Rasma. "Nationality, Policy and Ethnic Relations in the USSR", in *POLITICS, WORK, AND DAILY LIFE IN THE USSR: A SURVEY OF FORMER SOVIET CITIZENS*, edited by James R. Millar (Cambridge: Cambridge University Press, 1987), pp. 301-331.

☆Karpetz, Igor I. "International Criminal Law and International Crimes", 1 *TOURO JOURNAL OF TRANSNATIONAL LAW* 325-334 (1990).

A leading Soviet criminal law scholar comments on the Soviet attitude toward international crimes.

☆Kartashkin, Vladimir A. "Human Rights and the Emergence of the State of the Rule of Law in the USSR", 40 *EMORY LAW JOURNAL* 889-902 (1991).

This article by an eminent Soviet scholar briefly reviews the path of the Soviet Union from an absolute dictatorship to a state of some democratic values. This review is followed by comments on the draft constitution of the Russian Federation, the amendment of the Soviet Constitution, and the expansion of the rights of individuals by means of such laws as the one permitting exit from the USSR.

☆Kartashkin, Vladimir A. "International Protection of Minorities: The Soviet Perspective", 20 *ISRAEL YEARBOOK ON HUMAN RIGHTS* 309-317 (1990).

Kaser, Michael, and Aleksandar M. Vacic, eds. *REFORMS IN FOREIGN ECONOMIC RELATIONS OF EASTERN EUROPE AND THE SOVIET UNION*. New York: United Nations, 1991. xii, 202 pp. (United Nations Publications Sales No. E.91.II.E.5.)

Proceedings of a symposium conducted in association with Osteuropa-Institut and Südost-Institut on August 28-September 2, 1990, this publication describes in a fairly systematic manner the institutional frameworks for foreign economic relations and trade in all of the Eastern countries, including the former Soviet Union. The information on each country includes foreign trade payment data, exchange rate arrangements and systems, decentralization trends, export and import policies, foreign investment practices, joint venture developments, and other related issues. Directions and prospects of reforms in each of these areas are discussed as well. The information is arranged in a convenient manner. It is unfortunate that much of this information became dated as soon as it was published, especially for the Soviet Union, where the changes have been more extensive and frequent than in the other Eastern and Central European countries. The following papers deal directly with the Soviet Union:

"Economic Relations of the Soviet Union with Market Economies" by Boris M. Pichugin.

"Institutional Framework of Foreign Trade Relations of the Soviet Union" by Aleksandr N. Bykov.

"Integration of the Soviet Union and Eastern Europe into the World Economy" by Oleg T. Bogomolov.

Reviewed by Boris Pichugin in 199 *Foreign Trade* No. 10, 36-37.

☆Katkov, Alexander L. "Can Joint Ventures Help to Create a Market Economy in the Soviet Union", in *THE EMERGING RUSSIAN BEAR: INTEGRATING THE SOVIET UNION INTO THE WORLD ECONOMY*, edited by Josef C. Brada and Michael P. Claudon (New York: New York University Press, 1991), pp. 143-163.

The author, Professor of Economics at the Leningrad State University, takes a searching and critical look at the effect joint ventures and foreign enterprises located in the Soviet Union have on the development of the Soviet economy.

Kavass, Igor I. "Aspects of Soviet Law on Joint Ventures, Foreign Trade, and Investment: A Bibliographic Survey of Current Literature in English", 24 *VANDERBILT JOURNAL OF TRANSNATIONAL LAW* 415-448 (1991).

Kavass, Igor I., and Andrew T. Griffin. "Joint Ventures in the Soviet Union: A Review of Current Literature in English", 18 *INTERNATIONAL JOURNAL OF LEGAL INFORMATION* 177-204 (1990).

A survey of English-language writing on joint ventures in the Soviet Union through mid-1990.

☆Kazimirchuk, V.P. "On Constitutional Supervision in the USSR", in *PERESTROIKA AND THE RULE OF LAW: ANGLO-AMERICAN AND SOVIET PERSPECTIVES,* edited by William E. Butler (London: I.B. Tauris & Co., Ltd., 1991), pp. 148-156.

Kelley, Donald R.
See Huber, Robert T., and Donald R. Kelley.

Kellman, Barry. "Legal Implementation of the Multilateral Chemical Weapons Convention: Integrating International Security with the Constitution".
See Tanzman, Edward A., and Barry Kellman.

Kennedy, R. Cameron.
See Frenkel, William J., and R. Cameron Kennedy.

Khazanov, Anatoly. *THE KRYMCHAKS: A VANISHING GROUP IN THE SOVIET UNION.* Jerusalem: The Hebrew University of Jerusalem, The Marjorie Mayrock Center for Soviet and East European Research, 1989. 83 pp.

Krymchaks were originally a group of Tartar-speaking Jews who lived mainly on the Crimean Peninsula. This paper discusses their history under the Russian Czarist and then the Soviet regimes.

☆Khazova, O. "USSR: Recent Developments in Divorce and Its Consequences", 30 *JOURNAL OF FAMILY LAW* 439-445 (1991-92).

Brief reports of some recent judicial decision in Russia on child custody, support, marital property, and the rights of children.

☆Khazova, O. "U.S.S.R.: Some Problems of Soviet Family Law", 29 *JOURNAL OF FAMILY LAW* 463-470 (1990-91).

A discussion of the most significant problems facing the Soviet family due to inadequate legal reforms.

☆Khlestov, O.N. "The Origin and Prospects for Development of Control over Compliance with International Obligations of States", in *CONTROL OVER COMPLIANCE WITH INTERNATIONAL LAW,* edited by William E. Butler (Dordrecht, The Netherlands: Martinus Nijhoff Publishers, 1991), pp. 23-30.

☆Khudyakova, Lyudmila S.
See Sherr, Alan B., et al.

☆Kiselev, Sergei N.
See Stephan, Paul B. III, and Boris M. Klimenko.

Kitchin, William. "The Implications for Judicial Review in the Current Legal Reforms in the Soviet Union", 19 *POLICY STUDIES JOURNAL* No. 1, 96-105 (Fall 1990).

Kitching, Laurence P.A. *REGIONAL IDENTITY UNDER SOVIET RULE: THE CASE OF THE BALTIC STATES.*
See Loeber, Dietrich Andre, V. Stanley Vardys, and Laurence P.A. Kitching.

☆Klimenko, Boris M.
See Stephan, Paul B. III, and Boris M. Klimenko.

☆Klishin, Alexei A. "Doing Business in the U.S.S.R.: Welcome to the 'New Antipodes'".
See Glick, Steven M., and Alexei A. Klishin.

☆Klishin, Alexei A. "Federalist Fever: Economic and Banking Reform in the USSR".
See Glick, Steven M., and Alexei A. Klishin.

Knight, Amy W. "The Future of the KGB", 39 *PROBLEMS OF COMMUNISM* No. 6, 20-39 (November-December 1990).

This article is described as follows in the editorial abstract:

> Ever since Lenin created the infamous Cheka in 1917, a political police has served as the "sword and shield" of the party, or, more precisely, of the party leadership. Gorbachev—like other party leaders who lacked a public mandate—has made himself enormously dependent on the KGB. But the insistent demands of the reformers and the growing movement of the Soviet republics toward independence are outpacing Gorbachev's own program and chal-

lenging the prerogatives of a strong, centralized secret police. Gorbachev will find it increasingly difficult to maintain his association with this organization without losing his credibility as a reformist leader. In short, while the KGB may be crucial to maintaining Gorbachev's rule as discontent mounts, it is also a serious political liability.

Knudsen, Holger. *BIBLIOTHEK UND RECHT INTERNATIONAL/ LIBRARIES AND LAW—INTERNATIONAL, FESTSCHRIFT RALPH LANSKY.*
See Gödan, Jürgen Christoph, and Holger Knudsen.

☆Koldaeva, N.P. "Separation of Powers in the USSR: Emerging Theory", in *PERESTROIKA AND THE RULE OF LAW: ANGLO-AMERICAN AND SOVIET PERSPECTIVES,* edited by William E. Butler (London: I.B. Tauris & Co., Ltd., 1991), pp. 119-129.

Kolkey, Daniel M. "International Arbitration in East-West Trade", 12 *WHITTIER LAW REVIEW* 245-258 (1991).

A brief review of the main features of commercial arbitration involving parties in the Soviet Union and other Eastern European countries. Text of a speech at the 1990 International Law Symposium at Whittier College School of Law.

☆Kolodkin, Anatoly L. *MOSCOW SYMPOSIUM ON THE LAW OF THE SEA: PROCEEDINGS OF A WORKSHOP CO-SPONSORED BY THE LAW OF THE SEA INSTITUTE, THE SOVIET MARITIME LAW ASSOCIATION, THE SOVIET PEACE FUND.*
See Clingan, Thomas A., Jr., and Anatoly L. Kolodkin.

☆Kondrashov, Stanislav. "Out of the Darkness of Ignorance: Glimmers of *Glasnost*' in the Kingdom of Military Secrets", 29 *SOVIET LAW AND GOVERNMENT* No. 4, 21-77 (Spring 1991).

A discussion of the damaging domestic and international effects of secrecy with respect to Soviet military action in Cuba and Afghanistan and an argument for the end to the secrecy surrounding military affairs.

Published originally in *Norgi Mir*, 1989, No. 8 (July 20, 1989).

☆Korolev, Ivan S.
See Sherr, Alan B., et al.

☆Kortunov, Sergei V.
See Stephan, Paul B. III, and Boris M. Klimenko.

KPMG
See EASTERN EUROPE AND THE USSR: A GUIDE TO FOREIGN INVESTMENT LEGISLATION.

Kramer, John M. "Drug Abuse in the USSR", in *SOVIET SOCIAL PROBLEMS*, edited by Anthony Jones, et al. (Boulder, CO; San Francisco; Oxford: Westview Press, 1991), pp. 94-118.

☆Krans, Maksim. "The Miners' Alternative: A Few Questions for Reflection".
See Vasil'ev, Andrei, and Maksim Krans.

☆Krasnov, Mikhail.
See THE HEARTBEAT OF REFORM: SOVIET JURISTS AND POLITICAL SCIENTISTS DISCUSS THE PROGRESS OF PERESTROIKA.

☆Krupnik, Igor. "The Nationalities Question in the USSR: Looking for Explanations", 22 *SOCIAL SCIENCES* No. 4, 138-155 (1991).

The author, a senior researcher at the Institute of Ethnology and Anthropology of the USSR Academy of Sciences, examines in broad terms the nationality conflicts in the former Soviet Union. He concludes that the problems are long-standing, some of them caused by serious policy errors, and that solutions towards a peaceful coexistence are not likely to occur in the near future.

☆Krylov, Boris S. "Perestroika—Restructuring the Soviet Union", in *BEYOND PERESTROIKA: OPTIONS FOR A NEW SOVIET UNION,* edited by Laurence J. Aurbach (Chicago: American Bar Association, Section of Urban, State, and Local Government Law, 1991), pp. 15-22.

☆Kudryavtsev, Vladimir. "The Law-Based State: Society and the Individual", 22 *SOCIAL SCIENCES* No. 2, 7-14 (1991).

Many Soviet scholars still have the tendency to write in platitudes and slogans they learned during the intellectually stifling pre-Gorbachev times. This article belongs to that category. It talks about the establishment of a state based on law rather than arbitrary power, but it does not say very much on how this is to be achieved.

The author is a Vice-President of the USSR Academy of Sciences and a criminologist.

☆Kudryavtsev, Vladimir. *THE NUREMBERG TRIAL AND INTERNATIONAL LAW.*
See Ginsburgs, George, and Vladimir Kudryavtsev.

☆Kudryavtsev, Vladimir.
See also THE HEARTBEAT OF REFORM: SOVIET JURISTS AND POLITICAL SCIENTISTS DISCUSS THE PROGRESS OF PERESTROIKA.

Kuhlman, James A. "US-USSR Joint Ventures: An Examination of the Early Entrants".
See Nigh, Douglas, Peter Walters, and James A. Kuhlman.

Kuiper, W.G. "New Corporate Tax System Introduced", 30 *EUROPEAN TAXATION* 275-286 (1990).

This article describes the new taxes introduced for enterprises and joint ventures in 1990.

☆Kumanin, E.V. "Political Pluralism and Law", in *PERESTROIKA AND THE RULE OF LAW: ANGLO-AMERICAN AND SOVIET PERSPECTIVES,* edited by William E. Butler (London: I.B. Tauris & Co., Ltd., 1991), pp. 77-87.

☆Kurashvili, Boris.
See THE HEARTBEAT OF REFORM: SOVIET JURISTS AND POLITICAL SCIENTISTS DISCUSS THE PROGRESS OF PERESTROIKA.

Kuromiya, Hiroaki. "Stalinist Terror in the Donbas: A Note", 50 *Slavic Review* 157-162 (1991).

The losses in human lives during the Stalinist reign of terror continue to be counted. According to the report of the KGB task force appointed by Gorbachev, more than 3.7 million people were prosecuted by judicial and extrajudicial organs for counter-revolutionary activities and state crimes from 1930 to 1953. These figures, as the KGB itself admits, are incomplete.

This note, which deals more specifically with the scale of terror in the Donbas region, suggests that the number of persons executed or imprisoned throughout the whole USSR may have been much larger than is so far admitted by the KGB.

Kux, Stephan. *SOVIET FEDERALISM: A COMPARATIVE PERSPECTIVE.* New York: Institute for East-West Security Studies, 1990. vi, 117 pp.

In this carefully structured analytical study, Dr. Kux examines the feasibilities of a realistic federal system in the Soviet Union. He finds that the present relationship between the center in Moscow and the peripheries is seriously defective. He compares the Soviet situation with models of federalism developed in other parts of the world. After analyzing a variety of problems facing the Soviet Union, including the ethnic issue and the extensive economic disparity within the country, he concludes that "federalization can solve some, but not all of the Soviet Union's ethnic problems."

☆Kuznetsov, Valerii I.
See Stephan, Paul B. III, and Boris M. Klimenko.

☆Kvint, Vladimir. "Political, Economic and Legal Reform in the Soviet Union", 12 *WHITTIER LAW REVIEW* 143-146 (1991).

A very brief overview of the changes that took place in the Soviet Union during Gorbachev's rule until early 1990. At the time of these observations, the author was Vice Chairman of the Council for Regional Economy at the USSR Academy of Sciences. This is the text of a speech he presented at the 1990 International Law Symposium at Whittier College School of Law.

Kwiatkowska, Barbara. "Innocent Passage by Warships", 21 *OCEAN DEVELOPMENT AND INTERNATIONAL LAW* 447-450 (1990).

L

La Follette, Karen. *MELTDOWN: INSIDE THE SOVIET ECONOMY.* *See* Roberts, Paul Craig, and Karen La Follette.

Lampert, Nick. "The Socialist Legal State", in *GORBACHEV AND PERESTROIKA*, edited by Martin McCauley (New York: St. Martin's Press, 1990), pp. 116-134.

A brief survey of the Soviet legal system in the late 1980's. The author discusses changes taking place in Soviet attitudes towards the role of the law as well as the trends in the actual law reforms made during these years. The author's conclusions are surprisingly perceptive. After noting an increase in the Soviet rhetoric towards a greater rule of law, he goes on to say:

> It could indeed be argued that the legal state slogan corresponds above all to the interests of the intelligentsia broadly defined, who would be most likely to make use of a more independent legal system and for whom guarantees of professional autonomy are particularly important. Yet there is more than that at stake. The talk of the legal state arises from a sense of crisis of political authority and is part of a wider effort to strengthen the legitimacy of the Soviet state. Whether that is possible given the preservation of a monopoly of political power is a question that remains to be answered.

Lampert, Nick, and Gabor T. Rittersporn. *STALINISM: ITS NATURE AND AFTERMATH. ESSAYS IN HONOUR OF MOSHE LEWIN.* Armonk, NY: M.E. Sharpe, Inc., 1992. xv, 291 pp.

A collection of papers on a variety of topics which have as their central point the legacy of Stalinism in the Soviet Union.

Includes a paper on "Legality in Soviet Political Culture: A Perspective on Gorbachev's Reforms" by Peter H. Solomon, Jr.

Landfried, Christine, ed. *CONSTITUTIONAL REVIEW AND LEGISLATION: AN INTERNATIONAL COMPARISON.* Baden-Baden: Nomos Verlagsgesellschaft, 1988. 264 pp.

Includes a brief paper by Vladimir Tumanov on "Guarantees for Constitutionality of Legislation in the USSR".

Langer, Robert E. "USSR".
See Holland, William E., Mikhail Rozenberg, and Robert E. Langer.

Langrind, Peter M. "An Overview of Environmental Law in the USSR" (Note), 11 *NEW YORK LAW SCHOOL JOURNAL OF INTERNATIONAL AND COMPARATIVE LAW* 483-498 (1990).

A concise and clearly presented overview of the environmental problems of the Soviet Union and the legislation the Soviet government must introduce in order to remove and control such problems.

Lapidus, Gail W. "Can Gorbachev Manage the Nationalities Crisis?", in *CAN GORBACHEV'S REFORMS SUCCEED?*, edited by George W. Breslauer (Berkeley, CA: Center for Slavic and East European Studies and the Berkeley-Stanford Program in Soviet Studies, University of California of Berkeley, 1990), pp. 95-110.

Lapidus, Gail W. *THE GLASNOST PAPERS: VOICES ON REFORM FROM MOSCOW.*
See Melville, Andrei, and Gail W. Lapidus.

☆Larin, Aleksander M.
See Ginsburgs, George, and Vladimir Kudryavtsev.

THE LAW OF OWNERSHIP IN THE USSR.
See Butler, William E., ed. *THE LAW OF OWNERSHIP IN THE USSR.*

"The Law of the Union of Soviet Socialist Republics on Freedom of Conscience and Religious Organizations", 8 *JOURNAL OF LAW AND RELIGION* 385-395 (1990).

A compilation of translations of the Soviet laws on freedom of religion.

Lawrence, Paul R., and Charalambos A. Vlachoutsicos. *BEHIND THE FACTORY WALLS: DECISION MAKING IN SOVIET AND US ENTERPRISES.* Boston: Harvard Business School Press, 1990. xii, 352 pp.

A collection of papers about economic and industrial management in the United States and the Soviet Union. The appendices include two short papers on joint ventures:

"Aspects of Forming Joint Ventures in the USSR—Comments for the Western Investor" by Charalambos A. Vlachoutsicos.

"A Description of Soviet Laws and Policies on Joint Ventures" by Igor Faminsky and Alexander Naumov.

☆Lazarev, B.M. "The President of the USSR", 30 *SOVIET LAW AND GOVERNMENT* 7-26 (1991).

An analysis of the office of President of the USSR, which was established in 1990. The article explains the powers of the office as well as the reasons for its creation. Originally published in Russian in 1990 *Sovetskoye Gosudarstvo I Pravo*, No. 1, 3-14.

☆Lazarev, M.I. "On a Theoretical Concept of Control over the Fulfilment of International Obligations of States", in *CONTROL OVER COMPLIANCE WITH INTERNATIONAL LAW*, edited by William E. Butler (Dordrecht, The Netherlands: Martinus Nijhoff Publishers, 1991), pp. 17-22.

☆Lediakh, Irina A.
See Ginsburgs, George, and Vladimir Kudryavtsev.

LeDonne, G.P. "Police Reform in Russia: A Project of 1762", 32 *CAHIERS DU MONDE RUSSE ET SOVIETIQUE* 249-274 (1991).

Lee, Janet. "The Evolution of Cooperative Legislation: A Case Study of Reform in the Soviet Union", 27 *STANFORD JOURNAL OF INTERNATIONAL LAW* 155-187 (1990).

A discussion of the Soviet Law on Cooperatives, its effects on the Soviet economy and its participation in the world market, and the relationship of the legislation for cooperatives to the whole Soviet reform movement.

Lefeber, R., M. Fitzmaurice, and E.W. Vierdag, eds. *THE CHANGING POLITICAL STRUCTURE OF EUROPE: ASPECTS OF INTERNATIONAL LAW.* Dordrecht, The Netherlands: Martinus Nijhoff Publishers, 1991. xi, 286 pp.

These papers of a conference organized by the Department of International Law and Relations of the Faculty of Law at the University of Amsterdam in 1990 include the following contributions relating to the former Soviet Union or by Soviet scholars:

"International Cooperation in Respect of the Baltic Sea" by E. Franckx.
"The New Approach to the Law of Peaceful Coexistence" by Th. Schweisfurth.
"Reflections on the Future International Legal Problems of the USSR" by R.A. Mullerson.

LEGAL ASPECTS OF TRADE AND INVESTMENT IN THE SOVIET UNION AND EASTERN EUROPE. Commercial Law and Practice Course Handbook Series No. 549. New York: Practising Law Institute, 1990. 1036 pp.

Like its predecessors, this Practising Law Institute Course Handbook examines the latest legal developments pertaining to trade and investment in the Soviet Union. The emphasis is strongly practical. In addition to papers and outlines, the book also reproduces English translations of Soviet laws, decrees, and regulations enacted or promulgated mainly in 1987 and 1988 dealing with the formation and management of joint ventures. It includes also an English translation of the USSR Law on Income Tax of April 23, 1990, and the US-USSR Trade Relations Agreement of June 1, 1990.

The volume includes the following papers or outlines pertaining to the Soviet Union:

"A Case Study: The Soviet Union" by Eugene E. Madara.
"Considering Business Opportunities in the Soviet Union in the 1990s" by Richard N. Dean.
"Dispute Resolution and Choice of Law in United States-Soviet Trade" by Jonathan H. Hines.
"Doing Business in the Soviet Union: A Case Study" by R. Scott Toop.
"Doing Business in the Soviet Union: The Legal Environment" by Harold J. Berman.
"Introduction Guide to Joint Ventures in the Soviet Union" by Susan M. H. Lewenz.
"Investment Protection for Projects in Eastern Europe and the Soviet Union: OPIC, MIGA, and Bilateral Investment Treaties" by Robert B. Shanks.
"Tax, Investment, and Financing Issues in Projects in the USSR and Eastern Europe" by Richard C. Schneider, Jr.
"Technology Transfer Transactions with Soviet and Eastern European Enterprises: Experience in USA Companies" by Thomas J. Shillinglaw.

LEGAL AND PRACTICAL ASPECTS OF DOING BUSINESS IN THE SOVIET REPUBLICS. Commercial Law and Practice Course Handbook Series No. 604. New York: Practising Law Institute, 1992. 500 pp.

A collection of papers and outlines which attempt to explain conditions for foreign investment and trade in Russia and several of the other former Soviet republics. The contributors, all of them experts on legal issues of that part of the world, try very hard to make sense out of what in the early part of 1992 was a confusing and completely unstable situation. These papers and outlines were presented in New York City on February 20-21, 1992. A substantial part of the volume consists of texts of laws translated into English, legal forms, and other documents, including the text of a speech by the U.S. Secretary of State, James Baker.

The English translations of laws are those of a medley of legislation on foreign investments, companies, and business activities enacted in Russia, Kazakhstan, Ukraine, Belarus and Uzbekistan in 1990 and 1991. The papers and outlines are as follows:

"The Commonwealth of Independent States: Its Legal Status and Implication for Foreign Companies" by Preston M. Torbert.

"Financing Projects in the Territory of the Former USSR" by A. James Redway.

"First Soviet Free Zone Will Give Firms Access to Pacific Basin Markets" by Preston M. Torbert.

"Five Years Later: Evaluating Foreign Investment Experience in the 'Former USSR'" by Sarah C. Carey.

"Legal and Practical Aspects of Doing Business in the Soviet Republics" by Cole, Corette & Arbutyn.

"New Free Enterprise Zone Regulations Promote Investment" by Preston M. Torbert.

"Privatization: Opportunities, Risks, Prognosis" by Peter J. Pettibone.

"Structural Challenges Facing the Republics" by H. Michael Mears.

"A U.S. Perspective on the Legal Environment for Foreign Investment in Russia" by Paul B. Stephan, III.

☆Lemeshev, Mikhail. *BUREAUCRATS IN POWER—ECOLOGICAL COLLAPSE.* Moscow: Progress Publishers, 1990. 315 pp.

A forceful criticism of environmental protection management in the Soviet Union. The author, a Soviet economist, is an internationally-recognized expert on environmental problems. The book contains many illustrative case studies of critical pollution situations in the Soviet Union. Translated from the Russian by Sergei Chulaki.

Leonard, Edward S. "Investment in the Soviet Union in the Early Nineties: Diving into the Vortex" (Comment), 2 *TOURO JOURNAL OF TRANSNATIONAL LAW* 153-219 (1991).

The incentives as well as obstacles to foreign investment in the Soviet Union are thoroughly analyzed in this student comment.

☆Leont'eva, A.V. "New Aspects in the Structure and Jurisdiction of the COMECON Regarding the Protection of the Environment", 7 *PACE ENVIRONMENTAL LAW REVIEW* 179-183 (1989).

Levey, David H. "Models of Capital Market Development".
See Bohn, John A., Jr., and David H. Levey.

Levin, Martin P. "The Challenge of Doing Business in the Soviet Union", 11 *NEW YORK LAW SCHOOL JOURNAL OF INTERNATIONAL AND COMPARATIVE LAW* No. 3, 453-456 (1990).

An attorney's experience of conducting business negotiations in the Soviet Union. Presented at the Third Annual Ernst C. Stiefel Symposium: Practicing Law and Doing Business in the Soviet Union.

Lewenz, Susan M.H. "Introduction Guide to Joint Ventures in the Soviet Union", in *LEGAL ASPECTS OF TRADE AND INVESTMENT IN THE SOVIET UNION AND EASTERN EUROPE* (New York: Practising Law Institute, 1990), pp. 11-37.

Lisitsyn, Eugene N. "Environmental Law and Management in the USSR: A Reflection on Contemporary Reforms", 17 *REVIEW OF SOCIALIST LAW* 125-143 (1991).

A survey of recent policies towards environmental protection in the Soviet Union.

☆Litavrin, Petr. G.
See Stephan, Paul B. III, and Boris M. Klimenko.

Litman, Gary V. "Reinventing a Law on Inventions: International Aspects of the New Russian Patent Law" (Note), 25 *GEORGE WASHINGTON JOURNAL OF INTERNATIONAL LAW AND ECONOMICS* 171-226 (1991).

A student note about the new draft patent law of the Russian Federation.

☆Livshits, R.Z. "Jus and Lex: Evolution of Views", in *PERESTROIKA AND THE RULE OF LAW: ANGLO-AMERICAN AND SOVIET PERSPECTIVES,* edited by William E. Butler (London: I.B. Tauris & Co., Ltd., 1991), pp. 22-36.

Loeber, Dietrich André. "Latvia's 1937 Civil Code: A Quest for Cultural Identity", in *COMPARATIVE AND PRIVATE INTERNATIONAL LAW: ESSAYS IN HONOR OF JOHN HENRY MERRYMAN ON HIS SEVENTIETH BIRTHDAY*, edited by David S. Clark (Berlin: Duncker & Humblot, 1990), pp. 197-204.

Loeber, Dietrich André. *REGIONAL AND NATIONAL VARIATIONS: THE BALTIC FACTOR.* Washington: National Council for Soviet and East European Research, 1991. 30 pp.

Loeber, Dietrich André. "The Sobranie—A Challenge to Glasnost", in *THE SOVIET SOBRANIE OF LAWS*, edited by Richard M. Buxbaum and Kathryn Hendley (Berkeley, CA: University of California at Berkeley, 1991), pp. 1-25.

Loeber, Dietrich André, V. Stanley Vardys, and Laurence P.A. Kitching, eds. *REGIONAL IDENTITY UNDER SOVIET RULE: THE CASE OF THE BALTIC STATES.* Hackettstown, N.J.: Institute for the Study of Law, Politics and Society of Socialist States, 1990. xxiii, 470 pp.

According to a review by Toivu U. Raun in 50 *Slavic Review* 1048-49 (1991):

> This collection of papers on Baltic regional identity, originally presented at a conference at the University of Kiel in June 1987, is a useful addition to the scholarly literature on the Baltic states in the recent past. The thirty articles in the book, first published in six consecutive issues of the *Journal of Baltic Studies* in 1987-1988, are reproduced with virtually no changes, but non-subscribers to the journal will welcome this handy edition. The book has seven substantive sections: The first explores the issue of regionalism and the following sections relate this concept to political integration; social, cultural, and economic development; comparative law; and international dimensions. A concluding section of samizdat documents highlights Baltic regionalism and cooperation in dissent in the 1970s and 1980s.

Lowe, Vaughan. "USA/USSR: Uniform Interpretation of the Rules of International Law Governing Innocent Passage", 6 *INTERNATIONAL JOURNAL OF ESTUARINE AND COASTAL LAW* 73-76 (1991).

Ludwikowski, Rett R. "Searching for a New Constitutional Model for East-Central Europe", 17 *SYRACUSE JOURNAL OF INTERNATIONAL LAW AND COMMERCE* 91-170 (1991).

In a broad survey of historical and current constitutional developments in Eastern Europe, the author also discusses constitutional changes in the Soviet Union.

Ludwikowski, Rett R. "Soviet Constitutional Changes of the Glasnost Era: A Historical Perspective", 10 *NEW YORK LAW SCHOOL JOURNAL OF INTERNATIONAL AND COMPARATIVE LAW* 119-150 (1989).

A historical overview of changes in the Soviet Constitution, emphasizing changes made under glasnost and the political effects of these changes for Gorbachev.

☆Lukasheva, Yelena.
See THE HEARTBEAT OF REFORM: SOVIET JURISTS AND POLITICAL SCIENTISTS DISCUSS THE PROGRESS OF PERESTROIKA.

☆Lukashuk, Igor I. "Control in Contemporary International Law", in *CONTROL OVER COMPLIANCE WITH INTERNATIONAL LAW*, edited by William E. Butler (Dordrecht, The Netherlands: Martinus Nijhoff Publishers, 1991), pp. 5-16.

☆Lukashuk, Igor I.
See also Ginsburgs, George, and Vladimir Kudryavtsev.

Lukic, Reneo. "Twilight of the Federations in East Central Europe and the Soviet Union", 45 *JOURNAL OF INTERNATIONAL AFFAIRS* 575-598 (1992).

M

MacDonald, Bruce A. "An Introduction to Soviet Intellectual Property Law".
See Barschevsky, Mikhail, Sergo Selianovsky and Bruce A. MacDonald.

Madara, Eugene E. "A Case Study: The Soviet Union", in *LEGAL ASPECTS OF TRADE AND INVESTMENT IN THE SOVIET UNION AND EASTERN EUROPE* (New York: Practising Law Institute, 1990), pp. 75-94.

Maggs, Peter B. "Facilitating U.S.-Soviet Joint Ventures through Legislative Reform", in *THE EMERGING RUSSIAN BEAR: INTEGRATING THE SOVIET UNION INTO THE WORLD ECONOMY*, edited by Josef C. Brada and Michael P. Claudon (New York: New York University Press, 1991), pp. 129-141.

Professor Maggs offers a comprehensive list of the legal reforms that need to be introduced by the Soviet Union before it can effectively operate as a market economy with the incentives expected by foreign investors and enterpreneurs.

Maggs, Peter B. "Legislation on the Soviet National Economy in the Sobranie", in *THE SOVIET SOBRANIE OF LAWS,* edited by Richard M. Buxbaum and Kathryn Hendley (Berkeley, CA: University of California at Berkeley, 1991), pp. 55-67.

Maggs, Peter B. "Ownership Rights". A Paper presented at the Geonomics Institute Seminar, Middleburg, Vermont, May 10-13, 1991. 20 pp. Reprinted in *INVESTING IN REFORM: DOING BUSINESS IN A CHANGING SOVIET UNION,* edited by Michael P. Claudon and Tamar L. Gutner (New York: New York University Press, 1991), pp. 155-169.

In this excellent analysis of the murky and confusing state of the Soviet law relating to property and ownership, Professor Maggs postulates that "ownership rights are meaningless unless they can be traded for money in the context of a market". He then goes on to examine the worthlessness of the Soviet currency as well as the character of ownership within the Soviet Union. He offers practical advice on ownership matters to potential foreign investors.

Maggs, Peter B. "Post-Soviet Law: The Case of Intellectual Property Law", 5 *THE HARRIMAN INSTITUTE FORUM* No. 3 (November 1991). 9 pp.

In this short essay Professor Maggs surveys the law of intellectual property in the Soviet Union from a historical perspective, beginning with Imperial Russia. He also looks at the future, and his predictions are optimistic. He believes that a sound and healthy system of intellectual property protection will emerge from the chaos brought about by the collapse of the Soviet legal system. He is equally optimistic about the future of law in the Soviet Union in general.

Separate sections of the paper discuss intellectual property rights in the other republics, and specifically in the Baltic countries.

Maillet, Lynda L. *BUSINESS IN THE SOVIET UNION: A PRIMER AND OVERVIEW.*
See Barbanel, Jack A., and Lynda L. Maillet.

Maisto, G. "Double Taxation Treaty Italy-USSR with Particular Reference to Joint Ventures", 29 *EUROPEAN TAXATION* 113-119 (1989).

Makay, John J. "Gorbachev's Rhetoric of Glasnost: How Openness Intersects with Freedom of Expression."
See Bulsys, Joseph A., and John J. Makay.

☆Mamiofa, Iosif E. "Industrial Property Rights of Joint Ventures in the Soviet Union", 2 *INTERNATIONAL COMPANY AND COMMERCIAL LAW REVIEW* 242-246 (1991).

☆Mamiofa, Iosif E., and Corien Prins. "Protecting Computer Programs—The Soviet Perspective", 22 *INTERNATIONAL REVIEW OF INDUSTRIAL PROPERTY AND COPYRIGHT LAW* (IIC) 605-628 (1991).

This article examines the various alternatives for the protection of computer programs under Soviet copyright and patent laws respectively.

☆Mamoot, Leonid.
See THE HEARTBEAT OF REFORM: SOVIET JURISTS AND POLITICAL SCIENTISTS DISCUSS THE PROGRESS OF PERESTROIKA.

☆Mamutov, V.K. "The Miners' Strike and Improving Economic Legislation", 30 *SOVIET LAW AND GOVERNMENT* 80-92 (1991).

A discussion of the coal miner strikes in the Ukraine and Siberia including some economic proposals for improving the situation. A Russian version of this paper was originally published in 1990 *Sovetskoye Gosudarstvo I Pravo*, No. 1, 31-38.

Markovits, Inga. "Socialism and the Rule of Law: Some Speculations and Predictions", in *COMPARATIVE AND PRIVATE INTERNATIONAL LAW: ESSAYS IN HONOR OF JOHN HENRY MERRYMAN ON HIS SEVENTIETH BIRTHDAY*, edited by David S. Clark (Berlin: Duncker & Humblot, 1990), pp. 205-245.

A distinguished comparativist examines whether true judicial independence and general respect for the rights of individuals is really possible in socialist countries. With patience and remarkable lucidity the author explains the incompatibility of rule of law with the collectivist attitudes of the socialist state.

Marples, David R. "The Greening of Ukraine: Ecology and the Emergence of *Zelenyi svit*, 1986-1990", in *PERESTROIKA FROM BELOW: SOCIAL MOVEMENTS IN THE SOVIET UNION,* edited by Judith B. Sedaitis and Jim Butterfield (Boulder, CO: Westview Press, 1991), pp. 133-144.

☆Maslov, Alexander. "Bankrolling Soviet Joint Ventures", *4 EUROPEAN AFFAIRS* No. 3, 59-65 (Autumn 1990).

The Chairman of the Board of Directors of the Moscow Narodny Bank describes in practical terms the role of the Soviet banks in the promotion and formation of joint ventures in the Soviet Union. The financing practices of the banks are also explained. Comparisons are made with similar practices in selected Eastern European countries.

☆Maslov, Vyacheslav O.
See Sherr, Alan B., et al.

Mason, David S., and Svetlana Sydorenko. "Perestroyka, Social Justice, and Soviet Public Opinion", 39 *PROBLEMS OF COMMUNISM* No. 6, 34-43 (November-December 1990).

This article is described as follows in the editorial abstract:

> As Mikhail Gorbachev strives to improve the efficiency of the Soviet economy, he has invoked a perspective of social justice that points to the unfairness of slothful workers' receiving the same pay as productive fellow workers. However, a portion of the Soviet intelligentsia and a wide sector of the public at large are increasingly focusing on an egalitarian version of social justice that rejects increased differentiation in pay and worries about the state of those large numbers of people at the bottom of the social ladder. The tension between efficiency and social justice constitutes one of the Soviet leader's primary dilemmas.

Matthews, Mervyn. *PASSPORTS AND FREEDOM OF RESIDENCE IN THE USSR.* Palo Alto: Hoover Institution, Stanford University, 1990. 19 pp.

The author discusses the use of internal passports as a means to control and restrict the establishment of residence by individuals in Czarist Russia and the Soviet Union. He explains the reasons for limiting the number of residents in designated areas and for curtailing the freedom of movement in general. References are made to the requirements for "propiska" and the illegal practice of "limitchiki". The paper concludes with a brief description of the marginally liberalizing changes introduced during the first years of Gorbachev's rule.

☆Matyukhin, Georgy. "The Union of Soviet Socialist Republics and Other Socialist Countries in the International Monetary and Financial System", in *ECONOMIC REFORMS IN CENTRALLY PLANNED ECONOMIES AND THEIR IMPACT ON THE GLOBAL ECONOMY*, edited by Jozef M. van Brabant (New York: United Nations, 1990), pp. 269-278. (Published by the United Nations Department of International Economic and Social Affairs as *JOURNAL OF DEVELOPMENT PLANNING* No. 20; UN Classification No. ST/ESA/216; UN Sales No. e. 90. II. A.9.)

A paper by a senior economist of the USSR Academy of Sciences on the role of money in the socialist economies, the role of monopoly, ruble convertibility, and Soviet participation in international financial and monetary activities.

Maurins, A. "Problems of National Legislation for the Protection of the Environment".
See Strautmanis, J., and A. Maurins.

Mayer, Carl J. "Redefining Red", 17 *HUMAN RIGHTS* No. 3, 22-27, 45-46 (Fall/Winter 1990).

Observations on changes in attitudes towards human rights in the Soviet Union.

McAuley, Alastair, ed. *SOVIET FEDERALISM: NATIONALISM AND ECONOMIC DECENTRALISATION.* Leicester and London: Leicester University Press, 1991. ix, 214 pp.

A series of papers about the origins of the Soviet federal system, the forces leading towards its disintegration, the emergence and rise of nationalism, and the quest for decentralization and independence. The book was published prior to the Baltic states regaining their independence in early September 1991 and the subsequent collapse of the federal system.

Many papers seem to be directly relevant to legal and law-related research. They are—

"Baltic States Opt for Independence" by Kestutis Girnius.

"The Ethnodemographic Dimension" by Ann Sheehy.
"The Evolution of the Soviet Federation and the Independence of Latvia" by Andris Plotnieks.
"The Historical Background to Soviet Federalism" by Raymond Pearson.
"Legal Aspects of the Soviet Federal Structure" by Jane Henderson.
"Social and Economic Conditions for Ethnic Strife in the Soviet Union" by Klaus von Beyme.
"Socialist Federalism: Federalism and Democratic Centralism" by Miervaldis Ramans.
"The Soviet Federal System and the National Question in Comparative Perspective" by Ronald Watts.

McCauley, Martin, ed. *GORBACHEV AND PERESTROIKA*. New York: St. Martin's Press, 1990. xii, 222 pp.

A collection of essays on changes in the Soviet Union. Of particular interest to law-related research are—
"Nationalities" by Bohdan Nahaylo.
"The Socialist Legal State" by Nick Lampert.

McLure, Charles E., Jr. *INCOME TAX POLICY FOR THE RUSSIAN REPUBLIC.* Stanford, CA: Hoover Institution on War, Revolution and Peace, 1991. 17 pp.

The author was a member of a small Hoover Institution team advising the Supreme Economic Council of the Russian Republic in March-May, 1991, on the methods of transition to market economy. This brochure describes his recommendation to introduce a "Simplified Alternative Tax" in lieu of conventional income tax.

McNeill, John H. "America's Maritime Boundary with the Soviet Union", 154 *NAVAL WAR COLLEGE REVIEW* No. 3, 46-57 (Summer 1991).

By an agreement signed at Washington on June 1, 1990, the United States and the Soviet Union formally established an international boundary in the North Pacific Ocean and the Bering Sea and Straits. This article analyzes the historical antecedents of this agreement as well as its content and aims.

McWhinney, Edward. "The 'New Thinking' in Soviet International Law: Soviet Doctrines and Practice in the Post-Tunkin Era", 28 *CANADIAN YEARBOOK OF INTERNATIONAL LAW* 309-337 (1990).

An exceptionally interesting analysis of the changes in Soviet attitudes towards international law, presented by an eminent and experienced scholar.

McWhinney, Edward, et al. *FROM COEXISTENCE TO COOPERATION: INTERNATIONAL LAW AND ORGANIZATION IN THE POST-COLD WAR ERA*. Dordrecht, The Netherlands: Martinus Nijhoff Publishers, 1991. xiv, 297 pp.

A collection of papers dedicated to Grigory I. Tunkin on his eighty-fifth birthday. The following papers were contributed by Soviet scholars:

"Ecological Security in the Arctic: A Regional Approach" by Sergei V. Vinogradov.

"International Control and the Concept of 'Open Skies'" by Vladlen S. Vereshchetin.

"International Politics and International Law in the Nuclear Age" by Grigory I. Tunkin.

"The Legal Regime of Navigation in the Arctic: Problems of Soviet-Canadian Cooperation" by A.P. Movchan.

"The New Stage in International Economic Relations and the Foreign Trade Reforms in the USSR" by Marina P. Bardina.

"Options for Future Strategic Arms Reduction" by Sergei Fedorenko.

Mears, H. Michael. "Structural Challenges Facing the Republics", in *LEGAL AND PRACTICAL ASPECTS OF DOING BUSINESS IN THE SOVIET REPUBLICS* (New York: Practising Law Institute, 1992), pp. 15-25.

Melville, Andrei, and Gail W. Lapidus. *THE GLASNOST PAPERS: VOICES ON REFORM FROM MOSCOW.* Boulder, CO: Westview Press, 1990. vii, 359 pp.

The editors interviewed a number of eminent Russians about changes brought about by the freedom of expression and speech which emerged from Gorbachev's decision to introduce "glasnost".

One chapter deals with issues of justice and the protection of individual rights.

Meri, Lennart. "Estonia's Role in the New Europe", 67 *INTERNATIONAL AFFAIRS* 107-110 (1991).

A transcript of an address by the Estonian Foreign Minister to the Royal Institute of International Affairs on November 6, 1990. The Estonian Foreign Minister persuasively presents here his country's case for independence.

Meron, Theodor. "'Exclusive Preserves' and the New Soviet Policy toward the UN Secretariat" (Editorial Comment), 85 *AMERICAN JOURNAL OF INTERNATIONAL LAW* 322-329 (1991).

Many positions in the United Nations Secretariat are permanently filled by the nationals of specific countries. It is what the author of this detailed and exceptionally expert comment refers to as "exclusive preserves". Based on an accepted practice within the United Nations, such positions are usually filled by officials of particular countries, who are seconded to the United Nations for a period of years. At the end of their terms they are replaced by other officials from the same countries. The Soviet Union has rigidly adhered to this practice. The author examines past Soviet policy on this subject and discusses how it may be changing during Gorbachev's rule.

☆Meshkov, Aleksei Yu.
See Stephan, Paul B. III, and Boris M. Klimenko.

Mihalisko, Kathleen. "The Popular Movement in Belorussia and Baltic Influence", in *TOWARD INDEPENDENCE: THE BALTIC POPULAR MOVEMENTS*, edited by Jan Arveds Trapans (Boulder, CO; San Francisco; Oxford: Westview Press, 1991), pp. 123-132.

☆Milchakova, Natalia G. "An Examination of the New Soviet Income Tax on Individuals", 3 *TAX NOTES INTERNATIONAL* 237-243 (March 1991).

Millar, James R., ed. *POLITICS, WORK, AND DAILY LIFE IN THE USSR: A SURVEY OF FORMER SOVIET CITIZENS*. Cambridge: Cambridge University Press, 1987. xiv, 423 pp.

A collection of papers emerging from exhaustive interviews of Soviet emigrants who came to the United States between 1979 and 1982. Known as the Soviet Interview Project, the interviewing was conducted by a team of seasonal scholars.

Papers of interest to research of legal character relating to the Soviet Union include:

"Nationality, Policy and Ethnic Relations in the USSR" by Rasma Karklins.

"Perceptions of Social Status in the USSR" by Michael Swaford.

Mishchenko, Piotr. "New Political Thinking as a Tool of Soviet Foreign Policy."
See Gorin, Alexander and Piotr Mishchenko.

Misiunas, Romuald J. "Baltic Nationalism and Soviet Language Policy: From Russification to Constitutional Amendment", in *SOVIET NATIONALITY POLICIES: RULING ETHNIC GROUPS IN THE USSR*, edited by Henry R. Huttenbach (London: Mansell Publishing Limited, 1990), pp. 206-220.

Misiunas, Romuald J. "The Baltic Republics: Stagnation and Strikings for Sovereignty", in *THE NATIONALITIES FACTOR IN SOVIET POLITICS AND SOCIETY*, edited by Lubomyr Hajda and Mark Beissinger (Boulder, CO: Westview Press, 1990), pp. 204-227.

Moody, James E. "The Soviet Military Justice System". *See* Schmitt, Michael N., and James E. Moody.

Moon, David. *RUSSIAN PEASANTS AND TSARIST LEGISLATION ON THE EVE OF REFORM: THE INTERACTION OF THE PEASANTRY AND OFFICIAL RUSSIA, 1825-55.* London: Macmillan, 1991. 220 pp.

This contribution to the Studies in Soviet History and Society examines the interaction of peasants and official Russia in the period prior to the reforms of 1861. In a series of case studies, the author explores the methods of communication and understanding between the peasantry and officialdom, peasant aims, and their behavioral patterns.

Morgan, John. "Labour: Past Imperfect, Present Tense—Trade Unions and Labour in the Soviet State", in *THE IMPACT OF GORBACHEV: THE FIRST PHASE, 1985-1990,* edited by D. W. Spring (London and New York: Printer Publishers, 1991), pp. 37-48.

A useful summary of the changes which have taken place in trade union activity and labor relations in general during the first five years of Gorbachev's rule.

Morrison, John. *BORIS YELTSIN: FROM BOLSHEVIK TO DEMOCRAT.* New York: Dutton, 1991. 303 pp.

This book does not so much describe Boris Yeltsin, the elected president of the Russian Federation, as the first five years of Gorbachev's rule. In this respect it may be read as a general account of the events in the Soviet Union from 1985 until the abortive coup of August, 1991.

Morton, John.
See Sherr, Alan B., et al.

Motyl, Alexander J. "Russian Hegemony and Non-Russian Insecurity: Foreign Policy Dilemmas of the USSR's Successor States", 5 *HARRIMAN INSTITUTE FORUM* No. 4, 1-11 (December 1991).

Anticipating the imminent end of the Soviet Union, the author examines the different economic and political factors which preclude the formation of a meaningful and viable union among its republics. He believes an economic union to be unrealistic in view of the past coercive nature of the Soviet state as well as the manner in which it broke apart. In contrast, at least the republics in the western part of the Soviet Union are indicating both a strong desire as well as the ability to be independent. They can develop their own economic systems and establish their own international trade links.

This brings the author to the second and more important point of his paper. The demise of the Soviet Union will have an immense impact on international relations in that part of the world as well as globally.

Within a very short time the republics can be expected to establish their own international relations, which will lead to different alliances and commitments. The fear of Russia, still by far the largest sovereign entity within the region, will induce the other republics to seek their own defense arrangements. Russia, as the successor of the Soviet Union, will need to find its own place in the world, and this will not be easy. The author concludes that tensions and even conflicts between Russia and the other republics may be inevitable.

☆Movchan, A.P. "The Legal Regime of Navigation in the Arctic: Problems of Soviet-Canadian Cooperation", in *FROM COEXISTENCE TO COOPERATION: INTERNATIONAL LAW AND ORGANIZATION IN THE POST-COLD WAR ERA*, edited by Edward McWhinney, et al. (Dordrecht, The Netherlands: Martinus Nijhoff Publishers, 1991), pp. 167-176.

☆Mozolin, Viktor P. "The Positive Influence of Legal Reform on Soviet-U.S. Joint Ventures", in *THE EMERGING BEAR: INTEGRATING THE SOVIET UNION INTO THE WORLD ECONOMY*, edited by Josef C. Brada and Michael P. Claudon (New York: New York University Press, 1991), pp. 115-127.

The author, a senior member of the Institute of State and Law at the USSR Academy of Sciences, recognizes the need for radical legal reform as a prerequisite to the Soviet Union's development of a market economy with the necessary incentives to attract foreign investment, which it badly needs. He examines the development of legal problems encountered by the reformers and proposes a more radical reform strategy.

☆Muchlinski, P.T. "Dispute Settlement under the Washington Convention on the Settlement of Investment Disputes", in *CONTROL OVER COMPLIANCE WITH INTERNATIONAL LAW*, edited by William E. Butler (Dordrecht, The Netherlands: Martinus Nijhoff Publishers, 1991), pp. 175-193.

Muller, Peter-Michael. "Protection of Human Rights in the Administration of Criminal Justice in Central and Eastern Europe and the Soviet Union", 17 *INTERNATIONAL LEGAL PRACTITIONER* No. 1, 18-19 (March 1992).

A very brief evaluation of defendants' rights in criminal proceedings in the Soviet Union.

☆Mullerson, Ray.
See THE HEARTBEAT OF REFORM: SOVIET JURISTS AND POLITICAL SCIENTISTS DISCUSS THE PROGRESS OF PERESTROIKA.

☆Mullerson, Rein A. "The International Protection of Human Rights and the Domestic Jurisdiction of States", in *PERESTROIKA AND INTERNATIONAL LAW: CURRENT ANGLO-SOVIET APPROACHES TO INTERNATIONAL LAW*, edited by Anthony Carty and Gennady Danilenko (Edinburgh: Edinburg University Press, 1990), pp. 62-70.

☆Mullerson, Rein A. "Monitoring Compliance with International Human Rights Standards", in *CONTROL OVER COMPLIANCE WITH INTERNATIONAL LAW*, edited by William E. Butler. Dordrecht, The Netherlands: Martinus Nijhoff Publishers, 1991, pp. 125-137.

☆Mullerson, Rein A. "The Primacy of International Law in World Politics".
See Vereshchetin, Vladlen S., and Rein A. Mullerson.

☆Mullerson, Rein A. "Reflections on the Future International Legal Problems of the USSR", in *THE CHANGING POLITICAL STRUCTURE OF EUROPE: ASPECTS OF INTERNATIONAL LAW*, edited by R. Lefeber, M. Fitzmaurice, and E.W. Vierdag (Dordrecht, The Netherlands: Martinus Nijhoff Publishers, 1991), pp. 55-61.

☆Mullerson, Rein A.
See also Grzybowski, Kazimierz. "Soviet Theory of International Law for the Perestroika".

Muravina, Elena. "Copyright Transactions with Soviet Authors: The Role of VAAP" (Student Note), 11 *LOYOLA ENTERTAINMENT LAW JOURNAL* 421-451 (1991).

From the editorial abstract of this article:

> This Comment addresses the role of VAAP, the Soviet Copyright Agency, within the framework of Soviet copyright law. The author analyzes the legal position of the Agency, its relationship with the Soviet authors and the effects of VAAP's practices on the Western entertainment community interested in working with the Soviet Union. This Comment also assesses the effects of the changing Soviet political climate on copyright transactions with Soviet authors and entities.

☆Musatov, Vladimir. "The Soviet Credit and Enterprise Structure System under Reform", in *REFORMING THE RUBLE: MONETARY*

ASPECTS OF PERESTROIKA, edited by Josef C. Brada and Michael P. Claudon. New York: New York University Press, 1990, pp. 209-219.

The paper discusses the requirements for a banking reform and the development of a securities market in the Soviet Union.

N

Nahaylo, Bohdan. "Baltic Echoes in Ukraine", in *TOWARD INDEPENDENCE: THE BALTIC POPULAR MOVEMENTS*, edited by Jan Arveds Trapans (Boulder, CO; San Francisco; Oxford: Westview Press, 1991), pp. 108-122.

Nahaylo, Bohdan. "Nationalities", in *GORBACHEV AND PERESTROIKA*, edited by Martin McCauley (New York: St. Martin's Press, 1990), pp. 135-153.

A clear and concise survey of nationality developments and problems in the Soviet Union during the late 1980's.

☆Naumov, Alexander. "A Description of Soviet Laws and Policies on Joint Ventures".
See Faminsky, Igor, and Alexander Naumov.

☆Nersesyants, Vladik.
See THE HEARTBEAT OF REFORM: SOVIET JURISTS AND POLITICAL SCIENTISTS DISCUSS THE PROGRESS OF PERESTROIKA.

Newburg, Andre W.G. "U.S.-Soviet Trade Agreement and Investment Protection Treaties", 11 *NEW YORK LAW SCHOOL JOURNAL OF INTERNATIONAL AND COMPARATIVE LAW* No. 3, 447-451 (1990).

A brief description of the Agreement on Trade Relations signed by Presidents Bush and Gorbachev on June 1, 1990. There is also some discussion about the investment protection treaties the United States should make with the Soviet Union.

Presented at the Third Annual Ernst C. Stiefel Symposium: Practicing Law and Doing Business in the Soviet Union.

Newcity, Michael. *SOVIET TAXATION: STATUTES, REGULATIONS, AND TREATIES.* Ardsley-on-Hudson, NY: Transnational Juris Publications, Inc., 1991. Looseleaf.

A description of Soviet tax laws as they applied in 1990. Includes English-language translations of the relevant legislation, regulations, and treaties.

Newcity, Michael. "Tax Considerations in Foreign Trade and Investment in the USSR", 24 *VANDERBILT JOURNAL OF TRANSNATIONAL LAW* 235-267 (1991).

An exceptionally careful and detailed analysis of the taxes applied to foreign investments in the Soviet Union through 1990.

Newcity, Michael. "Tax Issues in Soviet Joint Ventures", 25 *TEXAS INTERNATIONAL LAW JOURNAL* 163-207 (1990).

An excellent article on the Soviet tax laws applicable to joint ventures. The author, who is the leading American expert on Soviet tax law, explains the theoretical underpinnings of the relevant Soviet provisions as well as their practical application. He also discusses the effect of the Law on the Taxes on Enterprises, Associations, and Organizations which was enacted in June 1990 and came into force on January 1, 1991. Detailed references are made to Soviet tax treaties with other countries and to the taxation of sources of income. There is also advice on practical tax savings and suggestions for special tax planning arrangements.

Nigh, Douglas, Peter Walters, and James A. Kuhlman. "US-USSR Joint Ventures: An Examination of the Early Entrants", 25 *COLUMBIA JOURNAL OF WORLD BUSINESS* No. 4, 20-27 (Winter 1990).

A follow-up study of the 105 US-USSR joint ventures in the Soviet Union formed between November, 1987 and October, 1989. In addition to a description of the economic, political, and legal circumstances encountered in the formation of these joint ventures, the study examines their status in late 1989. It also discusses the prospects for future US investment in joint ventures in the USSR. The authors assume an optimistic conclusion. Noting the receptiveness of the Soviet government toward large US corporations, they believe that an expansion of joint venturing in the USSR depends upon further improvement of relations between the US and the USSR and, even more so, on the convertibility of the ruble.

Nightingale, Christopher, and Stephen Tupper. *RUSSIAN AND SOVIET ECONOMIC CHANGE: THE NEW LAW.* London: Longman, 1991. 100 pp.

After a general description of the political and economic changes in the Soviet Union up to the end of 1990, this small booklet briefly discusses the new legislation on formation of business enterprises and the conduct of trade. It includes translations of Soviet laws enacted during the late 1980's relevant to foreign trade and investment. This publication is outrageously expensive.

☆Nikitinsky, Leonid.
See THE HEARTBEAT OF REFORM: SOVIET JURISTS AND POLITICAL SCIENTISTS DISCUSS THE PROGRESS OF PERESTROIKA.

"Normalization of the U.S.-Soviet Trade Relations", 46 *THE RECORD OF THE ASSOCIATION OF THE BAR OF THE CITY OF NEW YORK* 104-128 (1991).

A report prepared by the Committee on Soviet Affairs of the Bar of the City of New York.

O

Obláth, Gábor, and Peter Pete. "Mechanism and Institutional System of the Finnish-Soviet Economic Relations", in *FOREIGN TRADE IN EASTERN EUROPE AND THE SOVIET UNION,* edited by Michael Friedlaender (Boulder, CO; San Francisco; London: Westview Press, 1990), pp. 95-115.

Oda, Hiroshi. "Law Enforcement Agencies", in *THE SOVIET SOBRANIE OF LAWS,* edited by Richard M. Buxbaum and Kathryn Hendley (Berkeley, CA: University of California, 1991), pp. 127-139.

Oda, Hiroshi. *LAW AND POLITICS OF WEST-EAST TECHNOLOGY TRANSFER.* Dordrecht/Boston/London: Martinus Nijhoff/Graham & Trotman, 1991. viii, 265 pp.

Papers of a conference at the Faculty of Law of the University of Tokyo in October, 1988. Several of these papers deal specifically with different aspects of the Soviet legal system:

"Soviet Foreign Trade Reform and Technology Transfer" by William E. Butler.

"U.S. Governmental Controls over Technology Exports with Particular Reference to the Soviet Union" by Thomas W. Hoya.

"West-East Technology Transfer in the Context of Perestroika" by F.J.M. Feldbrugge.

Odom, William E.
See Commission on Security and Cooperation in Europe, *THE USSR IN CRISIS: STATE OF THE UNION.*

O'Donnell, Thomas A. *BUSINESS OPERATIONS IN THE U.S.S.R.*
See George, Arthur L., and Thomas A. O'Donnell.

O'Donnell, Thomas A. "The New Soviet Tax System: Moving into the Modern Age, with Growing Pains".
See George, Arthur L., and Thomas A. O'Donnell.

O'Donnell, Thomas A. "Russian Republic Joint-Stock Decree: Tidings of Great Joy?".
See George, Arthur L., and Thomas A. O'Donnell.

O'Donnell, Thomas A. "United States-Soviet Joint Ventures".
See George, Arthur L., and Thomas A. O'Donnell.

Olcott, Martha Brill. "Central Asia: The Reformers Challenge a Traditional Society", in *THE NATIONALITIES FACTOR IN SOVIET POLITICS AND SOCIETY*, edited by Lubomyr Hajda and Mark Beissinger (Boulder, CO: Westview Press, 1990), pp. 253-280.

Olcott, Martha Brill. "The Soviet (Dis)union", 82 *FOREIGN POLICY* 118-136 (Spring 1991).

A detailed analysis of the national movements in the Soviet Union during the late 1980's.

☆Orlov, Lev N. "Soviet Joint Enterprises with Capitalist Firms and Other Joint Ventures between East and West", 221 *RECUEIL DES COURS. HAGUE ACADEMY OF INTERNATIONAL LAW* 371-414 (1990-II).

An examination of Gorbachev's joint venture legislation from the Soviet standpoint by a professor at the Higher Commercial Management School of the USSR Ministry of Foreign Economic Relations.

Osakwe, Christopher. "The Harmonization of Soviet and EEC Trade Law in Anticipation of 1992", 12 *WHITTIER LAW REVIEW* 151-157 (1991).

A brief examination of an interesting and important issue, presented in a speech at the 1990 International Law Symposium at Whittier College School of Law.

Osakwe, Christopher. "The Host Country Perspective on Foreign Investments in the Soviet Union: Law and Policy", 24 *VANDERBILT JOURNAL OF TRANSNATIONAL LAW* 207-233 (1991).

A comprehensive examination of legal, political and economic conditions for foreign investment in the Soviet Union from 1985, when Gorbachev came to power, through 1990. The author concludes that such investment may bring worthwhile results despite bureaucratic obstacles, high taxes, and quite excessive overhead costs.

Osakwe, Christopher. *SOVIET BUSINESS LAW: INSTITUTIONS, PRINCIPLES, AND PROCESSES.* Salem, NH: Butterworth Legal Publishers, 1991. 2 Volumes, looseleaf, misc. pag.

The most definitive work to date on a new subject of law heretofore not known in the Soviet Union and emerging as a result of the country's turning towards a market economy. The coverage is broad and very extensive. The author discusses such topics as:

- the constitutional and structural bases of business law in the Soviet Union;
- the administrative apparatus empowered with the control of business;
- financial institutions;
- governmental agencies and enterprises in trade and commerce;
- the mechanism of settling commercial disputes in the Soviet Union;
- legal services in the Soviet Union;
- the concept of legal personality in the Soviet Law;
- contract law;
- law of torts;
- property law;
- commercial law;
- land law;
- labor law;
- law of foreign trade; and
- civil procedure and specialized procedural rules for commercial and maritime arbitrations.

The coverage permits this work to be used as a general manual on Soviet law. It is informative, and its presentation of the Soviet law is clear and easily understandable. There is an index. An English translation of the 1964 Civil Code of the Russian Federal Republic, as amended through January 16, 1990, is included as an appendix in the second volume of the work.

Of course, the demise of the Soviet Union at the end of 1991 makes the references in this book to the Soviet law obsolete. Nevertheless, the general description of the law is still useful and relevant because the Russian Federation and the other republics continue to retain most of the former legal framework. They will probably do so for quite some time.

Ostreng, Willy. "The Northern Sea Route: A New Era in Soviet Policy?", 22 *OCEAN DEVELOPMENT AND INTERNATIONAL LAW* 259-287 (1991).

The editorial abstract for this article by a member of The Fridtjof Nansen Institute in Lysaker, Norway, explains:

> Ever since the speech delivered by Soviet President Mikhail Gorbachev on October 1, 1987, in Murmansk, indications have multiplied to suggest that he was serious in his offer to open up the Northern Sea Route for international shipping. If this is the case, a dramatic shift in the thinking on Arctic security has taken place in the Kremlin. This article evaluates the relationship between various interests in Soviet policy concerning the utilization of the Northern Sea Route during the period 1917-1991. The aim is to discuss to what degree, and how, security-political, economic, and legal interests have influenced official Soviet evaluations of the right of other states to make use of the "shortcut" between the Atlantic and the Pacific. Four main questions are addressed: (1) What are the geopolitical realities and visions connected with economic and military use of the route? (2) How have these realities and visions been translated into practical policy? (3) How did cold war security-political tensions affect use of the route? (4) How will the new thaw in international politics influence the possibilities of multinational use of the Northern Sea Route in the future?

Owen, Thomas C. *THE CORPORATION UNDER RUSSIAN LAW, 1800-1917*. Cambridge: Cambridge University Press, 1991. xx, 234 pp.

The Imperial Russian government tended to have a generally restrictive policy towards corporations. The original law of 1836 on corporations was very stringent, but with minor modifications remained in force until the downfall of the Czarist regime in 1917. This book traces the history of thought and practice on the subject of corporations in Imperial Russia. Thoroughly researched, with access to Russian as well as Western sources, it makes a fascinating reading.

The author, a history professor at Louisiana State University, also wrote the important *Capitalism and Politics in Russia: A Social History of the Moscow Merchants, 1855-1905* (Cambridge University Press, 1981).

Reviewed by Albert J. Schmidt in 51 *Slavic Review* 170-171 (1992).

Oxenstierna, Susanne. "Labour Market Policies in the Baltic Republics", 130 *INTERNATIONAL LABOUR REVIEW* 255-274 (1991/2).

From the editorial abstract:

> Estonia, Latvia and Lithuania have their own policies for the transition to a market economy, but their integration with the rest of the USSR economy limits their scope for autonomous action. Restricted markets for supplies and output, the direct control of vital industries by ministries in Moscow and the high proportion of non-ethnic Balts in the industrial workforce all affect the transition. Various options for labour policies in the three republics are examined.

P

Palmer, Matthew S.R. "Privatization in Ukraine: Economics, Law, and Politics", 16 *YALE JOURNAL OF INTERNATIONAL LAW* 453-517 (1991).

A presentation of a theory for privatization in the Ukraine using self-determination rather than relying heavily on Western economists who may not fully understand the social and political ramifications of the privatization in the Ukraine.

Paul, Allen. *KATYN: THE UNTOLD STORY OF STALIN'S POLISH MASSACRE.* New York: Charles Scribner's Sons, 1991. 380 pp.

In 1990 Mikhail Gorbachev officially admitted that Stalin and his secret police shot 15,000 Polish prisoners of war in the Katyn forest in April and May, 1940. Prior to this admission the Soviet authorities had persistently denied responsibility for these numbers. An obvious reason for the executions was an attempt to destroy the Polish intellectual elite. Allen Paul, a journalist, presents a moving reconstruction of the human side of the Katyn murders. It adds another chapter to the emerging story about Stalin's bloodthirsty and cruel rule.

Pearson, Raymond. "The Historical Background to Soviet Federalism", in *SOVIET FEDERALISM: NATIONALISM AND ECONOMIC DECENTRALISATION*, edited by Alastair McAuley (Leicester and London: Leicester University Press, 1991), pp. 13-32.

A concise and clearly presented history of the origin and subsequent development of the Soviet federal system. According to the author, federalism was championed by Lenin and then deformed beyond recognition for his own political purposes by Stalin.

Pearson, Raymond. "Nationalities: Decolonizing the Last Empire", in *THE IMPACT OF GORBACHEV: THE FIRST PHASE, 1985-1990*, edited by D. W. Spring (London and New York: Pinter Publishers, 1991), pp. 92-115.

Pearson begins this paper by pointing out that the nationalities issue in the Soviet Union changed radically and dramatically in the early 1990's. Suddenly, there are different confrontations and different problems. The paper describes how this new situation came about through Gorbachev's "decolonization" policies.

Pearson, Thomas S. *RUSSIAN OFFICIALDOM IN CRISIS: AUTOCRACY AND LOCAL SELF-GOVERNMENT, 1861-1900*. Cambridge; New York; New Rochelle, NY: Cambridge University Press, 1989. xx, 284 pp.

This book examines the problems of local self-government in Imperial Russia after the reforms of 1861 and the subsequent changes in the structure of local government after the counter-reforms of 1889-90.

The book is favorably reviewed by Gary M. Hamburg in 50 *Slavic Review* 181-182 (1991).

Perkins, Roswell B., and Jonathan H. Hines. "Soviets Change Currency Rules", 10 *INTERNATIONAL FINANCIAL LAW REVIEW* No. 5, 22-24 (May 1991).

A brief discussion of the March 1, 1991, USSR Supreme Soviet Law "On Currency Regulation" which established operating rules for the possession and use of foreign currency in the Soviet Union.

Pete, Peter. "Mechanism and Institutional System of the Finnish-Soviet Economic Relations".
See Obláth, Gábor, and Peter Pete.

Pettibone, Peter J. "Privatization: Opportunities, Risks, Prognosis", in *LEGAL AND PRACTICAL ASPECTS OF DOING BUSINESS IN THE SOVIET REPUBLICS* (New York: Practising Law Institute, 1991), pp. 105-114.

Pettibone, Peter J. "What Congress and the Administration Can Do to Improve Soviet-U.S. Trade Relations", in *THE EMERGING RUS-*

SIAN BEAR: INTEGRATING THE SOVIET UNION INTO THE WORLD ECONOMY, edited by Josef C. Brada and Michael P. Claudon (New York: New York University Press, 1991), pp. 51-61.

The author discusses the repeal of various restrictive United States provisions which hamper more extensive trade with the Soviet Union. He also suggests that a new trade agreement with the Soviet Union should contain provisions conducive to a greater expansion of trade between the two countries.

Phillips, Jeremy. "Patents and Licensing in the USSR in Light of New Legislation", 3 *INTELLECTUAL PROPERTY IN BUSINESS* 26-28 (1991).

☆Piasheva, Larissa. *IN PURSUIT OF SOCIAL JUSTICE.* Moscow: Progress Publishers, 1991. 303 pp.

One of the cardinal issues of a Soviet Union as it changes towards a market economy is whether it will be able to offer economic and social security for the less-advantaged and lower-income segments of the society. Class disparities were always significant in the Soviet Union. In the late 1980's they became both more immense and obvious.

The author of this book, an economist and a political scientist, attempts to explain the prerequisites for a socially just state. Condemning communism as a totally wrong path towards improving the living conditions of mankind, she seems to suggest that the solution may be found in some kind of religious socialism.

Translated from the Russian by Vitaly Baskakov and Igor Kochubey. The Russian title of the book is *V Poiskah Sotzialnoi Spravedlivosti.*

☆Pichugin, Boris M. "Economic Relations of the Soviet Union with Market Economies", in *REFORMS IN FOREIGN ECONOMIC RELATIONS OF EASTERN EUROPE AND THE SOVIET UNION,* edited by Michael Kaser and Aleksandar M. Vacic (New York: United Nations, 1991), pp. 100-108.

☆Platonova, Natalya L.
See Sherr, Alan B., et al.

Plender, Richard, ed. *LEGAL HISTORY AND COMPARATIVE LAW: ESSAYS IN HONOR OF ALBERT KIRALFY.* London: Frank Cass and Co. Ltd., 1990. viii, 239 pp.

Includes an essay by Jane Henderson on "The Soviet Constitutional Reforms of December 1, 1988: An Analysis of the Changes from Draft to Law".

Plotnieks, Andris. "The Evolution of the Soviet Federation and the Independence of Latvia", in *SOVIET FEDERALISM: NATIONALISM AND ECONOMIC DECENTRALISATION,* edited by Alastair McAuley (Leicester and London: Leicester University Press, 1991), pp. 134-148.

A valuable historical account of the negotiations between Gorbachev and the representatives of the Baltic republics in 1988-90 concerning the reacquisition of independence by the three Baltic countries.

Pockney, B.P. *SOVIET STATISTICS SINCE 1950.* New York: St. Martin's Press, 1991. xviii, 333 pp.

Soviet statistics have always been imprecise. In many areas and for different periods of time they were not available at all. The data before 1950 is particularly scanty and unreliable.

This volume collects relevant Soviet statistics, derived from different (mainly Soviet) sources, in all areas of demography and economic activity from 1950 through the late 1980's (really 1988). It includes statistics on foreign trade. The volume is a convenient source for looking up the more general statistical data for the Soviet Union. Unfortunately, except for marriage and divorce rates, it does not contain any judicial or other law-related data.

☆Podlesnyi, Pavel T. "The Agenda of U.S.-Soviet Relations for the 1990s", 22 *NEW YORK UNIVERSITY JOURNAL OF INTERNATIONAL LAW AND POLITICS* 389-406 (1990).

An examination of future U.S.-Soviet relations. The author suggests an agenda of steps to be taken for successful development. The author is Head of Department, Institute for U.S.A. and Canadian Studies, Moscow.

☆Polenina, S.V. "The Supremacy of Lex and Legal Reform in the USSR", in *PERESTROIKA AND THE RULE OF LAW: ANGLO-AMERICAN AND SOVIET PERSPECTIVES,* edited by William E. Butler (London: I.B. Tauris & Co., Ltd., 1991), pp. 60-73.

☆Polubinskaya, Svetlana.
See THE HEARTBEAT OF REFORM: SOVIET JURISTS AND POLITICAL SCIENTISTS DISCUSS THE PROGRESS OF PERESTROIKA.

☆Popov, Vladimir. "Soviet Economic Reforms: Missed Opportunities and Remaining Hopes". A Paper presented at the Geonomics Institute Seminar, Middleburg, Vermont, May 10-13, 1991. 30 ll.

A pessimistic description of the Soviet economy as it stood in Spring, 1991. The author, a Soviet economist, urges foreign aid and a more extensive development of foreign trade and investment.

☆Portnoy, Mikhail A. "Major Financial Obstacles to the Formation and Operation of Joint Ventures", in *THE EMERGING RUSSIAN BEAR: INTEGRATING THE SOVIET UNION INTO THE WORLD ECONOMY*, edited by Josef C. Brada and Michael P. Claudon (New York: New York University Press, 1991), pp. 165-174.

The author, a senior research fellow at the USSR Institute for the Study of the U.S.A. and Canada, focuses his paper on the inadequate financing arrangements for joint ventures, which he believes to be one of the main obstacles to the formation of satisfactory economic and business relations between foreign investors and Soviet enterprises. In order to dispel the mistrust of foreign investors in the Soviet banking system, he explains in some detail the credit facilities and lending arrangements available in the Soviet Union.

Pospielovsky, Dimitry V. "Church-State Relations in the USSR in 1988: The Local Sobor of the Russian Orthodox Church", in *THE SOVIET UNION, 1988-1989: PERESTROIKA IN CRISIS?*, compiled by The Federal Institute for Soviet and International Studies (Boulder, CO: Westview Press, 1990), pp. 83-90.

Potichnyi, Peter J. *THE MULTI-PARTY SYSTEM IN UKRAINE.* Cologne: Bundesinstitut für ostwissenschaftliche und internationale Studien, 1992. iii, 39 pp. (Report 3-1992).

A detailed account of the development of political parties in Ukraine from 1987 to the end of 1991.

Powell, David E. *SOVIET SOCIAL PROBLEMS.*
See Jones, Anthony, Walter D. Connor, and David E. Powell.

Powell, David E. "Soviet Society", in *SOVIET UPDATE, 1989-1990*, edited by Anthony Jones and David E. Powell (Boulder, CO: Westview Press, 1991), pp. 54-74.

Contains a discussion of the church-state relations and crime.

Powell, David E. *SOVIET UPDATE, 1989-1990.*
See Jones, Anthony, and Daniel E. Powell.

Pravda, Alex. *DEVELOPMENTS IN SOVIET POLITICS.*
See White, Stephen, Alex Pravda and Zvi Gitelman.

Price Waterhouse.
See DOING BUSINESS IN THE UNION OF SOVIET SOCIALIST REPUBLICS.

Prins, Corien. *COMPUTER PROGRAM PROTECTION IN THE USSR: A NEW ERA FOR SOCIALIST COPYRIGHT LAW.* Deventer: Netherlands: Kluwer Law and Taxation Publishers, 1991. XVIII, 397 pp.

Prins, Corien. "Emile Zola Receives an Answer: The Soviet Union Is to Join the Berne Convention", 13 *EUROPEAN INTELLECTUAL PROPERTY REVIEW* 238-247 (1991).

Prins, Corien. "The New Civil Code of the Soviet Union: Major Changes in the Field of Intellectual Property Rights", 13 *EUROPEAN INTELLECTUAL PROPERTY REVIEW* 388-391 (1991).

Prins, Corien. "Protecting Computer Programs—The Soviet Perspective".
See Mamiofa, Iosif E., and Corien Prins.

PRIVATE INVESTMENTS ABROAD—PROBLEMS AND SOLUTIONS IN INTERNATIONAL BUSINESS IN 1991.
See Dean, Richard N.

Pryde, Philip R. *ENVIRONMENTAL MANAGEMENT IN THE SOVIET UNION.* Cambridge: Cambridge University Press, 1991. xx, 314 pp.

A thorough and detailed study of the environmental situation in the Soviet Union, this book describes the extensive destruction of the country by bad policy decisions and irresponsible industrial development. It contains extensive discussions of the Chernobyl incident as well as a detailed description of the unsuccessful control of toxic and urban wastes, and the pollution of water resources. Undoubtedly, this is one of the best books on the subject. Though the author is a geographer, he fully examines the pertinent legal issues in some detail.

Q

Quigley, John. "Freedom of Expression in the Soviet Media", 11 *LOYOLA ENTERTAINMENT LAW JOURNAL* 269-292 (1991).

From the editorial abstract of this article:

> The Soviet Union is in the midst of attempting radical reform of its political, social and economic institutions. Freedom of the press has been no exception. This article discusses the salient provisions of the recently passed Soviet press law. Although it is becoming increasingly obvious that there are no quick-fix solutions to Soviet woes, freedom of the press is openly recognized as essential to the promotion of glasnost, or openness. With this theme in mind, the author offers an objective presentation of the law as well as political and social analysis of the current atmosphere of the Soviet Union.

Quigley, John. "Soviet Immigration to the West Bank: Is It Legal?", 21 *GEORGIA JOURNAL OF INTERNATIONAL AND COMPARATIVE LAW* 387-413 (1991).

Though this article examines predominantly the international law right of Israel to settle the West Bank, it includes interesting references to the emigration of Jews from the Soviet Union.

Quigley, John. "The Soviet Presidency", 39 *AMERICAN JOURNAL OF COMPARATIVE LAW* 67-93 (1991).

A detailed examination of the emergence and powers of the Presidential office in the Soviet Union. Created by a constitutional amendment in 1990, the establishment of the Presidential office has been one of the most significant changes in the Soviet government system. The article describes in a clear and concise language the powers and responsibilities of the President of the USSR as set out in the USSR Constitution.

R

Racklin, Dimitri P. *BUSINESS VENTURES IN EASTERN EUROPE AND THE SOVIET UNION: THE EMERGING LEGAL FRAMEWORK FOR FOREIGN INVESTMENT.*
See Birenbaum, David E., and Dimitri P. Racklin.

Rácz, Margit, and Sándor Richter. "The Mechanism of Hungarian-Soviet Economic Relations", in *FOREIGN TRADE IN EASTERN EUROPE AND THE SOVIET UNION*, edited by Michael Friedlaender (Boulder, CO; San Francisco; London: Westview Press, 1990), pp. 83-94.

Radon, Jenik. "The Baltics: The Premier European Gateway to the Soviet Union". A Paper presented at the Geonomics Institute Seminar, Middleburg, Vermont, May 10-13, 1991. 37 pp. Reprinted in *INVESTING IN REFORM: DOING BUSINESS IN A CHANGING SOVIET UNION*, edited by Michael P. Claudon and Tamar L. Gutner (New York: New York University Press, 1991), pp. 207-231.

Predicating his presentation on the premise that international business is conducted through conveniently located geographic "gateways" (*e.g.* Hong Kong, Finland, Austria, etc.), the author predicts a bright economic future for the Baltic countries as the new "gateway" to the Russian hinterland. A very interesting thesis, presented in a workmanlike and a most readable manner.

Rakowska-Harmstone, Teresa. "Chickens Coming Home to Roost: A Perspective on Soviet Ethnic Relations", 45 *JOURNAL OF INTERNATIONAL AFFAIRS* 519-548 (1992).

A broad look at the emergence and victory of ethnic nationalism in the Soviet Union prior to its dissolution.

Rakowska-Harmstone, Teresa. "Nationalities and the Soviet Military", in *THE NATIONALITIES FACTOR IN SOVIET POLITICS AND SOCIETY*, edited by Lubomyr Hajda and Mark Beissinger (Boulder, CO: Westview Press, 1990), pp. 72-84.

Ramans, Miervaldis. "Socialist Federalism, Federalism and Democratic Centralism", in *SOVIET FEDERALISM: NATIONALISM AND ECONOMIC DECENTRALISATION*, edited by Alastair

McAuley (Leicester and London: Leicester University Press, 1991), pp. 128-133.

A legal analysis of the inconsistencies in the Soviet Constitution between the terms "federation" (Article 70) and "centralism" (Article 3).

☆Ranenko, Lyudmila A.
See Sherr, Alan, B., et al.

☆Ranenko, V., and A. Soloviev. "Experiences and Future Outlook of East-West Joint Ventures in the Soviet Union", in *EAST-WEST JOINT VENTURES: THE NEW BUSINESS ENVIRONMENT,* edited by Evka Razvigorova and Gottfried Wolf-Laudon (Cambridge, MA, and Oxford, England: Basil Blackwell, 1991), pp. 141-162.

Razvigorova, Evka, and Gottfried Wolf-Laudon. *EAST-WEST JOINT VENTURES: THE NEW BUSINESS ENVIRONMENT.* Cambridge, MA, and Oxford, England: Basil Blackwell, 1991. xviii, 327 pp.

This book on joint ventures in the Central and Eastern European countries includes a paper on the "Experiences and Future Outlook of East-West Joint Ventures in the Soviet Union" by V. Ranenko and A. Soloviev.

Redway, A. James. "Financing Projects in the Territory of the Former USSR", in *LEGAL AND PRACTICAL ASPECTS OF DOING BUSINESS IN THE SOVIET REPUBLICS* (New York: Practising Law Institute, 1992), pp. 117-124.

Remington, Thomas F. "Parliamentary Government in the USSR", in *PERESTROIKA-ERA POLITICS: THE NEW SOVIET LEGISLATURE AND GORBACHEV'S POLITICAL REFORMS,* edited by Robert T. Huber and Donald R. Kelley (Armonk, NY: M.E. Sharpe, Inc., 1991), pp. 175-204.

☆Reshetov, Lurii A.
See Ginsburgs, George, and Vladimir Kudryavtsev.

Richter, Sándor. "Four Small Countries' Relations with the Soviet Union", in *FOREIGN TRADE IN EASTERN EUROPE AND THE SOVIET UNION*, edited by Michael Friedlaender (Boulder, CO; San Francisco; London: Westview Press, 1990), pp. 63-82.

Richter, Sándor. "The Mechanism of Hungarian-Soviet Economic Relations".
See Rácz, Margit, and Sándor Richter.

Rigby, T.H. *POLITICAL ELITES IN THE USSR: CENTRAL LEADERS AND LOCAL CADRES FROM LENIN TO GORBACHEV.* Aldershot, Hants, England: Edward Elgar Publishing Ltd., 1990. vii, 301 pp.

The development of a political elite in the Soviet Union and the selection and elevation of its members have always been questions fundamental to the survival (and now the collapse) of the communist regime in that country. In this fascinating book, Dr. Rigby traces the emergence and subsequent growth of the political elite.

Though the book may now be of historical interest only, it is nevertheless important for a proper understanding of the Soviet regime. It may also help to understand more clearly the personalities of many of the new leaders who have emerged in the various republics of the former Soviet Union. After all, most of them had been quite successful members of the former political elite. They may have changed their ideologies and allegiances when the Soviet Union began to disintegrate, but their habits and political methods reflect the training they received during the time of the Soviet Union.

Rigby, T.H. "Staffing USSR Incorporated: The Origins of the Nomenklatura System", 40 *SOVIET STUDIES* 523-537 (1988).

An examination of the origins and operation of the Soviet system of nomenklatura, by which the Communist Party controlled the selection of personnel in important government, industrial and military positions, and the socio-political implications of its use.

Rittersporn, Gabor T. *STALINISM: ITS NATURE AND AFTERMATH. ESSAYS IN HONOUR OF MOSHE LEWIN.*
See Lampert, Nick, and Gabor T. Rittersporn, eds.

Roberts, Geoffrey R. *THE UNHOLY ALLIANCE: STALIN'S PACT WITH HITLER*. Bloomington and Indianapolis: Indiana University Press, 1991. xi, 296 pp.

This is a book about the Soviet-German Pact of August 23, 1939. According to J. Calvit Clarke III in 17 *Soviet Union/Union Sovietique* (Nos. 1-2, 146-149 (1990)):

> Over the last several years, a number of scholars have written important books on Stalinist foreign policy; and Geoffrey Roberts' *The Unholy Alliance: Stalin's Pact with Hitler* will take its place among them. He begins his discussion with a solid description of Soviet historiography on the pact. Displaying a wide range of reading and an ability to synthesize, he admirably fulfills one of his purposes, that is, to show that a credible history, even on sensitive topics, can be written by extensively using Soviet sources.

Roberts, Paul Craig, and Karen La Follette. *MELTDOWN: INSIDE THE SOVIET ECONOMY.* Washington: Cato Institute, 1990. xi, 152 pp.

Perhaps the most surprising and unexpected event of 1990 was the virtual collapse of the Soviet economy. Most Western observers and experts had viewed the Soviet economic system as being stronger than it turned out to be in reality, and during the late 1980's many Western business enterprises were hoping to find new and lucrative markets in that country. In this relatively brief book two American economists explain in a clear and concise manner the reasons for the failure of the Soviet economy. Their predictions for the Soviet Union are not overly optimistic. Eschewing technical jargon, this is a valuable book for anyone trying to understand the economic problems of the Soviet Union.

Robinson, Nicholas A. "Soviet Environmental Law and Perestroika: A Challenge for Joint Ventures", 2 *LAND MANAGEMENT AND ENVIRONMENTAL LAW REPORT* 195-201 (1990-91).

Robinson, Nicholas A. "Soviet Environmental Protection: The Challenge for Legal Studies", 7 *PACE ENVIRONMENTAL LAW REVIEW* 117-150 (1989).

A very useful survey of environmental protection developments in the Soviet Union during the late 1980's. The author refers to a report by Goskompriroda for 1988, published in English and Russian in 1990, which he describes as the first comprehensive survey of Soviet environmental problems (bibliographic information for the Goskompriroda report is not available).

☆Rodina, Lyudmila A.
See Sherr, Alan B., et al.

Ro'i, Yaacov. *THE STRUGGLE FOR SOVIET JEWISH EMIGRATION 1948-1967.* Cambridge: Cambridge University Press, 1991. 457 pp.

A detailed historical review of the Jewish determination and perseverance to emigrate from the Soviet Union after World War II.

☆Romanova, O.B. "Tourism and Environmental Protection", 7 *PACE ENVIRONMENTAL LAW REVIEW* 185-191 (1989).

A brief survey of a serious problem in the Soviet Union. The author stresses that "natural resources are 'consumed' by the tourist industry . . ." She then suggests some solutions towards accommodating both.

Rosencranz, Armin, and Antony Scott. "Siberia, Environmentalism and Problems of Environmental Protection", 14 *HASTINGS*

INTERNATIONAL AND COMPARATIVE LAW REVIEW 929-967 (1991).

This article discusses from a historical perspective some of the inadequacies of Soviet environmental control systems in reference to its application in Siberia. Current economic concerns of the local Siberian communities are examined in the light of the regulatory effectiveness of the Soviet environmental agencies, as are the dangers posed by joint United States-Soviet economic ventures.

Rossi, Jacques. *THE GULAG HANDBOOK: AN ENCYCLOPEDIA DICTIONARY OF SOVIET PENITENTIARY INSTITUTIONS AND TERMS RELATED TO THE FORCED LABOR CAMPS.* New York: Paragon House, 1989. 610 pp.

Predominantly, this book is a dictionary of Soviet prison and concentration camp language. Appendices include extensive information about prison regulations, etc.

Rosten, Keith A. "Soviet-U.S. Joint Ventures: Problems, Challenges, and Opportunities", in *THE EMERGING RUSSIAN BEAR: INTEGRATING THE SOVIET UNION INTO THE WORLD ECONOMY,* edited by Josef C. Brada and Michael P. Claudon (New York: New York University Press, 1991), pp. 87-113.

A survey of joint ventures in the Soviet Union and the legal mechanisms by which they operate.

Roth, Stephan J. "The New Soviet Law on Religion", 20 *SOVIET JEWISH AFFAIRS* No. 2-3, 27-37 (Autumn-Winter 1990).

☆Roulko, Eugeniy T. "Soviet Joint Enterprise Legislation", 5 *FLORIDA INTERNATIONAL LAW JOURNAL* 221-234 (1990).

A brief overview of the 1987 USSR joint venture legislation. The author is an associate professor at the Kiev State University.

☆Rozenberg, Mikhail. "USSR".

See Holland, William E., Mikhail Rozenberg, and Robert E. Langer.

☆Rubanov, A.A.

See Butler, William E., *FUNDAMENTAL PRINCIPLES OF LEGISLATION ON INVESTMENT ACTIVITY IN THE USSR AND REPUBLICS.*

See also Butler, William E., *THE LAW OF OWNERSHIP IN THE USSR.*

☆Rubanov, Vladimir.

See THE HEARTBEAT OF REFORM: SOVIET JURISTS AND POLITICAL SCIENTISTS DISCUSS THE PROGRESS OF PERESTROIKA.

Rubin, Gary E. "The United States and Soviet Jews: Refugee Policy and Acculturation", 13 *IN DEFENSE OF THE ALIEN* 98-102 (1990).

A brief account of the United States policy towards offering a home to Jewish refugees from the Soviet Union where, as the author alleges, they continue to be persecuted. Rubin is a member of the American Jewish Committee.

☆"Rules of the Communist Party of the Soviet Union. Ratified by the Twenty-eighth Congress of the CPSU", 30 *SOVIET LAW AND GOVERNMENT* No. 2, 7-25 (Fall 1991).

This is an English translation of the *Rules of the Communist Party of the Soviet Union*, ratified by its 28th Congress in July, 1990.

Rush, Myron. *THE FATE OF THE PARTY APPARATUS UNDER GORBACHEV*. Santa Monica, CA: Rand, 1991. ix, 29 pp.

A very interesting analysis of the gradual demolition of the Communist Party's governing structure by Gorbachev.

S

☆Sadovoy, Eugene. "Television and the Law in the Soviet Union". *See* Bazyler, Michael J., and Eugene Sadovoy.

☆Saguirion, Artemy A. "The U.S.S.R. and the New Law of the Sea Convention: In Search of Practical Solutions", 84 *AMERICAN SOCIETY OF INTERNATIONAL LAW PROCEEDINGS* 295-300 (1990).

Saliman, S. Gerald. "An Analysis of the Changing Legal Environment in the USSR for Foreign Investment", 22 *LAW AND POLICY IN INTERNATIONAL BUSINESS* 1-36 (1991).

A relatively optimistic and sympathetic review of Gorbachev's programs of the late 1980's directed towards the expansion of Soviet foreign trade and the luring of foreign investors. In particular the article examines:

The USSR Council of Ministers Decree of December 2, 1988 "On the Further Developments of the Foreign

Economic Activity of the State, Cooperative and Other Public Enterprises, Associations and Organizations";

The USSR Council of Ministers Decree of March 7, 1989 "On Measures for Regulation of Foreign Economic Activities";

The March 14, 1989 Annex to Instruction of the USSR Ministry of Foreign Economic Relations on "The Procedure for the Registration of Enterprises, Associations, Production Cooperatives and Other Organizations Carrying Out Export-Import Operations".

The March 18, 1989 "Instructions on the Procedure for the Registration and Distribution of Applications for the Issuance of Licenses and Presentation of the Licenses Received to the State Customs Central Authorities of the USSR Ministry of Foreign Economic Relations";

and several other 1989 legislative and administrative measures relating to foreign trade and joint ventures.

Salter, Leonard M. "Can the Soviet Union Use a Chapter 11? Would It Be Effective?", 96 *COMMERCIAL LAW JOURNAL* 90-98 (1991).

A discussion of the Soviet Union's financial trouble using the analogy of a device available under the United States bankruptcy law (known as Chapter 11) to show a need for an alternative method to obtain relief for debts it cannot pay off to foreign creditors.

☆Samorodov, A. "Conversion of the Soviet Defence Industry and Its Consequences for Labour", 129 *INTERNATIONAL LABOUR REVIEW* 555-572 (1990).

From the article's editorial abstract:

> Current disarmament talks and agreements increase the urgency of converting defence industry plants to peaceful uses. Overall, the conditions for such conversion are favourable in the USSR—not least because most defence plants already produce civilian goods—but major problems exist. Conversion prospects are affected by the self-financing system introduced under the economic reforms, as well as by greater autonomy in trading and price-setting, and the switch from earlier, non-competitive tender procedures. Redeployment of workers at all staffing levels is problematic, and higher wages have drawn many better-qualified workers away into the private and co-operative sectors. The defence industry's technological capacities may be greater than are required for consumer goods production but the great shortages of the latter facilitate conversion.

Samuelian, Thomas J. "Cultural Ecology and Gorbachev's Restructured Union", 32 *HARVARD INTERNATIONAL LAW JOURNAL* 159-200 (1991).

A very original and pioneering article about the different nationalities of the Soviet Union, their aspirations for independence or autonomy, their present conditions, and Gorbachev's attempts to hold on to them within the framework of a union.

Sanjian, Andrea Stevenson. "Prostitution, the Press, and Agenda-Building in the Soviet Policy Process", in *SOVIET SOCIAL PROBLEMS*, edited by Anthony Jones, et al. (Boulder, CO; San Francisco: Oxford: Westview Press, 1991), pp. 270-295.

☆Savinkin, Alexander.
See THE HEARTBEAT OF REFORM: SOVIET JURISTS AND POLITICAL SCIENTISTS DISCUSS THE PROGRESS OF PERESTROIKA.

☆Savitskii, Valerii. "Democratization in the USSR: Toward the Freedom of the Individual through Law and Courts", 2 *CRIMINAL LAW FORUM* 85-110 (1990).

A survey of changes in the Soviet law under Gorbachev, the developments in the approach to the rule of law, and the expansion of the freedoms of individuals. The author is Director of the Sector on Problems of Justice, the Institute of State and Law, USSR Academy of Sciences. The article was translated by Professor George Ginsburgs.

☆Savitskii, Valerii. "Selected Problems of Judicial Reform, Criminal Justice, and the Protection of Individual Rights in the USSR", 2 *CRIMINAL LAW FORUM* 269-292 (1991).

The author, Director of the Sector on Problems of Justice at the Institute of State and Law, USSR Academy of Sciences, discusses various problems facing the reforms of Soviet administrative and criminal justice. He mentions the progress that has already been made, such as the rights of citizens to seek judicial protection against administrative abuse, the introduction of the rule of presumption of innocence and of other procedural safeguards into the criminal process, and the reorganization of the criminal investigation mechanism and surveillance.

☆Savitskii, Valerii
See also "Fear: Confessions of a Well-Known Legal Expert Who Has Criticized the Draft Law on the KGB".

Schmid, Karin. "Legal Reform as a Means of Perestroika", in *THE SOVIET UNION, 1988-1989: PERESTROIKA IN CRISIS?*, compiled by The Federal Institute for Soviet and International Studies (Boulder, CO: Westview Press, 1990), pp. 54-60.

Schmidt, Gustav. "Happy Moments: Solving the Special German-Soviet Russian Conflict", 24 *CORNELL INTERNATIONAL LAW JOURNAL* 437-455 (1991).

A survey of German-Soviet relations prior to the unification of Germany.

Schmitt, Michael N., and James E. Moody. "The Soviet Military Justice System", 34 *AIR FORCE LAW REVIEW* 1-108 (1991).

An excellently organized and very detailed examination of the Soviet military justice system. The authors discuss the regime of discipline in the Soviet Army, judicial and non-judicial punishment, the system and operation of military tribunals, as well as the substantive and procedural laws applied in the Soviet military courts. The authors underscore that the military courts apply the substantive and procedural laws of the republics where they sit. This presents interesting ramifications for the Soviet armed forces in light of the Soviet Union's political restructuring.

Schneider, Eberhard. "The Nineteenth Party Conference: Reform of the Political System", in *THE SOVIET UNION 1988-1989: PERESTROIKA IN CRISIS?*, compiled by The Federal Institute for Soviet and International Studies (Boulder, CO: Westview Press, 1990), pp. 30-39.

Schneider, Richard C., Jr. "Tax, Investment, and Financing Issues in Projects in the USSR and Eastern Europe", in *LEGAL ASPECTS OF TRADE AND INVESTMENT IN THE SOVIET UNION AND EASTERN EUROPE* (New York: Practising Law Institute, 1990), pp. 235-295.

Schroeder, Gertrude E. "The Dismal Fate of Soviet-Type Economies: Mises Was Right", 11 *CATO JOURNAL* 13-25 (1991).

In this concisely and clearly written article the author explains why the Soviet economy could not survive. The main causes of its failure are identified and explained in a pithy manner.

Schroeder, Gertrude E. "Economic Relations among the Soviet Republics". A Paper presented at the Geonomics Institute Seminar, Middleburg, Vermont, May 10-13, 1991. 23 ll.

An interesting paper on an important and not widely researched topic. The author points out the extensive economic interdependence of the republics due to past policies of centralized economic planning and management of the Soviet Union as a whole. She predicts that stabilizing the economy and creating market institutions will present a gargantuan task for the individual republics.

Schroeder, Gertrude E. "Nationalities and the Soviet Economy" in *NATIONALITIES FACTOR IN SOVIET POLITICS AND SOCIETY*, edited by Lubomyr Hajda and Mark Beissinger (Boulder, CO: Westview Press, 1990), pp. 43-71.

Schroeder, Gertrude E. "On the Economic Viability of New Nation-States", 45 *JOURNAL OF INTERNATIONAL AFFAIRS* 549-574 (1992).

This is the first article which seriously examines the economic viability of the individual republics which began to break off from the Soviet Union in August, 1991. Many western politicans as well as scholars believed in the necessity of keeping the Soviet Union intact simply in order to preserve its economic integrity. This author is optimistic about most of the republics being able to make it on their own.

Schuler, Kurt. "Ruble Reform: A Lesson from Keynes". *See* Hanke, Steve H., and Kurt Schuler.

Schwartz, Eric J. "Recent Developments in the Copyright Regimes of the Soviet Union and Eastern Europe", 38 *JOURNAL OF THE COPYRIGHT SOCIETY OF THE U.S.A.* 123-226 (1991).

Schweisfurth, Theodor. "The Acceptance of the Soviet Union of the Compulsory Jurisdiction of the ICJ for Six Human Rights Conventions", 2 *EUROPEAN JOURNAL OF INTERNATIONAL LAW* 110-117 (1991).

Schweisfurth, Theodor "The New Approach to the Law of Peaceful Coexistence", in *THE CHANGING POLITICAL STRUCTURE OF EUROPE: ASPECTS OF INTERNATIONAL LAW*, edited by R. Lefeber, M. Fitzmaurice, and E.W. Vierdag (Dordrecht, The Netherlands: Martinus Nijhoff Publishers, 1991), pp. 29-49.

An interesting analysis of the changes in the Soviet attitudes toward international relations during the time of the Gorbachev rule.

Scotland, Francis A. "Soviet Financial Reform: Money and Credit", in *THE EMERGING RUSSIAN BEAR: INTEGRATING THE SOVIET UNION INTO THE WORLD ECONOMY*, edited by Josef C. Brada and Michael P. Claudon (New York: New York University Press, 1991), pp. 63-72.

Brief proposals for a market-based financial reform.

Scott, Antony. "Siberia, Environmentalism and Problems of Environmental Protection".
See Rosencranz, Armin, and Antony Scott.

Sedaitis, Judith B. "Worker Activism: Politics at the Grass Roots", in *PERESTROIKA FROM BELOW: SOCIAL MOVEMENTS IN THE SOVIET UNION*, edited by Judith B. Sedaitis and Jim Butterfield (Boulder, CO: Westview Press, 1991), pp. 13-27.

Sedaitis, Judith B., and Jim Butterfield, eds. *PERESTROIKA FROM BELOW: SOCIAL MOVEMENTS IN THE SOVIET UNION* (Boulder, CO: Westview Press, Inc., 1991). xii, 220 pp.

A collection of papers originally presented at a Symposium on Social Movements in the Soviet Union, organized by the Nationalities and Siberian Studies Program of the W. Averell Harriman Institute for Advanced Study of the Soviet Union in November, 1989. Most of the papers discuss the emergence of a political consciousness among the people of the Soviet Union. Though many of the issues have been made irrelevant by subsequent events, the papers offer valuable insights into the historical origins of movements and political activities which came into existence during the mid-years of Gorbachev's term of office as the leader of the Soviet Union (in the late 1980s).

Papers of particular interest to legal and law-related research are—

"Environmental Politics and Policy under *Perestroika*" by Charles E. Ziegler.
"The Greening of Ukraine: Ecology and the Emergence of *Zelenyi svit*, 1986-1990" by David R. Marples.
"Nationalism, Movement Groups, and Party Formation" by Paul A. Goble.
"Worker Activism: Politics at the Grass Roots" by Judith B. Sedaitis.
"Worker Activism: The Role of the State" by Russell Bova.

Selianovsky, Sergo. "An Introduction to Soviet Intellectual Property Law".
See Barschevsky, Mikhail, Sergo Selianovsky, and Bruce A. MacDonald.

☆Semeyko, Aleksei L.
See Stephan, Paul B. III, and Boris M. Klimenko.

☆Semilutina, Natalya G.
See Sherr, Alan B., et al.

Shadbolt, R.A. "Contracting for Construction Projects with the U.S.S.R.", 7 *INTERNATIONAL CONSTRUCTION LAW REVIEW* 379-385 (1990).

A look at the organizational structure of the Soviet construction industry and the prospects for foreigners to obtain construction contracts in the Soviet Union. A useful article on a subject heretofore not examined in any detail.

☆Shakhnazarov, Georgy.
See THE HEARTBEAT OF REFORM: SOVIET JURISTS AND POLITICAL SCIENTISTS DISCUSS THE PROGRESS OF PERESTROIKA.

Shanks, Robert B. "Investment Protection for Projects in Eastern Europe and the Soviet Union: OPIC, MIGA, and Bilateral Investment Treaties", in *LEGAL ASPECTS OF TRADE AND INVESTMENT IN THE SOVIET UNION AND EASTERN EUROPE* (New York: Practising Law Institute, 1990), pp. 391-408.

☆Sharafetdinov, Nuriman.
See THE HEARTBEAT OF REFORM: SOVIET JURISTS AND POLITICAL SCIENTISTS DISCUSS THE PROGRESS OF PERESTROIKA.

Sharlet, Robert. "The Path of Constitutional Reform in the USSR", in *PERESTROIKA-ERA POLITICS: THE NEW SOVIET LEGISLATURE AND GORBACHEV'S POLITICAL REFORMS,* edited by Robert Huber and Donald R. Kelley (Armonk, NY: M.E. Sharpe, Inc., 1991), pp. 17-32.

☆Shcherbak, Iurii. *CHERNOBYL: A DOCUMENTARY STORY.* New York: St. Martin's Press, 1989. xvi, 168 pp.

Translated from the Ukrainian by Ian Press, this book is a Soviet journalistic account of the Chernobyl nuclear energy plant disaster.

☆Shcherbakov, V.I. "Remuneration of Labour in the USSR: Problems and Prospects", 130 *INTERNATIONAL LABOUR REVIEW* 227-236 (1991/2).

From the editorial abstract:

> The Soviet Union is in a process of transition from an administrative-command economy to one based on different forms of ownership, but many problems remain. Wage differentials and incentives were eroded over the years, leading to the rise of the so-called "shadow economy". Previous reforms in 1987 were not sufficiently wide-ranging and radical changes in the labour market are now being introduced. Collective bargaining and individual

contracts appear to be indispensable if workers are truly to profit from their labour.

Sheedy, John F., and Richard N. Dean. "Gaining a Foothold in the Soviet Market: How to Establish a Representative Office", *25 INTERNATIONAL LAWYER* 103-125 (1991).

Opening a representative office in Moscow has for many years been the most practical means of establishing relatively permanent contacts in the Soviet Union for foreign businesses. In this article the practicalities and techniques of opening such representative offices are discussed by two members of the international law firm of Coudert Brothers. The discussion is detailed and thorough. It offers many useful hints, yet it also manages to deal with serious theoretical and policy issues. The value of the article is further enhanced by the inclusion of an English translations of the relatively unknown USSR Council of Ministers Decree of November 30, 1989 "On Approval of the Statute on the Procedure for the Opening and Activity in the USSR of Representative Offices of Foreign Firms, Banks and Organizations" as well as a translation of the text of the statute.

Sheehy, Ann. "The Ethnodemographic Dimension", in *SOVIET FEDERALISM: NATIONALISM AND ECONOMIC DECENTRALISATION*, edited by Alastair McAuley (Leicester and London: Leicester University Press, 1991), pp. 56-88.

Exceptionally useful statistical information about the ethnic and national makeup of the Soviet Union.

☆Sheinis, Zinovy. *MAXIM LITVINOV.* Moscow: Progress Publishers, 1990. 356 pp.

A biography of an early Soviet People's Commissar for Foreign Affairs and a leading diplomat. The book is a valuable historical study of an important period in Soviet international relations.

Shelley, Louise I. "Crime in the Soviet Union", in *SOVIET SOCIAL PROBLEMS,* edited by Anthony Jones, et al. (Boulder, CO; San Francisco; Oxford: Westview Press, 1991), pp. 252-269.

Shelley, Louise I. "Soviet Criminal Law and Justice: Are There or Were There Secrets?", in *THE SOVIET SOBRANIE OF LAWS,* edited by Richard M. Buxbaum and Kathryn Hendley (Berkeley, CA: University of California at Berkeley, 1991), pp. 140-155.

☆Sheremet, Konstantin. "Law and Social Change in the USSR of the 1990s", 27 *SOCIETY* 90-97 (1990).

A look at trends in legal theory since perestroika outlining issues to be given top priority by lawyers and law schools in the future. The author is a well-known Soviet legal scholar.

Sherr, Alan B., et al. *INTERNATIONAL JOINT VENTURES: SOVIET AND WESTERN PERSPECTIVES.* New York: Quorum Books, 1991. xv, 351 pp. (A project of the Center for Foreign Policy Development at Brown University, the Institute for World Economy and International Relations of the USSR Academy of Sciences and the All-Union Research Institute for Foreign Economic Relations, State Foreign Economies Commission of the USSR Council of Ministers).

This book deals with the legislative and economic attempts of Gorbachev's government to improve the Soviet economy through joint ventures with foreign participants and capital. Though the Soviet Union does not exist any more and Gorbachev is no longer the head of government in any part of the former Soviet Union, many of the observations in the book apply with equal force to joint ventures in Russia, Ukraine, the Baltic, etc.

Contributions to this book were made by the following persons—

Soviet authors:	Western authors:
☆Artemova, Tatyana M.	Butler, William E.
☆Doronin, Igor G.	Cooper, Julian
☆Eventov, Zinoviy M.	Gotbaum, Noah E.
☆Faminsky, Igor P.	Hanson, Philip
☆Khudyakova, Lyudmila S.	Kalicki, Jan H.
☆Korolev, Ivan S.	Morton, John
☆Maslov, Vyacheslav O.	Sherr, Alan B.
☆Platonova, Natalya L.	Stubbs, Eric A.
☆Ranenko, Vladimir V.	
☆Rodina, Lyudmila A.	
☆Semilutina, Natalya G.	
☆Yakovleva, Evgeniya L.	

☆Shevardnadze, Eduard. "Consolidation of the CPSU in a Multiparty System", 29 *SOVIET LAW AND GOVERNMENT* No. 4, 5-20 (Spring 1991).

A speech by the former Soviet foreign minister in which he discusses the successes and the failures of perestroika. Shevardnadze, at the time of giving the speech, still believed that a reformed Communist Party had a role in a pluralist political system emerging in the Soviet Union.

Published originally in *Literaturnaia Gazeta*, 1990, No. 16 (April 18, 1990).

☆Shevardnadze, Eduard. *THE FUTURE BELONGS TO FREEDOM.* New York: The Free Press, 1991. xx, 237 pp.

It has become fashionable for the new Soviet political celebrities to publish semi-autobiographical books which are quickly translated into French, German, English, and other major languages (frequently before they are published in Russian). Through clever marketing such books become bestsellers, though it is highly doubtful whether they are really read (and understood) by a majority of the people who buy them. It is all clever enterpreneurship which exploits public curiosity in anything that purports to be "Soviet". Books by such Soviet public figures as Gorbachev, Yeltsin and Sobchak have sold as extensively as the biographies of Marilyn Monroe. Yet they generally say little, and the little they say is not very convincing.

Eduard Shevardnadze was Gorbachev's Foreign Minister. In December, 1990 he resigned his office as a protest against the dictatorship he believed was developing in the Soviet Union. This almost turned out to be true when in August, 1991 several close Gorbachev collaborators tried to take power by staging a coup against Gorbachev. They did not succeed, and Shevardnadze's resignation acquired a symbolic meaning.

This book is Shevardnadze's political testament. Unfortunately it is badly written, ponderous, rather simplistic in its political statements, and astonishingly vague and sketchy in factual descriptions of Shevardnadze's life and work as a Party functionary and a high government official. Reviewing it for the *New York Times Book Review* (September 13, 1991), Bernard Gwertzman comments that "unfortunately, the book lacks the kind of detail that would have made it something special." In the opinion of most people with whom Shevardnadze came into contact as the Soviet Foreign Minister, he is supposed to be an engaging man. This book, unfortunately, demonstrates that he is no great intellect.

Shillinglaw, Thomas J. "Technology Transfer Transactions with Soviet and Eastern European Enterprises: Experience in USA Companies", in *LEGAL ASPECTS OF TRADE AND INVESTMENT IN THE SOVIET UNION AND EASTERN EUROPE* (New York: Practising Law Institute, 1990), pp. 205-233.

☆Shinkaretskaya, Galina G. "Changing Attitude towards International Adjudication in the Soviet Union", 3 *LEIDEN JOURNAL OF INTERNATIONAL LAW* No. 3, 59-66 (Special Issue, December 1990).

The author presents an overview of Russian and Soviet attitudes to the settlement of disputes by means of international adjudication. She discusses the readiness of the Russian Czarist government to participate in international arbitrations and mediations, and the complete turn-around in that attitude during the Sòviet period. She notes the development of a more receptive approach by the current governments.

☆Shinkaretskaya, Galina G. "International Arbitration in the External Policy of the Soviet Union", in *PERESTROIKA AND INTERNATIONAL LAW: CURRENT ANGLO-SOVIET APPROACHES TO INTERNATIONAL LAW*, edited by Anthony Carty and Gennady Danilenko (Edinburgh: Edinburg University Press, 1990), pp. 110-118.

Silliman, Emily. "Local Government: Structure and Economic Regulation". A Paper presented at the Geonomics Institute Seminar, Middleburg, Vermont, May 10-13, 1991. 22 pp. Reprinted in *INVESTING IN REFORM: DOING BUSINESS IN A CHANGING SOVIET UNION,* edited by Michael P. Claudon and Tamar L. Gutner (New York: New York University Press, 1991), pp. 139-157.

A very valuable and interesting paper about the functions and powers of local governments in the Soviet Union through 1990.

Simes, Dimitry. "Gorbachev's Time of Troubles", 82 *FOREIGN POLICY* 97-117 (Spring 1991).

Simes is a highly respected and an unusually perceptive commentator on current events in the Soviet Union. In this article he takes Gorbachev to task for missing opportunities and pursuing contradictory courses of action. According to Simes, Gorbachev, despite his good intentions, did not truly appreciate the dynamics of the changes he unleashed in the Soviet Union. Much of this was due to his deeply ingrained loyalty to the communist system of the USSR and perhaps less clearly to the ideological aspects of communism. This brilliant article discusses Gorbachev's misperceptions and choices.

☆Simkin, Lev.
See THE HEARTBEAT OF REFORM: SOVIET JURISTS AND POLITICAL SCIENTISTS DISCUSS THE PROGRESS OF PERESTROIKA.

Simmons, David M. "Recognition of Illegalities, Proposals for Reform, and Implemented Reforms in the Soviet Criminal Justice System under Gorbachev, Glasnost and Perestroika", 5 *AMERICAN UNIVERSITY JOURNAL OF INTERNATIONAL LAW AND POLICY* 921-953 (1990).

An overview of the reforms of the Soviet criminal justice system during Gorbachev's period of perestroika.

Simon, Gerhard. *NATIONALISM AND POLICY TOWARD THE NATIONALITIES IN THE SOVIET UNION.* Boulder, CO: Westview, 1991. 483 pp.

According to the booknote in 70 *FOREIGN AFFAIRS* No. 5, 197-198 (Winter 1991/92):

> This was a prescient book when first published in German in 1986. Sensitive to the growing self-assertion of national elites in the Soviet Union, Simon's study traces better than any other the background of this summer's [1991] Soviet collapse. With a minimum of fuss and excess, he leads the reader from the 1920s and the original Bolshevik notions of nation-building in the non-Russian lands through the 1970s and the flowering of a "new nationalism" in the republics. By then Stalin's harsh policies of modernization and integration, like Khrushchev's more sophisticated and moderate sequel, were proving to contain the seeds of their own failure. The drama, as Simon correctly foresaw, would begin in the Baltic and spread west to east.

Simons, William B. "Foreign Investment Laws in the Republics of the USSR: Lithuania and Kazakhstan", 17 *REVIEW OF SOCIALIST LAW* 161-190 (1991).

Beginning with a concise, but exceptionally clear and helpful, introduction by William B. Simons, this set of documents consists of the author's English translations of: the Lithuanian Law on Foreign Investments of December 29, 1990 (including the decree on the procedure for enacting it), the Lithuanian Law on the Prohibition and Restrictions of Spheres of Activity for Foreign Investments of May 2, 1991 (including enacting decree), and the Kazakhstan Law on Foreign Investments of January 17, 1991 (including its enacting decree).

Simons, William B. "Foreign Investment Laws of Kazakhstan", 17 *REVIEW OF SOCIALIST LAW* 81-94 (1991).

This brief survey of legislation enacted by the Kazakhstan Supreme Soviet in the fall of 1990 includes full English translations of the Law on Free Economic Zones and the decree of its entry into force (texts of both of these laws were published in the *Kazakhstanskaia Pravda in* January, 1991 when they entered into force). Kazakhstan also enacted legislation on foreign economic activity, foreign investments, entrepreneurship, banking, property, and land ownership and use at about the same time, but English translations of these laws are not made available by the author.

Skolnick, Joanne. "When Soviet Lawyers Meet American Law", 17 *HUMAN RIGHTS* No. 3, 20-21 (Fall/Winter 1990).

A short report on the experience of Soviet lawyers in the United States during a 1990 visit under the sponsorship of the Soviet Lawyer Internship Project, administered by the Section of Individual Rights and Responsibilities of the American Bar Association.

☆Slavin, M.M. "Inviolability of the Individual in a Rule-of-Law State", in *PERESTROIKA AND THE RULE OF LAW: ANGLO-AMERICAN AND SOVIET PERSPECTIVES,* edited by William E. Butler (London: I.B. Tauris & Co., Ltd., 1991), pp. 186-199.

Slider, Darrell. "Embattled Enterpreneurs: Soviet Cooperatives in an Unreformed Society", 43 *SOVIET STUDIES* 797-822 (1991).

☆Smagin, Mikhail.
See THE HEARTBEAT OF REFORM: SOVIET JURISTS AND POLITICAL SCIENTISTS DISCUSS THE PROGRESS OF PERESTROIKA.

☆Smidovich, Nikita P.
See Stephan, Paul B. III, and Boris M. Klimenko.

Smith, Cynthia M. "Soviet Republics' Demand for Autonomy: The Need for Constitutional Reform and the Institution of Canadian-Style Judicial Review".
See Blase, John C., and Cynthia M. Smith.

Smith, Gordon B. *SOVIET POLITICS: STRUGGLING WITH CHANGE.* 2d ed. New York: St. Martin's Press; London: The MacMillan Press, 1992. xx, 396 pp.

This book by Gordon B. Smith, Professor of Government and International Studies of the University of South Carolina and one of the leading experts on the Soviet Union in the United States, is an introductory text about the political and economic structure of the Soviet Union. It is very comprehensive. Unfortunately, despite the 1992 publication date and the author's attempts to describe the mysterious and unsuccesful coup of August 1991, the book became substantially dated as soon as it was published. Quite clearly, like everyone else, the author could not predict the disintegration of the Soviet Union in December 1991. Nevertheless, the book is not without value. Its descriptions of the major forces of change and leading new political personalities offer, in the absence of more current texts, a convenient and useful introduction to the changes which brought about the end of the Soviet Union. More to the point for lawyers, there is an informative and well-organized chapter on the Soviet legal system as it existed in early 1991.

Smith, Graham. *THE NATIONALITIES QUESTION IN THE SOVIET UNION.* London and New York: Longman, 1990. ix, 389 pp.

An excellent overview of the different nationalities in the Soviet Union immediately before its fragmentation and the emergence of fifteen independent republics. The book consists of separate chapters, each written by a different contributor, on the major nationalities of the Soviet Union. Though the papers do not discuss issues of direct relevance to legal research, the book is a useful reference source on the major challenges facing each of the nationalities.

Smith, Hedrick. *THE NEW RUSSIANS.* New York: Random House, 1990. xxxi, 621 pp. Revised paperbound edition: New York: Avon Books, 1991. xxxi, 734 pp.

The author of the much-acclaimed book *The Russians* (1984) presents here a popularized history of the changes taking place in the Soviet Union from 1985, when Gorbachev became the leader of the country, through late 1990. The paperback edition, extensively revised, also discusses the important and crucial events of 1991, including a brief account of the unsuccessful coup against Gorbachev in August of that year which resulted in a drastic reshaping of the Soviet Union.

Smith's book is not a scholarly work, and it is not intended to be. Journalistic in style, it is rather wordy, but it is immensely readable. It succeeds very well in explaining the crumbling of the Soviet Union and the collapse of its former power structure. It also happens to be a very handy reference work on the history of the Soviet Union from 1985 through August, 1991.

Sneider, Carolyn M. "The Slepak Principles Act and Soviet Union-United States Joint Ventures: Profits or People?" (Note), 13 *LOYOLA OF LOS ANGELES INTERNATIONAL AND COMPARATIVE LAW JOURNAL* 365-392 (1990).

This note discusses the participation of United States corporations and individuals in trade with the Soviet Union and investment in that country in the light of the United States' commitment to international human rights. Several bills (known as the Slepak Principles Act) were introduced in the United States Congress in 1989 for the purpose of discouraging United States trading or investment activity in the Soviet Union until that country establishes a better human rights record. The bills did not pass. The note examines the reasons for the Congressional reluctance to enact legislation of this kind. It also urges a firmer United States attitude towards the Soviet Union on questions of human rights.

Snowe, Olympia J. "The Moscow Embassy: A Study of Congressional Response to Crisis", 16 *JOURNAL OF LEGISLATION* 35-46 (1989).

In the spring of 1987, much to the amazement of the State Department and the American government in general, it was discovered that security at the United States Embassy in Moscow had been breached. Particularly distressing were allegations that members of the Marine Security Guard Detachment, whose members are charged with the guarding of embassies, had permitted Soviet nationals to penetrate the facility. Equally distressing were allegations that the new United States embassy complex was riddled with listening devices. Congresswoman Olympia J. Snowe was appointed to lead a delegation to Moscow and investigate the situation. This article describes the Soviet behavior, the United States responses, and negotiations between the two countries.

☆Sobchak, Anatoly A. "The Changing Role of Lawyers in the Soviet Union", 3 *INTERNATIONAL LEGAL PERSPECTIVES* 40-50 (1990).

Dr. Anatoly A. Sobchak is one of the prominent modern politicians in the USSR. In the late 1980's he was elected Mayor of Leningrad, and it was due mainly to his efforts that the name of the city was changed back to St. Petersburg. Formerly a professor of law at the Leningrad State University, he became one of the more influential members of the USSR Supreme Soviet and an outspoken critic of Gorbachev's policies. In late 1990 he resigned his membership in the Communist Party of the USSR. This is a transcript of his commencement address at Lewis and Clark Law School on May 27, 1990. The speech addresses in general terms the changes required to be made in the Soviet Union to establish a rule of law and to enable the development of an independent legal profession.

☆Sobchak, Anatoly A. *FOR A NEW RUSSIA: THE MAYOR OF ST. PETERSBURG'S OWN STORY OF THE STRUGGLE FOR JUSTICE AND DEMOCRACY.* New York: The Free Press, 1991. 191 pp.

The author of this book, a law professor, became a member of the USSR Supreme Soviet, then the Mayor of St. Petersburg, and one of the leading political figures in the disintegrating Soviet Union. In this book he writes about his election to the Soviet legislature in 1989 and his subsequent experience there. The book is extremely self-centered. The author describes himself as the wisest and smartest politician in the Soviet Union. Nevertheless, there are interesting and valuable descriptions of the procedures, dynamics, and behind-the-scenes activities of the Soviet legislature.

☆Sobchak, Anatoly A. "The New Soviet Union—Challenges in the Development of a Law-Abiding State", 20 *STETSON LAW REVIEW* 211-216 (1990).

Observations about political changes and legal reforms in the Sovet Union by the popular mayor of St. Petersburg.

Soderquist, Larry D. "Private Companies in the Soviet Union: Cooperatives in the Era of Perestroika".
See Griffin, Andrew T., and Larry D. Soderquist.

Soderquist, Larry D. "The Soviet Cooperative before Perestroika: The Leninist versus the Stalinist Concept".
See Griffin, Andrew T., and Larry D. Soderquist.

Solchanyk, Roman. "Ukraine, Belorussia, and Moldavia: Imperial Integration, Russification, and the Struggle for National Survival", in *THE NATIONALITIES FACTOR IN SOVIET POLITICS AND SOCIETY*, edited by Lubomyr Hajda and Mark Beissinger (Boulder, CO: Westview Press, 1990), pp. 175-203.

Solomon, Peter H., Jr. "Gorbachev's Legal Revolution", 17 *CANADIAN BUSINESS LAW JOURNAL* 184-194 (1990).

An examination of Gorbachev's commitment to make the USSR a law-based state, discussing the components of this reform as well as problems in the implementation.

Solomon, Peter H., Jr. "Legality in Soviet Political Culture: A Perspective on Gorbachev's Reforms", in *STALINISM: ITS NATURE AND AFTERMATH. ESSAYS IN HONOUR OF MOSHE LEWIN*, edited by Nick Lampert and Gabor T. Rittersporn (Armonk, NY: M.E. Sharpe, Inc., 1992), pp. 260-287.

☆Soloviev, A. "Experiences and Future Outlook of East-West Joint Ventures in the Soviet Union."
See Ranenko, V., and A. Soloviev.

Solzhenitzyn, Aleksandr. *REBUILDING RUSSIA: REFLECTIONS AND TENTATIVE PROPOSALS.* New York: Farrer, Straus and Giroux, 1991. 119 pp.

Though this small book does not specifically examine either the law or the legal system of the Soviet Union, it is a work of sufficiently profound importance to be included among books useful to know as a general background to legal research. It discusses the causes for the decline and breakup of the Soviet Union, followed by Solzhenitsyn's view of how this part of the world should look in the future. He recognizes the conflict between the various nationalities and ethnic groups as one of the key obstacles to keeping the Soviet Union together. His proposal is that all of the individual nations should go their own ways, if they so wish. The entity he would like to see emerge from the ruins of the former system is a culturally and ethnically strong "Rus", consisting of Great Russia, Little Russia (Ukraine) and Byelorussia. It is not likely that even this will happen.

Published originally in Russian as a supplement to the newspaper *Komsomolskaya Pravda* in September 1990, the book is superbly translated by Alexis Klimoff. For a favorable review, see Daniel Patrick Moynihan, *New York Times Book Review*, November 24, 1991, p. 9.

Soros, George. *A PERSPECTIVE ON THE COLLAPSE OF THE SOVIET SYSTEM.* Baltimore: The Paul H. Nitze School for

Advanced International Studies, The John Hopkins University, 1990. 11 pp.

George Soros is an American philanthropist who has donated extensive funds toward the democratization of the Soviet Union and the improvement of its economy. Among his many projects of this kind, he has funded lengthy study visits by Soviet lawyers in the United States.

In this short presentation Soros comments upon the future of the Soviet Union. Coming straight to the point, he advocates the establishment of a free market economy and recognition of national self-expression as the best solutions for the problems suffered by the people of that unfortunate part of the world.

Speekhard, Rebecca A. "Soviet Union".
See White, Walter H., and Rebecca A. Speekhard.

Sperber, Jeffrey. "From Borscht to Bits: Transfer of Technology and Industrial Property in the Soviet Union".
See Frenkel, William J., and Jeffrey Sperber.

Spring, D.W., ed. *THE IMPACT OF GORBACHEV: THE FIRST PHASE, 1985-1990.* London and New York: Pinter Publishers, 1991. ix, 244 pp.

A collection of papers reviewing the first five years of Gorbachev's rule in the Soviet Union. The papers deal with different topics. Two are of possible interest in law-related research:

"Labour: Past Imperfect, Present Tense—Trade Unions and Labour in the Soviet State" by John Morgan.

"Nationalities: Decolonizing the Last Empire" by Raymond Pearson.

Sprudzs, Adolf. "The Rule of Law and the Baltic States", in *BIBLIOTHEK UND RECHT INTERNATIONAL/LIBRARIES AND LAW—INTERNATIONAL, FESTSCHRIFT RALPH LANSKY*, edited by Jürgen Christoph Gödan and Holger Knudsen (Hamburg and Augsburg: Arbeitsgemeinschaft für juristisches Bibliotheks- und Dokumentationswesen, 1991), pp. 231-241.

A brief historical account of the forceful and treacherous annexation of the Baltic States by the Soviet Union in 1940 and comments about the intrinsic illegality thereof under the general principles and rules of international law. Includes an English translation of the Declaration of Restoration of Latvian Independence, pronounced in Riga on May 4, 1990.

Standing, Guy. "Wages and Work Motivation in the Soviet Labour Market. Why a 'BIP', not a 'TIP' Is Required", 130 *INTERNATIONAL LABOUR REVIEW* 237-253 (1991/2).

From the editorial abstract:

Labor productivity and wages have been very low in the USSR, and although efforts have been made to raise both, the tax-based income policy (TIP) recommended by many foreign economists and international institutions has only compounded the problem. This article examines the evidence and draws on an enterprise survey in progress; it concludes by recommending a benefits-based incomes policy (BIP) for the transitional period, coupled with fiscal encouragement of voluntary saving from wage increases in a "privatization fund", which would be counter-inflationary and would boost investment.

Starr, S. Frederick. "Voluntary Groups and Initiatives", in *SOVIET UPDATE, 1989-1990,* edited by Anthony Jones and David E. Powell (Boulder, CO: Westview Press, 1991), pp. 97-116.

A complete and clearly formulated overview of the emergence and development of independent movements and parties in the Soviet Union during the 1989-90 period.

Steckelman, Peter D. "Advancing Soviet-American Trade: The Legal Steps Necessary to Further Economic Relations" (Note), 11 *NEW YORK LAW SCHOOL JOURNAL OF INTERNATIONAL AND COMPARATIVE LAW* 463-481 (1990).

A rather ambitious student note on the improvement of trade relations between the United States and the Soviet Union. Topics discussed include changes in the Soviet emigration policies, the Jackson-Vanik Amendment, the most favored nation status, and the June 1, 1990 Trade Agreement between the United States and Soviet Union.

Stephan, Paul B., III. "*Perestroyka* and Property: The Law of Ownership in the Post-Socialist Soviet Union", 39 *AMERICAN JOURNAL OF COMPARATIVE LAW* 35-65 (1991).

Beginning with a brief outline of the Soviet property law prior to Gorbachev, this article then describes the various reform attempts through 1990 to introduce the notion of broader private ownership in the Soviet Union. The prospects of such reforms are evaluated in the context of economic and political developments. The author also discusses some of the unresolved issues within the Soviet society which present serious obstacles to the privatization movement and the establishment of a functioning market economy. He concludes that the ultimate success of privatization in the Soviet Union will depend on the liberalization of its economy.

Note: This is one of very few publications where the Russian word "reconstruction" is transliterated as "perestroyka" rather than "perestroika".

Stephan, Paul B., III. "The Restructuring of Soviet Commercial Law and Its Impact on International Business Transactions", 24 *GEORGE WASHINGTON JOURNAL OF INTERNATIONAL LAW AND ECONOMICS* 89-102 (1990).

A careful and thorough survey of Soviet legislative activities in the late 1980's which intended to create, as the author describes (p. 89), "a more hospitable climate for private and foreign business relations". The author discusses the problems these new laws bring about as well as the old barriers they have not removed. In a perceptive conclusion he warns against half measures which may endanger rather than help the Soviet economy.

Stephan, Paul B., III. "Revisiting the Incorporation Debate: The Role of Domestic Political Structure", 31 *VIRGINIA JOURNAL OF INTERNATIONAL LAW* 417-436 (1991).

The author discusses how domestic courts, particularly in the United States, employ principles and rules of international law in order to achieve more just and humane results. In comparing the United States practice on this issue with that of the Soviet Union, he notes some similarities, but a less constructive general approach towards the internal use of international law in the Soviet Union.

Stephan, Paul B., III. *SOVIET ECONOMIC LAW: THE PARADOX OF PERESTROYKA*. Pittsburgh, PA: University of Pittsburgh Center for Russian and East European Studies, 1990. 90 pp. (The Carl Beck Papers in Russian and East European Studies, No. 805).

A highly penetrating and serious study of the changes which have taken place in the Soviet legal infrastructure as a part of Gorbachev's quest for wholesale economic reform. The author looks first at the origins of the Soviet economic law under Lenin and Stalin, subsequent reform efforts under Khrushchev and Brezhnev, and the ultimate collapse of this unwieldy and monstrous regime. He then describes, step by step, Gorbachev's efforts to build a new economic system. Considerable attention is given to the conflict between the ideological attractions of a state-operated economy and the advantages of privatization. The author questions the validity of economic data as the main criteria in measuring the successes of reforms. In his opinion, social and institutional factors are equally or even more important. The laws Gorbachev introduced for the implementation of the changes he wanted to bring about in the Soviet economic system are scrutinized in the context of such criteria.

Stephan, Paul B., III. "Soviet Law and Foreign Investment: Perestroyka's Gordian Knot", 25 *INTERNATIONAL LAWYER* 741-754 (1991).

Professor Stephan takes a critical look at the Soviet attempts to attract foreign investment. He claims that "the Soviet leadership has not succeeded in creating a legal infrastructure" sufficiently clear and straightforward for potential investors from abroad. He finds that the existing Soviet laws and international agreements (as of early 1991) on the formation of business organizations, acquisition and ownership of property, banking and foreign exchange, etc., "send conflicting signals", and further confusion is created by the legislative activities of individual republics which are frequently in conflict with the all-Union legislation.

Stephan, Paul B., III. "A U.S. Perspective on the Legal Environment for Foreign Investment in Russia", in *LEGAL AND PRACTICAL ASPECTS OF DOING BUSINESS IN THE SOVIET REPUBLICS* (New York: Practising Law Institute, 1992), pp. 29-34.

Portions of this paper are excerpted from the author's "Soviet Law and Foreign Investment: Perestroyka's Gordian Knot", 25 *International Lawyer* 741-754 (1991).

Stephan, Paul B., III, and Boris M. Klimenko, eds. *INTERNATIONAL LAW AND INTERNATIONAL SECURITY: MILITARY AND POLITICAL DIMENSIONS—A U.S.-SOVIET DIALOGUE.* Armonk, NY: M.E. Sharpe, Inc., 1991. xxii, 362 pp.

In this exceptionally interesting volume (simultaneously published in the Russian language) different issues of international law are discussed side-by-side by Soviet and American experts. The issues include renunciation of military aggression, the scope of legitimate self-defense, internal conflicts and international law, limitations on the development and use of nuclear, chemical, biological, and other mass destruction weapons, limitations on military use of space, reduction of military forces, verification of arms control agreements, principles of sovereignty, prevention and peaceful resolution of international disputes, performance of international obligations, methods for the strengthening of mutual guarantees of non-aggression, and prevention of international terrorism. Soviet scholars participating in this work are—

Agayev, Ednan T.
Fedorov, Vladimir N.
Kiselev, Sergei N.
Klimenko, Boris M.
Kortunov, Sergei V.
Kuznetsov, Valerii I.
Litavrin, Petr. G.
Meshkov, Aleksei Yu.
Semeyko, Aleksei L.
Smidovich, Nikita P.
Tuzmukhamedov, Bakhtiyar
Ul'yanov, Mikhail I.
Yegorov, Sergei A.
Zmeyevskii, Aleksandr V.

Strautmanis, J., and A. Maurins. "Problems of National Legislation for the Protection of the Environment: The Case of Latvia", 38 *OSTEUROPA RECHT* 72-73 (1992).

Stubbs, Eric A.
See Sherr, Alan B., et al.

A STUDY OF THE SOVIET ECONOMY. Paris: International Monetary Fund, The World Bank, Organization for Economic Co-Operation and Development, and the European Bank for Reconstruction and Development, 1991. 3 volumes.

This is the monumental study of the Soviet economy prepared by the staff of the International Monetary Fund, the World Bank, Organization for Economic Co-Operation and Development and the European Bank for Reconstruction and Development in late 1990 and early 1991. Volume I examines general economic issues, reform attempts, macro-economic policies, and structural changes. Volume II deals with systemic reforms, including property, prices, formation of enterprises, legal and institutional reforms and enterpreneurial or business activities in general. Volume III focuses on specific issues in different key sectors of the Soviet economy.

Sunstein, Cass R. "Constitutionalism and Secession", 58 *UNIVERSITY OF CHICAGO LAW REVIEW* 633-670 (1991).

The author discusses the right to secession from a comparative perspective within the framework of the Soviet and Eastern European constitutional structures. His thesis is that constitutions ought not to include provisions which permit secession, and that the issue is moral and political rather than legal.

Suny, Ronald G. "Transcaucasia: Cultural Cohesion and Ethnic Revival in a Multinational Society", in *THE NATIONALITIES FACTOR IN SOVIET POLITICS AND SOCIETY*, edited by Lubomyr Hajda and Mark Beissinger. Boulder, CO: Westview Press, 1990, pp. 228-252.

☆Sviridenko, Oleg. "Counter-Trade Operations with the Republics of the Former USSR", 1992 *REVUE DE DROIT DES AFFAIRES INTERNATIONALES/INTERNATIONAL BUSINESS LAW JOURNAL* No. 1, 69-78.

This brief article contains some interesting examples of recent countertrade dealings by Russia.

Swaford, Michael. "Perceptions of Social Stations in the USSR", in *POLITICS, WORK, AND DAILY LIFE IN THE USSR: A SURVEY OF FORMER SOVIET CITIZENS*, edited by James R. Millar (Cambridge: Cambridge University Press, 1987), pp. 279-300.

☆Sydorenko, Svetlana. "Perestroyka, Social Justice, and Soviet Public Opinion".
See Mason, David S., and Svetlana Sydorenko.

"Symposium on U.S.-Soviet Military and Economic Relations", 22 *NEW YORK UNIVERSITY JOURNAL OF INTERNATIONAL LAW AND POLITICS* 373-595 (1990).

A symposium on miscellaneous topics: U.S.-Soviet relations, joint ventures and other trading arrangements within the Soviet Union, and military or disarmament issues. It includes the following articles on topics relevant to legal research:

"Anti-Satellite Weapons and U.S. National Security" by Gordon Goldstein.

"A Few Things U.S. Businesspeople Should Know about Joint Ventures in the Soviet Union: A Lawyer's View" by Daniel J. Arbess.

"Insurance and Risk Management of Joint Ventures in the USSR" by Larisa Afanasyeva.

"Joint Venture Experience: Observations on the Business and Legal Challenges" by Jeffrey A. Burt.

"Legal Implementation of the Multilateral Chemical Weapons Convention: Integrating International Security with the Constitution" by Edward A. Tanzman and Barry Kellman.

"Opportunities and Problems for Joint Ventures in Soviet Law" by John N. Hazard.

"Unconventional Forms of Financing: Buy-Back/Compensation/Barter" by Leo G. B. Welt.

T

Tanzman, Edward A., and Barry Kellman. "Legal Implementation of the Multilateral Chemical Weapons Convention: Integrating International Security with the Constitution", 22 *NEW YORK UNIVERSITY JOURNAL OF INTERNATIONAL LAW AND POLITICS* 475-518 (1990).

The authors of this article focus much of their discussion on the negotiations between the Soviet Union and the United States.

Tatu, Michel. *MIKHAIL GORBACHEV: THE ORIGINS OF PERESTROIKA*. Boulder, CO: East European Monographs, 1981 (distributed by Columbia University Press). xi, 155 pp.

An interesting biography of Gorbachev by one of the top Sovietologists in France; full of detail and zest. Originally written in French, the English language translation was done by A.P.M. Bradley. The book has many typographical and even factual errors, but these do not seriously affect its value as an exceptionally interesting account of Gorbachev's ascent to the leadership of the Soviet Union. It is unfortunate that the account of Gorbachev's life in this book ends in about mid-1987.

Theroux, Eugene, and Arthur L. George. *JOINT VENTURES IN THE SOVIET UNION: LAW AND PRACTICE.* Washington, DC: Baker & McKenzie, 1991. 165 pp.

"Third Annual Ernst C. Stiefel Symposium: Practicing Law and Doing Business in the Soviet Union", 11 *NEW YORK LAW SCHOOL JOURNAL OF INTERNATIONAL AND COMPARATIVE LAW* No. 3, 433-518 (1990).

Papers presented at the symposium include:

"Advancing Soviet-American Trade: The Legal Steps Necessary to Further Economic Relations" by Peter D. Steckelman.

"The Challenge of Doing Business in the Soviet Union" by Martin P. Levin.

"Joint Venture Law in the Soviet Union" by Nicole M. Houri.

"An Overview of Environmental Law in the USSR" by Peter M. Langrind.

"Practicing Law and Doing Business in the Soviet Union" by Richard N. Dean.
"Risks in Investing in the USSR: Can There Be Protection against Them?" by John N. Hazard.
"The Triple Crisis of the Soviet Union Today" by Richard N. Gardner.
"U.S.-Soviet Trade Agreement and Investment Protection Treaties" by Andre W.G. Newburg.

Thompson, Kenneth W., ed. *NEGOTIATING ARMS CONTROL: MISSED OPPORTUNITIES AND LIMITED SUCCESSES.* Lanham, MD: University Press of America, Inc., 1991. xii, 142 pp. (W. Alton Jones Foundation Series on Arms Control, vol. 17).

Includes an address by Max M. Kampelman on "Negotiating with the Soviets".

Thompson, Lorri M. "Soviet Straitjacket Psychiatry: New Legislation to End the Reign of Terror in the USSR" (Note), 16 *SYRACUSE JOURNAL OF INTERNATIONAL LAW AND COMMERCE,* 271-91 (1990).

This student note begins with a brief history of psychiatric abuse in the Soviet Union. The bulk of the note consists of a description of the criminal commitment process prescribed in articles 403-413 of the RSFSR Code of Criminal Procedure and the civil commitment procedure (entitled "The Conditions and Procedures for Providing Psychiatric Care") introduced by the Presidium of the USSR Supreme Soviet in January, 1988. The note concludes with a criticism of the new procedures and with comments about the amelioration of Criminal Code provisions on state crimes.

Tiefenbrun, Susan W. "A Legal Framework for Soviet Privatization." *See* Floroff, Olga, and Susan Tiefenbrun.

Tiefenbrun, Susan W. "New Soviet Fundamentals of Law on Land Ownership".
See Floroff, Olga, and Susan W. Tiefenbrun.

Timmermans, Wim A. "Union of Soviet Socialist Republics", in *GUIDE TO THE COMMERCIAL AND CORPORATE LAW OF EASTERN EUROPE*, edited by David Winter (Bicester, Oxfordshire, England: CCH Editions Limited, 1991), pp. 63-122.

A surprisingly helpful overview of the business-related legislation enacted in the USSR during the first five years of the Gorbachev regime (through early 1991). Very useful as a quick reference source.

☆Timoshenko, Alexandre S. "Control Machinery in the Ecological Security System", in *CONTROL OVER COMPLIANCE WITH INTERNATIONAL LAW*, edited by William E. Butler (Dordrecht, The Netherlands: Martinus Nijhoff Publishers, 1991), pp. 51-59.

☆Timoshenko, Alexandre S. "Ecological Security: The International Aspect", 7 *PACE ENVIRONMENTAL LAW REVIEW* 151-160 (1989).

A brief description of the main international activities relating to the protection of the environment.

Tolz, Vera. *THE USSR'S EMERGING MULTIPARTY SYSTEM*. New York: Praeger, 1990. xvi, 123 pp. (The Center for Strategic and International Studies, Washington Papers No. 148).

Published in 1990, this is the first comprehensive survey of new political parties emerging during the Gorbachev regime in the former Soviet Union. The book is an excellent reference source on the movements and ideologies which dominate political activities in Russia and some of the other newly-emerging independent republics.

Toop, R. Scott. "Doing Business in the Soviet Union: A Case Study", in *LEGAL ASPECTS OF TRADE AND INVESTMENT IN THE SOVIET UNION AND EASTERN EUROPE* (New York: Practising Law Institute, 1990), pp. 57-74.

Torbert, Preston M. "The Commonwealth of Independent States: Its Legal Status and Implications for Foreign Companies", in *LEGAL AND PRACTICAL ASPECTS OF DOING BUSINESS IN THE SOVIET REPUBLICS* (New York: Practising Law Institute, 1992), pp. 127-137.

A brief account of the formation of the Commonwealth of Independent States and other developments.

Torbert, Preston M. "First Soviet Free Zone Will Give Firms Access to Pacific Basin Markets", in *LEGAL AND PRACTICAL ASPECTS OF DOING BUSINESS IN THE SOVIET REPUBLICS* (New York: Practising Law Institute, 1992), pp. 483-494.

Previously published in the *East Asian Executive Reports* (March 1991), this brief article discusses the establishment of a free trade zone in Nakhodka. It includes an English translation of the Nakhodka Free Trade Zone Regulations.

Torbert, Preston M. "New Free Enterprise Zone Regulations Promote Investment", in *LEGAL AND PRACTICAL ASPECTS OF DOING BUSINESS IN THE SOVIET REPUBLICS.* Commercial Law and Practice Course Handbook Series No. 604. New York: Practising Law Institute, 1992, pp. 477-482.

Previously published in *East Europe/Soviet Union Executive Guide* (October 1991).

Trapans, Andris. "Moscow, Economics and the Baltic Republics", in *TOWARD INDEPENDENCE: THE BALTIC POPULAR MOVEMENTS,* edited by Jan Arveds Trapans (Boulder, CO; San Francisco; Oxford: Westview Press, 1991), pp. 85-98.

Trapans, Jan Arveds. "The Sources of Latvia's Popular Movement", in *TOWARD INDEPENDENCE: THE BALTIC POPULAR MOVEMENTS,* edited by Jan Arveds Trapans (Boulder, CO; San Francisco; Oxford: Westview Press, 1991), pp. 25-41.

Trapans, Jan Arveds, ed. *TOWARD INDEPENDENCE: THE BALTIC POPULAR MOVEMENTS* (Boulder, CO; San Francisco; Oxford: Westview Press, 1991), vii, 166 pp.

A study of independence movements in the Baltic during the late 1980's. There are also research papers examining such movements in other Soviet Republics. The papers in this volume were presented at a conference convened by Radio Free Europe/Radio Liberty in September, 1989. Papers relevant or helpful to legal research include:

"Baltic Echoes in Ukraine" by Bohdan Nahaylo.

"Moscow, Economics and the Baltic Republics" by Andris Trapans.

"The Party and Popular Movements in the Baltic" by Kestutis Giruins.

"The Popular Movement in Belorussia and Baltic Influence" by Kathleen Mihalisko.

"Reaction: The Intermovements in Estonia" by Toomas Hendrik Ilves.

"Sajudis: National Revolution in Lithuania" by V. Stanley Vardys.

"The Sources of Latvia's Popular Movement" by Jan Arveds Trapans.

Reviewed by Toivo V. Raun in 51 *Slavic Review* 156-157 (1992).

Treml, Vladimir G. "Drinking and Alcohol Abuse in the USSR in the 1980's", in *SOVIET SOCIAL PROBLEMS,* edited by Anthony Jones, et al. (Boulder, CO; San Francisco; Oxford: Westview Press, 1991), pp. 119-136.

☆Trofimov, Vladimir. *LEGAL STATUS OF ANTARKTICA*. Moscow: Publishing House "Prometey", 1990. 141 pp.

The author, a member of the Commission on Antarctic Rescarch at the USSR Academy of Sciences, describes the international aspects relating to the legal status of Antarctica, including the regulation of its development and the protection of its environment. The book is written from a Soviet standpoint, and special emphasis is placed on an examination of the Soviet rights and interests in the Antarctic. The author devotes much attention to detail, and his work is suprisingly thorough. Unfortunately there is no index.

Tucker, Robert C. *STALIN IN POWER: THE REVOLUTION FROM ABOVE, 1928-1941*. New York: Norton, 1990. xix, 707 pp.

A thorough and authoritative account of the system created by Stalin to acquire complete power over the Soviet Union. Exceptionally well-written and documented. A compulsory reading for any serious student of the history of the Soviet Union. In terms of its style and depth, this is a much more detailed work on Stalin than the recent biographies of Conquest and Volkogonov (also listed in this volume).

☆Tumanov, Vladimir. "Guarantees for Constitutionality of Legislation in the U.S.S.R.", in *CONSTITUTIONAL REVIEW AND LEGISLATION: AN INTERNATIONAL COMPARISON*, edited by Christine Landfried (Baden-Baden: Nomos Verlagsgesellschaft, 1988), pp. 213-217.

A brief and now outdated explanation of how constitutional review is incompatible with the principle of political supremacy in the Soviet Union. The author advances a rather unconvincing explanation that the constitutionality of legislation is adequately controlled by the Presidium of the USSR Supreme Soviet and, on a different level, by the Procurator's Office.

☆Tumanov, Vladimir.

See also THE HEARTBEAT OF REFORM: SOVIET JURISTS AND POLITICAL SCIENTISTS DISCUSS THE PROGRESS OF PERESTROIKA.

☆Tunkin, Grigory I. "International Politics and International Law in the Nuclear Age", in *FROM COEXISTENCE TO COOPERATION: INTERNATIONAL LAW AND ORGANIZATION IN THE POST-COLD WAR ERA*, edited by Edward McWhinney, et al. (Dordrecht, The Netherlands: Martinus Nijhoff Publishers, 1991), pp. 9-17.

Tupper, Stephen. *RUSSIAN AND SOVIET ECONOMIC CHANGE: THE NEW LAW.*
See Nightingale, Christopher, and Stephen Tupper.

Turro, John. "Soviet Union Adopts New Tax System", 2 *TAX NOTES INTERNATIONAL* 793-796 (August 1990).

☆Tuzmukhamedov, Bakhtiar R. "Verification of Disarmament", in *PERESTROIKA AND INTERNATIONAL LAW: CURRENT ANGLO-SOVIET APPROACHES TO INTERNATIONAL LAW*, edited by Anthony Carty and Gennady Danilenko (Edinburgh: Edinburg University Press, 1990), pp. 48-61.

☆Tuzmukhamedov, Bakhtiyar R.
See also Stephan, Paul B. III, and Boris M. Klimenko.

U

☆Uljanov, Eugene. "The Latest Developments in the Foreign Currency Practices and Regulations of the Soviet Union". A Paper presented at the Geonomics Institute Seminar, Middleburg, Vermont, May 10-13, 1991. 20 pp. Also published in *INVESTING IN REFORM: DOING BUSINESS IN A CHANGING SOVIET UNION,* edited by Michael P. Claudon and Tamar L. Gutner (New York: New York University Press, 1991), pp. 61-73.

Eugene Uljanov, of the Bank for Foreign Economic Affairs of the USSR, explains the banking situation in the USSR, ruble convertibility, and currency exchange problems as they existed in Spring, 1991.

☆Ul'yanov, Mikhail I.
See Stephan, Paul B. III, and Boris M. Klimenko.

United Nations Centre on Transnational Corporations Advisory Studies.
See JOINT VENTURE ACCOUNTING IN THE USSR: DIRECTION FOR CHANGE.

UNITED NATIONS ECONOMIC COMMISSION FOR EUROPE.
See Kaser, Michael, and Aleksandar M. Vacic.

United States Congress. House of Representatives Committee on Foreign Affairs. *SOVIET DIPLOMACY AND NEGOTIATING BEHAVIOR—1988-90: GORBACHEV-REAGAN-BUSH MEETINGS AT THE SUMMIT.* Washington, D.C.: U.S. Government Printing Office, 1991. xvii, 478 pp.

This is Volume III of the excellent study prepared by Dr. Joseph G. Whelen of the Congressional Research Service.

The first two volumes are described in this author's *Gorbachev's Law: A Bibliographic Survey Of English Writings On Soviet Legal Developments 1987-1990* (Buffalo, NY: William S. Hein & Co., Inc., 1991).

USSR: FIRST STEPS TOWARDS REFORM OF THE CRIMINAL JUSTICE SYSTEM. London: Amnesty International, International Secretariat, 1990. 10 pp.

An Amnesty International report about reforms of criminal justice in the USSR from mid-1989 through mid-1990. The reform legislation, enacted by the Supreme Soviet, includes such measures as greater independence of the judiciary, fairer procedure, protection of the rights of the accused, and procedures for bringing actions against government officials who infringe the rights of citizens. The report also notes the emergence of religious freedom and the establishment of the Committee on Constitutional Supervision. It concludes that there is considerable progress in the USSR towards the establishment of a true "rule of law" and a more visible observance of human rights.

V

Vacic, Aleksandar M. *REFORMS IN FOREIGN ECONOMIC RELATIONS OF EASTERN EUROPE AND THE SOVIET UNION.* *See* Kaser, Michael, and Aleksandar M. Vacic.

Vaksberg, Arkady. *THE SOVIET MAFIA.* New York: St. Martin's Press, 1991. ix, 275 pp.

Organized crime predominates in all parts of the Soviet Union. Referred to as "the Mafia", it emerged in the early 1960's as a direct result of a system of privileges created by Stalin during the terror-ridden period of his rule. Today "the Mafia" permeates the whole society in literally every one of the countries which previously constituted the Soviet Union. It encompasses government agencies, police and security forces (including the KGB), economic organizations of the state, as well as many ordinary citizens who work in partnership with criminal elements.

Arkady Vaksberg, who has written extensively about the miscarriage of justice in the Soviet Union, exposes in this book the corrupt and dissolute conduct of the Soviet leadership from the time of Brezhnev to 1990. He paints an ugly picture of high-level officials cheating and stealing public property in partnership with professional criminals. According to Vaksberg, "the Mafia" stranglehold over the economy of all of the republics of the former Soviet Union is as widespread as it was in the past. This view is shared by many informed persons in the former Soviet Union.

Unfortunately, the book must have been written in a hurry when it was first published in Russian. It tends to be repetitive and tedious; short on facts, it contains lengthy speculations by the author. The translation by John and Elizabeth Roberts does not improve the original. This is regrettable because the topic is important.

Vaksberg, Arkadii. *STALIN'S PROSECUTOR: THE LIFE OF ANDRE VYSHINSKY.* New York; London: Weidenfeld, 1990. xi, 374 pp.

Vyshinsky was Stalin's ruthless Procurator-General during the period of terror in the 1930's, and he subsequently rose to the position of the Soviet foreign minister. Demoted after Stalin's death, he became the Soviet representative to the United Nations in New York. It is one of the ironies of fate that this great enemy of the West died in New York, the center of capitalism.

In this thoroughly researched biography, based on previously suppressed documents, Vaksberg presents a compelling picture of a ruthless and unprincipled man who rose to a position of great powers in the terrible era of Stalin's reign and who was responsible for the deaths of many innocent people. Exceptionally readable, this is one of the most penetrating books about the injustice and horror of the mass persecution unleashed by Stalin during his terror-filled reign of the Soviet Union.

van Brabant, Jozef M.
See Brabant, Jozef M. van.

van den Berg, Ger P.
See Berg, Ger P. van den.

Vardys, V. Stanley. *REGIONAL IDENTITY UNDER SOVIET RULE: THE CASE OF THE BALTIC STATES.*
See Loeber, Dietrich Andre, V. Stanley Vardys, and Laurence P.A. Kitching.

Vardys, V. Stanley. "Sajudis: National Revolution in Lithuania", in *TOWARD INDEPENDENCE: THE BALTIC POPULAR MOVEMENTS*, edited by Jan Arveds Trapans (Boulder, CO; San Francisco; Oxford: Westview Press, 1991), pp. 11-23.

☆Vasil'ev, Andrei, and Maksim Krans. "The Miners' Alternative: A Few Questions for Reflection", 30 *SOVIET LAW AND GOVERNMENT* No. 2, 45-61 (Fall 1991).

Translated from *Kommunist* 1990 No. 13, pp. 59-67, this article examines the miners' movement which began with strikes in Summer 1989 and has since developed into a strong labor organization.

Vause, W. Gary. "The Coming End of Perestroika's Golden Age of Law Reform?", 20 *STETSON LAW REVIEW* 201-209 (1990).

A brief comment on the future of reforms in the Soviet Union after Gorbachev's swing to conservatism and Shevardnadze's resignation from his post as the Soviet foreign minister in late 1990.

Vecchio, Mark S. "Soviet Joint Ventures: Keeping an Eye on the Goalposts", 9 *INTERNATIONAL FINANCIAL LAW REVIEW* No. 4, 37-38 (April 1990).

A brief comment about the May 6, 1989 USSR Council of Ministers decree which amends and classifies several provisions of the January, 1987 Soviet joint venture law. The amendment attempts to make the original joint venture law more attractive for foreign investors.

☆Vereshchetin, Vladlen S. "International Control and the Concept of 'Open Skies'", in *FROM COEXISTENCE TO COOPERATION: INTERNATIONAL LAW AND ORGANIZATION IN THE POST-COLD WAR ERA*, edited by Edward McWhinney, et al. (Dordrecht, The Netherlands: Martinus Nijhoff Publishers, 1991), pp. 31-43.

☆Vereshchetin, Vladlen S. "'Open Skies'—The Metamorphoses of One Concept", in *CONTROL OVER COMPLIANCE WITH INTERNATIONAL LAW*, edited by William E. Butler (Dordrecht, The Netherlands: Martinus Nijhoff Publishers, 1991), pp. 41-50.

☆Vereshchetin, Vladlen S., and Rein A. Mullerson. "The Primacy of International Law in World Politics", in *PERESTROIKA AND INTERNATIONAL LAW: CURRENT ANGLO-SOVIET APPROACHES TO INTERNATIONAL LAW*, edited by Anthony Carty and Gennady Danilenko (Edinburgh: Edinburg University Press, 1990), pp. 6-14.

☆Vereschchetin, Vladlen S.
See also Grzybowski, Kazimierz. "Soviet Theory of International Law for the Perestroika"; and
THE HEARTBEAT OF REFORM: SOVIET JURISTS AND POLITICAL SCIENTISTS DISCUSS THE PROGRESS OF PERESTROIKA.

Vierdag, E.W. *THE CHANGING POLITICAL STRUCTURE OF EUROPE: ASPECTS OF INTERNATIONAL LAW.*
See Lefeber, R., M. Fitzmaurice, and E.W. Vierdag.

☆Vilegjanina, Elena E. "The Principle of Peaceful Settlement of Disputes: A New Soviet Approach", in *PERESTROIKA AND INTERNATIONAL LAW: CURRENT ANGLO-SOVIET APPROACHES TO INTERNATIONAL LAW*, edited by Anthony Carty and Gennady Danilenko (Edinburgh: Edinburg University Press, 1990), pp. 119-128.

☆Vinogradov, Sergei V. "Ecological Security in the Arctic: A Regional Approach", in *FROM COEXISTENCE TO COOPERATION: INTERNATIONAL LAW AND ORGANIZATION IN THE POST-COLD WAR ERA*, edited by Edward McWhinney, et al. (Dordrecht, The Netherlands: Martinus Nijhoff Publishers, 1991), pp. 155-166.

☆Vinogradov, Sergei V. "International Environmental Security: The Concept and Its Implementation", in *PERESTROIKA AND INTERNATIONAL LAW: CURRENT ANGLO-SOVIET APPROACHES TO INTERNATIONAL LAW*, edited by Anthony Carty and Gennady Danilenko (Edinburgh: Edinburg University Press, 1990), pp. 196-207.

☆Vinogradov, Sergei V. "Verification Machinery in the Antarctic Treaty System", in *CONTROL OVER COMPLIANCE WITH INTERNATIONAL LAW*, edited by William E. Butler (Dordrecht, The Netherlands: Martinus Nijhoff Publishers, 1991), pp. 97-105.

Vizulis, Izidors Joseph. *THE MOLOTOV-RIBBENTROP PACT OF 1939: THE BALTIC CASE.* New York: Praeger, 1990. vi, 176 pp.

Describes Soviet-German arrangements which led to the Soviet annexation of the Baltic countries in 1940.

Reviewing the book in 17 *Soviet Union/Union Sovietique,* Nos. 1-2, 146-149 (1990), J. Calvit Clarke III describes it as "... a polemic, haphazardly thrown together presumably for its commercial appeal."

Vlachoutsicos, Charalambos A. "Aspects of Forming Joint Ventures in the USSR—Comments for the Western Investor", in *BEHIND THE FACTORY WALLS: DECISION MAKING IN SOVIET AND US ENTERPRISES,* edited by Paul R. Lawrence and Charalambos A. Vlachoutsicos (Boston: Harvard Business School Press, 1990), pp. 307-319.

Vlachoutsicos, Charalambos A. *BEHIND THE FACTORY WALLS: DECISION MAKING IN SOVIET AND U.S. ENTERPRISES.*
See Lawrence, Paul R., and Charalambos A. Vlachoutsicos.

☆Volkogonov, Dmitri. *STALIN: TRIUMPH AND TRAGEDY.* New York; London: Weidenfeld, 1991.

This is the first openly critical biography of Joseph Stalin written and published in the Soviet Union. Though historical in character, the book may interest legal researchers because it describes in great detail the lawlessness of Stalin's rule. With chilling objectivity it documents the system of terror he brought into existence and the subsequent extermination of millions of people. The author, a leading Soviet military historian, carefully traces Stalin's ascent to power, and explains how he built a huge bureaucratic apparatus which helped to create one of the most terrible tyrannies in the history of mankind. The book is translated into English by Harold Shukman.

For a brief review by David W. Benn, see 67 *International Affairs* 596 (1991).

☆Volkov, F.M., ed. *INTERNATIONAL LAW.* Moscow: Progress Publishers, 1990. 285 pp.

A general work on international law reflective of the changes in the Soviet attitude during the late 1980's.

von Beyme, Klaus.
See Beyme, Klaus von.

von Borcke, Astrid.
See Borcke, Astrid von.

☆Vorobyova, Olga V. "Transfer of Technology: Recent Developments".
See Boguslavskii[y], Mark M., and Olga V. Vorobyova.

W

Wädekin, Karl-Eugen. "Agriculture", in *THE SOVIET SOBRANIE OF LAWS,* edited by Richard M. Buxbaum and Kathryn Hendley (Berkeley, CA: University of California at Berkeley, 1991), pp. 102-120.

Wädekin, Karl-Eugen. "The Re-Emergence of the Kolkhoz Principle", 41 *SOVIET SUTDIES* 20-38 (1989).

An analysis of the trend in legislation on collective farms toward smaller production units where incentives can be more effective.

Walker, Edward. *PERESTROIKA IN THE SOVIET REPUBLICS: DOCUMENTS ON THE NATIONAL QEUSTION.*
See Furtado, Charles F., Jr., and Andrea Chandler.

Waller, Robert L. "Soviet Countertrade", 1 *THE UNITED STATES AIR FORCE ACADEMY JOURNAL OF LEGAL STUDIES* 87-103 (1990).

This article advocates the use of countertrade as a means towards the encouragement of greater Soviet participation in international trade. It explains the mechanics of countertrade, but it does not discuss either the historical record of past countertrade transactions or its present practices.

Walters, Peter. "US-USSR Joint Ventures: An Examination of the Early Entrants".
See Nigh, Douglas, Peter Walters, and James A. Kuhlman.

Watts, Ronald. "The Soviet Federal System and the National Question in Comparative Perspective", in *SOVIET FEDERALISM: NATIONALISM AND ECONOMIC DECENTRALISATION*, edited by Alastair McAuley (Leicester and London: Leicester University Press, 1991), pp. 196-207.

Comparison of the Soviet federal system with other federations. The author notes the "pathological" form of the Soviet federalism which in reality was no more than concealed centralism.

Wcislo, Francis W. "Soslovie or Class? Bureaucratic Reformers and Provincial Gentry in Conflict, 1906-1908", 4 *RUSSIAN REVIEW* 1-24 (1988).

The author examines the impact of the historical conflict between the landowning aristocracy and the government bureaucrats in Czarist Russia.

Webb, William T. "The International Legal Aspects of the Lithuanian Secession" (Note), 17 *JOURNAL OF LEGISLATION* 309-330 1991).

A student note on the legality of the Lithuanian declaration of independence of March 11, 1990.

Welt, Leo G.B. "Unconventional Forms of Financing: Buy-Back/Compensation/Barter", "Symposium on U.S.-Soviet Military and Economic Relations", *22 NEW YORK UNIVERSITY JOURNAL OF INTERNATIONAL LAW AND POLITICS* 461-473 (1990).

In the context of trade with the Soviet Union, the author examines different forms of financing and trading. The article contains illustrations of actual transactions. Very interesting and of great practical value.

Whelen, Joseph G.
See United States Congress.

White, Stephen, ed. *POLITICAL AND ECONOMIC ENCYCLOPAEDIA OF THE SOVIET UNION AND EASTERN EUROPE.* Marlow, Essex, England: Longman Group UK Ltd., 1990. xxii, 328 pp.

A handy reference work. Includes brief information on government, politics, economics, religion, nationality issues, international relations, etc., as well as longer notes on individual countries, short biographies of leading political figures, and chronology of events. Unfortunately, rapidly occurring and sweeping changes within the region covered by this book have made much of the information obsolete or inaccurate.

White, Stephen, Alex Pravda, and Zvi Gitelman, eds. *DEVELOPMENTS IN SOVIET POLITICS*. Durham, NC: Duke University Press, 1990. 310 pp.

A general survey of the Soviet political system in 1990. Includes "The Rule of Law and the Legal System" by William E. Butler.

White, Walter H., and Rebecca A. Speekhard. "Soviet Union", 25 *INTERNATIONAL LAWYER* 549-553 (1991).

A brief note on legislation enacted by the Soviet Union in 1990 for the purpose of encouraging foreign investment. There are also references to the legislation of the Russian Federation pertaining to the easing of restrictions on investment in general.

Whitman, Sylvia. "'These Are Bridges That Have to Be Built': The American Law Center in Moscow Provides a Groundbreaking Link between U.S. and Soviet Lawyers", 20 *STUDENT LAWYER* No. 5, 8-10 (January 1992).

A brief story about the American Law Center in Moscow, a joint project of Emory University School of Law and the Moscow Law Institute. A brainchild of Professor Harold J. Berman, the Center aims to educate Russian lawyers about the U.S. legal system. Berman, a leading American expert on the Soviet law, teaches at Emory University School of Law.

Winiecki, Jan. "Buying Out Property Rights to the Economy from the Ruling Stratum: The Case of Soviet-Type States", 9 *INTERNATIONAL REVIEW OF LAW AND ECONOMICS* 79-85 (1989).

An interesting analysis of the proposition that the members of the ruling elite of communist countries should be compensated for making reforms because it is in their best interests to keep the status quo, and that only by compensating them will they effectively cooperate in the making of useful economic changes.

Winter, David, ed. *GUIDE TO THE COMMERCIAL AND CORPORATE LAW OF EASTERN EUROPE*. Bicester, Oxfordshire, England: CCH Editions Limited, 1991. xiv, 164 pp.

Includes a helpful overview of commercial and corporate law developments in the USSR by Wim A. Timmermans.

Wolf-Laudon, Gottfried. *EAST-WEST JOINT VENTURES: THE NEW BUSINESS ENVIRONMENT.*
See Razvigorova, Evka, and Gottfried Wolf-Laudon.

World Bank.
See A STUDY OF THE SOVIET ECONOMY.

Wyman, Lowry. "Crime and Punishment in the USSR: How Is It Really Changing?", 29 *THE JUDGE'S JOURNAL* 14-19 (1990).

A discussion of the role of *glasnost* in the reform of the Soviet criminal justice system, asserting that *glasnost* is only the first step towards more meaningful reforms.

Y

☆Yablokov, A.V. "The Current State of the Soviet Environment", 4 *ENVIRONMENTAL POLICY REVIEW* 1-19 (1990).

The journal where this article appears is published by the Marjorie Mayrock Center for Soviet and European Research in Jerusalem, Israel. The article contains a general description of the environmental problems in the Soviet Union.

☆Yakovlev, Alexander M. "Transforming the Soviet Union into a Rule of Law Democracy: A Report from the Front Lines", 46 *THE RECORD OF THE ASSOCIATION OF THE BAR OF THE CITY OF NEW YORK* 129-148 (1991).

A report given by a member of the Congress of People's Deputies of the U.S.S.R. outlining the chances for success in building a new state based on the rule of law. This article focuses on reforms in the political, economic and judicial systems.

☆Yakovlev, Alexander M.

See also THE HEARTBEAT OF REFORM: SOVIET JURISTS AND POLITICAL SCIENTISTS DISCUSS THE PROGRESS OF PERESTROIKA.

☆Yakovleva, Evgeniya L.

See Sherr, Alan B., et al.

☆Yakushev, L.P. "New Approaches to Social Security Provision in the USSR", 130 *INTERNATIONAL LABOUR REVIEW* 329-337 (1991).

According to the abstract of this article:

> Although providing all the basic types of social security cover, the Soviet system has tended to favour some groups at the expense of others. The author attributes such distortions to state financing

and the associated absence of adequate links between the level of contributions paid and benefits received. He traces the movement away from the social insurance approach of the 1920s and gives details of recent legislation which is removing anomalies and re-establishing the link between funding and benefits. Particularly topical is the account of measures to ensure Union-wide respect for basic social security standards now that the republics are becoming increasingly independent.

☆Yegorov, Sergei A.
See Stephan, Paul B. III, and Boris M. Klimenko.

Yuan, Cheng. *EAST-WEST TRADE: CHANGING PATTERNS IN CHINESE FOREIGN TRADE LAW AND INSTITUTIONS.* New York: Oceana Publications, Inc., 1991. xxvi, 357 pp.

Includes a chapter on the historical development of the state-operated foreign trade monopoly in the Soviet Union.

☆Yudin, Alexei.
See THE HEARTBEAT OF REFORM: SOVIET JURISTS AND POLITICAL SCIENTISTS DISCUSS THE PROGRESS OF PERESTROIKA.

Z

Zanft, Oksanna. "Arms Control and Chemical Weapons—Agreement on Destruction and Non-Production of Chemical Weapons, June 1, 1990, United States-U.S.S.R." (Note), 32 *HARVARD INTERNATIONAL LAW JOURNAL* 497-507 (1991).

Zeidman, Philip F., and Michael Avner. "Franchising in Eastern Europe and the Soviet Union", 3 *DE PAUL BUSINESS LAW JOURNAL* 307-338 (1991).

Throughout this thorough and informative article on business franchises in Eastern Europe there are references to franchising practices and experiences in the Soviet Union.

Ziegler, Charles E. "Environmental Politics and Policy under Perestroika", in *PERESTROIKA FROM BELOW: SOCIAL MOVEMENTS IN THE SOVIET UNION*, edited by Judith B. Sedaitis and Jim Butterfield (Boulder, CO: Westview Press, 1991), pp. 113-131.

Zile, Zigurds L. "Of Laws, Secrecy, and Environmental Quality in the USSR", in *THE SOVIET SOBRANIE OF LAWS,* edited by Richard M. Buxbaum and Kathryn Hendley (Berkeley, CA: University of California at Berkeley, 1991), pp. 121-126.

Zimbler, Brian L. "Soviet Foreign Investment Laws and Practices, 1987-1990: A Practicioner's Perspective", 4 *TRANSNATIONAL LAWYER* 85-122 (1991).

This is not just another survey of Soviet efforts to improve foreign trade and attract foreign investment through the mere enactment of laws and regulations. Zimbler, who practices law in San Francisco, also includes many examples of trade deals and joint ventures betweeen Soviet enterprises and their foreign partners. He explores the reasons for the success of some ventures and the failure of others. He also notes that the Soviet enterpreneurs are rapidly becoming more sophisticated in their dealings. Joint ventures, for example, are evolving into what he identifies as four different types, and at best from the Soviet standpoint their formation and management are becoming sounder. This is an interesting article, well worth reading by anyone wanting to know how foreign trade operates in the Soviet Union.

Zisk, Kimberly Marten. "Soviet Academic Theories on International Conflict and Negotiation", 34 *JOURNAL OF CONFLICT RESOLUTION* 678-693 (1990).

The author of this article argues that Soviet scholars are exercising an increasingly greater influence on changes in the Soviet foreign policy. The ideas about international conflict and cooperation Gorbachev has expressed in his speeches and writings repeatedly reflect the views of such scholars. In general the scholars advocate cooperation and peaceful resolution of disputes. This article examines the different scholarly trends on international relations and international law which currently prevail in the Soviet Union.

☆Zmeyevskii, Aleksandr V.
See Stephan, Paul B. III, and Boris M. Klimenko.

Zuljan, Ralph. "A Conflict Analysis of the Armenian-Azerbaijan Dispute".
See Fraser, Niall M., Keith W. Hipel, John Jaworsky and Ralph Zuljan.

DEMISE OF THE SOVIET UNION:
Subject Bibliography

CHECKLIST OF SUBJECT HEADINGS

SUBJECT BIBLIOGRAPHY: CHECKLIST OF SUBJECT HEADINGS

DEMISE OF THE SOVIET UNION:

SUBJECT BIBLIOGRAPHY

Administration of Justice

See also Legal Profession and Procuracy

Subheadings:

Judicial Opinions
Scope and Character

Judicial Opinions

Baker, John H., ed. *JUDICIAL RECORDS, LAW REPORTS, AND THE GROWTH OF CASE LAW.* Berlin: Duncker & Humblot, 1989. 353 pp.

Butler, William E. "The Role of Case-Law in the Russian Legal System", in *JUDICIAL RECORDS, LAW REPORTS, AND THE GROWTH OF CASE LAW,* edited by John H. Baker (Berlin: Duncker & Humblot, 1989), pp. 337-352.

Scope and Character

Henderson, Jane. "Law of the USSR: On the Status of Judges in the USSR", 16 *REVIEW OF SOCIALIST LAW* 305-338 (1990).

Markovits, Inga. "Socialism and the Rule of Law: Some Speculations and Predictions", in *COMPARATIVE AND PRIVATE INTERNATIONAL LAW: ESSAYS IN HONOR OF JOHN HENRY MERRYMAN ON HIS SEVENTIETH BIRTHDAY*, edited by David S. Clark (Berlin: Duncker & Humblot, 1990), pp. 205-245.

Oda, Hiroshi. "Law Enforcement Agencies", in *THE SOVIET SOBRANIE OF LAWS,* edited by Richard M. Buxbaum and Kathryn Hendley (Berkeley, CA: University of California, 1991), pp. 127-139.

Advokatura

See Legal Profession

Aggression

See International Law

Agriculture and Collectivization

☆Emelyanov, Alexei. "Agrarian Reform and the Village Today", 22 *SOCIAL SCIENCES* No. 3, 85-97 (1991).

Wädekin, Karl-Eugen. "Agriculture", in *THE SOVIET SOBRANIE OF LAWS*, edited by Richard M. Buxbaum and Kathryn Hendley (Berkeley, CA: University of California at Berkeley, 1991), pp. 102-120.

Wädekin, Karl-Eugen. "The Re-Emergence of the Kolkhoz Principle", 41 *SOVIET STUDIES* 20-38 (1989).

Alcoholism

Treml, Vladimir G. "Drinking and Alcohol Abuse in the USSR in the 1980's", in *SOVIET SOCIAL PROBLEMS*, edited by Anthony Jones, et al. (Boulder, CO; San Francisco; Oxford: Westview Press, 1991), pp. 119-136.

Antarctica

See International Law

Arbitration

Subheadings:
Commercial
International
Maritime

Commercial

Osakwe, Christopher. *SOVIET BUSINESS LAW: INSTITUTIONS, PRINCIPLES, AND PROCESSES.* Salem, NH: Butterworth Legal Publishers, 1991. 2 Volumes, looseleaf, misc. pag.

International

Hines, Jonathan H. "Dispute Resolution and Choice of Law in United States-Soviet Trade", in *LEGAL ASPECTS OF TRADE AND INVESTMENT IN THE SOVIET UNION AND EASTERN EUROPE 1990* (New York: Practising Law Institute, 1990), pp. 117-187.

Kolkey, Daniel M. "International Arbitration in East-West Trade", 12 *WHITTIER LAW REVIEW* 245-258 (1991).

☆Muchlinski, P.T. "Dispute Settlement under the Washington Convention on the Settlement of Investment Disputes", in *CONTROL OVER COMPLIANCE WITH INTERNATIONAL LAW*, edited by William E. Butler (Dordrecht, The Netherlands: Martinus Nijhoff Publishers, 1991), pp. 175-193.

☆Shinkaretskaya, Galina G. "Changing Attitude towards International Adjudication in the Soviet Union", 3 *LEIDEN JOURNAL OF INTERNATIONAL LAW* No. 3, 59-66 (Special Issue, December 1990).

☆Shinkaretskaya, Galina G. "International Arbitration in the External Policy of the Soviet Union", in *PERESTROIKA AND INTERNATIONAL LAW: CURRENT ANGLO-SOVIET APPROACHES TO INTERNATIONAL LAW*, edited by Anthony Carty and Gennady Danilenko (Edinburgh: Edinburg University Press, 1990), pp. 110-118.

Maritime

Osakwe, Christopher. *SOVIET BUSINESS LAW: INSTITUTIONS, PRINCIPLES, AND PROCESSES.* Salem, NH: Butterworth Legal Publishers, 1991. 2 Volumes, looseleaf, misc. pag.

Arctic

See International Law *and*
Maritime Law

Armenia

Blaustein, Albert P., ed. *CONSTITUTIONS OF DEPENDENCIES AND SPECIAL SOVEREIGNTIES.* Dobbs Ferry, NY: Oceana Publications, 1977- .

Fraser, Niall M., Keith W. Hipel, John Jaworsky, and Ralph Zuljan. "A Conflict Analysis of the Armenian-Azerbaijan Dispute", 34 *JOURNAL OF CONFLICT RESOLUTION* 652-677 (1990).

Heitman, Sidney. "Soviet Emigration Policies toward Germans and Armenians", in *SOVIET NATIONALITY POLICIES: RULING ETHNIC GROUPS IN THE USSR*, edited by Henry R. Huttenbach (London: Mansell Publishing Limited, 1990), pp. 235-259.

Suny, Ronald G. "Transcaucasia: Cultural Cohesion and Ethnic Revival in a Multinational Society", in *THE NATIONALITIES FACTOR IN SOVIET POLITICS AND SOCIETY*, edited by Lubomyr Hajda and Mark Beissinger. Boulder, CO: Westview Press, 1990, pp. 228-252.

Arms Control

See International Law

Autonomy

See Baltic *and*
Nationalities and Nationalism

Azerbaizhan

Blaustein, Albert P., ed. *CONSTITUTIONS OF DEPENDENCIES AND SPECIAL SOVEREIGNTIES.* Dobbs Ferry, NY: Oceana Publications, 1977- .

Commission on Security and Cooperation in Europe. *ELECTIONS IN THE BALTIC STATES AND SOVIET REPUBLICS: A COMPENDIUM OF REPORTS ON PARLIAMENTARY ELECTIONS HELD IN 1990.* Compiled by the Staff of the Commission on Security and Cooperation in Europe. Washington: U.S. Government Printing Office, 1990. x, 188 pp.

Fraser, Niall M., Keith W. Hipel, John Jaworsky, and Ralph Zuljan. "A Conflict Analysis of the Armenian-Azerbaijan Dispute", 34 *JOURNAL OF CONFLICT RESOLUTION* 652-677 (1990).

Suny, Ronald G. "Transcaucasia: Cultural Cohesion and Ethnic Revival in a Multinational Society", in *THE NATIONALITIES FACTOR IN SOVIET POLITICS AND SOCIETY*, edited by Lubomyr Hajda and Mark Beissinger. Boulder, CO: Westview Press, 1990, pp. 228-252.

Baltic

Allison, William C., V. "Self-Determination and Recent Developments in the Baltic States" (Comment), 19 *DENVER JOURNAL OF INTERNATIONAL LAW AND POLICY* 625-640 (1991).

Anderson, Edgar. "How Narva, Petersi, and Abrene Came to Be in the RSFSR", 19 *JOURNAL OF BALTIC STUDIES* 197-214 (1988).

Blase, John C., and Cynthia M. Smith. "Soviet Republics' Demand for Autonomy: The Need for Constitutional Reform and the Institution of Canadian-Style Judicial Review" (Note), 17 *JOURNAL OF LEGISLATION* 237-260 (1991).

Blaustein, Albert P., ed. *CONSTITUTIONS OF DEPENDENCIES AND SPECIAL SOVEREIGNTIES.* Dobbs Ferry, NY: Oceana Publications, 1977- .

Blueger, Valentin. "Observations of a Latvian Practitioner", 24 *VANDERBILT JOURNAL OF TRANSNATIONAL LAW* 389-393 (1991).

BALTIC, *continued*

Boczek, Boleslaw Adam. "The Baltic Sea: An International Legal Profile", 38 *OSTEUROPA RECHT* 25-51 (1992).

Clark, David S., ed. *COMPARATIVE AND PRIVATE INTERNATIONAL LAW: ESSAYS IN HONOR OF JOHN HENRY MERRYMAN ON HIS SEVENTIETH BIRTHDAY*. Berlin: Duncker & Humblot, 1990. xxii, 450 pp.

Commission on Security and Cooperation in Europe. *ELECTIONS IN THE BALTIC STATES AND SOVIET REPUBLICS: A COMPENDIUM OF REPORTS ON PARLIAMENTARY ELECTIONS HELD IN 1990*. Compiled by the Staff of the Commission on Security and Cooperation in Europe. Washington: U.S. Government Printing Office, 1990. x, 188 pp.

Fitzmaurice, M. *INTERNATIONAL LEGAL PROBLEMS OF THE ENVIRONMENTAL PROTECTION OF THE BALTIC SEA*. Dordrecht, The Netherlands: Martinus Nijhoff/Graham & Trotman, 1992. xxix, 328 pp.

Fogelklou, Anders. *SOVIET FEDERALISM AND BALTIC CLAIMS FOR SOVEREIGNTY*. Uppsala, Sweden: Uppsala University, Department of Soviet and East European Studies, 1990. 21 pp. (Working Papers, 3).

Franckx, Erik. "First Trijunction Point Agreed upon in the Baltic between Poland, Sweden, and the USSR", 5 *INTERNATIONAL JOURNAL OF ESTUARINE AND COASTAL LAW* 394-397 (1990).

Franckx, Erik. "International Cooperation in Respect of the Baltic Sea", in *THE CHANGING POLITICAL STRUCTURE OF EUROPE: ASPECTS OF INTERNATIONAL LAW*, edited by R. Lefeber, M. Fitzmaurice, and E.W. Vierdag (Dordrecht, The Netherlands: Martinus Nijhoff Publishers, 1991), pp. 245-277.

Furtado, Charles F., Jr., and Andrea Chandler. *PERESTROIKA IN THE SOVIET REPUBLICS: DOCUMENTS ON THE NATIONAL QUESTION*. Boulder, CO: Westview Press, 1992. xxvi, 646 pp.

Ginsburgs, George. "The Citizenship of the Baltic States", 21 *JOURNAL OF BALTIC STUDIES* 3-26 (1990).

Ginsburgs, George. "Soviet International Law and Baltic Environmental Protection", 38 *OSTEUROPA RECHT* 52-64 (1992).

BALTIC, *continued*

Girnius, Kestutis. "Baltic States Opt for Independence", in *SOVIET FEDERALISM: NATIONALISM AND ECONOMIC DECENTRALISATION,* edited by Alastair McAuley (Leicester and London: Leicester University Press, 1991), pp. 160-177.

Girnius, Kestutis. "The Party and Popular Movements in the Baltic", in *TOWARD INDEPENDENCE: THE BALTIC POPULAR MOVEMENTS*, edited by Jan Arveds Trapans (Boulder, CO; San Francisco; Oxford: Westview Press, 1991), pp. 57-69.

Grazin, Igor. "The International Recognition of National Rights: The Baltic States' Case", 66 *NOTRE DAME LAW REVIEW* 1385-1419 (1991).

Gureckas, Algimantas P. "Lithuania's Boundaries and Territorial Claims between Lithuania and Neighboring States", 12 *NEW YORK LAW SCHOOL JOURNAL OF INTERNATIONAL AND COMPARATIVE LAW* 107-150 (1991).

Ilves, Toomas Hendrik. "Reaction: The Intermovements in Estonia", in *TOWARD INDEPENDENCE: THE BALTIC POPULAR MOVEMENTS*, edited by Jan Arveds Trapans (Boulder, CO; San Francisco; Oxford: Westview Press, 1991), pp. 71-83.

Loeber, Dietrich André. "Latvia's 1937 Civil Code: A Quest for Cultural Identity", in *COMPARATIVE AND PRIVATE INTERNATIONAL LAW: ESSAYS IN HONOR OF JOHN HENRY MERRYMAN ON HIS SEVENTIETH BIRTHDAY,* edited by David S. Clark (Berlin: Duncker & Humblot, 1990), pp. 197-204.

Loeber, Dietrich André. *REGIONAL AND NATIONAL VARIATIONS: THE BALTIC FACTOR.* Washington: National Council for Soviet and East European Research, 1991. 30 pp.

Loeber, Dietrich André, V. Stanley Vardys, and Laurence P.A. Kitching, eds. *REGIONAL IDENTITY UNDER SOVIET RULE: THE CASE OF THE BALTIC STATES.* Hackettstown, N.J.: Institute for the Study of Law, Politics and Society of Socialist States, 1990. xxiii, 470 pp.

Meri, Lennart. "Estonia's Role in the New Europe", 67 *INTERNATIONAL AFFAIRS* 107-110 (1991).

Mihalisko, Kathleen. "The Popular Movement in Belorussia and Baltic Influence", in *TOWARD INDEPENDENCE: THE BALTIC POPULAR MOVEMENTS*, edited by Jan Arveds Trapans (Boulder, CO; San Francisco; Oxford: Westview Press, 1991), pp. 123-132.

BALTIC, *continued*

Misiunas, Romuald J. "Baltic Nationalism and Soviet Language Policy: From Russification to Constitutional Amendment", in *SOVIET NATIONALITY POLICIES: RULING ETHNIC GROUPS IN THE USSR*, edited by Henry R. Huttenbach (London: Mansell Publishing Limited, 1990), pp. 206-220.

Misiunas, Romuald J. "The Baltic Republics: Stagnation and Strikings for Sovereignty", in *THE NATIONALITIES FACTOR IN SOVIET POLITICS AND SOCIETY*, edited by Lubomyr Hajda and Mark Beissinger (Boulder, CO: Westview Press, 1990), pp. 204-227.

Nahaylo, Bohdan. "Baltic Echoes in Ukraine", in *TOWARD INDEPENDENCE: THE BALTIC POPULAR MOVEMENTS,* edited by Jan Arveds Trapans (Boulder, CO; San Francisco; Oxford: Westview Press, 1991), pp. 108-122.

Olcott, Martha Brill. "The Soviet (Dis)union", 82 *FOREIGN POLICY* 118-136 (Spring 1991).

Oxenstierna, Susanne. "Labour Market Policies in the Baltic Republics", 130 *INTERNATIONAL LABOUR REVIEW* 255-274 (1991/2).

Plotnieks, Andris. "The Evolution of the Soviet Federation and the Independence of Latvia", in *SOVIET FEDERALISM: NATIONALISM AND ECONOMIC DECENTRALISATION,* edited by Alastair McAuley (Leicester and London: Leicester University Press, 1991), pp. 134-148.

Radon, Jenik. "The Baltics: The Premier European Gateway to the Soviet Union". A Paper presented at the Geonomics Institute Seminar, Middleburg, Vermont, May 10-13, 1991. 37 pp. Reprinted in *INVESTING IN REFORM: DOING BUSINESS IN A CHANGING SOVIET UNION*, edited by Michael P. Claudon and Tamar L. Gutner (New York: New York University Press, 1991), pp. 207-231.

Schroeder, Gertrude E. "On the Economic Viability of New Nation-States", 45 *JOURNAL OF INTERNATIONAL AFFAIRS* 549-574 (1992).

Simons, William B. "Foreign Investment Laws in the Republics of the USSR: Lithuania and Kazakhstan", 17 *REVIEW OF SOCIALIST LAW* 161-190 (1991).

BALTIC, *continued*

Sprudzs, Adolf. "The Rule of Law and the Baltic States", in *BIBLIOTHEK UND RECHT INTERNATIONAL/LIBRARIES AND LAW —INTERNATIONAL, FESTSCHRIFT RALPH LANSKY*, edited by Jürgen Christoph Gödan and Holger Knudsen (Hamburg and Augsburg: Arbeitsgemeinschaft für juristisches Bibliotheks- und Dokumentationswesen, 1991), pp. 231-241.

Strautmanis, J., and A. Maurins. "Problems of National Legislation for the Protection of the Environment: The Case of Latvia", 38 *OSTEUROPA RECHT* 72-73 (1992).

Trapans, Andris. "Moscow, Economics and the Baltic Republics", in *TOWARD INDEPENDENCE: THE BALTIC POPULAR MOVEMENTS*, edited by Jan Arveds Trapans (Boulder, CO; San Francisco; Oxford: Westview Press, 1991), pp. 85-98.

Trapans, Jan Arveds. "The Sources of Latvia's Popular Movement", in *TOWARD INDEPENDENCE: THE BALTIC POPULAR MOVEMENTS*, edited by Jan Arveds Trapans (Boulder, CO; San Francisco; Oxford: Westview Press, 1991), pp. 25-41.

Trapans, Jan Arveds, ed. *TOWARD INDEPENDENCE: THE BALTIC POPULAR MOVEMENTS* (Boulder, CO; San Francisco; Oxford: Westview Press, 1991), vii, 166 pp.

Vardys, V. Stanley. "Sajudis: National Revolution in Lithuania", in *TOWARD INDEPENDENCE: THE BALTIC POPULAR MOVEMENTS*, edited by Jan Arveds Trapans (Boulder, CO; San Francisco; Oxford: Westview Press, 1991), pp. 11-23.

Vizulis, Izidors Joseph. *THE MOLOTOV-RIBBENTROP PACT OF 1939: THE BALTIC CASE*. New York: Praeger, 1990. vi, 176 pp.

Webb, William T. "The International Legal Aspects of the Lithuanian Secession" (Note), 17 *JOURNAL OF LEGISLATION* 309-330 1991).

Banking and Finance
See also Currency

Bohn, John A., Jr., and David H. Levey. "Models of Capital Market Development", in *THE EMERGING RUSSIAN BEAR: INTEGRATING THE SOVIET UNION INTO THE WORLD ECONOMY*, edited by Josef C. Brada and Michael P. Claudon (New York: New York University Press, 1991), pp. 73-85.

Brada, Josef C., and Michael P. Claudon, eds. *REFORMING THE RUBLE: MONETARY ASPECTS OF PERESTROIKA*. New York: New York University Press, 1990. x, 228 pp.

Frenkel, William G. "Growth of Commercial Banking in the USSR", 9 *INTERNATIONAL FINANCIAL LAW REVIEW* No. 8, 27-28 (August 1990).

Frenkel, William G. "Soviet Bank Legislation Enacted", 5 *JOURNAL OF INTERNATIONAL BANKING LAW* 507-510 (1991).

Glick, Steven M., and Alexei A. Klishin. "Federalist Fever: Economic and Banking Reform in the USSR", 10 *INTERNATIONAL FINANCIAL LAW REVIEW* No. 1, 32-34 (January 1991).

☆Maslov, Alexander. "Bankrolling Soviet Joint Ventures", *4 EUROPEAN AFFAIRS* No. 3, 59-65 (Autumn 1990).

☆Musatov, Vladimir. "The Soviet Credit and Enterprise Structure System under Reform", in *REFORMING THE RUBLE: MONETARY ASPECTS OF PERESTROIKA*, edited by Josef C. Brada and Michael P. Claudon. New York: New York University Press, 1990, pp. 209-219.

Osakwe, Christopher. *SOVIET BUSINESS LAW: INSTITUTIONS, PRINCIPLES, AND PROCESSES.* Salem, NH: Butterworth Legal Publishers, 1991. 2 Volumes, looseleaf, misc. pag.

Perkins, Roswell B., and Jonathan H. Hines. "Soviets Change Currency Rules", 10 *INTERNATIONAL FINANCIAL LAW REVIEW* No. 5, 22-24 (May 1991).

☆Portnoy, Mikhail A. "Major Financial Obstacles to the Formation and Operation of Joint Ventures", in *THE EMERGING RUSSIAN BEAR: INTEGRATING THE SOVIET UNION INTO THE WORLD ECONOMY*, edited by Josef C. Brada and Michael P. Claudon (New York: New York University Press, 1991), pp. 165-174.

BANKING AND FINANCE, *continued*

Scotland, Francis A. "Soviet Financial Reform: Money and Credit", in *THE EMERGING RUSSIAN BEAR: INTEGRATING THE SOVIET UNION INTO THE WORLD ECONOMY*, edited by Josef C. Brada and Michael P. Claudon (New York: New York University Press, 1991), pp. 63-72.

☆Uljanov, Eugene. "The Latest Developments in the Foreign Currency Practices and Regulations of the Soviet Union". A Paper presented at the Geonomics Institute Seminar, Middleburg, Vermont, May 10-13, 1991. 20 pp. Also published in *INVESTING IN REFORM: DOING BUSINESS IN A CHANGING SOVIET UNION*, edited by Michael P. Claudon and Tamar L. Gutner (New York: New York University Press, 1991), pp. 61-73.

Belorussia

Blaustein, Albert P., ed. *CONSTITUTIONS OF DEPENDENCIES AND SPECIAL SOVEREIGNTIES*. Dobbs Ferry, NY: Oceana Publications, 1977- .

Furtado, Charles F., Jr., and Andrea Chandler. *PERESTROIKA IN THE SOVIET REPUBLICS: DOCUMENTS ON THE NATIONAL QUESTION*. Boulder, CO: Westview Press, 1992. xxvi, 646 pp.

LEGAL AND PRACTICAL ASPECTS OF DOING BUSINESS IN THE SOVIET REPUBLICS. Commercial Law and Practice Course Handbook Series No. 604. New York: Practising Law Institute, 1992. 500 pp.

Solchanyk, Roman. "Ukraine, Belorussia, and Moldavia: Imperial Integration, Russification, and the Struggle for National Survival", in *THE NATIONALITIES FACTOR IN SOVIET POLITICS AND SOCIETY*, edited by Lubomyr Hajda and Mark Beissinger (Boulder, CO: Westview Press, 1990), pp. 175-203.

Bibliographies, Bibliographic Studies and Reference Works

See also Dictionaries and Encyclopedias

Kavass, Igor I. "Aspects of Soviet Law on Joint Ventures, Foreign Trade, and Investment: A Bibliographic Survey of Current Literature in English", 24 *VANDERBILT JOURNAL OF TRANSNATIONAL LAW* 415-448 (1991).

Kavass, Igor I., and Andrew T. Griffin. "Joint Ventures in the Soviet Union: A Review of Current Literature in English", 18 *INTERNATIONAL JOURNAL OF LEGAL INFORMATION* 177-204 (1990).

Pockney, B.P. *SOVIET STATISTICS SINCE 1950.* New York: St. Martin's Press, 1991. xviii, 333 pp.

Bureaucracy

See Government System *and* Political System

Business Law

See Commercial Law *and* Business Organizations

Business Organizations

Floroff, Olga, and Susan W. Tiefenbrun. "A Legal Framework for Soviet Privatization", 18 *PEPPERDINE LAW REVIEW* No. 4, 849-892 (1991).

Frenkel, William G. "Soviet Company Law: An Overview", 1 *INTERNATIONAL COMPANY AND COMMERCIAL LAW REVIEW* 153-157 (1990).

George, Arthur L., and Thomas A. O'Donnell. "Russian Republic Joint-Stock Decree: Tidings of Great Joy?", 18 *TAX PLANNING INTERNATIONAL REVIEW* No. 8, 14-16 (August, 1991).

BUSINESS ORGANIZATIONS, *continued*

Hogan, James E. "New Tax and Companies Legislation in the USSR", 16 *REVIEW OF SOCIALIST LAW* 351-362 (1990).

Timmermans, Wim A. "Union of Soviet Socialist Republics", in *GUIDE TO THE COMMERCIAL AND CORPORATE LAW OF EASTERN EUROPE*, edited by David Winter (Bicester, Oxfordshire, England: CCH Editions Limited, 1991), pp. 63-122.

Winter, David, ed. *GUIDE TO THE COMMERCIAL AND CORPORATE LAW OF EASTERN EUROPE*. Bicester, Oxfordshire, England: CCH Editions Limited, 1991. xiv, 164 pp.

Censorship

☆Baturin, Yuriy M., Vladimir L. Entin, and Mikhail A. Fedotov. "The Road to Freedom for the Soviet Press", 12 *JOURNAL OF MEDIA LAW AND PRACTICE* 43-47 (1991).

Berkowitz, Julie S. "A Look into Glasnost's Impact on the Soviet Art World" (Student Note), 11 *LOYOLA ENTERTAINMENT LAW JOURNAL* 453-477 (1991).

Goldstein, Irving. "Telecommunications in the Soviet Union", 5 *JOURNAL OF LAW AND TECHNOLOGY* 21-23 (Winter 1990).

Quigley, John. "Freedom of Expression in the Soviet Media", 11 *LOYOLA ENTERTAINMENT LAW JOURNAL* 269-292 (1991).

Central Asia

Critchlow, James. "'Corruption', Nationalism, and the Native Elites in Soviet Central Asia", 4 *JOURNAL OF COMMUNIST STUDIES* 142-159 (1988).

Critchlow, James. "Islam in Soviet Central Asia: Renaissance or Revolution?", 18 *RELIGION IN COMMUNIST LANDS* 196-211 (1990).

CENTRAL ASIA, *continued*

Furtado, Charles F., Jr., and Andrea Chandler. *PERESTROIKA IN THE SOVIET REPUBLICS: DOCUMENTS ON THE NATIONAL QUESTION*. Boulder, CO: Westview Press, 1992. xxvi, 646 pp.

Olcott, Martha Brill. "Central Asia: The Reformers Challenge a Traditional Society", in *THE NATIONALITIES FACTOR IN SOVIET POLITICS AND SOCIETY*, edited by Lubomyr Hajda and Mark Beissinger (Boulder, CO: Westview Press, 1990), pp. 253-280.

Churches

See Religion

Citizens' Rights

See Human Rights *and*
Individual and the Law

Citizenship

Ginsburgs, George. "The Citizenship of the Baltic States", 21 *JOURNAL OF BALTIC STUDIES* 3-26 (1990).

Ginsburgs, George. "Soviet Citizenship Law: Recent Practices and Proposed Reforms", 36 *OSTEURAPA RECHT* 251-275 (1990).

Civil Law and Procedure

Subheadings:
Civil Code—General
Procedure
Property

Civil Code — General

Frenkel, William G. "U.S.S.R. Legislation: Proposed Amendments to Soviet Civil Law Concerning Property, Legal Personality, and Commerce", 2 *INTERNATIONAL COMPANY AND COMMERCIAL LAW REVIEW* 46-48 (1991).

Osakwe, Christopher. *SOVIET BUSINESS LAW: INSTITUTIONS, PRINCIPLES, AND PROCESSES.* Salem, NH: Butterworth Legal Publishers, 1991. 2 Volumes, looseleaf, misc. pag.

Procedure

Ginsburgs, George. *THE SOVIET UNION AND INTERNATIONAL COOPERATION IN LEGAL MATTERS—PART II: CIVIL LAW.* (Law in Eastern Europe No. 43). Dordrecht, The Netherlands: Martinus Nijhoff Publishers, 1991. xiv, 393 pp.

Property

Butler, William E. ed. *THE LAW OF OWNERSHIP IN THE USSR.* London: Intershelf, Ltd., 1991. viii, 392 pp. (The Butler Commentaries on Soviet Law).

Floroff, Olga, and Susan W. Tiefenbrun. "New Soviet Fundamentals of Law on Land Ownership", 4 *NEW YORK INTERNATIONAL LAW REVIEW* 92-106 (1991).

Maggs, Peter B. "Ownership Rights". A Paper presented at the Geonomics Institute Seminar, Middleburg, Vermont, May 10-13, 1991. 20 pp. Reprinted in *INVESTING IN REFORM: DOING BUSINESS IN A CHANGING SOVIET UNION,* edited by Michael P. Claudon and Tamar L. Gutner (New York: New York University Press, 1991), pp. 155-169.

Stephan, Paul B., III. "*Perestroyka* and Property: The Law of Ownership in the Post-Socialist Soviet Union", 39 *AMERICAN JOURNAL OF COMPARATIVE LAW* 35-65 (1991).

Civil Rights

See Human Rights *and* Individual and the Law

Codification

Ajani, Gianmaria. "The Soviet Experience with Codification: Theoretical and Comparative Perspectives", in *THE SOVIET SOBRANIE OF LAWS*, edited by Richard M. Buxbaum and Kathryn Hendley (Berkeley, CA: University of California at Berkeley, 1991), pp. 184-196.

Barry, Donald B. "State and Social Structure: Part I of the Sobranie", in *THE SOVIET SOBRANIE OF LAWS*, edited by Richard M. Buxbaum and Kathryn Hendley (Berkeley, CA: University of California at Berkeley, 1991), pp. 26-44.

Berg, Ger P. van den. "Soviet Labor Law in the Collection of USSR Laws", in *THE SOVIET SOBRANIE OF LAWS*, edited by Richard M. Buxbaum and Kathryn Hendley (Berkeley, CA: University of California at Berkeley, 1991), pp. 68-101.

Berman, Harold J. "Some Jurisprudential Implications of the Codification of Soviet Laws", in *THE SOVIET SOBRANIE OF LAWS*, edited by Richard M. Buxbaum and Kathryn Hendley (Berkeley, CA: University of California at Berkeley, 1991), pp. 172-183.

Brunner, Georg. "State Structure, Part 2: Organizational Matters", in *THE SOVIET SOBRANIE OF LAWS*, edited by Richard M. Buxbaum and Kathryn Hendley (Berkeley, CA: University of California at Berkeley, 1991), pp. 45-54.

Buxbaum, Richard M. "The Sobranie: A Postscript", in *THE SOVIET SOBRANIE OF LAWS*, edited by Richard M. Buxbaum and Kathryn Hendley (Berkeley, CA: University of California at Berkeley, 1991), pp. 211-226.

Buxbaum, Richard M., and Kathryn Hendley, eds. *THE SOVIET SOBRANIE OF LAWS*. Berkeley, CA: University of California at Berkeley, 1991. xii, 226 pp. (Research Series No. 78).

Ginsburgs, George. "Earlier Publication Practice: The Case of the 1959 Sbornik", in *THE SOVIET SOBRANIE OF LAWS*, edited by Richard M. Buxbaum and Kathryn Hendley (Berkeley, CA: University of California at Berkeley, 1991), pp. 197-210.

CODIFICATION, *continued*

Juviler, Peter. "Secret Justice and Personal Rights", in *THE SOVIET SOBRANIE OF LAWS*, edited by Richard M. Buxbaum and Kathryn Hendley (Berkeley, CA: University of California at Berkeley, 1991), pp. 156-172.

Loeber, Dietrich André. "The Sobranie—A Challenge to Glasnost", in *THE SOVIET SOBRANIE OF LAWS*, edited by Richard M. Buxbaum and Kathryn Hendley (Berkeley, CA: University of California at Berkeley, 1991), pp. 1-25.

Maggs, Peter B. "Legislation on the Soviet National Economy in the Sobranie", in *THE SOVIET SOBRANIE OF LAWS*, edited by Richard M. Buxbaum and Kathryn Hendley (Berkeley, CA: University of California at Berkeley, 1991), pp. 55-67.

Oda, Hiroshi. "Law Enforcement Agencies", in *THE SOVIET SOBRANIE OF LAWS*, edited by Richard M. Buxbaum and Kathryn Hendley (Berkeley, CA: University of California, 1991), pp. 127-139.

Shelley, Louise I. "Soviet Criminal Law and Justice: Are There or Were There Secrets?", in *THE SOVIET SOBRANIE OF LAWS*, edited by Richard M. Buxbaum and Kathryn Hendley (Berkeley, CA: University of California at Berkeley, 1991), pp. 140-155.

Wädekin, Karl-Eugen. "Agriculture", in *THE SOVIET SOBRANIE OF LAWS*, edited by Richard M. Buxbaum and Kathryn Hendley (Berkeley, CA: University of California at Berkeley, 1991), pp. 102-120.

Zile, Zigurds L. "Of Laws, Secrecy, and Environmental Quality in the USSR", in *THE SOVIET SOBRANIE OF LAWS*, edited by Richard M. Buxbaum and Kathryn Hendley (Berkeley, CA: University of California at Berkeley, 1991), pp. 121-126.

Collective Farms

See Agriculture and Collectivization

COMECON

☆Leont'eva, A.V. "New Aspects in the Structure and Jurisdiction of the COMECON Regarding the Protection of the Environment", 7 *PACE ENVIRONMENTAL LAW REVIEW* 179-183 (1989).

Commercial Law

See also Business Organizations *and* Foreign Trade

Butler, William E. "Soviet Business Law: Training the Rising Generation", 2 *EUROPEAN BUSINESS LAW REVIEW* 79-80 (1991).

Nightingale, Christopher, and Stephen Tupper. *RUSSIAN AND SOVIET ECONOMIC CHANGE: THE NEW LAW*. London: Longman, 1991. 100 pp.

Osakwe, Christopher. *SOVIET BUSINESS LAW: INSTITUTIONS, PRINCIPLES, AND PROCESSES*. Salem, NH: Butterworth Legal Publishers, 1991. 2 Volumes, looseleaf, misc. pag.

Stephan, Paul B., III. "The Restructuring of Soviet Commercial Law and Its Impact on International Business Transactions", 24 *GEORGE WASHINGTON JOURNAL OF INTERNATIONAL LAW AND ECONOMICS* 89-102 (1990).

Timmermans, Wim A. "Union of Soviet Socialist Republics", in *GUIDE TO THE COMMERCIAL AND CORPORATE LAW OF EASTERN EUROPE*, edited by David Winter (Bicester, Oxfordshire, England: CCH Editions Limited, 1991), pp. 63-122.

Winter, David, ed. *GUIDE TO THE COMMERCIAL AND CORPORATE LAW OF EASTERN EUROPE*. Bicester, Oxfordshire, England: CCH Editions Limited, 1991. xiv, 164 pp.

Committee of Constitutional Supervision

See Constitution

Commonwealth of Independent States

Torbert, Preston M. "The Commonwealth of Independent States: Its Legal Status and Implications for Foreign Companies", in *LEGAL AND PRACTICAL ASPECTS OF DOING BUSINESS IN THE SOVIET REPUBLICS* (New York: Practising Law Institute, 1992), pp. 127-137.

Communist Party

Rigby, T.H. *POLITICAL ELITES IN THE USSR: CENTRAL LEADERS AND LOCAL CADRES FROM LENIN TO GORBACHEV.* Aldershot, Hants, England: Edward Elgar Publishing Ltd., 1990. vii, 301 pp.

☆"Rules of the Communist Party of the Soviet Union. Ratified by the Twenty-eighth Congress of the CPSU", 30 *SOVIET LAW AND GOVERNMENT* No. 2, 7-25 (Fall 1991).

Rush, Myron. *THE FATE OF THE PARTY APPARATUS UNDER GORBACHEV.* Santa Monica, CA: Rand, 1991. ix, 29 pp.

Schneider, Eberhard. "The Nineteenth Party Conference: Reform of the Political System", in *THE SOVIET UNION 1988-1989: PERESTROIKA IN CRISIS?,* compiled by The Federal Institute for Soviet and International Studies (Boulder, CO: Westview Press, 1990), pp. 30-39.

Computerization

☆Mamiofa, Iosif E., and Corien Prins. "Protecting Computer Programs—The Soviet Perspective", 22 *INTERNATIONAL REVIEW OF INDUSTRIAL PROPERTY AND COPYRIGHT LAW* (IIC) 605-628 (1991).

Prins, Corien. *COMPUTER PROGRAM PROTECTION IN THE USSR: A NEW ERA FOR SOCIALIST COPYRIGHT LAW.* Deventer: Netherlands: Kluwer Law and Taxation Publishers, 1991. XVIII, 397 pp.

Concentration Camps

See Prison System *and*
Stalinist Terror

Constitution

Barry, Donald B. "State and Social Structure: Part I of the Sobranie", in *THE SOVIET SOBRANIE OF LAWS*, edited by Richard M. Buxbaum and Kathryn Hendley (Berkeley, CA: University of California at Berkeley, 1991), pp. 26-44.

Berman, Harold J. "The Rule of Law and the Law-Based State (Rechtstaat) (with Special Reference to the Developments in the Soviet Union)", 4 *HARRIMAN INSTITUTE FORUM* No. 5, 1-12 (May 1991).

Blase, John C., and Cynthia M. Smith. "Soviet Republics' Demand for Autonomy: The Need for Constitutional Reform and the Institution of Canadian-Style Judicial Review" (Note), 17 *JOURNAL OF LEGISLATION* 237-260 (1991).

Blaustein, Albert P., ed. *CONSTITUTIONS OF DEPENDENCIES AND SPECIAL SOVEREIGNTIES*. Dobbs Ferry, NY: Oceana Publications, 1977- .

Blaustein, Albert P., and Gisbert H. Flanz, eds. *CONSTITUTIONS OF THE COUNTRIES OF THE WORLD*. Dobbs Ferry, NY: Oceana Publications, 1970- .

CONSTITUTION (FUNDAMENTAL LAW) OF THE UNION OF SOVIET SOCIALIST REPUBLICS: ADOPTED AT THE SEVENTH (SPECIAL) SESSION OF THE SUPREME SOVIET OF THE USSR, NINTH CONVOCATION, ON OCTOBER 7, 1977. London: Novosti Press Agency, 1990. 58 pp.

D'Zurilla, William T. "Farewell to Lenin: The Story of Russia's New, Non-Communist Constitution", 38 *FEDERAL BAR NEWS AND JOURNAL* 410-412 (1991).

☆Entin, Vladimir L. "Law and Glasnost", in *PERESTROIKA AND THE RULE OF LAW: ANGLO-AMERICAN AND SOVIET PERSPECTIVES,* edited by William E. Butler (London: I.B. Tauris & Co., Ltd., 1991), pp. 101-116.

CONSTITUTION, *continued*

Getty, J. Arch. "State and Society under Stalin: Constitutions and Elections in the 1930s", 50 *Slavic Review* 18-35 (1991).

Henderson, Jane. "The 1988 Soviet Constitutional Reforms and Sources of Law", 1 *KINGS COLLEGE LAW JOURNAL* 59-77 (1990).

Henderson, Jane. "The Soviet Constitutional Reforms of December 1, 1988: An Analysis of the Changes from Draft to Law", in *LEGAL HISTORY AND COMPARATIVE LAW: ESSAYS IN HONOR OF ALBERT KIRALFY*, edited by Richard Plender (London: Frank Cass and Co. Ltd., 1990), pp. 73-97.

☆Kartashkin, Vladimir A. "Human Rights and the Emergence of the State of the Rule of Law in the USSR", 40 *EMORY LAW JOURNAL* 889-902 (1991).

☆Kazimirchuk, V.P. "On Constitutional Supervision in the USSR", in *PERESTROIKA AND THE RULE OF LAW: ANGLO-AMERICAN AND SOVIET PERSPECTIVES,* edited by William E. Butler (London: I.B. Tauris & Co., Ltd., 1991), pp. 148-156.

Kitchin, William. "The Implications for Judicial Review in the Current Legal Reforms in the Soviet Union", 19 *POLICY STUDIES JOURNAL* No. 1, 96-105 (Fall 1990).

☆Koldaeva, N.P. "Separation of Powers in the USSR: Emerging Theory", in *PERESTROIKA AND THE RULE OF LAW: ANGLO-AMERICAN AND SOVIET PERSPECTIVES,* edited by William E. Butler (London: I.B. Tauris & Co., Ltd., 1991), pp. 119-129.

Landfried, Christine, ed. *CONSTITUTIONAL REVIEW AND LEGISLATION: AN INTERNATIONAL COMPARISON*. Baden-Baden: Nomos Verlagsgesellschaft, 1988. 264 pp.

Ludwikowski, Rett R. "Searching for a New Constitutional Model for East-Central Europe", 17 *SYRACUSE JOURNAL OF INTERNATIONAL LAW AND COMMERCE* 91-170 (1991).

Ludwikowski, Rett R. "Soviet Constitutional Changes of the Glasnost Era: A Historical Perspective", 10 *NEW YORK LAW SCHOOL JOURNAL OF INTERNATIONAL AND COMPARATIVE LAW* 119-150 (1989).

☆Polenina, S.V. "The Supremacy of Lex and Legal Reform in the USSR", in *PERESTROIKA AND THE RULE OF LAW: ANGLO-AMERICAN AND SOVIET PERSPECTIVES,* edited by William E. Butler (London: I.B. Tauris & Co., Ltd., 1991), pp. 60-73.

CONSTITUTION, *continued*

Ramans, Miervaldis. "Socialist Federalism, Federalism and Democratic Centralism", in *SOVIET FEDERALISM: NATIONALISM AND ECONOMIC DECENTRALISATION*, edited by Alastair McAuley (Leicester and London: Leicester University Press, 1991), pp. 128-133.

Sharlet, Robert. "The Path of Constitutional Reform in the USSR", in *PERESTROIKA-ERA POLITICS: THE NEW SOVIET LEGISLATURE AND GORBACHEV'S POLITICAL REFORMS*, edited by Robert Huber and Donald R. Kelley (Armonk, NY: M.E. Sharpe, Inc., 1991), pp. 17-32.

Sunstein, Cass R. "Constitutionalism and Secession", 58 *UNIVERSITY OF CHICAGO LAW REVIEW* 633-670 (1991).

☆Tumanov, Vladimir. "Guarantees for Constitutionality of Legislation in the U.S.S.R.", in *CONSTITUTIONAL REVIEW AND LEGISLATION: AN INTERNATIONAL COMPARISON*, edited by Christine Landfried (Baden-Baden: Nomos Verlagsgesellschaft, 1988), pp. 213-217.

Contract Law

See Commercial Law *and* Foreign Trade

Control

See Internal Control

Cooperatives

Belkindas, Misha. *PRIVATIZATION OF THE SOVIET ECONOMY UNDER GORBACHEV II: 1. THE CAMPAIGN AGAINST UNEARNED INCOME. 2. THE DEVELOPMENT OF PRIVATE COOPERATIVES*. Durham, NC: Department of Economics, Duke University, 1989. ii, 97 pp. (Berkeley-Duke Occasional Papers on the Second Economy in the USSR, 14).

COOPERATIVES, *continued*

Bonnell, Victoria E. "Voluntary Associations in Gorbachev's Reform Program", in *CAN GORBACHEV'S REFORMS SUCCEED?*, edited by George W. Breslauer (Berkeley, CA: Center for Slavic and East European Studies and the Berkeley-Stanford Program in Soviet Studies, University of California at Berkeley, 1990), pp. 63-76.

Griffin, Andrew T., and Larry D. Soderquist. "Private Companies in the Soviet Union: Cooperatives in the Era of Perestroika", 32 *HARVARD INTERNATIONAL LAW JOURNAL* 201-225 (1991).

Griffin, Andrew T., and Larry D. Soderquist. "The Soviet Cooperative before Perestroika: The Leninist versus the Stalinist Concept", 39 *AMERICAN JOURNAL OF COMPARATIVE LAW* 599-609 (1991).

Lee, Janet. "The Evolution of Cooperative Legislation: A Case Study of Reform in the Soviet Union", 27 *STANFORD JOURNAL OF INTERNATIONAL LAW* 155-187 (1990).

Slider, Darrell. "Embattled Enterpreneurs: Soviet Cooperatives in an Unreformed Society", 43 *SOVIET STUDIES* 797-822 (1991).

Copyright

Barschevsky, Mikhail, Sergo Selianovsky, and Bruce A. MacDonald. "An Introduction to Soviet Intellectual Property Law," 1 *INTELLECTUAL PROPERTY LAW* 227-238 (1990).

COPYRIGHT LAWS OF EASTERN EUROPE AND THE U.S.S.R. A Report from the International Intellectual Property Alliance by Proskauer, Rose, Goetz and Mendelsohn. Washington, D.C.: November, 1990. 60 and 4 pp.

Maggs, Peter B. "Post-Soviet Law: The Case of Intellectual Property Law", 5 *THE HARRIMAN INSTITUTE FORUM* No. 3 (November 1991). 9 pp.

☆Mamiofa, Iosif E., and Corien Prins. "Protecting Computer Programs—The Soviet Perspective", 22 *INTERNATIONAL REVIEW OF INDUSTRIAL PROPERTY AND COPYRIGHT LAW* (IIC) 605-628 (1991).

Muravina, Elena. "Copyright Transactions with Soviet Authors: The Role of VAAP" (Student Note), 11 *LOYOLA ENTERTAINMENT LAW JOURNAL* 421-451 (1991).

COPYRIGHT, *continued*

Prins, Corien. *COMPUTER PROGRAM PROTECTION IN THE USSR: A NEW ERA FOR SOCIALIST COPYRIGHT LAW.* Deventer: Netherlands: Kluwer Law and Taxation Publishers, 1991. XVIII, 397 pp.

Prins, Corien. "Emile Zola Receives an Answer: The Soviet Union Is to Join the Berne Convention", 13 *EUROPEAN INTELLECTUAL PROPERTY REVIEW* 238-247 (1991).

Prins, Corien. "The New Civil Code of the Soviet Union: Major Changes in the Field of Intellectual Property Rights", 13 *EUROPEAN INTELLECTUAL PROPERTY REVIEW* 388-391 (1991).

Schwartz, Eric J. "Recent Developments in the Copyright Regimes of the Soviet Union and Eastern Europe", 38 *JOURNAL OF THE COPYRIGHT SOCIETY OF THE U.S.A.* 123-226 (1991).

Corporations

See Business Organizations *and* Foreign Trade

Corrective Labor Camps

See Prison System

Countertrade

See Foreign Trade

Courts

See Administration of Justice

Crime

See Criminal Law and Procedure

Criminal Law and Procedure

See also Stalinist Terror

Subheadings:
Crime and Criminology
General
Policy
Procedure
State Crimes

Crime and Criminology

Dobson, Richard B. "Youth Problems in the Soviet Union", in *SOVIET SOCIAL PROBLEMS*, edited by Anthony Jones, et al. (Boulder, CO; San Francisco; Oxford: Westview Press, 1991), pp. 227-251.

Jones, Anthony, Walter D. Connor, and David E. Powell, eds. *SOVIET SOCIAL PROBLEMS*. Boulder, CO; San Franciso; Oxford: Westview Press, 1991. ix, 337 pp.

Powell, David E. "Soviet Society", in *SOVIET UPDATE, 1989-1990*, edited by Anthony Jones and David E. Powell (Boulder, CO: Westview Press, 1991), pp. 54-74.

Sanjian, Andrea Stevenson. "Prostitution, the Press, and Agenda-Building in the Soviet Policy Process", in *SOVIET SOCIAL PROBLEMS*, edited by Anthony Jones, et al. (Boulder, CO; San Francisco: Oxford: Westview Press, 1991), pp. 270-295.

☆Savitskii, Valerii. "Democratization in the USSR: Toward the Freedom of the Individual through Law and Courts", 2 *CRIMINAL LAW FORUM* 85-110 (1990).

Shelley, Louise I. "Crime in the Soviet Union", in *SOVIET SOCIAL PROBLEMS,* edited by Anthony Jones, et al. (Boulder, CO; San Francisco; Oxford: Westview Press, 1991), pp. 252-269.

Vaksberg, Arkady. *THE SOVIET MAFIA*. New York: St. Martin's Press, 1991. ix, 275 pp.

General

☆Gutsenko, Konstantin. "The Right to a Defense", 30 *SOVIET LAW AND GOVERNMENT* No. 3, 78-95 (Winter, 1991-92).

CRIMINAL LAW AND PROCEDURE—General, *continued*

Simmons, David M. "Recognition of Illegalities, Proposals for Reform, and Implemented Reforms in the Soviet Criminal Justice System under Gorbachev, Glasnost and Perestroika", 5 *AMERICAN UNIVERSITY JOURNAL OF INTERNATIONAL LAW AND POLICY* 921-953 (1990).

Wyman, Lowry. "Crime and Punishment in the USSR: How Is It Really Changing?", 29 *THE JUDGE'S JOURNAL* 14-19 (1990).

Policy

Ginsburgs, George. "The Soviet Union and International Co-operation in Penal Matters", 41 *INTERNATIONAL AND COMPARATIVE LAW QUARTERLY* 85-116 (1992).

Ginsburgs, George. "The USSR and the Socialist Model of International Cooperation in Criminal Matters", 17 *REVIEW OF SOCIALIST LAW* 199-278 (1991).

☆Savitskii, Valerii. "Selected Problems of Judicial Reform, Criminal Justice, and the Protection of Individual Rights in the USSR", 2 *CRIMINAL LAW FORUM* 269-292 (1991).

Shelley, Louise I. "Soviet Criminal Law and Justice: Are There or Were There Secrets?", in *THE SOVIET SOBRANIE OF LAWS,* edited by Richard M. Buxbaum and Kathryn Hendley (Berkeley, CA: University of California at Berkeley, 1991), pp. 140-155.

USSR: FIRST STEPS TOWARDS REFORM OF THE CRIMINAL JUSTICE SYSTEM. London: Amnesty International, International Secretariat, 1990. 10 pp.

Procedure

Muller, Peter-Michael. "Protection of Human Rights in the Administration of Criminal Justice in Central and Eastern Europe and the Soviet Union", 17 *INTERNATIONAL LEGAL PRACTITIONER* No. 1, 18-19 (March 1992).

State Crimes

Georgopoulos, Zach. "Soviet and Chinese Dissent Laws: Glasnost v. Tienanmen" (Note), 14 *HASTINGS INTERNATIONAL AND COMPARATIVE LAW REVIEW* 475-503 (1991).

Criminology

See Criminal Law and Procedure
—Crime and Criminology

Currency

See also Banking and Finance

Brada, Josef C., and Michael P. Claudon, eds. *REFORMING THE RUBLE: MONETARY ASPECTS OF PERESTROIKA*. New York: New York University Press, 1990. x, 228 pp.

Feige, Edgar L. "Perestroika and Ruble Convertibility", 10 *CATO JOURNAL* 631-653 (1991).

Frenkel, William G., and R. Cameron Kennedy. "The Soviet Ruble: How Convertible is Convertible?" 10 *INTERNATIONAL FINANCIAL LAW REVIEW* No. 3, 29-31 (March 1991).

Hanke, Steve H., and Kurt Schuler. "Ruble Reform: A Lesson from Keynes", 10 *CATO JOURNAL* 655-666 (1991).

Perkins, Roswell B., and Jonathan H. Hines. "Soviets Change Currency Rules", 10 *INTERNATIONAL FINANCIAL LAW REVIEW* No. 5, 22-24 (May 1991).

☆Uljanov, Eugene. "The Latest Developments in the Foreign Currency Practices and Regulations of the Soviet Union". A Paper presented at the Geonomics Institute Seminar, Middleburg, Vermont, May 10-13, 1991. 20 pp. Also published in *INVESTING IN REFORM: DOING BUSINESS IN A CHANGING SOVIET UNION*, edited by Michael P. Claudon and Tamar L. Gutner (New York: New York University Press, 1991), pp. 61-73.

Customs

See Foreign Trade

Dictionaries and Encyclopedias

Brown, Archie, ed. *THE SOVIET UNION: A BIOGRAPHICAL DICTIONARY.* London: George Weidenfeld and Nicolson Ltd., 1990; New York: Macmillan Publishing Co., 1991. xiv, 489 pp.

Rossi, Jacques. *THE GULAG HANDBOOK: AN ENCYCLOPEDIA DICTIONARY OF SOVIET PENITENTIARY INSTITUTIONS AND TERMS RELATED TO THE FORCED LABOR CAMPS.* New York: Paragon House, 1989. 610 pp.

White, Stephen, ed. *POLITICAL AND ECONOMIC ENCYCLOPAEDIA OF THE SOVIET UNION AND EASTERN EUROPE.* Marlow, Essex, England: Longman Group UK Ltd., 1990. xxii, 328 pp.

Documents

See Laws and Official Documents in English Translation

Drugs

Kramer, John M. "Drug Abuse in the USSR", in *SOVIET SOCIAL PROBLEMS*, edited by Anthony Jones, et al. (Boulder, CO; San Francisco; Oxford: Westview Press, 1991), pp. 94-118.

Treml, Vladimir G. "Drinking and Alcohol Abuse in the USSR in the 1980's", in *SOVIET SOCIAL PROBLEMS,* edited by Anthony Jones, et al. (Boulder, CO; San Francisco; Oxford: Westview Press, 1991), pp. 119-136.

Economic System

See also Private Economic Activity *and* Privatization

Åslund, Anders. "Gorbachev, Perestroyka, and Economic Crisis", *40 PROBLEMS OF COMMUNISM* No. 1-2, 18-41 (January-April, 1991).

Åslund, Anders. *GORBACHEV'S STRUGGLE FOR ECONOMIC REFORM*. 2d ed. Ithaca, NY: Cornell University Press, 1991. x, 219 pp.

Atkinson, Scott. "The USSR and the Pacific Century", 30 *ASIAN SURVEY* 629-642 (1990).

Belkindas, Misha. *PRIVATIZATION OF THE SOVIET ECONOMY UNDER GORBACHEV II: 1. THE CAMPAIGN AGAINST UNEARNED INCOME. 2. THE DEVELOPMENT OF PRIVATE COOPERATIVES*. Durham, NC: Department of Economics, Duke University, 1989. ii, 97 pp. (Berkeley-Duke Occasional Papers on the Second Economy in the USSR, 14).

Brada, Josef C., and Michael P. Claudon, eds. *THE EMERGING RUSSIAN BEAR: INTEGRATING THE SOVIET UNION INTO THE WORLD ECONOMY*. New York: New York University Press, 1991. xiii, 228 pp. (Geonomics Institute for International Economic Advancement Series).

Claudon, Michael P., and Tamar L. Gutner, eds. *INVESTING IN REFORM: DOING BUSINESS IN A CHANGING SOVIET UNION*. New York: New York University Press, 1991. xix, 279 pp.

Desai, Padma. "Soviet Economic Reform", 3 *HARRIMAN INSTITUTE FORUM* No. 12, 1-12 (Dec. 1990).

THE ECONOMY OF THE USSR: A STUDY UNDERTAKEN IN RESPONSE TO A REQUEST BY THE HOUSTON SUMMIT: SUMMARY AND RECOMMENDATIONS. Washington, DC: The World Bank, 1990. iv, 51 pp.

English, Richard D. "Privatization by General Fund: Economic Empowerment for Central and Eastern Europe", 24 *GEORGE WASHINGTON JOURNAL OF INTERNATIONAL LAW AND ECONOMICS* 527-586 (1991).

ECONOMIC SYSTEM, *continued*

Geron, Leonard. *SOVIET FOREIGN ECONOMIC POLICY UNDER PERESTROIKA*. London: The Royal Institute of International Affairs; New York: Council on Foreign Relations Press, 1990. x, 126 pp. (Chatham House Papers).

Goldman, Marshall I. *WHAT WENT WRONG WITH PERESTROIKA*. New York: W.W. Norton & Company, 1991. 258 pp.

Kaser, Michael, and Aleksandar M. Vacic, eds. *REFORMS IN FOREIGN ECONOMIC RELATIONS OF EASTERN EUROPE AND THE SOVIET UNION.* New York: United Nations, 1991. xii, 202 pp. (United Nations Publications Sales No. E.91.II.E.5.)

Lawrence, Paul R. and Charalambos A. Vlachoutsicos. *BEHIND THE FACTORY WALLS: DECISION MAKING IN SOVIET AND US ENTERPRISES.* Boston: Harvard Business School Press, 1990. xii, 352 pp.

Maggs, Peter B. "Facilitating U.S.-Soviet Joint Ventures through Legislative Reform", in *THE EMERGING RUSSIAN BEAR: INTEGRATING THE SOVIET UNION INTO THE WORLD ECONOMY,* edited by Josef C. Brada and Michael P. Claudon (New York: New York University Press, 1991), pp. 129-141.

Maggs, Peter B. "Legislation on the Soviet National Economy in the Sobranie", in *THE SOVIET SOBRANIE OF LAWS,* edited by Richard M. Buxbaum and Kathryn Hendley (Berkeley, CA: University of California at Berkeley, 1991), pp. 55-67.

☆Mozolin, Viktor P. "The Positive Influence of Legal Reform on Soviet-U.S. Joint Ventures", in *THE EMERGING BEAR: INTEGRATING THE SOVIET UNION INTO THE WORLD ECONOMY,* edited by Josef C. Brada and Michael P. Claudon (New York: New York University Press, 1991), pp. 115-127.

☆Piasheva, Larissa. *IN PURSUIT OF SOCIAL JUSTICE.* Moscow: Progress Publishers, 1991. 303 pp.

☆Popov, Vladimir. "Soviet Economic Reforms: Missed Opportunities and Remaining Hopes". A Paper presented at the Geonomics Institute Seminar, Middleburg, Vermont, May 10-13, 1991. 30 ll.

Roberts, Paul Craig, and Karen La Follette. *MELTDOWN: INSIDE THE SOVIET ECONOMY.* Washington: Cato Institute, 1990. xi, 152 pp.

Salter, Leonard M. "Can the Soviet Union Use a Chapter 11? Would It Be Effective?", 96 *COMMERCIAL LAW JOURNAL* 90-98 (1991).

ECONOMIC SYSTEM, *continued*

☆Samorodov, A. "Conversion of the Soviet Defence Industry and Its Consequences for Labour", 129 *INTERNATIONAL LABOUR REVIEW* 555-572 (1990).

Schroeder, Gertrude E. "The Dismal Fate of Soviet-Type Economies: Mises Was Right", 11 *CATO JOURNAL* 13-25 (1991).

Schroeder, Gertrude E. "Economic Relations among the Soviet Republics". A Paper presented at the Geonomics Institute Seminar, Middleburg, Vermont, May 10-13, 1991. 23 ll.

Stephan, Paul B., III. *SOVIET ECONOMIC LAW: THE PARADOX OF PERESTROYKA*. Pittsburgh, PA: University of Pittsburgh Center for Russian and East European Studies, 1990. 90 pp. (The Carl Beck Papers in Russian and East European Studies, No. 805).

A STUDY OF THE SOVIET ECONOMY. Paris: International Monetary Fund, The World Bank, Organization for Economic Co-Operation and Development, and the European Bank for Reconstruction and Development, 1991. 3 volumes.

Winiecki, Jan. "Buying Out Property Rights to the Economy from the Ruling Stratum: The Case of Soviet-Type States", 9 *INTERNATIONAL REVIEW OF LAW AND ECONOMICS* 79-85 (1989).

Education

See Legal Profession

Elections

Commission on Security and Cooperation in Europe. *ELECTIONS IN THE BALTIC STATES AND SOVIET REPUBLICS: A COMPENDIUM OF REPORTS ON PARLIAMENTARY ELECTIONS HELD IN 1990*. Compiled by the Staff of the Commission on Security and Cooperation in Europe. Washington: U.S. Government Printing Office, 1990. x, 188 pp.

ELECTIONS, *continued*

Commission on Security and Cooperation in Europe. *REFERENDUM IN THE SOVIET UNION. A COMPENDIUM OF REPORTS ON THE MARCH 17, 1991 REFERENDUM ON THE FUTURE OF THE USSR.* Compiled by the Staff of the Commission on Security and Cooperation in Europe. Washington: U.S. Government Printing Office, 1991. viii, 46 pp.

☆Danilenko, Viktor. "Electoral Reform", in *PERESTROIKA-ERA POLITICS: THE NEW SOVIET LEGISLATURE AND GORBACHEV'S POLITICAL REFORMS,* edited by Robert Huber and Donald R. Kelley (Armonk, NY: M.E. Sharpe, Inc., 1991), pp. 33-49.

Getty, J. Arch. "State and Society under Stalin: Constitutions and Elections in the 1930s", 50 *Slavic Review* 18-35 (1991).

Emigration

Heitman, Sidney. *THE RIGHT TO LEAVE: THE NEW SOVIET DRAFT LAW ON EMIGRATION.* Cologne: Bundesinstitut für ostwissenschaftliche und internationale Studien, 1990. iii, 53 pp. (Report 26-1990).

Heitman, Sidney. *SOVIET EMIGRATION IN 1990.* Cologne: Bundesinstitut für ostwissenschaftliche und internationale Studien, 1991. iii, 45 pp. (Report 33-1991).

Heitman, Sidney. "Soviet Emigration Policies toward Germans and Armenians", in *SOVIET NATIONALITY POLICIES: RULING ETHNIC GROUPS IN THE USSR*, edited by Henry R. Huttenbach (London: Mansell Publishing Limited, 1990), pp. 235-259.

Irwin, Zachary. "Soviet-Jewish Emigration Policy: Anti-Zionism and Philo-Semitism", in *SOVIET NATIONALITY POLICIES: RULING ETHNIC GROUPS IN THE USSR,* edited by Henry R. Huttenbach (London: Mansell Publishing Limited, 1990), pp. 260-285.

Ro'i, Yaacov. *THE STRUGGLE FOR SOVIET JEWISH EMIGRATION 1948-1967.* Cambridge: Cambridge University Press, 1991. 457 pp.

Environmental Law and Policy

☆Bondarenko, V.S. "Coastal Management in the USSR: Perestroika on the Coast", 18 *COASTAL MANAGEMENT* 337-363 (1990).

☆Brinchuk, M.M. "Ecological and Legal Problems of Agro-Chemicalization", 7 *PACE ENVIRONMENTAL LAW REVIEW* 171-177 (1989).

French, Hillary F. "Green Revolution: Environmental Reconstruction in Eastern Europe and the Soviet Union", 26 *THE COLUMBIA JOURNAL OF WORLD BUSINESS* 28-52 (1991).

Fitzmaurice, M. *INTERNATIONAL LEGAL PROBLEMS OF THE ENVIRONMENTAL PROTECTION OF THE BALTIC SEA*. Dordrecht, The Netherlands: Martinus Nijhoff/Graham & Trotman, 1992. xxix, 328 pp.

Ginsburgs, George. "Soviet International Law and Baltic Environmental Protection", 38 *OSTEUROPA RECHT* 52-64 (1992).

Goldman, Marshall I. "Pollution in the Soviet Union: The Growth of Environmentalism and Its Consequences", in *SOVIET SOCIAL PROBLEMS*, edited by Anthony Jones, et al. (Boulder, CO; San Francisco; Oxford: Westview Press, 1991), pp. 39-56.

☆Ikonitskaya, I.A. "Legal Protection of Land in the USSR", 7 *PACE ENVIRONMENTAL LAW REVIEW* 161-170 (1989).

Langrind, Peter M. "An Overview of Environmental Law in the USSR" (Note), 11 *NEW YORK LAW SCHOOL JOURNAL OF INTERNATIONAL AND COMPARATIVE LAW* 483-498 (1990).

☆Lemeshev, Mikhail. *BUREAUCRATS IN POWER—ECOLOGICAL COLLAPSE*. Moscow: Progress Publishers, 1990. 315 pp.

☆Leont'eva, A.V. "New Aspects in the Structure and Jurisdiction of the COMECON Regarding the Protection of the Environment", 7 *PACE ENVIRONMENTAL LAW REVIEW* 179-183 (1989).

Lisitsyn, Eugene N. "Environmental Law and Management in the USSR: A Reflection on Contemporary Reforms", 17 *REVIEW OF SOCIALIST LAW* 125-143 (1991).

Marples, David R. "The Greening of Ukraine: Ecology and the Emergence of *Zelenyi svit*, 1986-1990", in *PERESTROIKA FROM BELOW: SOCIAL MOVEMENTS IN THE SOVIET UNION*, edited by Judith B. Sedaitis and Jim Butterfield (Boulder, CO: Westview Press, 1991), pp. 133-144.

ENVIRONMENTAL LAW AND POLICY, *continued*

Pryde, Philip R. *ENVIRONMENTAL MANAGEMENT IN THE SOVIET UNION.* Cambridge: Cambridge University Press, 1991. xx, 314 pp.

Robinson, Nicholas A. "Soviet Environmental Law and Perestroika: A Challenge for Joint Ventures", 2 *LAND MANAGEMENT AND ENVIRONMENTAL LAW REPORT* 195-201 (1990-91).

Robinson, Nicholas A. "Soviet Environmental Protection: The Challenge for Legal Studies", 7 *PACE ENVIRONMENTAL LAW REVIEW* 117-150 (1989).

☆Romanova, O.B. "Tourism and Environmental Protection", 7 *PACE ENVIRONMENTAL LAW REVIEW* 185-191 (1989).

Rosencranz, Armin, and Antony Scott. "Siberia, Environmentalism and Problems of Environmental Protection", 14 *HASTINGS INTERNATIONAL AND COMPARATIVE LAW REVIEW* 929-967 (1991).

☆Shcherbak, Iurii. *CHERNOBYL: A DOCUMENTARY STORY.* New York: St. Martin's Press, 1989. xvi, 168 pp.

Strautmanis, J., and A. Maurins. "Problems of National Legislation for the Protection of the Environment: The Case of Latvia", 38 *OSTEUROPA RECHT* 72-73 (1992).

☆Timoshenko, Alexandre S. "Control Machinery in the Ecological Security System", in *CONTROL OVER COMPLIANCE WITH INTERNATIONAL LAW*, edited by William E. Butler (Dordrecht, The Netherlands: Martinus Nijhoff Publishers, 1991), pp. 51-59.

☆Timoshenko, Alexandre S. "Ecological Security: The International Aspect", 7 *PACE ENVIRONMENTAL LAW REVIEW* 151-160 (1989).

☆Vinogradov, Sergei V. "Ecological Security in the Arctic: A Regional Approach", in *FROM COEXISTENCE TO COOPERATION: INTERNATIONAL LAW AND ORGANIZATION IN THE POST-COLD WAR ERA*, edited by Edward McWhinney, et al. (Dordrecht, The Netherlands: Martinus Nijhoff Publishers, 1991), pp. 155-166.

ENVIRONMENTAL LAW AND POLICY, *continued*

☆Vinogradov, Sergei V. "International Environmental Security: The Concept and Its Implementation", in *PERESTROIKA AND INTERNATIONAL LAW: CURRENT ANGLO-SOVIET APPROACHES TO INTERNATIONAL LAW*, edited by Anthony Carty and Gennady Danilenko (Edinburgh: Edinburg University Press, 1990), pp. 196-207.

☆Yablokov, A.V. "The Current State of the Soviet Environment", 4 *ENVIRONMENTAL POLICY REVIEW* 1-19 (1990).

Ziegler, Charles E. "Environmental Politics and Policy under Perestroika", in *PERESTROIKA FROM BELOW: SOCIAL MOVEMENTS IN THE SOVIET UNION*, edited by Judith B. Sedaitis and Jim Butterfield (Boulder, CO: Westview Press, 1991), pp. 113-131.

Zile, Zigurds L. "Of Laws, Secrecy, and Environmental Quality in the USSR", in *THE SOVIET SOBRANIE OF LAWS,* edited by Richard M. Buxbaum and Kathryn Hendley (Berkeley, CA: University of California at Berkeley, 1991), pp. 121-126.

Equality

☆Piasheva, Larissa. *IN PURSUIT OF SOCIAL JUSTICE.* Moscow: Progress Publishers, 1991. 303 pp.

Estonia

See Baltic

Ethnic Minorities

See Nationalities and Nationalism

Extradition

Ginsburgs, George. "The USSR and the Socialist Model of International Cooperation in Criminal Matters", 17 *REVIEW OF SOCIALIST LAW* 199-278 (1991).

Family Law

Bazyler, Michael J. "Soviet Family Law", 39 *UNIVERSITY OF KANSAS LAW REVIEW* 125-174 (1990).

Harwin, Judith. "Union of Soviet Socialist Republics: Child Care in the Soviet Union—Law, Policy and Practice", 28 *JOURNAL OF FAMILY LAW* 627-635 (1990).

Jones, Anthony, Walter D. Connor, and David E. Powell, eds. *SOVIET SOCIAL PROBLEMS.* Boulder, CO; San Franciso; Oxford: Westview Press, 1991. ix, 337 pp.

Juviler, Peter. "No End of a Problem: Perestroika for the Family?" in *SOVIET SOCIAL PROBLEMS,* edited by Anthony Jones, et al. (Boulder, CO; San Francisco; Oxford: Westview Press, 1991), pp. 194-212.

☆Khazova, O. "USSR: Recent Developments in Divorce and Its Consequences", 30 *JOURNAL OF FAMILY LAW* 439-445 (1991-92).

☆Khazova, O. "U.S.S.R.: Some Problems of Soviet Family Law", 29 *JOURNAL OF FAMILY LAW* 463-470 (1990-91).

Federalism and Federation

See Government System

Finance

See Banking and Finance

Foreign Policy

See Foreign Trade—Policy and Relations *and* International Law—Foreign Relations

Foreign Trade

Subheadings:
Countertrade
Customs
Finance
Franchise
Free Trade Zones
Investment
Joint Ventures
Policy and Relations
Practice and "How-To"
Technology Transfers

Countertrade

☆Sviridenko, Oleg. "Counter-Trade Operations with the Republics of the Former USSR", 1992 *REVUE DE DROIT DES AFFAIRES INTERNATIONALES/INTERNATIONAL BUSINESS LAW JOURNAL* No. 1, 69-78.

Waller, Robert L. "Soviet Countertrade", 1 *THE UNITED STATES AIR FORCE ACADEMY JOURNAL OF LEGAL STUDIES* 87-103 (1990).

Customs

Butler, William E. *THE CUSTOMS CODE OF THE USSR AND THE LAW ON THE CUSTOMS TARIFF OF THE USSR*. London: Interlist, 1991. xxvi, 210 pp.

Finance

☆Maslov, Alexander. "Bankrolling Soviet Joint Ventures", *4 EUROPEAN AFFAIRS* No. 3, 59-65 (Autumn 1990).

Perkins, Roswell B., and Jonathan H. Hines. "Soviets Change Currency Rules", 10 *INTERNATIONAL FINANCIAL LAW REVIEW* No. 5, 22-24 (May 1991).

☆Portnoy, Mikhail A. "Major Financial Obstacles to the Formation and Operation of Joint Ventures", in *THE EMERGING RUSSIAN BEAR: INTEGRATING THE SOVIET UNION INTO THE WORLD ECONOMY*, edited by Josef C. Brada and Michael P. Claudon (New York: New York University Press, 1991), pp. 165-174.

FOREIGN TRADE—Finance, *continued*

Redway, A. James. "Financing Projects in the Territory of the Former USSR", in *LEGAL AND PRACTICAL ASPECTS OF DOING BUSINESS IN THE SOVIET REPUBLICS* (New York: Practising Law Institute, 1992), pp. 117-124.

Salter, Leonard M. "Can the Soviet Union Use a Chapter 11? Would It Be Effective?", 96 *COMMERCIAL LAW JOURNAL* 90-98 (1991).

☆Uljanov, Eugene. "The Latest Developments in the Foreign Currency Practices and Regulations of the Soviet Union". A Paper presented at the Geonomics Institute Seminar, Middleburg, Vermont, May 10-13, 1991. 20 pp. Also published in *INVESTING IN REFORM: DOING BUSINESS IN A CHANGING SOVIET UNION,* edited by Michael P. Claudon and Tamar L. Gutner (New York: New York University Press, 1991), pp. 61-73.

Welt, Leo G.B. "Unconventional Forms of Financing: Buy-Back/Compensation/Barter", "Symposium on U.S.-Soviet Military and Economic Relations", *22 NEW YORK UNIVERSITY JOURNAL OF INTERNATIONAL LAW AND POLITICS* 461-473 (1990).

Franchise

Zeidman, Philip F., and Michael Avner. "Franchising in Eastern Europe and the Soviet Union", 3 *DE PAUL BUSINESS LAW JOURNAL* 307-338 (1991).

Free Trade Zones

☆Boguslavskii, Mark M. "The Legal Status of Free Economic Zones in the USSR", 29 *SOVIET LAW AND GOVERNMENT* 78-91 (1991).

Torbert, Preston M. "First Soviet Free Zone Will Give Firms Access to Pacific Basin Markets", in *LEGAL AND PRACTICAL ASPECTS OF DOING BUSINESS IN THE SOVIET REPUBLICS* (New York: Practising Law Institute, 1992), pp. 483-494.

FOREIGN TRADE—Free Trade Zones, *continued*

Torbert, Preston M. "New Free Enterprise Zone Regulations Promote Investment", in *LEGAL AND PRACTICAL ASPECTS OF DOING BUSINESS IN THE SOVIET REPUBLICS.* Commercial Law and Practice Course Handbook Series No. 604. New York: Practising Law Institute, 1992, pp. 477-482.

Investment

Augustyn, Francene M. "Foreign Investment in the Soviet Union: The Dawning of a New Era", 2 *TAX NOTES INTERNATIONAL* 1115-1120 (November 1990).

Birenbaum, David E., and Dimitri P. Racklin. *BUSINESS VENTURES IN EASTERN EUROPE AND THE SOVIET UNION: THE EMERGING LEGAL FRAMEWORK FOR FOREIGN INVESTMENT.* Englewood Cliffs, NJ: Prentice Hall, 1990- . 2 volumes, looseleaf.

Butler, William E. *FUNDAMENTAL PRINCIPLES OF LEGISLATION ON INVESTMENT ACTIVITY IN THE USSR AND REPUBLICS.* London: Interlist, 1991. viii, 302 pp. (The Butler Commentaries on Soviet Law).

Carey, Sarah C. "Five Years Later: Evaluating Foreign Investment Experience in the 'Former USSR'", in *LEGAL AND PRACTICAL ASPECTS OF DOING BUSINESS IN THE SOVIET REPUBLICS* (New York: Practising Law Institute, 1992), pp. 51-68.

EASTERN EUROPE AND THE USSR: A GUIDE TO FOREIGN INVESTMENT LEGISLATION, 3d. ed. KPMG, March 1991. 32 pp.

Felker, Timothy L. "Perestroyka and Western Direct Investment: The Task of Integrating a Western Company into the Changing Soviet Economy", 12 *UNIVERSITY OF PENNSYLVANIA JOURNAL OF INTERNATIONAL BUSINESS LAW* 219-244 (1991).

Fitch, Stephen D. "The Harriman Manganese Concession in the Soviet Union: Lessons for Today", 9 *INTERNATIONAL TAX AND BUSINESS LAWYER* 209-271 (1991).

FREE MARKET TAKEOVER: A LEGAL GUIDE TO INVESTING IN EASTERN EUROPE, USSR, CHINA AND VIETNAM, a Special Supplement to the July 1981 issue of *INTERNATIONAL FINANCIAL LAW REVIEW.*

FOREIGN TRADE—Investment, *continued*

Hazard, John N. "Risks in Investing in the USSR: Can There Be Protection against Them?", 11 *NEW YORK LAW SCHOOL JOURNAL OF INTERNATIONAL AND COMPARATIVE LAW* No. 3, 457-461 (1990).

Holland, William E., Mikhail Rozenberg, and Robert E. Langer. "USSR", in *FREE MARKET TAKEOVER: A LEGAL GUIDE TO INVESTING IN EASTERN EUROPE, USSR, CHINA AND VIETNAM*, a Special Supplement to the July 1991 issue of *INTERNATIONAL FINANCIAL LAW REVIEW*, pp. 55-61.

International Chamber of Commerce. *FOREIGN INVESTMENT IN THE USSR. KEY 1990 LEGISLATION*. Paris: ICC Publications, 1991.

Leonard, Edward S. "Investment in the Soviet Union in the Early Nineties: Diving into the Vortex" (Comment), 2 *TOURO JOURNAL OF TRANSNATIONAL LAW* 153-219 (1991).

☆Muchlinski, P.T. "Dispute Settlement under the Washington Convention on the Settlement of Investment Disputes", in *CONTROL OVER COMPLIANCE WITH INTERNATIONAL LAW*, edited by William E. Butler (Dordrecht, The Netherlands: Martinus Nijhoff Publishers, 1991), pp. 175-193.

Newcity, Michael. "Tax Considerations in Foreign Trade and Investment in the USSR", 24 *VANDERBILT JOURNAL OF TRANSNATIONAL LAW* 235-267 (1991).

Osakwe, Christopher. "The Host Country Perspective on Foreign Investments in the Soviet Union: Law and Policy", 24 *VANDERBILT JOURNAL OF TRANSNATIONAL LAW* 207-233 (1991).

Saliman, S. Gerald. "An Analysis of the Changing Legal Environment in the USSR for Foreign Investment", 22 *LAW AND POLICY IN INTERNATIONAL BUSINESS* 1-36 (1991).

Schneider, Richard C., Jr. "Tax, Investment, and Financing Issues in Projects in the USSR and Eastern Europe", in *LEGAL ASPECTS OF TRADE AND INVESTMENT IN THE SOVIET UNION AND EASTERN EUROPE* (New York: Practising Law Institute, 1990), pp. 235-295.

Shanks, Robert B. "Investment Protection for Projects in Eastern Europe and the Soviet Union: OPIC, MIGA, and Bilateral Investment Treaties", in *LEGAL ASPECTS OF TRADE AND INVESTMENT IN THE SOVIET UNION AND EASTERN EUROPE* (New York: Practising Law Institute, 1990), pp. 391-408.

FOREIGN TRADE—Investment, *continued*

Simons, William B. "Foreign Investment Laws in the Republics of the USSR: Lithuania and Kazakhstan", 17 *REVIEW OF SOCIALIST LAW* 161-190 (1991).

Simons, William B. "Foreign Investment Laws of Kazakhstan", 17 *REVIEW OF SOCIALIST LAW* 81-94 (1991).

Stephan, Paul B., III. "A U.S. Perspective on the Legal Environment for Foreign Investment in Russia", in *LEGAL AND PRACTICAL ASPECTS OF DOING BUSINESS IN THE SOVIET REPUBLICS* (New York: Practising Law Institute, 1992), pp. 29-34.

Stephan, Paul B., III. "Soviet Law and Foreign Investment: Perestroyka's Gordian Knot", 25 *INTERNATIONAL LAWYER* 741-754 (1991).

Toop, R. Scott. "Doing Business in the Soviet Union: A Case Study", in *LEGAL ASPECTS OF TRADE AND INVESTMENT IN THE SOVIET UNION AND EASTERN EUROPE* (New York: Practising Law Institute, 1990), pp. 57-74.

White, Walter H., and Rebecca A. Speekhard. "Soviet Union", 25 *INTERNATIONAL LAWYER* 549-553 (1991).

Joint Ventures

☆Afanasyeva, Larisa. "Insurance and Risk Management of Joint Ventures in the USSR", *22 NEW YORK UNIVERSITY JOURNAL OF INTERNATIONAL LAW AND POLITICS* 447-459 (1990).

Arbess, Daniel J. "A Few Things U.S. Businesspeople Should Know about Joint Ventures in the Soviet Union: A Lawyer's View", *22 NEW YORK JOURNAL OF INTERNATIONAL LAW AND POLITICS* 411-434 (1990).

Aulin, Lisen. *ESTABLISHING JOINT VENTURES IN THE USSR.* Deventer, The Netherlands; Boston: Kluwer Law and Taxation Publishers, 1990. ix, 149 pp.

Block, Kevin P. "The Disciplining and Dismissal of Employees by Joint Ventures in the USSR", 23 *GEORGE WASHINGTON JOURNAL OF INTERNATIONAL LAW AND ECONOMICS* 619-667 (1990).

☆Boguslavskii, Mark M. *JOINT VENTURES IN THE USSR: A GUIDE TO SOVIET LAW.* London: W.H. Everett and Son Ltd, 1991. 192 pp.

FOREIGN TRADE—Joint Ventures, *continued*

Brada, Josef C., and Michael P. Claudon, eds. *THE EMERGING RUSSIAN BEAR: INTEGRATING THE SOVIET UNION INTO THE WORLD ECONOMY.* New York: New York University Press, 1991. xiii, 228 pp. (Geonomics Institute for International Economic Advancement Series).

☆Braginskii[y], Mikhail I. *JOINT VENTURES: BENEFIT FOR ALL.* Moscow: Novosti Press Agency Publishing House, 1988. 15 pp.

Burt, Jeffrey A. "Joint Venture Experience: Observations on the Business and Legal Challenges", *22 NEW YORK UNIVERSITY JOURNAL OF INTERNATIONAL LAW AND POLITICS* 435-445 (1990).

Carey, Sarah C. "The Process of Negotiating a Joint Venture in the USSR: Questions Resolved and Unresolved", *10 INTERNATIONAL QUARTERLY* 42-52 (1989).

Carpenter, Russell H., Jr. "Soviet Joint Enterprises with Capitalist Firms and Other Joint Ventures between East and West: The Western Point of View", 222 *RECUEIL DES COURS. HAGUE ACADEMY OF INTERNATIONAL LAW* 365-421 (1990 III).

Dean, Richard N. "Considering Business Opportunities in the Soviet Union in the 1990s", in *LEGAL ASPECTS OF TRADE AND INVESTMENT IN THE SOVIET UNION AND EASTERN EUROPE.* Commercial Law and Practice Course Handbook Series No. 549. (New York: Practising Law Institute, 1990), pp. 95-116.

Dean, Richard N. "Considering Business Opportunities in the Soviet Union in the 1990s", 26 *VANDERBILT JOURNAL OF TRANSNATIONAL LAW* 325-343 (1991). Reprinted in *PRIVATE INVESTMENTS ABROAD—PROBLEMS AND SOLUTIONS IN INTERNATIONAL BUSINESS IN 1991* (The Southwestern Legal Foundation) (New York: Matthew Bender, 1992), Chapter 11 (24 pp.).

☆Faminsky, Igor P., and Alexander Naumov. "A Description of Soviet Laws and Policies on Joint Ventures", in *BEHIND THE FACTORY WALLS: DECISION MAKING IN SOVIET AND US ENTERPRISES,* edited by Paul R. Lawrence and Charalambos A. Vlachoutsicos (Boston: Harvard Business School Press, 1990), pp. 301-306.

George, Arthur L., and Thomas A. O'Donnell. "United States-Soviet Joint Ventures", 20 *TAX MANAGEMENT INTERNATIONAL JOURNAL* 73-85 and 99-114 (1991).

Geron, Leonard. *JOINT VENTURES IN THE USSR: DATA BASE 1991 EDITION,* 2d ed. Oxford: D.G. Oxford Consultants, 1991. 432 pp.

FOREIGN TRADE—Joint Ventures, *continued*

Giuliani, Federico. "Recent Trends in Soviet Legislation: Joint Ventures, Ownership, and Leasing", 2 *INTERNATIONAL COMPANY AND COMMERCIAL LAW REVIEW* 202-206 (1991).

Hazard, John N. "Opportunities and Problems for Joint Ventures in Soviet Law", 22 *NEW YORK UNIVERSITY JOURNAL OF INTERNATIONAL LAW AND POLITICS* 407-410 (1990).

Herlach, Mark D., and Lucille A. Barale, eds. *JOINT VENTURES IN EASTERN EUROPE*. London: Euromoney Publications PLC, 1990. xi, 183 pp.

Hertzfeld, Jeffrey M. "Joint Ventures: Saving the Soviets from Perestroika", 69 *HARVARD BUSINESS REVIEW* No. 1, 80-91 (January-February 1991).

Hobér, Kaj. "Joint Ventures with the Soviet Union", 6 *INTERNATIONAL FINANCIAL LAW REVIEW* 15-18 (1987). Reprinted in *INVESTING IN REFORM: DOING BUSINESS IN A CHANGING SOVIET UNION,* edited by Michael P. Claudon and Tamar L. Gutner, eds. (New York: New York University Press, 1991), pp. 99-137.

Houri, Nicole M. "Joint Venture Law in the Soviet Union" (Note), 11 *NEW YORK LAW SCHOOL JOURNAL OF INTERNATIONAL AND COMPARATIVE LAW* 499-518 (1990).

JOINT VENTURE ACCOUNTING IN THE USSR: DIRECTION FOR CHANGE. New York: United Nations, 1990. v, 46 pp. (United Nations Centre on Transnational Corporations Advisory Studies, Series B, No. 7; UN Classification No. St/CTC/SER.B/7; UN Sales No. E.90.II.A.26).

☆Katkov, Alexander L. "Can Joint Ventures Help to Create a Market Economy in the Soviet Union", in *THE EMERGING RUSSIAN BEAR: INTEGRATING THE SOVIET UNION INTO THE WORLD ECONOMY*, edited by Josef C. Brada and Michael P. Claudon (New York: New York University Press, 1991), pp. 143-163.

Kavass, Igor I. "Aspects of Soviet Law on Joint Ventures, Foreign Trade, and Investment: A Bibliographic Survey of Current Literature in English", 24 *VANDERBILT JOURNAL OF TRANSNATIONAL LAW* 415-448 (1991).

Kavass, Igor I., and Andrew T. Griffin. "Joint Ventures in the Soviet Union: A Review of Current Literature in English", 18 *INTERNATIONAL JOURNAL OF LEGAL INFORMATION* 177-204 (1990).

FOREIGN TRADE—Joint Ventures, *continued*

LEGAL ASPECTS OF TRADE AND INVESTMENT IN THE SOVIET UNION AND EASTERN EUROPE. Commercial Law and Practice Course Handbook Series No. 549. New York: Practising Law Institute, 1990. 1036 pp.

Lewenz, Susan M.H. "Introduction Guide to Joint Ventures in the Soviet Union", in *LEGAL ASPECTS OF TRADE AND INVESTMENT IN THE SOVIET UNION AND EASTERN EUROPE* (New York: Practising Law Institute, 1990), pp. 11-37.

Madara, Eugene E. "A Case Study: The Soviet Union", in *LEGAL ASPECTS OF TRADE AND INVESTMENT IN THE SOVIET UNION AND EASTERN EUROPE* (New York: Practising Law Institute, 1990), pp. 75-94.

Maggs, Peter B. "Facilitating U.S.-Soviet Joint Ventures through Legislative Reform", in *THE EMERGING RUSSIAN BEAR: INTEGRATING THE SOVIET UNION INTO THE WORLD ECONOMY*, edited by Josef C. Brada and Michael P. Claudon (New York: New York University Press, 1991), pp. 129-141.

Maisto, G. "Double Taxation Treaty Italy-USSR with Particular Reference to Joint Ventures", 29 *EUROPEAN TAXATION* 113-119 (1989).

☆Mamiofa, Iosif E. "Industrial Property Rights of Joint Ventures in the Soviet Union", 2 *INTERNATIONAL COMPANY AND COMMERCIAL LAW REVIEW* 242-246 (1991).

☆Maslov, Alexander. "Bankrolling Soviet Joint Ventures", *4 EUROPEAN AFFAIRS* No. 3, 59-65 (Autumn 1990).

☆Mozolin, Viktor P. "The Positive Influence of Legal Reform on Soviet-U.S. Joint Ventures", in *THE EMERGING BEAR: INTEGRATING THE SOVIET UNION INTO THE WORLD ECONOMY*, edited by Josef C. Brada and Michael P. Claudon (New York: New York University Press, 1991), pp. 115-127.

Newcity, Michael. "Tax Issues in Soviet Joint Ventures", 25 *TEXAS INTERNATIONAL LAW JOURNAL* 163-207 (1990).

Nigh, Douglas, Peter Walters, and James A. Kuhlman. "US-USSR Joint Ventures: An Examination of the Early Entrants", 25 *COLUMBIA JOURNAL OF WORLD BUSINESS* No. 4, 20-27 (Winter 1990).

FOREIGN TRADE—Joint Ventures, *continued*

☆Orlov, Lev N. "Soviet Joint Enterprises with Capitalist Firms and Other Joint Ventures between East and West", 221 *RECUEIL DES COURS. HAGUE ACADEMY OF INTERNATIONAL LAW* 371-414 (1990-II).

☆Portnoy, Mikhail A. "Major Financial Obstacles to the Formation and Operation of Joint Ventures", in *THE EMERGING RUSSIAN BEAR: INTEGRATING THE SOVIET UNION INTO THE WORLD ECONOMY*, edited by Josef C. Brada and Michael P. Claudon (New York: New York University Press, 1991), pp. 165-174.

☆Ranenko, V., and A. Soloviev. "Experiences and Future Outlook of East-West Joint Ventures in the Soviet Union", in *EAST-WEST JOINT VENTURES: THE NEW BUSINESS ENVIRONMENT*, edited by Evka Razvigorova and Gottfried Wolf-Laudon (Cambridge, MA, and Oxford, England: Basil Blackwell, 1991), pp. 141-162.

Razvigorova, Evka, and Gottfried Wolf-Laudon. *EAST-WEST JOINT VENTURES: THE NEW BUSINESS ENVIRONMENT*. Cambridge, MA, and Oxford, England: Basil Blackwell, 1991. xviii, 327 pp.

Rosten, Keith A. "Soviet-U.S. Joint Ventures: Problems, Challenges, and Opportunities", in *THE EMERGING RUSSIAN BEAR: INTEGRATING THE SOVIET UNION INTO THE WORLD ECONOMY*, edited by Josef C. Brada and Michael P. Claudon (New York: New York University Press, 1991), pp. 87-113.

☆Roulko, Eugeniy T. "Soviet Joint Enterprise Legislation", 5 *FLORIDA INTERNATIONAL LAW JOURNAL* 221-234 (1990).

Sherr, Alan B., ed. *INTERNATIONAL JOINT VENTURES: SOVIET AND WESTERN PERSPECTIVES*. New York: Quorum Books, 1991. 351 pp.

Sherr, Alan B., et al. *INTERNATIONAL JOINT VENTURES: SOVIET AND WESTERN PERSPECTIVES*. New York: Quorum Books, 1991. xv, 351 pp. (A project of the Center for Foreign Policy Development at Brown University, the Institute for World Economy and International Relations of the USSR Academy of Sciences and the All-Union Research Institute for Foreign Economic Relations, State Foreign Economies Commission of the USSR Council of Ministers).

Sneider, Carolyn M. "The Slepak Principles Act and Soviet Union-United States Joint Ventures: Profits or People?" (Note), 13 *LOYOLA OF LOS ANGELES INTERNATIONAL AND COMPARATIVE LAW JOURNAL* 365-392 (1990).

FOREIGN TRADE—Joint Ventures, *continued*

"Symposium on U.S.-Soviet Military and Economic Relations", 22 *NEW YORK UNIVERSITY JOURNAL OF INTERNATIONAL LAW AND POLITICS* 373-595 (1990).

Theroux, Eugene, and Arthur L. George. *JOINT VENTURES IN THE SOVIET UNION: LAW AND PRACTICE.* Washington, DC: Baker & McKenzie, 1991. 165 pp.

Toop, R. Scott. "Doing Business in the Soviet Union: A Case Study", in *LEGAL ASPECTS OF TRADE AND INVESTMENT IN THE SOVIET UNION AND EASTERN EUROPE* (New York: Practising Law Institute, 1990), pp. 57-74.

Vecchio, Mark S. "Soviet Joint Ventures: Keeping an Eye on the Goalposts", 9 *INTERNATIONAL FINANCIAL LAW REVIEW* No. 4, 37-38 (April 1990).

Vlachoutsicos, Charalambos A. "Aspects of Forming Joint Ventures in the USSR—Comments for the Western Investor", in *BEHIND THE FACTORY WALLS: DECISION MAKING IN SOVIET AND US ENTERPRISES,* edited by Paul R. Lawrence and Charalambos A. Vlachoutsicos (Boston: Harvard Business School Press, 1990), pp. 307-319.

Policy and Relations

☆Bardina, Marina P. "The New Shape in International Economic Relations and the Foreign Trade Reforms in the USSR", in *FROM COEXISTENCE TO COOPERATION: INTERNATIONAL LAW AND ORGANIZATION IN THE POST-COLD WAR ERA*, edited by Edward McWhinney, et al. (Dordrecht, The Netherlands: Martinus Nijhoff Publishers, 1991), pp. 211-240.

Berman, Harold J. "Doing Business in the Soviet Union: The Legal Environment", in *LEGAL ASPECTS OF TRADE AND INVESTMENT IN THE SOVIET UNION AND EASTERN EUROPE* (New York: Practising Law Institute, 1990), pp. 39-49.

☆Bogomolov, Oleg T. "Integration of the Soviet Union and Eastern Europe into the World Economy", in *REFORMS IN FOREIGN ECONOMIC RELATIONS OF EASTERN EUROPE AND THE SOVIET UNION*, edited by Michael Kaser and Aleksandar M. Vacic (New York: United Nations, 1991), pp. 162-166.

☆Boguslavskii, Mark M. "The Legal Status of Free Economic Zones in the USSR", 29 *SOVIET LAW AND GOVERNMENT* 78-91 (1991).

FOREIGN TRADE—Policy and Relations, *continued*

Brabant, Jozef M. van, ed. *ECONOMIC REFORMS IN CENTRALLY PLANNED ECONOMIES AND THEIR IMPACT ON THE GLOBAL ECONOMY.* New York: United Nations, 1990 (Published by the United Nations Department of International Economic and Social Affairs as *JOURNAL OF DEVELOPMENT PLANNING* No. 20. UN Classification No. ST/ESA/216; UN Sales No. e. 90. II. A.9).

☆Bykov, Aleksandr N. "Institutional Framework of Foreign Trade Relations of the Soviet Union", in *REFORMS IN FOREIGN ECONOMIC RELATIONS OF EASTERN EUROPE AND THE SOVIET UNION,* edited by Michael Kaser and Aleksandar M. Vacic (New York: United Nations, 1991), pp. 37-44.

Claudon, Michael P., and Tamar L. Gutner, eds. *INVESTING IN REFORM: DOING BUSINESS IN A CHANGING SOVIET UNION.* New York: New York University Press, 1991. xix, 279 pp.

Friedlaender, Michael, ed. *FOREIGN TRADE IN EASTERN EUROPE AND THE SOVIET UNION.* Boulder, CO; San Francisco; London: Westview Press, 1990. xiii, 241 pp. (Published in cooperation with the Vienna Institute for Comparative Economic Studies as its "Yearbook II").

Garbrisch, Hubert. "Finnish-Soviet Economic Relations", in *FOREIGN TRADE IN EASTERN EUROPE AND THE SOVIET UNION,* edited by Michael Friedlaender (Boulder, CO; San Francisco; London: Westview Press, 1990), pp. 117-126.

Geron, Leonard. *SOVIET FOREIGN ECONOMIC POLICY UNDER PERESTROIKA.* London: The Royal Institute of International Affairs; New York: Council on Foreign Relations Press, 1990. x, 126 pp. (Chatham House Papers).

Havlik, Peter. "Soviet Perestroika and Foreign Trade", in *FOREIGN TRADE IN EASTERN EUROPE AND THE SOVIET UNION,* edited by Michael Friedlaender (Boulder, CO; San Francisco; London: Westview Press, 1990), pp. 7-18.

Hobér, Kaj. "Recent Trends in Foreign Trade and Investment". A paper presented at the Geonomics Institute Seminar, Middlebury, Vermont, May 10-13, 1991. 43 + 5 pp. Also published in *INVESTING IN REFORM: DOING BUSINESS IN A CHANGING SOVIET UNION,* edited by Michael P. Claudon and Tamar L. Gutner (New York: New York University Press, 1991).

FOREIGN TRADE—Policy and Relations, *continued*

Kaser, Michael, and Aleksandar M. Vacic, eds. *REFORMS IN FOREIGN ECONOMIC RELATIONS OF EASTERN EUROPE AND THE SOVIET UNION.* New York: United Nations, 1991. xii, 202 pp. (United Nations Publications Sales No. E.91.II.E.5.)

Kolkey, Daniel M. "International Arbitration in East-West Trade", 12 *WHITTIER LAW REVIEW* 245-258 (1991).

☆Matyukhin, Georgy. "The Union of Soviet Socialist Republics and Other Socialist Countries in the International Monetary and Financial System", in *ECONOMIC REFORMS IN CENTRALLY PLANNED ECONOMIES AND THEIR IMPACT ON THE GLOBAL ECONOMY*, edited by Jozef M. van Brabant (New York: United Nations, 1990), pp. 269-278. (Published by the United Nations Department of International Economic and Social Affairs as *JOURNAL OF DEVELOPMENT PLANNING* No. 20; UN Classification No. ST/ESA/216; UN Sales No. e. 90. II. A.9.)

Newburg, Andre W.G. "U.S.-Soviet Trade Agreement and Investment Protection Treaties", 11 *NEW YORK LAW SCHOOL JOURNAL OF INTERNATIONAL AND COMPARATIVE LAW* No. 3, 447-451 (1990).

"Normalization of the U.S.-Soviet Trade Relations", 46 *THE RECORD OF THE ASSOCIATION OF THE BAR OF THE CITY OF NEW YORK* 104-128 (1991).

Obláth, Gábor, and Peter Pete. "Mechanism and Institutional System of the Finnish-Soviet Economic Relations", in *FOREIGN TRADE IN EASTERN EUROPE AND THE SOVIET UNION,* edited by Michael Friedlaender (Boulder, CO; San Francisco; London: Westview Press, 1990), pp. 95-115.

Osakwe, Christopher. "The Harmonization of Soviet and EEC Trade Law in Anticipation of 1992", 12 *WHITTIER LAW REVIEW* 151-157 (1991).

Pettibone, Peter J. "What Congress and the Administration Can Do to Improve Soviet-U.S. Trade Relations", in *THE EMERGING RUSSIAN BEAR: INTEGRATING THE SOVIET UNION INTO THE WORLD ECONOMY*, edited by Josef C. Brada and Michael P. Claudon (New York: New York University Press, 1991), pp. 51-61.

FOREIGN TRADE—Policy and Relations, *continued*

☆Pichugin, Boris M. "Economic Relations of the Soviet Union with Market Economies", in *REFORMS IN FOREIGN ECONOMIC RELATIONS OF EASTERN EUROPE AND THE SOVIET UNION,* edited by Michael Kaser and Aleksandar M. Vacic (New York: United Nations, 1991), pp. 100-108.

☆Popov, Vladimir. "Soviet Economic Reforms: Missed Opportunities and Remaining Hopes". A Paper presented at the Geonomics Institute Seminar, Middleburg, Vermont, May 10-13, 1991. 30 ll.

Rácz, Margit, and Sándor Richter. "The Mechanism of Hungarian-Soviet Economic Relations", in *FOREIGN TRADE IN EASTERN EUROPE AND THE SOVIET UNION*, edited by Michael Friedlaender (Boulder, CO; San Francisco; London: Westview Press, 1990), pp. 83-94.

Radon, Jenik. "The Baltics: The Premier European Gateway to the Soviet Union". A Paper presented at the Geonomics Institute Seminar, Middleburg, Vermont, May 10-13, 1991. 37 pp. Reprinted in *INVESTING IN REFORM: DOING BUSINESS IN A CHANGING SOVIET UNION*, edited by Michael P. Claudon and Tamar L. Gutner (New York: New York University Press, 1991), pp. 207-231.

Richter, Sándor. "Four Small Countries' Relations with the Soviet Union", in *FOREIGN TRADE IN EASTERN EUROPE AND THE SOVIET UNION*, edited by Michael Friedlaender (Boulder, CO; San Francisco; London: Westview Press, 1990), pp. 63-82.

Steckelman, Peter D. "Advancing Soviet-American Trade: The Legal Steps Necessary to Further Economic Relations" (Note), 11 *NEW YORK LAW SCHOOL JOURNAL OF INTERNATIONAL AND COMPARATIVE LAW* 463-481 (1990).

Stephan, Paul B., III. "The Restructuring of Soviet Commercial Law and Its Impact on International Business Transactions", 24 *GEORGE WASHINGTON JOURNAL OF INTERNATIONAL LAW AND ECONOMICS* 89-102 (1990).

Yuan, Cheng. *EAST-WEST TRADE: CHANGING PATTERNS IN CHINESE FOREIGN TRADE LAW AND INSTITUTIONS.* New York: Oceana Publications, Inc., 1991. xxvi, 357 pp.

FOREIGN TRADE, *continued*

Practice and "How To"

Barbanel, Jack A., and Lynda L. Maillet. *BUSINESS IN THE SOVIET UNION: A PRIMER AND OVERVIEW.* Ardsley-on-Hudson, NY: Transnational Juris Publications, Inc., 1991. xxiv, 287 pp.

Birenbaum, David E., and Dimitri P. Racklin. *BUSINESS VENTURES IN EASTERN EUROPE AND THE SOVIET UNION: THE EMERGING LEGAL FRAMEWORK FOR FOREIGN INVESTMENT.* Englewood Cliffs, NJ: Prentice Hall, 1990- . 2 volumes, looseleaf.

Blueger, Valentin. "Observations of a Latvian Practitioner", 24 *VANDERBILT JOURNAL OF TRANSNATIONAL LAW* 389-393 (1991).

Carr, Josephine. "The Decline and Fall of the Soviet Empire", 10 *INTERNATIONAL FINANCIAL LAW REVEIW* No. 12, 14-20 (December 1991).

THE CUSTOMS CODE OF THE USSR AND THE LAW ON THE CUSTOMS TARIFF OF THE USSR: IN FORCE AS OF 1 JULY, 1991. Staines, England: Intershelf Ltd., 1991. xxvi, 210 pp.

Dean, Richard N. "Considering Business Opportunities in the Soviet Union in the 1990s", in *LEGAL ASPECTS OF TRADE AND INVESTMENT IN THE SOVIET UNION AND EASTERN EUROPE.* Commercial Law and Practice Course Handbook Series No. 549. (New York: Practising Law Institute, 1990), pp. 95-116.

Dean, Richard N. "Considering Business Opportunities in the Soviet Union in the 1990s". 26 *VANDERBILT JOURNAL OF TRANSNATIONAL LAW* 325-343 (1991). Reprinted in *PRIVATE INVESTMENTS ABROAD—PROBLEMS AND SOLUTIONS IN INTERNATIONAL BUSINESS IN 1991* (The Southwestern Legal Foundation) (New York: Matthew Bender, 1992), Chapter 11 (24 pp.).

Dean, Richard N. "Practicing Law and Doing Business in the Soviet Union", 11 *NEW YORK LAW SCHOOL JOURNAL OF INTERNATIONAL AND COMPARATIVE LAW* No. 3, 439-446 (1990).

DOING BUSINESS IN EASTERN EUROPE AND THE SOVIET UNION: COURSE MANUAL. Washington, DC: Federal Publications, 1990. 1 vol., looseleaf.

DOING BUSINESS IN THE UNION OF SOVIET SOCIALIST REPUBLICS. New York, Moscow, London: Price Waterhouse, 1991. xii, 134 pp.

FOREIGN TRADE—Practice and "How To", *continued*

DOING BUSINESS IN THE USSR. London: Ernst & Whinney (Ernst and Young), 1988. 67 pp.

DOING BUSINESS WITH THE SOVIET UNION. St. Paul, MN: Advanced Legal Education, Hamline University School of Law, 1991. 369 pp.

George, Arthur L., and Thomas A. O'Donnell. *BUSINESS OPERATIONS IN THE U.S.S.R.* Washington, DC: Tax Management, Inc., 1991 (Tax Management, Foreign Income Portfolios, 990).

Glick, Steven M., and Alexei A. Klishin. "Doing Business in the U.S.S.R.: Welcome to the 'New Antipodes'", 9 *INTERNATIONAL FINANCIAL LAW REVIEW* No. 12, 28-31 (December 1990).

Hines, Jonathan H. "Dispute Resolution and Choice of Law in United States-Soviet Trade", in *LEGAL ASPECTS OF TRADE AND INVESTMENT IN THE SOVIET UNION AND EASTERN EUROPE 1990* (New York: Practising Law Institute, 1990), pp. 117-187.

LEGAL ASPECTS OF TRADE AND INVESTMENT IN THE SOVIET UNION AND EASTERN EUROPE. Commercial Law and Practice Course Handbook Series No. 549. New York: Practising Law Institute, 1990. 1036 pp.

LEGAL AND PRACTICAL ASPECTS OF DOING BUSINESS IN THE SOVIET REPUBLICS. Commercial Law and Practice Course Handbook Series No. 604. New York: Practising Law Institute, 1992. 500 pp.

Levin, Martin P. "The Challenge of Doing Business in the Soviet Union", 11 *NEW YORK LAW SCHOOL JOURNAL OF INTERNATIONAL AND COMPARATIVE LAW* No. 3, 453-456 (1990).

Madara, Eugene E. "A Case Study: The Soviet Union", in *LEGAL ASPECTS OF TRADE AND INVESTMENT IN THE SOVIET UNION AND EASTERN EUROPE* (New York: Practising Law Institute, 1990), pp. 75-94.

Maggs, Peter B. "Ownership Rights". A Paper presented at the Geonomics Institute Seminar, Middleburg, Vermont, May 10-13, 1991. 20 pp. Reprinted in *INVESTING IN REFORM: DOING BUSINESS IN A CHANGING SOVIET UNION,* edited by Michael P. Claudon and Tamar L. Gutner (New York: New York University Press, 1991), pp. 155-169.

FOREIGN TRADE—Practice and "How To", *continued*

Mears, H. Michael. "Structural Challenges Facing the Republics", in *LEGAL AND PRACTICAL ASPECTS OF DOING BUSINESS IN THE SOVIET REPUBLICS* (New York: Practising Law Institute, 1992), pp. 15-25.

Nightingale, Christopher, and Stephen Tupper. *RUSSIAN AND SOVIET ECONOMIC CHANGE: THE NEW LAW.* London: Longman, 1991. 100 pp.

Osakwe, Christopher. *SOVIET BUSINESS LAW: INSTITUTIONS, PRINCIPLES, AND PROCESSES.* Salem, NH: Butterworth Legal Publishers, 1991. 2 Volumes, looseleaf, misc. pag.

Shadbolt, R.A. "Contracting for Construction Projects with the U.S.S.R.", 7 *INTERNATIONAL CONSTRUCTION LAW REVIEW* 379-385 (1990).

Sheedy, John F., and Richard N. Dean. "Gaining a Foothold in the Soviet Market: How to Establish a Representative Office", *25 INTERNATIONAL LAWYER* 103-125 (1991).

"Third Annual Ernst C. Stiefel Symposium: Practicing Law and Doing Business in the Soviet Union", 11 *NEW YORK LAW SCHOOL JOURNAL OF INTERNATIONAL AND COMPARATIVE LAW* No. 3, 433-518 (1990).

Timmermans, Wim A. "Union of Soviet Socialist Republics", in *GUIDE TO THE COMMERCIAL AND CORPORATE LAW OF EASTERN EUROPE*, edited by David Winter (Bicester, Oxfordshire, England: CCH Editions Limited, 1991), pp. 63-122.

Welt, Leo G.B. "Unconventional Forms of Financing: Buy-Back/Compensation/Barter", "Symposium on U.S.-Soviet Military and Economic Relations", *22 NEW YORK UNIVERSITY JOURNAL OF INTERNATIONAL LAW AND POLITICS* 461-473 (1990).

Winter, David, ed. *GUIDE TO THE COMMERCIAL AND CORPORATE LAW OF EASTERN EUROPE.* Bicester, Oxfordshire, England: CCH Editions Limited, 1991. xiv, 164 pp.

Zimbler, Brian L. "Soviet Foreign Investment Laws and Practices, 1987-1990: A Practicioner's Perspective", 4 *TRANSNATIONAL LAWYER* 85-122 (1991).

FOREIGN TRADE, *continued*

Technology Transfers

Apostolakis, Bobby E. "Technology Transfer to USSR: Exaggerations, Myths, or Utopia?", 37 *RIVISTA INTERNAZIONALE DI SCIENZE ECONOMICHE E COMMERCIALI* 289-306 (1990).

☆Boguslavskii[y], Mark M., and Olga V. Vorobyova. "Transfer of Technology: Recent Developments", in *PERESTROIKA AND INTERNATIONAL LAW: CURRENT ANGLO-SOVIET APPROACHES TO INTERNATIONAL LAW,* edited by Anthony Carty and Gennady Danilenko (Edinburgh: Edinburg University Press, 1990), pp. 147-157.

Butler, William E. "Soviet Foreign Trade Reform and Technology Transfer", in *LAW AND POLITICS OF WEST-EAST TECHNOLOGY TRANSFER,* edited by Hiroshi Oda (Dordrecht/Boston/London: Martinus Nijhoff/Graham & Trotman, 1991), pp. 211-231.

Feldbrugge, F.J.M. "West-East Technology Transfer in the Context of Perestroika", in *LAW AND POLITICS OF WEST-EAST TECHNOLOGY TRANSFER,* edited by Hiroshi Oda (Dordrecht/Boston/London: Martinus Nijhoff/Graham & Trotman, 1991), pp. 265-269.

Frenkel, William G., and Jeffrey Sperber. "From Borscht to Bits: Transfer of Technology and Industrial Property in the Soviet Union", 4 *DE PAUL BUSINESS LAW JOURNAL* 3-48 (1991).

Hoya, Thomas W. "U.S. Governmental Controls over Technology Exports with Particular Reference to the Soviet Union", in *LAW AND POLITICS OF WEST-EAST TECHNOLOGY TRANSFER,* edited by Hiroshi Oda (Dordrecht/Boston/London: Martinus Nijhoff/Graham & Trotman, 1991), pp. 65-89.

Oda, Hiroshi. *LAW AND POLITICS OF WEST-EAST TECHNOLOGY TRANSFER.* Dordrecht/Boston/London: Martinus Nijhoff/Graham & Trotman, 1991. viii, 265 pp.

Shillinglaw, Thomas J. "Technology Transfer Transactions with Soviet and Eastern European Enterprises: Experience in USA Companies", in *LEGAL ASPECTS OF TRADE AND INVESTMENT IN THE SOVIET UNION AND EASTERN EUROPE* (New York: Practising Law Institute, 1990), pp. 205-233.

Free Economic Zones

See Foreign Trade

Freedom of Speech

See Censorship *and* Human Rights

Future of the USSR

Aurbach, Laurence J., ed. *BEYOND PERESTROIKA: OPTIONS FOR A NEW SOVIET UNION*. Chicago: American Bar Association, Section of Urban, State, and Local Government Law, 1991. iv, 40 pp.

Commission on Security and Cooperation in Europe. *REFERENDUM IN THE SOVIET UNION. A COMPENDIUM OF REPORTS ON THE MARCH 17, 1991 REFERENDUM ON THE FUTURE OF THE USSR*. Compiled by the Staff of the Commission on Security and Cooperation in Europe. Washington: U.S. Government Printing Office, 1991. viii, 46 pp.

Gardner, Richard N. "The Triple Crisis of the Soviet Union Today", 11 *NEW YORK LAW SCHOOL JOURNAL OF INTERNATIONAL AND COMPARATIVE LAW* 435-437 (1990).

Hobér, Kaj. "Recent Trends in Foreign Trade and Investment". A paper presented at the Geonomics Institute Seminar, Middlebury, Vermont, May 10-13, 1991. 43 + 5 pp. Also published in *INVESTING IN REFORM: DOING BUSINESS IN A CHANGING SOVIET UNION*, edited by Michael P. Claudon and Tamar L. Gutner (New York: New York University Press, 1991).

Jones, Anthony, Walter D. Connor, and David E. Powell, eds. *SOVIET SOCIAL PROBLEMS*. Boulder, CO; San Francisco; Oxford: Westview Press, 1991. ix, 337 pp.

Motyl, Alexander J. "Russian Hegemony and Non-Russian Insecurity: Foreign Policy Dilemmas of the USSR's Successor States", 5 *HARRIMAN INSTITUTE FORUM* No. 4, 1-11 (December 1991).

Solzhenitzyn, Aleksandr. *REBUILDING RUSSIA: REFLECTIONS AND TENTATIVE PROPOSALS*. New York: Farrer, Straus and Giroux, 1991. 119 pp.

General Studies

Subheadings:
General Information on Soviet Union
Impressions of Soviet Law
Law versus Reality
Policy and Development
Research on Soviet Law
Surveys of Soviet Law

General Information on Soviet Union

Barbanel, Jack A., and Lynda L. Maillet. *BUSINESS IN THE SOVIET UNION: A PRIMER AND OVERVIEW.* Ardsley-on-Hudson, NY: Transnational Juris Publications, Inc., 1991. xxiv, 287 pp.

Cole Corette & Arbutyn. "Legal and Practical Aspects of Doing Business in the Soviet Republics", in *LEGAL AND PRACTICAL ASPECTS OF DOING BUSINESS IN THE SOVIET REPUBLICS* (New York: Practising Law Institute, 1992), pp. 71-102.

Doder, Dusko, and Louise Branson. *GORBACHEV: HERETIC IN THE KREMLIN.* New York: Viking, 1990. x, 450 pp.

DOING BUSINESS IN THE UNION OF SOVIET SOCIALIST REPUBLICS. New York, Moscow, London: Price Waterhouse, 1991. xii, 134 pp.

The Federal Institute for Soviet and International Studies. *THE SOVIET UNION, 1988-1989: PERESTROIKA IN CRISIS?* Boulder, CO: Westview Press, 1990. xv, 410 pp.

Hosking, Geoffrey. *THE AWAKENING OF THE SOVIET UNION.* Cambridge: Harvard University Press, 1990. ix, 182 pp.

Jones, Anthony, and David E. Powell, eds. *SOVIET UPDATE, 1989-1990.* Boulder, CO: Westview Press, 1991. vii, 152 pp.

Smith, Hedrick. *THE NEW RUSSIANS.* New York: Random House, 1990. xxxi, 621 pp. Revised paperbound edition: New York: Avon Books, 1991. xxxi, 734 pp.

Soros, George. *A PERSPECTIVE ON THE COLLAPSE OF THE SOVIET SYSTEM.* Baltimore: The Paul H. Nitze School for Advanced International Studies, The John Hopkins University, 1990. 11 pp.

GENERAL STUDIES—General Information on Soviet Union, *continued*

Spring, D.W., ed. *THE IMPACT OF GORBACHEV: THE FIRST PHASE, 1985-1990.* London and New York: Pinter Publishers, 1991. ix, 244 pp.

Impressions of Soviet Law

Berman, Harold J. "Counter-Revolution or Transition: A Response to Human Rights and the Emergence of the State of the Rule of Law in the USSR", 40 *EMORY LAW JOURNAL* 903-909 (1991).

Law versus Reality

☆Feofanov, Iurii. "A Return to Origins: Reflections on Power and Law", 29 *SOVIET LAW AND GOVERNMENT* No. 3, 15-52 (Winter 1990-91).

Solomon, Peter H., Jr. "Legality in Soviet Political Culture: A Perspective on Gorbachev's Reforms", in *STALINISM: ITS NATURE AND AFTERMATH. ESSAYS IN HONOUR OF MOSHE LEWIN*, edited by Nick Lampert and Gabor T. Rittersporn (Armonk, NY: M.E. Sharpe, Inc., 1992), pp. 260-287.

Policy and Development

Hazard, John N. "Soviet Law Takes a Fresh Breath", 5 *HARRIMAN INSTITUTE FORUM* No. 6 (February 1992). 13 pp.

Lampert, Nick, and Gabor T. Rittersporn. *STALINISM: ITS NATURE AND AFTERMATH. ESSAYS IN HONOUR OF MOSHE LEWIN.* Armonk, NY: M.E. Sharpe, Inc., 1992. xv, 291 pp.

McCauley, Martin, ed. *GORBACHEV AND PERESTROIKA*. New York: St. Martin's Press, 1990. xii, 222 pp.

☆Sheremet, Konstantin. "Law and Social Change in the USSR of the 1990s", 27 *SOCIETY* 90-97 (1990).

☆Yakovlev, Alexander M. "Transforming the Soviet Union into a Rule of Law Democracy: A Report from the Front Lines", 46 *THE RECORD OF THE ASSOCIATION OF THE BAR OF THE CITY OF NEW YORK* 129-148 (1991).

GENERAL STUDIES, *continued*

Research on Soviet Law

Butler, William E. ed. *PERESTROIKA AND THE RULE OF LAW: ANGLO-AMERICAN AND SOVIET PERSPECTIVES*. London: I.B. Tauris & Co., Ltd., 1991. 199 pp.

Huskey, Eugene. "A Framework for the Analysis of Soviet Law", 50 *RUSSIAN REVIEW* 53-70 (1991).

Surveys of Soviet Law

☆Alexeyev, Sergei. *LAW AND LEGAL CULTURE IN SOVIET SOCIETY*. Moscow: Progress Publishers, 1991. 214 pp.

Barry, Donald B. "State and Social Structure: Part I of the Sobranie", in *THE SOVIET SOBRANIE OF LAWS*, edited by Richard M. Buxbaum and Kathryn Hendley (Berkeley, CA: University of California at Berkeley, 1991), pp. 26-44.

Butler, William E. "Perestroika and the Rule of Law", in *PERESTROIKA AND THE RULE OF LAW: ANGLO-AMERICAN AND SOVIET PERSPECTIVES,* edited by William E. Butler (London: I.B. Tauris & Co., Ltd., 1991), pp. 7-21.

Butler, William E. "The Rule of Law and the Legal System", in *DEVELOPMENTS IN SOVIET POLITICS*, edited by Stephen White, Alex Pravda and Zvi Gitelman (Durham, NC: Duke University Press, 1990), pp. 104-119.

Buxbaum, Richard M., and Kathryn Hendley, eds. *THE SOVIET SOBRANIE OF LAWS*. Berkeley, CA: University of California at Berkeley, 1991. xii, 226 pp. (Research Series No. 78).

Lampert, Nick. "The Socialist Legal State", in *GORBACHEV AND PERESTROIKA*, edited by Martin McCauley (New York: St. Martin's Press, 1990), pp. 116-134.

Loeber, Dietrich André. "The Sobranie—A Challenge to Glasnost", in *THE SOVIET SOBRANIE OF LAWS*, edited by Richard M. Buxbaum and Kathryn Hendley (Berkeley, CA: University of California at Berkeley, 1991), pp. 1-25.

Osakwe, Christopher. *SOVIET BUSINESS LAW: INSTITUTIONS, PRINCIPLES, AND PROCESSES*. Salem, NH: Butterworth Legal Publishers, 1991. 2 Volumes, looseleaf, misc. pag.

Georgia

Commission on Security and Cooperation in Europe. *ELECTIONS IN THE BALTIC STATES AND SOVIET REPUBLICS: A COMPENDIUM OF REPORTS ON PARLIAMENTARY ELECTIONS HELD IN 1990*. Compiled by the Staff of the Commission on Security and Cooperation in Europe. Washington: U.S. Government Printing Office, 1990. x, 188 pp.

Suny, Ronald G. "Transcaucasia: Cultural Cohesion and Ethnic Revival in a Multinational Society", in *THE NATIONALITIES FACTOR IN SOVIET POLITICS AND SOCIETY*, edited by Lubomyr Hajda and Mark Beissinger. Boulder, CO: Westview Press, 1990, pp. 228-252.

Germans

Buchsweiler, Meir. *A COLLECTION OF SOVIET DOCUMENTS CONCERNING GERMANS IN THE USSR*. Jerusalem: The Hebrew University of Jerusalem, The Marjorie Mayrock Center for Soviet and East European Research, 1991. 26 pp. (Research Paper No. 73).

Heitman, Sidney. "Soviet Emigration Policies toward Germans and Armenians", in *SOVIET NATIONALITY POLICIES: RULING ETHNIC GROUPS IN THE USSR*, edited by Henry R. Huttenbach (London: Mansell Publishing Limited, 1990), pp. 235-259.

Glasnost

Editorial Note: Glasnost has become a much-used "catchword" in popular writing, and is included in the titles of many works which have only a vague connection with the concept of Glasnost. Such publications have been omitted from the following list.

Berkowitz, Julie S. "A Look into Glasnost's Impact on the Soviet Art World" (Student Note), 11 *LOYOLA ENTERTAINMENT LAW JOURNAL* 453-477 (1991).

GLASNOST, *continued*

Bulsys, Joseph A., and John J. Makay. "Gorbachev's Rhetoric of Glasnost: How Openness Intersects with Freedom of Expression", 27 *FREE SPEECH YEARBOOK* 55-67 (1989).

Melville, Andrei, and Gail W. Lapidus. *THE GLASNOST PAPERS: VOICES ON REFORM FROM MOSCOW.* Boulder, CO: Westview Press, 1990. vii, 359 pp.

Quigley, John. "Freedom of Expression in the Soviet Media", 11 *LOYOLA ENTERTAINMENT LAW JOURNAL* 269-292 (1991).

Gorbachev

Åslund, Anders. *GORBACHEV'S STRUGGLE FOR ECONOMIC REFORM.* 2d ed. Ithaca, NY: Cornell University Press, 1991. x, 219 pp.

Doder, Dusko, and Louise Branson. *GORBACHEV: HERETIC IN THE KREMLIN.* New York: Viking, 1990. x, 450 pp.

☆Gorbachev, Mikhail. *THE AUGUST COUP: THE TRUTH AND THE LESSONS.* New York: Harper Collins, 1991. 127 pp.

Tatu, Michel. *MIKHAIL GORBACHEV: THE ORIGINS OF PERESTROIKA.* Boulder, CO: East European Monographs, 1981 (distributed by Columbia University Press). xi, 155 pp.

Government System

Subheadings:
Federalism and Federation
Legislatures
Local Government
Powers and Structure
President
Reorganization

Federalism and Federation

Gleason, Gregory. *FEDERALISM AND NATIONALISM: THE STRUGGLE FOR REPUBLICAN RIGHTS IN THE USSR.* Boulder, CO: Westview Press, Inc., 1990. xiii, 170 pp.

Grazin, Igor. "The Problems of Federalism in the Former Soviet Union: The Parallels with Pre-Civil War America", 18 *JOURNAL OF LEGISLATION* 69-85 (1991).

Henderson, Jane. "Legal Aspects of the Soviet Federal Structure", in *SOVIET FEDERALISM: NATIONALISM AND ECONOMIC DECENTRALISATION*, edited by Alastair McAuley (Leicester and London: Leicester University Press, 1991), pp. 33-55.

Kux, Stephan. *SOVIET FEDERALISM: A COMPARATIVE PERSPECTIVE.* New York: Institute for East-West Security Studies, 1990. vi, 117 pp.

Lukic, Reneo. "Twilight of the Federations in East Central Europe and the Soviet Union", 45 *JOURNAL OF INTERNATIONAL AFFAIRS* 575-598 (1992).

McAuley, Alastair, ed. *SOVIET FEDERALISM: NATIONALISM AND ECONOMIC DECENTRALISATION.* Leicester and London: Leicester University Press, 1991. ix, 214 pp.

Pearson, Raymond. "The Historical Background to Soviet Federalism", in *SOVIET FEDERALISM: NATIONALISM AND ECONOMIC DECENTRALISATION*, edited by Alastair McAuley (Leicester and London: Leicester University Press, 1991), pp. 13-32.

Ramans, Miervaldis. "Socialist Federalism, Federalism and Democratic Centralism", in *SOVIET FEDERALISM: NATIONALISM AND ECONOMIC DECENTRALISATION,* edited by Alastair McAuley (Leicester and London: Leicester University Press, 1991), pp. 128-133.

GOVERNMENT SYSTEM—Federalism and Federation, *continued*

Samuelian, Thomas J. "Cultural Ecology and Gorbachev's Restructured Union", 32 *HARVARD INTERNATIONAL LAW JOURNAL* 159-200 (1991).

Watts, Ronald. "The Soviet Federal System and the National Question in Comparative Perspective", in *SOVIET FEDERALISM: NATIONALISM AND ECONOMIC DECENTRALISATION*, edited by Alastair McAuley (Leicester and London: Leicester University Press, 1991), pp. 196-207.

Legislatures

Goldman, Stuart. "The New Soviet Legislative Branch", in *PERESTROIKA-ERA POLITICS: THE NEW SOVIET LEGISLATURE AND GORBACHEV'S POLITICAL REFORMS,* edited by Robert Huber and Donald R. Kelley (Armonk, NY: M.E. Sharpe, Inc., 1991), pp. 51-75.

Huskey, Eugene. "Legislative-Executive Relations in the New Soviet Political Order", in *PERESTROIKA-ERA POLITICS: THE NEW SOVIET LEGISLATURE AND GORBACHEV'S POLITICAL REFORMS,* edited by Robert Huber and Donald R. Kelley (Armonk, NY: M.E. Sharpe, Inc., 1991), pp. 53-173.

Local Government

Silliman, Emily. "Local Government: Structure and Economic Regulation". A Paper presented at the Geonomics Institute Seminar, Middleburg, Vermont, May 10-13, 1991. 22 pp. Reprinted in *INVESTING IN REFORM: DOING BUSINESS IN A CHANGING SOVIET UNION,* edited by Michael P. Claudon and Tamar L. Gutner (New York: New York University Press, 1991), pp. 139-157.

Powers and Structure

Brunner, Georg. "State Structure, Part 2: Organizational Matters", in *THE SOVIET SOBRANIE OF LAWS*, edited by Richard M. Buxbaum and Kathryn Hendley (Berkeley, CA: University of California at Berkeley, 1991), pp. 45-54.

Hazard, John N. "Prospects for a New Type of Federation", in *BEYOND PERESTROIKA: OPTIONS FOR A NEW SOVIET UNION*, edited by Laurence J. Aurbach (Chicago: American Bar Association, Section of Urban, State, and Local Government Law, 1991), pp. 5-14.

GOVERNMENT SYSTEM—Powers and Structure, *continued*

Huber, Robert T., and Donald R. Kelley. *PERESTROIKA-ERA POLITICS: THE NEW SOVIET LEGISLATURE AND GORBACHEV'S POLITICAL REFORMS.* Armonk, NY: M.E. Sharpe, Inc., 1991. viii, 246 pp.

☆Krylov, Boris S. "Perestroika—Restructuring the Soviet Union", in *BEYOND PERESTROIKA: OPTIONS FOR A NEW SOVIET UNION,* edited by Laurence J. Aurbach (Chicago: American Bar Association, Section of Urban, State, and Local Government Law, 1991), pp. 15-22.

Remington, Thomas F. "Parliamentary Government in the USSR", in *PERESTROIKA-ERA POLITICS: THE NEW SOVIET LEGISLATURE AND GORBACHEV'S POLITICAL REFORMS,* edited by Robert T. Huber and Donald R. Kelley (Armonk, NY: M.E. Sharpe, Inc., 1991), pp. 175-204.

President

Juviler, Peter. "Presidential Power and Presidential Character", 16 *SOVIET UNION/UNION SOVIETIQUE* 245-256 (1989).

☆Lazarev, B.M. "The President of the USSR", 30 *SOVIET LAW AND GOVERNMENT* 7-26 (1991).

Quigley, John. "The Soviet Presidency", 39 *AMERICAN JOURNAL OF COMPARATIVE LAW* 67-93 (1991).

Reorganization

DeBenedictis, Don J. "The Coup's Legal Aftermath", 77 *ABA JOURNAL* No. 11, 22 (November 1991).

History (Pre-1917)

Baker, John H., ed. *JUDICIAL RECORDS, LAW REPORTS, AND THE GROWTH OF CASE LAW.* Berlin: Duncker & Humblot, 1989. 353 pp.

Bryner, Cyril. "The Issue of Capital Punishment in the Reign of Elizabeth Petrovka", 49 *RUSSIAN REVIEW* 389-416 (1990).

HISTORY (Pre-1917), *continued*

Butler, William E. "The 1867 Russo-American Convention: Some Textual Issues", 40 *INTERNATIONAL AND COMPARATIVE LAW QUARTERLY* 457-463 (1991).

Butler, William E. "The Role of Case-Law in the Russian Legal System", in *JUDICIAL RECORDS, LAW REPORTS, AND THE GROWTH OF CASE LAW*, edited by John H. Baker (Berlin: Duncker & Humblot, 1989), pp. 337-352.

LeDonne, G.P. "Police Reform in Russia: A Project of 1762", 32 *CAHIERS DU MONDE RUSSE ET SOVIETIQUE* 249-274 (1991).

Moon, David. *RUSSIAN PEASANTS AND TSARIST LEGISLATION ON THE EVE OF REFORM: THE INTERACTION OF THE PEASANTRY AND OFFICIAL RUSSIA, 1825-55*. London: Macmillan, 1991. 220 pp.

Owen, Thomas C. *THE CORPORATION UNDER RUSSIAN LAW, 1800-1917*. Cambridge: Cambridge University Press, 1991. xx, 234 pp.

Pearson, Thomas S. *RUSSIAN OFFICIALDOM IN CRISIS: AUTOCRACY AND LOCAL SELF-GOVERNMENT, 1861-1900*. Cambridge; New York; New Rochelle, NY: Cambridge University Press, 1989. xx, 284 pp.

Wcislo, Francis W. "Soslovie or Class? Bureaucratic Reformers and Provincial Gentry in Conflict, 1906-1908", 4 *RUSSIAN REVIEW* 1-24 (1988).

Human Rights

See also Individual and the Law

Berliner, Rochelle S. "The Disappearance of Raoul Wallenberg: A Resolution Is Possible" (Note), 11 *NEW YORK LAW SCHOOL JOURNAL OF INTERNATIONAL AND COMPARATIVE LAW* 381-432 (1990).

Bonnie, Richard J. "Coercive Psychiatry and Human Rights: An Assessment of Recent Changes in the Soviet Union", 1 *CRIMINAL LAW FORUM* 319-346 (1990).

Bulsys, Joseph A., and John J. Makay. "Gorbachev's Rhetoric of Glasnost: How Openness Intersects with Freedom of Expression", 27 *FREE SPEECH YEARBOOK* 55-67 (1989).

HUMAN RIGHTS, *continued*

Copeland, Emily A. "Perestroika and Human Rights: Steps in the Right Direction", 15 *FLETCHER FORUM OF WORLD AFFAIRS* No. 2, 101-119 (Summer 1991).

Ginsburgs, George. "Perestroika in the Soviet Union and the Common Law of Mankind", 17 *REVIEW OF SOCIALIST LAW* 1-49 (1991).

Juviler, Peter. "Human Rights after Perestroika: Progress and Perils", 4 *HARRIMAN INSTITUTE FORUM* No. 6, 1-10 (June 1991).

☆Kartashkin, Vladimir A. "Human Rights and the Emergence of the State of the Rule of Law in the USSR", 40 *EMORY LAW JOURNAL* 889-902 (1991).

☆Kartashkin, Vladimir A. "International Protection of Minorities: The Soviet Perspective", 20 *ISRAEL YEARBOOK ON HUMAN RIGHTS* 309-317 (1990).

Matthews, Mervyn. *PASSPORTS AND FREEDOM OF RESIDENCE IN THE USSR.* Palo Alto: Hoover Institution, Stanford University, 1990. 19 pp.

Mayer, Carl J. "Redefining Red", 17 *HUMAN RIGHTS* No. 3, 22-27, 45-46 (Fall/Winter 1990).

Muller, Peter-Michael. "Protection of Human Rights in the Administration of Criminal Justice in Central and Eastern Europe and the Soviet Union", 17 *INTERNATIONAL LEGAL PRACTITIONER* No. 1, 18-19 (March 1992).

☆Mullerson, Rein A. "The International Protection of Human Rights and the Domestic Jurisdiction of States", in *PERESTROIKA AND INTERNATIONAL LAW: CURRENT ANGLO-SOVIET APPROACHES TO INTERNATIONAL LAW*, edited by Anthony Carty and Gennady Danilenko (Edinburgh: Edinburg University Press, 1990), pp. 62-70.

☆Mullerson, Rein A. "Monitoring Compliance with International Human Rights Standards", in *CONTROL OVER COMPLIANCE WITH INTERNATIONAL LAW*, edited by William E. Butler (Dordrecht, The Netherlands: Martinus Nijhoff Publishers, 1991), pp. 125-137.

Schweisfurth, Theodor. "The Acceptance of the Soviet Union of the Compulsory Jurisdiction of the ICJ for Six Human Rights Conventions", 2 *EUROPEAN JOURNAL OF INTERNATIONAL LAW* 110-117 (1991).

HUMAN RIGHTS, *continued*

☆Slavin, M.M. "Inviolability of the Individual in a Rule-of-Law State", in *PERESTROIKA AND THE RULE OF LAW: ANGLO-AMERICAN AND SOVIET PERSPECTIVES,* edited by William E. Butler (London: I.B. Tauris & Co., Ltd., 1991), pp. 186-199.

Sneider, Carolyn M. "The Slepak Principles Act and Soviet Union-United States Joint Ventures: Profits or People?" (Note), 13 *LOYOLA OF LOS ANGELES INTERNATIONAL AND COMPARATIVE LAW JOURNAL* 365-392 (1990).

USSR: FIRST STEPS TOWARDS REFORM OF THE CRIMINAL JUSTICE SYSTEM. London: Amnesty International, International Secretariat, 1990. 10 pp.

Immunity

See International Law

Individual and the Law

See also Human Rights

Clark, David S., ed. *COMPARATIVE AND PRIVATE INTERNATIONAL LAW: ESSAYS IN HONOR OF JOHN HENRY MERRYMAN ON HIS SEVENTIETH BIRTHDAY.* Berlin: Duncker & Humblot, 1990. xxii, 450 pp.

☆Feofanov, Iurii. "A Return to Origins: Reflections on Power and Law", 29 *SOVIET LAW AND GOVERNMENT* No. 3, 15-52 (Winter 1990-91).

Juviler, Peter. "Secret Justice and Personal Rights", in *THE SOVIET SOBRANIE OF LAWS,* edited by Richard M. Buxbaum and Kathryn Hendley (Berkeley, CA: University of California at Berkeley, 1991), pp. 156-172.

☆Kartashkin, Vladimir A. "Human Rights and the Emergence of the State of the Rule of Law in the USSR", 40 *EMORY LAW JOURNAL* 889-902 (1991).

☆Kudryavtsev, Vladimir. "The Law-Based State: Society and the Individual", 22 *SOCIAL SCIENCES* No. 2, 7-14 (1991).

INDIVIDUAL AND THE LAW, *continued*

Markovits, Inga. "Socialism and the Rule of Law: Some Speculations and Predictions", in *COMPARATIVE AND PRIVATE INTERNATIONAL LAW: ESSAYS IN HONOR OF JOHN HENRY MERRYMAN ON HIS SEVENTIETH BIRTHDAY*, edited by David S. Clark (Berlin: Duncker & Humblot, 1990), pp. 205-245.

Melville, Andrei, and Gail W. Lapidus. *THE GLASNOST PAPERS: VOICES ON REFORM FROM MOSCOW.* Boulder, CO: Westview Press, 1990. vii, 359 pp.

☆Savitskii, Valerii. "Democratization in the USSR: Toward the Freedom of the Individual through Law and Courts", 2 *CRIMINAL LAW FORUM* 85-110 (1990).

☆Slavin, M.M. "Inviolability of the Individual in a Rule-of-Law State", in *PERESTROIKA AND THE RULE OF LAW: ANGLO-AMERICAN AND SOVIET PERSPECTIVES,* edited by William E. Butler (London: I.B. Tauris & Co., Ltd., 1991), pp. 186-199.

Industrial Property

See Patents and Trademarks

Insurance

☆Afanasyeva, Larisa. "Insurance and Risk Management of Joint Ventures in the USSR", 22 *NEW YORK UNIVERSITY JOURNAL OF INTERNATIONAL LAW AND POLITICS* 447-459 (1990).

Frenkel, William G. "Soviet Insurance Market Open to New Business", 9 *INTERNATIONAL FINANCIAL LAW REVIEW* No. 11, 36-38 (November 1990).

Insurance, Social

See Social Security

Intellectual Property

See Copyright

Internal Control

Juviler, Peter. "Secret Justice and Personal Rights", in *THE SOVIET SOBRANIE OF LAWS*, edited by Richard M. Buxbaum and Kathryn Hendley (Berkeley, CA: University of California at Berkeley, 1991), pp. 156-172.

Matthews, Mervyn. *PASSPORTS AND FREEDOM OF RESIDENCE IN THE USSR*. Palo Alto: Hoover Institution, Stanford University, 1990. 19 pp.

International Court of Justice

See International Law

International Law

Subheadings:

Aggression

Butler, William E., ed. *CONTROL OVER COMPLIANCE WITH INTERNATIONAL LAW*. Dordrecht, The Netherlands: Martinus Nijhoff Publishers, 1991. vi, 209 pp.

INTERNATIONAL LAW—Aggression, *continued*

☆Khlestov, O.N. "The Origin and Prospects for Development of Control over Compliance with International Obligations of States", in *CONTROL OVER COMPLIANCE WITH INTERNATIONAL LAW*, edited by William E. Butler (Dordrecht, The Netherlands: Martinus Nijhoff Publishers, 1991), pp. 23-30.

☆Lazarev, M.I. "On a Theoretical Concept of Control over the Fulfilment of International Obligations of States", in *CONTROL OVER COMPLIANCE WITH INTERNATIONAL LAW*, edited by William E. Butler (Dordrecht, The Netherlands: Martinus Nijhoff Publishers, 1991), pp. 17-22.

☆Lukashuk, Igor I. "Control in Contemporary International Law", in *CONTROL OVER COMPLIANCE WITH INTERNATIONAL LAW*, edited by William E. Butler (Dordrecht, The Netherlands: Martinus Nijhoff Publishers, 1991), pp. 5-16.

Antarctica

☆Trofimov, Vladimir. *LEGAL STATUS OF ANTARKTICA*. Moscow: Publishing House "Prometey", 1990. 141 pp.

☆Vinogradov, Sergei V. "Verification Machinery in the Antarctic Treaty System", in *CONTROL OVER COMPLIANCE WITH INTERNATIONAL LAW*, edited by William E. Butler (Dordrecht, The Netherlands: Martinus Nijhoff Publishers, 1991), pp. 97-105.

Application in Domestic Proceedings

Stephan, Paul B., III. "Revisiting the Incorporation Debate: The Role of Domestic Political Structure", 31 *VIRGINIA JOURNAL OF INTERNATIONAL LAW* 417-436 (1991).

Arctic

Elferink, Alex Oude. "The 1990 USSR-USA Maritime Boundary Agreement", 6 *INTERNATIONAL JOURNAL OF ESTUARINE AND COASTAL LAW* 41-52 (1991).

Jorgensen-Dahl, Arnfinn. "The Soviet-Norwegian Maritime Disputes in the Arctic: Law and Politics", 21 *OCEAN DEVELOPMENT AND INTERNATIONAL LAW* 411-429 (1990).

McNeill, John H. "America's Maritime Boundary with the Soviet Union", 154 *NAVAL WAR COLLEGE REVIEW* No. 3, 46-57 (Summer 1991).

INTERNATIONAL LAW—Arctic, *continued*

☆Movchan, A.P. "The Legal Regime of Navigation in the Arctic: Problems of Soviet-Canadian Cooperation", in *FROM COEXISTENCE TO COOPERATION: INTERNATIONAL LAW AND ORGANIZATION IN THE POST-COLD WAR ERA*, edited by Edward McWhinney, et al. (Dordrecht, The Netherlands: Martinus Nijhoff Publishers, 1991), pp. 167-176.

Ostreng, Willy. "The Northern Sea Route: A New Era in Soviet Policy?", 22 *OCEAN DEVELOPMENT AND INTERNATIONAL LAW* 259-287 (1991).

☆Vinogradov, Sergei V. "Ecological Security in the Arctic: A Regional Approach", in *FROM COEXISTENCE TO COOPERATION: INTERNATIONAL LAW AND ORGANIZATION IN THE POST-COLD WAR ERA*, edited by Edward McWhinney, et al. (Dordrecht, The Netherlands: Martinus Nijhoff Publishers, 1991), pp. 155-166.

Arms Control

Calingaert, Daniel. *SOVIET NUCLEAR POLICY UNDER GORBACHEV: A POLICY OF DISARMAMENT.* New York: Praeger, 1991. x, 180 pp.

☆Fedorenko, Sergei. "Options for Future Strategic Arms Reduction", in *FROM COEXISTENCE TO COOPERATION: INTERNATIONAL LAW AND ORGANIZATION IN THE POST-COLD WAR ERA*, edited by Edward McWhinney, et al. (Dordrecht, The Netherlands: Martinus Nijhoff Publishers, 1991), pp. 79-93.

Goldstein, Gordon. "Anti-Satellite Weapons and U.S. National Security", 22 *NEW YORK UNIVERSITY JOURNAL OF INTERNATIONAL LAW AND POLITICS* 519-555 (1990).

"Symposium on U.S.-Soviet Military and Economic Relations", 22 *NEW YORK UNIVERSITY JOURNAL OF INTERNATIONAL LAW AND POLITICS* 373-595 (1990).

Tanzman, Edward A., and Barry Kellman. "Legal Implementation of the Multilateral Chemical Weapons Convention: Integrating International Security with the Constitution", 22 *NEW YORK UNIVERSITY JOURNAL OF INTERNATIONAL LAW AND POLITICS* 475-518 (1990).

INTERNATIONAL LAW—Arms Control, *continued*

☆Tuzmukhamedov, Bakhtiar R. "Verification of Disarmament", in *PERESTROIKA AND INTERNATIONAL LAW: CURRENT ANGLO-SOVIET APPROACHES TO INTERNATIONAL LAW*, edited by Anthony Carty and Gennady Danilenko (Edinburgh: Edinburg University Press, 1990), pp. 48-61.

☆Vereshchetin, Vladlen S. "International Control and the Concept of 'Open Skies'", in *FROM COEXISTENCE TO COOPERATION: INTERNATIONAL LAW AND ORGANIZATION IN THE POST-COLD WAR ERA*, edited by Edward McWhinney, et al. (Dordrecht, The Netherlands: Martinus Nijhoff Publishers, 1991), pp. 31-43.

Zanft, Oksanna. "Arms Control and Chemical Weapons—Agreement on Destruction and Non-Production of Chemical Weapons, June 1, 1990, United States-U.S.S.R." (Note), 32 *HARVARD INTERNATIONAL LAW JOURNAL* 497-507 (1991).

Doctrine and Practice

Carty, Anthony, and Gennady Danilenko, eds. *PERESTROIKA AND INTERNATIONAL LAW: CURRENT ANGLO-SOVIET APPROACHES TO INTERNATIONAL LAW.* Edinburgh: Edinburg University Press, 1990. ix, 231 pp.

☆Czaplinski, W. and Danilenko, G. "Conflicts of Norms in International Law", 21 *NETHERLANDS YEARBOOK OF INTERNATIONAL LAW* 3-42 (1990).

☆Danilenko, Gennady M. "International Jus Cogens: Issues of Law-Making", 2 *EUROPEAN JOURNAL OF INTERNATIONAL LAW* 42-65 (1991).

☆Danilenko, Gennady M. "International Law-Making: Issues of Law and Policy", in *PERESTROIKA AND INTERNATIONAL LAW: CURRENT ANGLO-SOVIET APPROACHES TO INTERNATIONAL LAW,* edited by Anthony Carty and Gennady Danilenko (Edinburgh: Edinburg University Press, 1990), pp. 15-26.

Ginsburgs, George. "Perestroika in the Soviet Union and the Common Law of Mankind", 17 *REVIEW OF SOCIALIST LAW* 1-49 (1991).

Grzybowski, Kazimierz. "Soviet Theory of International Law for the Perestroika", 36 *OSTEUROPA-RECHT* 276-282 (1990).

☆*INTERNATIONAL LAW*. Moscow: Progress Publishers, 1990. 285 pp. (Student's Library).

INTERNATIONAL LAW—Doctrine and Practice, *continued*

McWhinney, Edward. "The 'New Thinking' in Soviet International Law: Soviet Doctrines and Practice in the Post-Tunkin Era", 28 *CANADIAN YEARBOOK OF INTERNATIONAL LAW* 309-337 (1990).

☆Mullerson, Rein A. "The International Protection of Human Rights and the Domestic Jurisdiction of States", in *PERESTROIKA AND INTERNATIONAL LAW: CURRENT ANGLO-SOVIET APPROACHES TO INTERNATIONAL LAW*, edited by Anthony Carty and Gennady Danilenko (Edinburgh: Edinburg University Press, 1990), pp. 62-70.

☆Mullerson, Rein A. "Reflections on the Future International Legal Problems of the USSR", in *THE CHANGING POLITICAL STRUCTURE OF EUROPE: ASPECTS OF INTERNATIONAL LAW*, edited by R. Lefeber, M. Fitzmaurice, and E.W. Vierdag (Dordrecht, The Netherlands: Martinus Nijhoff Publishers, 1991), pp. 55-61.

Schweisfurth, Theodor "The New Approach to the Law of Peaceful Coexistence", in *THE CHANGING POLITICAL STRUCTURE OF EUROPE: ASPECTS OF INTERNATIONAL LAW,* edited by R. Lefeber, M. Fitzmaurice, and E.W. Vierdag (Dordrecht, The Netherlands: Martinus Nijhoff Publishers, 1991), pp. 29-49.

☆Sheinis, Zinovy. *MAXIM LITVINOV.* Moscow: Progress Publishers, 1990. 356 pp.

☆Shinkaretskaya, G.G. "Changing Attitude towards International Adjudication in the Soviet Union", 3 *LEIDEN JOURNAL OF INTERNATIONAL LAW* No. 3, 59-66 (Special Issue, December 1990).

Stephan, Paul B., III, and Boris M. Klimenko, eds. *INTERNATIONAL LAW AND INTERNATIONAL SECURITY: MILITARY AND POLITICAL DIMENSIONS—A U.S.-SOVIET DIALOGUE.* Armonk, NY: M.E. Sharpe, Inc., 1991. xxii, 362 pp.

☆Tunkin, Grigory I. "International Politics and International Law in the Nuclear Age", in *FROM COEXISTENCE TO COOPERATION: INTERNATIONAL LAW AND ORGANIZATION IN THE POST-COLD WAR ERA*, edited by Edward McWhinney, et al. (Dordrecht, The Netherlands: Martinus Nijhoff Publishers, 1991), pp. 9-17.

INTERNATIONAL LAW—Doctrine and Practice, *continued*

☆Vereshchetin, Vladlen S., and Rein A. Mullerson. "The Primacy of International Law in World Politics", in *PERESTROIKA AND INTERNATIONAL LAW: CURRENT ANGLO-SOVIET APPROACHES TO INTERNATIONAL LAW*, edited by Anthony Carty and Gennady Danilenko (Edinburgh: Edinburg University Press, 1990), pp. 6-14.

☆Volkov, F.M., ed. *INTERNATIONAL LAW.* Moscow: Progress Publishers, 1990. 285 pp.

Zisk, Kimberly Marten. "Soviet Academic Theories on International Conflict and Negotiation", 34 *JOURNAL OF CONFLICT RESOLUTION* 678-693 (1990).

Environment

Fitzmaurice, M. *INTERNATIONAL LEGAL PROBLEMS OF THE ENVIRONMENTAL PROTECTION OF THE BALTIC SEA.* Dordrecht, The Netherlands: Martinus Nijhoff/Graham & Trotman, 1992. xxix, 328 pp.

☆Timoshenko, Alexandre S. "Ecological Security: The International Aspect", 7 *PACE ENVIRONMENTAL LAW REVIEW* 151-160 (1989).

☆Vinogradov, Sergei V. "Ecological Security in the Arctic: A Regional Approach", in *FROM COEXISTENCE TO COOPERATION: INTERNATIONAL LAW AND ORGANIZATION IN THE POST-COLD WAR ERA*, edited by Edward McWhinney, et al. (Dordrecht, The Netherlands: Martinus Nijhoff Publishers, 1991), pp. 155-166.

☆Vinogradov, Sergei V. "International Environmental Security: The Concept and Its Implementation", in *PERESTROIKA AND INTERNATIONAL LAW: CURRENT ANGLO-SOVIET APPROACHES TO INTERNATIONAL LAW*, edited by Anthony Carty and Gennady Danilenko (Edinburgh: Edinburg University Press, 1990), pp. 196-207.

Foreign Relations

Beichman, Arnold. *THE LONG PRETENSE: SOVIET TREATY DIPLOMACY FROM LENIN TO GORBACHEV.* New Brunswick, NJ and London, England: Transaction Publishers, 1991. xiv, 303 pp.

INTERNATIONAL LAW—Foreign Relations, *continued*

☆Gorin, Alexander, and Piotr Mishchenko. "New Political Thinking as a Tool of Soviet Foreign Policy", 17 *JOURNAL OF LEGISLATION* 13-21 (1990).

Lefeber, R., M. Fitzmaurice, and E.W. Vierdag, eds. *THE CHANGING POLITICAL STRUCTURE OF EUROPE: ASPECTS OF INTERNATIONAL LAW.* Dordrecht, The Netherlands: Martinus Nijhoff Publishers, 1991. xi, 286 pp.

McWhinney, Edward, et al. *FROM COEXISTENCE TO COOPERATION: INTERNATIONAL LAW AND ORGANIZATION IN THE POST-COLD WAR ERA.* Dordrecht, The Netherlands: Martinus Nijhoff Publishers, 1991. xiv, 297 pp.

Motyl, Alexander J. "Russian Hegemony and Non-Russian Insecurity: Foreign Policy Dilemmas of the USSR's Successor States", 5 *HARRIMAN INSTITUTE FORUM* No. 4, 1-11 (December 1991).

☆Podlesnyi, Pavel T. "The Agenda of U.S.-Soviet Relations for the 1990s", 22 *NEW YORK UNIVERSITY JOURNAL OF INTERNATIONAL LAW AND POLITICS* 389-406 (1990).

Roberts, Geoffrey R. *THE UNHOLY ALLIANCE: STALIN'S PACT WITH HITLER.* Bloomington and Indianapolis: Indiana University Press, 1991. xi, 296 pp.

Schmidt, Gustav. "Happy Moments: Solving the Special German-Soviet Russian Conflict", 24 *CORNELL INTERNATIONAL LAW JOURNAL* 437-455 (1991).

Vizulis, Izidors Joseph. *THE MOLOTOV-RIBBENTROP PACT OF 1939: THE BALTIC CASE.* New York: Praeger, 1990. vi, 176 pp.

Webb, William T. "The International Legal Aspects of the Lithuanian Secession" (Note), 17 *JOURNAL OF LEGISLATION* 309-330 1991).

Immunity

Berliner, Rochelle S. "The Disappearance of Raoul Wallenberg: A Resolution Is Possible" (Note), 11 *NEW YORK LAW SCHOOL JOURNAL OF INTERNATIONAL AND COMPARATIVE LAW* 381-432 (1990).

INTERNATIONAL LAW, *continued*

International Court of Justice

Schweisfurth, Theodor. "The Acceptance of the Soviet Union of the Compulsory Jurisdiction of the ICJ for Six Human Rights Conventions", 2 *EUROPEAN JOURNAL OF INTERNATIONAL LAW* 110-117 (1991).

International Legal Cooperation

Ginsburgs, George. *THE SOVIET UNION AND INTERNATIONAL COOPERATION IN LEGAL MATTERS—PART II: CIVIL LAW.* (Law in Eastern Europe No. 43). Dordrecht, The Netherlands: Martinus Nijhoff Publishers, 1991. xiv, 393 pp.

Ginsburgs, George. "The Soviet Union and International Co-operation in Penal Matters", 41 *INTERNATIONAL AND COMPARATIVE LAW QUARTERLY* 85-116 (1992).

Ginsburgs, George. "The USSR and the Socialist Model of International Cooperation in Criminal Matters", 17 *REVIEW OF SOCIALIST LAW* 199-278 (1991).

☆Karpetz, Igor I. "International Criminal Law and International Crimes", 1 *TOURO JOURNAL OF TRANSNATIONAL LAW* 325-334 (1990).

International Organizations

☆Danilenko, Gennady M. "The Changing Structure of the International Community: Constitutional Implications", 32 *HARVARD INTERNATIONAL LAW JOURNAL* 353-361 (1991).

☆Ivanov, S.A. "The International Labour Organisation: Control over Application of the Conventions and Recommendations on Labour", in *CONTROL OVER COMPLIANCE WITH INTERNATIONAL LAW*, edited by William E. Butler (Dordrecht, The Netherlands: Martinus Nijhoff Publishers, 1991), pp. 153-163.

Meron, Theodor. "'Exclusive Preserves' and the New Soviet Policy toward the UN Secretariat" (Editorial Comment), 85 *AMERICAN JOURNAL OF INTERNATIONAL LAW* 322-329 (1991).

INTERNATIONAL LAW, *continued*

Negotiating Behavior

Kampelman, Max M. "Negotiating with the Soviets", in *NEGOTIATING ARMS CONTROL: MISSED OPPORTUNITIES AND LIMITED SUCCESSES*, edited by Kenneth W. Thompson (Lanham, MD: University Press of America, Inc. 1991), pp. 3-26.

Snowe, Olympia J. "The Moscow Embassy: A Study of Congressional Response to Crisis", 16 *JOURNAL OF LEGISLATION* 35-46 (1989).

Thompson, Kenneth W., ed. *NEGOTIATING ARMS CONTROL: MISSED OPPORTUNITIES AND LIMITED SUCCESSES.* Lanham, MD: University Press of America, Inc., 1991. xii, 142 pp. (W. Alton Jones Foundation Series on Arms Control, vol. 17).

United States Congress. House of Representatives Committee on Foreign Affairs. *SOVIET DIPLOMACY AND NEGOTIATING BEHAVIOR—1988-90: GORBACHEV-REAGAN-BUSH MEETINGS AT THE SUMMIT.* Washington, D.C.: U.S. Government Printing Office, 1991. xvii, 478 pp.

Settlement of Disputes

☆Shinkaretskaya, Galina G. "Changing Attitude towards International Adjudication in the Soviet Union", 3 *LEIDEN JOURNAL OF INTERNATIONAL LAW* No. 3, 59-66 (Special Issue, December 1990).

☆Shinkaretskaya, Galina G. "International Arbitration in the External Policy of the Soviet Union", in *PERESTROIKA AND INTERNATIONAL LAW: CURRENT ANGLO-SOVIET APPROACHES TO INTERNATIONAL LAW*, edited by Anthony Carty and Gennady Danilenko (Edinburgh: Edinburg University Press, 1990), pp. 110-118.

☆Vilegjanina, Elena E. "The Principle of Peaceful Settlement of Disputes: A New Soviet Approach", in *PERESTROIKA AND INTERNATIONAL LAW: CURRENT ANGLO-SOVIET APPROACHES TO INTERNATIONAL LAW,* edited by Anthony Carty and Gennady Danilenko (Edinburgh: Edinburg University Press, 1990), pp. 119-128.

International Legal Cooperation

See International Law

International Trade

See COMECON *and*
Foreign Trade

Investment

See Foreign Trade—Investment

Jews

Artz, Donna E. "Soviet Anti-Semitism: Legal Responses in an Age of Glasnost", 4 *TEMPLE INTERNATIONAL AND COMPARATIVE LAW JOURNAL* 163-183 (1990).

Gitelman, Zvi. "Glasnost, Perestroika and Antisemitism", 70 *FOREIGN AFFAIRS* No. 2, 141-159 (Spring 1991).

Heitman, Sidney. *THE RIGHT TO LEAVE: THE NEW SOVIET DRAFT LAW ON EMIGRATION.* Cologne: Bundesinstitut für ostwissenschaftliche und internationale Studien, 1990. iii, 53 pp. (Report 26-1990).

Heitman, Sidney. *SOVIET EMIGRATION IN 1990.* Cologne: Bundesinstitut für ostwissenschaftliche und internationale Studien, 1991. iii, 45 pp. (Report 33-1991).

Irwin, Zachary. "Soviet-Jewish Emigration Policy: Anti-Zionism and Philo-Semitism", in *SOVIET NATIONALITY POLICIES: RULING ETHNIC GROUPS IN THE USSR,* edited by Henry R. Huttenbach (London: Mansell Publishing Limited, 1990), pp. 260-285.

Khazanov, Anatoly. *THE KRYMCHAKS: A VANISHING GROUP IN THE SOVIET UNION.* Jerusalem: The Hebrew University of Jerusalem, The Marjorie Mayrock Center for Soviet and East European Research, 1989. 83 pp.

JEWS, *continued*

Quigley, John. "Soviet Immigration to the West Bank: Is It Legal?", 21 *GEORGIA JOURNAL OF INTERNATIONAL AND COMPARATIVE LAW* 387-413 (1991).

Ro'i, Yaacov. *THE STRUGGLE FOR SOVIET JEWISH EMIGRATION 1948-1967.* Cambridge: Cambridge University Press, 1991. 457 pp.

Rubin, Gary E. "The United States and Soviet Jews: Refugee Policy and Acculturation", 13 *IN DEFENSE OF THE ALIEN* 98-102 (1990).

Joint Stock Companies

See Business Organizations

Joint Ventures

See Foreign Trade

Judges

See Administration of Justice

Judicial Opinions

Baker, John H., ed. *JUDICIAL RECORDS, LAW REPORTS, AND THE GROWTH OF CASE LAW.* Berlin: Duncker & Humblot, 1989. 353 pp.

Butler, William E. "The Role of Case-Law in the Russian Legal System", in *JUDICIAL RECORDS, LAW REPORTS, AND THE GROWTH OF CASE LAW*, edited by John H. Baker (Berlin: Duncker & Humblot, 1989), pp. 337-352.

Jurisprudence

See Administration of Justice, Legal Profession, *and* Philosophy of Law

Kazakhstan

☆Balkina, M.A., ed. *NEW POLITICAL PARTIES AND MOVEMENTS IN THE SOVIET UNION*. Commack, N.Y.: Nova Science Publishers, Inc., 1991. 156 pp.

LEGAL AND PRACTICAL ASPECTS OF DOING BUSINESS IN THE SOVIET REPUBLICS. Commercial Law and Practice Course Handbook Series No. 604. New York: Practising Law Institute, 1992. 500 pp.

Simons, William B. "Foreign Investment Laws in the Republics of the USSR: Lithuania and Kazakhstan", 17 *REVIEW OF SOCIALIST LAW* 161-190 (1991).

Simons, William B. "Foreign Investment Laws of Kazakhstan", 17 *REVIEW OF SOCIALIST LAW* 81-94 (1991).

KGB

See Police

Kolkhoz Law

See Agriculture and Collectivization

Labor Camps

See Prison System

Labor and Labor Law

Block, Kevin P. "The Disciplining and Dismissal of Employees by Joint Ventures in the USSR", 23 *GEORGE WASHINGTON JOURNAL OF INTERNATIONAL LAW AND ECONOMICS* 619-667 (1990).

Berg, Ger P. van den. "Soviet Labor Law in the Collection of USSR Laws", in *THE SOVIET SOBRANIE OF LAWS,* edited by Richard M. Buxbaum and Kathryn Hendley (Berkeley, CA: University of California at Berkeley, 1991), pp. 68-101.

Bonnell, Victoria E. "Voluntary Associations in Gorbachev's Reform Program", in *CAN GORBACHEV'S REFORMS SUCCEED?*, edited by George W. Breslauer (Berkeley, CA: Center for Slavic and East European Studies and the Berkeley-Stanford Program in Soviet Studies, University of California at Berkeley, 1990), pp. 63-76.

Bova, Russell. "Worker Activism: The Role of the State", in *PERESTROIKA FROM BELOW: SOCIAL MOVEMENTS IN THE SOVIET UNION,* edited by Judith B. Sedaitis and Jim Butterfield (Boulder, CO: Westview Press, 1991), pp. 29-42.

Connor, Walter D. "Equality of Opportunity", in *SOVIET SOCIAL PROBLEMS*, edited by Anthony Jones, et al. (Boulder, CO; San Francisco; Oxford: Westview Press, 1991), pp. 137-153.

Cook, Linda J. "Lessons of Soviet Coal Miners' Strike of Summer 1989", 4 *HARRIMAN INSTITUTE FORUM* No. 3, 1-10 (March 1991).

Grancelli, Bruno. *SOVIET MANAGEMENT AND LABOR RELATIONS.* Boston: Allen and Unwin, 1988. xvi, 248 pp.

☆Mamutov, V.K. "The Miners' Strike and Improving Economic Legislation", 30 *SOVIET LAW AND GOVERNMENT* 80-92 (1991).

Mason, David S., and Svetlana Sydorenko. "Perestroyka, Social Justice, and Soviet Public Opinion", 39 *PROBLEMS OF COMMUNISM* No. 6, 34-43 (November-December 1990).

Morgan, John. "Labour: Past Imperfect, Present Tense—Trade Unions and Labour in the Soviet State", in *THE IMPACT OF GORBACHEV: THE FIRST PHASE, 1985-1990,* edited by D. W. Spring (London and New York: Printer Publishers, 1991), pp. 37-48.

LABOR AND LABOR LAW, *continued*

Osakwe, Christopher. *SOVIET BUSINESS LAW: INSTITUTIONS, PRINCIPLES, AND PROCESSES.* Salem, NH: Butterworth Legal Publishers, 1991. 2 Volumes, looseleaf, misc. pag.

Oxenstierna, Susanne. "Labour Market Policies in the Baltic Republics", 130 *INTERNATIONAL LABOUR REVIEW* 255-274 (1991/2).

☆Samorodov, A. "Conversion of the Soviet Defence Industry and Its Consequences for Labour", 129 *INTERNATIONAL LABOUR REVIEW* 555-572 (1990).

Sedaitis, Judith B. "Worker Activism: Politics at the Grass Roots", in *PERESTROIKA FROM BELOW: SOCIAL MOVEMENTS IN THE SOVIET UNION*, edited by Judith B. Sedaitis and Jim Butterfield (Boulder, CO: Westview Press, 1991), pp. 13-27.

☆Shcherbakov, V.I. "Remuneration of Labour in the USSR: Problems and Prospects", 130 *INTERNATIONAL LABOUR REVIEW* 227-236 (1991/2).

Standing, Guy. "Wages and Work Motivation in the Soviet Labour Market. Why a 'BIP', not a 'TIP' Is Required", 130 *INTERNATIONAL LABOUR REVIEW* 237-253 (1991/2).

☆Vasil'ev, Andrei, and Maksim Krans. "The Miners' Alternative: A Few Questions for Reflection", 30 *SOVIET LAW AND GOVERNMENT* No. 2, 45-61 (Fall 1991).

Latvia

See Baltic

Law Enforcement

See Police *and* Procuracy

Law of the Sea

See Maritime Law

Law Reform

See Codification *and* Legal Reform

Law Sources

See Laws and Official Documents in English Translation

Laws and Official Documents in English Translation

Subheadings:

Civil Code—Russian Republic
Collections of Laws and Documents
Communist Party
Constitution
Customs
Draft Union Treaty
Foreign Trade
Judges
Latvian Independence
Press
Property Law
Religion
Taxation

Civil Code—Russian Republic

Osakwe, Christopher. *SOVIET BUSINESS LAW: INSTITUTIONS, PRINCIPLES, AND PROCESSES.* Salem, NH: Butterworth Legal Publishers, 1991. 2 Volumes, looseleaf, misc. pag.

Collections of Laws and Documents

Black, J.L., ed. *USSR DOCUMENTS ANNUAL 1989. THE GORBACHEV REFORMS CONTINUE. THE END OF THE EMPIRE?* Gulf Breeze, FL: Academic International Press, 1990. xii, 435 pp.

Black, J.L., ed. *USSR DOCUMENTS ANNUAL 1990. RESTRUCTURING PERESTROIKA.* Gulf Breeze, FL: Academic International Press, 1991. 2 Vols. (ix, 335 and vii, 379 pp. respectively).

Butler, William E. *BASIC DOCUMENTS ON THE SOVIET LEGAL SYSTEM*, 2nd ed. New York: Oceana Publications, Inc., 1991. v, 492 pp.

LAWS AND OFFICIAL DOCUMENTS IN ENGLISH TRANSLATION—Collections of Laws and Documents, *continued*

Furtado, Charles F., Jr., and Andrea Chandler. *PERESTROIKA IN THE SOVIET REPUBLICS: DOCUMENTS ON THE NATIONAL QUESTION*. Boulder, CO: Westview Press, 1992. xxvi, 646 pp.

Communist Party

☆"Rules of the Communist Party of the Soviet Union. Ratified by the Twenty-eighth Congress of the CPSU", 30 *SOVIET LAW AND GOVERNMENT* No. 2, 7-25 (Fall 1991).

Constitution

Blaustein, Albert P., ed. *CONSTITUTIONS OF DEPENDENCIES AND SPECIAL SOVEREIGNTIES*. Dobbs Ferry, NY: Oceana Publications, 1977- .

Blaustein, Albert P., and Gisbert H. Flanz, eds. *CONSTITUTIONS OF THE COUNTRIES OF THE WORLD*. Dobbs Ferry, NY: Oceana Publications, 1970- .

CONSTITUTION (FUNDAMENTAL LAW) OF THE UNION OF SOVIET SOCIALIST REPUBLICS: ADOPTED AT THE SEVENTH (SPECIAL) SESSION OF THE SUPREME SOVIET OF THE USSR, NINTH CONVOCATION, ON OCTOBER 7, 1977. London: Novosti Press Agency, 1990. 58 pp.

Customs

Butler, William E. *THE CUSTOMS CODE OF THE USSR AND THE LAW ON THE CUSTOMS TARIFF OF THE USSR*. London: Interlist, 1991. xxvi, 210 pp.

Draft Union Treaty

Aurbach, Laurence J., ed. *BEYOND PERESTROIKA: OPTIONS FOR A NEW SOVIET UNION*. Chicago: American Bar Association, Section of Urban, State, and Local Government Law, 1991. iv, 40 pp.

LAWS AND OFFICIAL DOCUMENTS IN ENGLISH TRANSLATION, *continued*

Foreign Trade

Aulin, Lisen. *ESTABLISHING JOINT VENTURES IN THE USSR.* Deventer, The Netherlands; Boston: Kluwer Law and Taxation Publishers, 1990. ix, 149 pp.

Birenbaum, David E., and Dimitri P. Racklin. *BUSINESS VENTURES IN EASTERN EUROPE AND THE SOVIET UNION: THE EMERGING LEGAL FRAMEWORK FOR FOREIGN INVESTMENT.* Englewood Cliffs, NJ: Prentice Hall, 1990- . 2 volumes, looseleaf.

Brada, Josef C., and Michael P. Claudon, eds. *THE EMERGING RUSSIAN BEAR: INTEGRATING THE SOVIET UNION INTO THE WORLD ECONOMY.* New York: New York University Press, 1991. xiii, 228 pp. (Geonomics Institute for International Economic Advancement Series).

Butler, William E. *FUNDAMENTAL PRINCIPLES OF LEGISLATION ON INVESTMENT ACTIVITY IN THE USSR AND REPUBLICS.* London: Interlist, 1991. viii, 302 pp. (The Butler Commentaries on Soviet Law).

George, Arthur L., and Thomas A. O'Donnell. *BUSINESS OPERATIONS IN THE U.S.S.R.* Washington, DC: Tax Management, Inc., 1991 (Tax Management, Foreign Income Portfolios, 990).

Herlach, Mark D., and Lucille A. Barale, eds. *JOINT VENTURES IN EASTERN EUROPE.* London: Euromoney Publications PLC, 1990. xi, 183 pp.

International Chamber of Commerce. *FOREIGN INVESTMENT IN THE USSR. KEY 1990 LEGISLATION.* Paris: ICC Publications, 1991.

LEGAL ASPECTS OF TRADE AND INVESTMENT IN THE SOVIET UNION AND EASTERN EUROPE. Commercial Law and Practice Course Handbook Series No. 549. New York: Practising Law Institute, 1990. 1036 pp.

LAWS AND OFFICIAL DOCUMENTS IN ENGLISH TRANSLATION—Foreign Trade, *continued*

LEGAL AND PRACTICAL ASPECTS OF DOING BUSINESS IN THE SOVIET REPUBLICS. Commercial Law and Practice Course Handbook Series No. 604. New York: Practising Law Institute, 1992. 500 pp.

Nightingale, Christopher, and Stephen Tupper. *RUSSIAN AND SOVIET ECONOMIC CHANGE: THE NEW LAW*. London: Longman, 1991. 100 pp.

Sheedy, John F., and Richard N. Dean. "Gaining a Foothold in the Soviet Market: How to Establish a Representative Office", *25 INTERNATIONAL LAWYER* 103-125 (1991).

Simons, William B. "Foreign Investment Laws in the Republics of the USSR: Lithuania and Kazakhstan", 17 *REVIEW OF SOCIALIST LAW* 161-190 (1991).

Simons, William B. "Foreign Investment Laws of Kazakhstan", 17 *REVIEW OF SOCIALIST LAW* 81-94 (1991).

Torbert, Preston M. "First Soviet Free Zone Will Give Firms Access to Pacific Basin Markets", in *LEGAL AND PRACTICAL ASPECTS OF DOING BUSINESS IN THE SOVIET REPUBLICS* (New York: Practising Law Institute, 1992), pp. 483-494.

Judges

Henderson, Jane. "Law of the USSR: On the Status of Judges in the USSR", 16 *REVIEW OF SOCIALIST LAW* 305-338 (1990).

Latvian Independence

Sprudzs, Adolf. "The Rule of Law and the Baltic States", in *BIBLIOTHEK UND RECHT INTERNATIONAL/LIBRARIES AND LAW—INTERNATIONAL, FESTSCHRIFT RALPH LANSKY*, edited by Jürgen Christoph Gödan and Holger Knudsen (Hamburg and Augsburg: Arbeitsgemeinschaft für juristisches Bibliotheks- und Dokumentationswesen, 1991), pp. 231-241.

Press

Bazyler, Michael J., and Eugene Sadovoy. "Television and the Law in the Soviet Union", 11 *LOYOLA ENTERTAINMENT JOURNAL* 293-351 (1991).

LAWS AND OFFICIAL DOCUMENTS IN ENGLISH TRANSLATION, *continued*

Property Law

Butler, William E. ed. *THE LAW OF OWNERSHIP IN THE USSR.* London: Intershelf, Ltd., 1991. viii, 392 pp. (The Butler Commentaries on Soviet Law).

Religion

"The Law of the Union of Soviet Socialist Republics on Freedom of Conscience and Religious Organizations", 8 *JOURNAL OF LAW AND RELIGION* 385-395 (1990).

Taxation

George, Arthur L., and Thomas A. O'Donnell. *BUSINESS OPERATIONS IN THE U.S.S.R.* Washington, DC: Tax Management, Inc., 1991 (Tax Management, Foreign Income Portfolios, 990).

Hogan, James E. "New Tax and Companies Legislation in the USSR", 16 *REVIEW OF SOCIALIST LAW* 351-362 (1990).

Newcity, Michael. *SOVIET TAXATION: STATUTES, REGULATIONS, AND TREATIES.* Ardsley-on-Hudson, NY: Transnational Juris Publications, Inc., 1991. Looseleaf.

Legal Education

See Legal Profession

Legal History

See History (Pre-1917)

Legal Profession

☆Drugueva, Olga. "Legal Education in the USSR", 17 *CORNELL LAW FORUM* 10-11 (July 1990).

Gifford, Donald C. "Glasnost and Perestroika at West Virginia University: The College of Law's Soviet Exchange Program", 94 *WEST VIRGINIA LAW REVIEW* 165-177 (1991).

Osakwe, Christopher. *SOVIET BUSINESS LAW: INSTITUTIONS, PRINCIPLES, AND PROCESSES.* Salem, NH: Butterworth Legal Publishers, 1991. 2 Volumes, looseleaf, misc. pag.

Skolnick, Joanne. "When Soviet Lawyers Meet American Law", 17 *HUMAN RIGHTS* No. 3, 20-21 (Fall/Winter 1990).

☆Sobchak, Anatoly A. "The Changing Role of Lawyers in the Soviet Union", 3 *INTERNATIONAL LEGAL PERSPECTIVES* 40-50 (1990).

Whitman, Sylvia. "'These Are Bridges That Have to Be Built': The American Law Center in Moscow Provides a Groundbreaking Link between U.S. and Soviet Lawyers", 20 *STUDENT LAWYER* No. 5, 8-10 (January 1992).

Legal Reform

☆*THE HEARTBEAT OF REFORM: SOVIET JURISTS AND POLITICAL SCIENTISTS DISCUSS THE PROGRESS OF PERESTROIKA.* Compiled by Juri Baturin. Moscow: Progress Publishers, 1990. 368 pp.

☆Kvint, Vladimir. "Political, Economic and Legal Reform in the Soviet Union", 12 *WHITTIER LAW REVIEW* 143-146 (1991).

Schmid, Karin. "Legal Reform as a Means of Perestroika", in *THE SOVIET UNION, 1988-1989: PERESTROIKA IN CRISIS?,* compiled by The Federal Institute for Soviet and International Studies (Boulder, CO: Westview Press, 1990), pp. 54-60.

☆Sheremet, Konstantin. "Law and Social Change in the USSR of the 1990s", 27 *SOCIETY* 90-97 (1990).

Solomon, Peter H., Jr. "Gorbachev's Legal Revolution", 17 *CANADIAN BUSINESS LAW JOURNAL* 184-194 (1990).

LEGAL REFORM, *continued*

Solomon, Peter H., Jr. "Legality in Soviet Political Culture: A Perspective on Gorbachev's Reforms", in *STALINISM: ITS NATURE AND AFTERMATH. ESSAYS IN HONOUR OF MOSHE LEWIN*, edited by Nick Lampert and Gabor T. Rittersporn (Armonk, NY: M.E. Sharpe, Inc., 1992), pp. 260-287.

☆Yakovlev, Alexander M. "Transforming the Soviet Union into a Rule of Law Democracy: A Report from the Front Lines", 46 *THE RECORD OF THE ASSOCIATION OF THE BAR OF THE CITY OF NEW YORK* 129-148 (1991).

Legal System

See Administration of Justice, General Studies—Surveys of Soviet Law, Legal Reform, *and* Perestroika

Legal Translations

See Laws and Official Documents in English Translation

Legislation

See Government System—Legislature *and* Laws and Official Documents in English Translation

Lithuania

See Baltic

Litvinov

☆Sheinis, Zinovy. *MAXIM LITVINOV.* Moscow: Progress Publishers, 1990. 356 pp.

Local Government

See Government System—Local Government

Mafia

Vaksberg, Arkady. *THE SOVIET MAFIA.* New York: St. Martin's Press, 1991. ix, 275 pp.

Maritime Law

See also Arbitration—Maritime

Boczek, Boleslaw Adam. "The Baltic Sea: An International Legal Profile", 38 *OSTEUROPA RECHT* 25-51 (1992).

Clingan, Thomas A., Jr., and Anatoly L. Kolodkin, eds. *MOSCOW SYMPOSIUM ON THE LAW OF THE SEA: PROCEEDINGS OF A WORKSHIP CO-SPONSORED BY THE LAW OF THE SEA INSTITUTE, THE SOVIET MARITIME LAW ASSOCIATION, THE SOVIET PEACE FUND*, November 28-December 2, 1988 in Moscow. Honolulu: The Law of the Sea Institute, William S. Richardson School of Law, University of Hawaii, 1991. xi, 394 pp.

Elferink, Alex Oude. "The 1990 USSR-USA Maritime Boundary Agreement", 6 *INTERNATIONAL JOURNAL OF ESTUARINE AND COASTAL LAW* 41-52 (1991).

Fitzmaurice, M. *INTERNATIONAL LEGAL PROBLEMS OF THE ENVIRONMENTAL PROTECTION OF THE BALTIC SEA.* Dordrecht, The Netherlands: Martinus Nijhoff/Graham & Trotman, 1992. xxix, 328 pp.

Franckx, Erik. "First Trijunction Point Agreed upon in the Baltic between Poland, Sweden, and the USSR", 5 *INTERNATIONAL JOURNAL OF ESTUARINE AND COASTAL LAW* 394-397 (1990).

MARITIME LAW, *continued*

Franckx, Erik. "Further Steps in the Clarification of the Soviet Position on the Innocent Passage of Foreign Warships through Its Territorial Waters", 19 *GEORGIA JOURNAL OF INTERNATIONAL AND COMPARATIVE LAW* 535-563 (1989).

Franckx, Erik. "International Cooperation in Respect of the Baltic Sea", in *THE CHANGING POLITICAL STRUCTURE OF EUROPE: ASPECTS OF INTERNATIONAL LAW,* edited by R. Lefeber, M. Fitzmaurice, and E.W. Vierdag (Dordrecht, The Netherlands: Martinus Nijhoff Publishers, 1991), pp. 245-277.

☆Gureyev, S. *THE ECONOMIC ZONE: AN INTERNATIONAL LEGAL ASPECT.* Moscow: Progress Publishers, 1990. 164 pp.

Jorgensen-Dahl, Arnfinn. "The Soviet-Norwegian Maritime Disputes in the Arctic: Law and Politics", 21 *OCEAN DEVELOPMENT AND INTERNATIONAL LAW* 411-429 (1990).

Kwiatkowska, Barbara. "Innocent Passage by Warships", 21 *OCEAN DEVELOPMENT AND INTERNATIONAL LAW* 447-450 (1990).

Lowe, Vaughan. "USA/USSR: Uniform Interpretation of the Rules of International Law Governing Innocent Passage", 6 *INTERNATIONAL JOURNAL OF ESTUARINE AND COASTAL LAW* 73-76 (1991).

McNeill, John H. "America's Maritime Boundary with the Soviet Union", 154 *NAVAL WAR COLLEGE REVIEW* No. 3, 46-57 (Summer 1991).

☆Movchan, A.P. "The Legal Regime of Navigation in the Arctic: Problems of Soviet-Canadian Cooperation", in *FROM COEXISTENCE TO COOPERATION: INTERNATIONAL LAW AND ORGANIZATION IN THE POST-COLD WAR ERA*, edited by Edward McWhinney, et al. (Dordrecht, The Netherlands: Martinus Nijhoff Publishers, 1991), pp. 167-176.

Ostreng, Willy. "The Northern Sea Route: A New Era in Soviet Policy?", 22 *OCEAN DEVELOPMENT AND INTERNATIONAL LAW* 259-287 (1991).

☆Saguirion, Artemy A. "The U.S.S.R. and the New Law of the Sea Convention: In Search of Practical Solutions", 84 *AMERICAN SOCIETY OF INTERNATIONAL LAW PROCEEDINGS* 295-300 (1990).

Market Economy

See also Economic System *and* Privatization

Bohn, John A., Jr., and David H. Levey. "Models of Capital Market Development", in *THE EMERGING RUSSIAN BEAR: INTEGRATING THE SOVIET UNION INTO THE WORLD ECONOMY*, edited by Josef C. Brada and Michael P. Claudon (New York: New York University Press, 1991), pp. 73-85.

Floroff, Olga, and Susan W. Tiefenbrun. "A Legal Framework for Soviet Privatization", 18 *PEPPERDINE LAW REVIEW* No. 4, 849-892 (1991).

☆Katkov, Alexander L. "Can Joint Ventures Help to Create a Market Economy in the Soviet Union", in *THE EMERGING RUSSIAN BEAR: INTEGRATING THE SOVIET UNION INTO THE WORLD ECONOMY*, edited by Josef C. Brada and Michael P. Claudon (New York: New York University Press, 1991), pp. 143-163.

Military Law

Schmitt, Michael N., and James E. Moody. "The Soviet Military Justice System", 34 *AIR FORCE LAW REVIEW* 1-108 (1991).

Minorities

See Baltic,
Jews, *and*
Nationalities and Nationalism

Moldavia

Blaustein, Albert P., ed. *CONSTITUTIONS OF DEPENDENCIES AND SPECIAL SOVEREIGNTIES.* Dobbs Ferry, NY: Oceana Publications, 1977- .

Commission on Security and Cooperation in Europe. *ELECTIONS IN THE BALTIC STATES AND SOVIET REPUBLICS: A COMPENDIUM OF REPORTS ON PARLIAMENTARY ELECTIONS HELD IN 1990.* Compiled by the Staff of the Commission on Security and Cooperation in Europe. Washington: U.S. Government Printing Office, 1990. x, 188 pp.

Furtado, Charles F., Jr., and Andrea Chandler. *PERESTROIKA IN THE SOVIET REPUBLICS: DOCUMENTS ON THE NATIONAL QUESTION.* Boulder, CO: Westview Press, 1992. xxvi, 646 pp.

Solchanyk, Roman. "Ukraine, Belorussia, and Moldavia: Imperial Integration, Russification, and the Struggle for National Survival", in *THE NATIONALITIES FACTOR IN SOVIET POLITICS AND SOCIETY*, edited by Lubomyr Hajda and Mark Beissinger (Boulder, CO: Westview Press, 1990), pp. 175-203.

Money

See Currency

Narcotic Drugs

See Drugs

National Independence

See Baltic *and*
Nationalities and Nationalism

Nationalities and Nationalism

Allworth, Edward. "A Theory of Soviet Nationality Policies", in *SOVIET NATIONALITY POLICIES: RULING ETHNIC GROUPS IN THE USSR*, edited by Henry R. Huttenbach (London: Mansell Publishing Ltd., 1990), pp. 24-46.

Beyme, Klaus von. "Social and Economic Conditions for Ethnic Strife in the Soviet Union", in *SOVIET FEDERALISM: NATIONALISM AND ECONOMIC DECENTRALISATION,* edited by Alastair McAuley (Leicester and London: Leicester University Press, 1991), pp. 89-109.

Blase, John C., and Cynthia M. Smith. "Soviet Republics' Demand for Autonomy: The Need for Constitutional Reform and the Institution of Canadian-Style Judicial Review" (Note), 17 *JOURNAL OF LEGISLATION* 237-260 (1991).

Blaustein, Albert P., ed. *CONSTITUTIONS OF DEPENDENCIES AND SPECIAL SOVEREIGNTIES.* Dobbs Ferry, NY: Oceana Publications, 1977- .

Bociurkiw, R. Bohdan. "Nationalities and Soviet Religious Policies", in *THE NATIONALITIES FACTOR IN SOVIET POLITICS AND SOCIETY*, edited by Lubomyr Hajda and Mark Beissinger (Boulder, CO: Westview Press, 1990), pp. 148-174.

Buchsweiler, Meir. *A COLLECTION OF SOVIET DOCUMENTS CONCERNING GERMANS IN THE USSR.* Jerusalem: The Hebrew University of Jerusalem, The Marjorie Mayrock Center for Soviet and East European Research, 1991. 26 pp. (Research Paper No. 73).

Carlisle, Donald S. "Uzbekistan and the Uzbeks", 40 *PROBLEMS OF COMMUNISM* No. 5, 23-44 (Sept.-Oct. 1991).

Carter, Stephen K. *RUSSIAN NATIONALISM: YESTERDAY, TODAY, TOMORROW.* London: Pinter Publishers, 1990. 175 pp.

Commission on Security and Cooperation in Europe. *ELECTIONS IN THE BALTIC STATES AND SOVIET REPUBLICS: A COMPENDIUM OF REPORTS ON PARLIAMENTARY ELECTIONS HELD IN 1990.* Compiled by the Staff of the Commission on Security and Cooperation in Europe. Washington: U.S. Government Printing Office, 1990. x, 188 pp.

Critchlow, James. "'Corruption', Nationalism, and the Native Elites in Soviet Central Asia", 4 *JOURNAL OF COMMUNIST STUDIES* 142-159 (1988).

NATIONALITIES AND NATIONALISM, *continued*

Diuk, Nadia, and Adrian Karatnycky. *THE HIDDEN NATIONS: THE PEOPLE CHALLENGE THE SOVIET UNION*. New York: William Morrow and Co., 1990. 286 pp.

Fraser, Niall M., Keith W. Hipel, John Jaworsky, and Ralph Zuljan. "A Conflict Analysis of the Armenian-Azerbaijan Dispute", 34 *JOURNAL OF CONFLICT RESOLUTION* 652-677 (1990).

Furtado, Charles F., Jr., and Andrea Chandler. *PERESTROIKA IN THE SOVIET REPUBLICS: DOCUMENTS ON THE NATIONAL QUESTION*. Boulder, CO: Westview Press, 1992. xxvi, 646 pp.

Girnius, Kestutis. "The Party and Popular Movements in the Baltic", in *TOWARD INDEPENDENCE: THE BALTIC POPULAR MOVEMENTS*, edited by Jan Arveds Trapans (Boulder, CO; San Francisco; Oxford: Westview Press, 1991), pp. 57-69.

Gleason, Gregory. *FEDERALISM AND NATIONALISM: THE STRUGGLE FOR REPUBLICAN RIGHTS IN THE USSR*. Boulder, CO: Westview Press, Inc., 1990. xiii, 170 pp.

Goble, Paul A. "Nationalism, Movement Groups, and Party Formation", in *PERESTROIKA FROM BELOW: SOCIAL MOVEMENTS IN THE SOVIET UNION*, edited by Judith Sedaitis and Jim Butterfield (Boulder, CO: Westview Press, 1991), pp. 165-174.

Hajda, Lubomyr, and Mark Beissinger. *THE NATIONALITIES FACTOR IN SOVIET POLITICS AND SOCIETY*. Boulder, CO: Westview Press, 1990. vii, 331 pp.

Halbach, Uwe. "Anatomy of an Escalation: The Nationality Question", in *THE SOVIET UNION, 1988-1989: PERESTROIKA IN CRISIS?*, compiled by The Federal Institute for Soviet and International Studies (Boulder, CO: Westview Press, 1990), pp. 73-82.

Hazard, John N. "Codification of Soviet Nationality Policies", in *SOVIET NATIONALITY POLICIES: RULING ETHNIC GROUPS IN THE USSR*, edited by Henry R. Huttenbach (London: Mansell Publishing Limited, 1990), pp. 47-61.

Huttenbach, Henry R., ed. *SOVIET NATIONALITY POLICIES: RULING ETHNIC GROUPS IN THE USSR*. London: Mansell Publishing Ltd., 1990. xvi, 302 pp.

Ilves, Toomas Hendrik. "Reaction: The Intermovements in Estonia", in *TOWARD INDEPENDENCE: THE BALTIC POPULAR MOVEMENTS*, edited by Jan Arveds Trapans (Boulder, CO; San Francisco; Oxford: Westview Press, 1991), pp. 71-83.

NATIONALITIES AND NATIONALISM, *continued*

Karklins, Rasma. "Nationalities and Ethnic Issues", in *SOVIET UPDATE, 1989-1990,* edited by Anthony Jones and David E. Powell (Boulder, CO: Westview Press, 1991), pp. 75-96.

Karklins, Rasma. "Nationality, Policy and Ethnic Relations in the USSR", in *POLITICS, WORK, AND DAILY LIFE IN THE USSR: A SURVEY OF FORMER SOVIET CITIZENS*, edited by James R. Millar (Cambridge: Cambridge University Press, 1987), pp. 301-331.

☆Krupnik, Igor. "The Nationalities Question in the USSR: Looking for Explanations", 22 *SOCIAL SCIENCES* No. 4, 138-155 (1991).

Kux, Stephan. *SOVIET FEDERALISM: A COMPARATIVE PERSPECTIVE*. New York: Institute for East-West Security Studies, 1990. vi, 117 pp.

Lapidus, Gail W. "Can Gorbachev Manage the Nationalities Crisis?", in *CAN GORBACHEV'S REFORMS SUCCEED?*, edited by George W. Breslauer (Berkeley, CA: Center for Slavic and East European Studies and the Berkeley-Stanford Program in Soviet Studies, University of California of Berkeley, 1990), pp. 95-110.

Loeber, Dietrich André. *REGIONAL AND NATIONAL VARIATIONS: THE BALTIC FACTOR*. Washington: National Council for Soviet and East European Research, 1991. 30 pp.

Lukic, Reneo. "Twilight of the Federations in East Central Europe and the Soviet Union", 45 *JOURNAL OF INTERNATIONAL AFFAIRS* 575-598 (1992).

McAuley, Alastair, ed. *SOVIET FEDERALISM: NATIONALISM AND ECONOMIC DECENTRALISATION*. Leicester and London: Leicester University Press, 1991. ix, 214 pp.

Mihalisko, Kathleen. "The Popular Movement in Belorussia and Baltic Influence", in *TOWARD INDEPENDENCE: THE BALTIC POPULAR MOVEMENTS*, edited by Jan Arveds Trapans (Boulder, CO; San Francisco; Oxford: Westview Press, 1991), pp. 123-132.

Millar, James R., ed. *POLITICS, WORK, AND DAILY LIFE IN THE USSR: A SURVEY OF FORMER SOVIET CITIZENS*. Cambridge: Cambridge University Press, 1987. xiv, 423 pp.

NATIONALITIES AND NATIONALISM, *continued*

Misiunas, Romuald J. "Baltic Nationalism and Soviet Language Policy: From Russification to Constitutional Amendment", in *SOVIET NATIONALITY POLICIES: RULING ETHNIC GROUPS IN THE USSR*, edited by Henry R. Huttenbach (London: Mansell Publishing Limited, 1990), pp. 206-220.

Misiunas, Romuald J. "The Baltic Republics: Stagnation and Strikings for Sovereignty", in *THE NATIONALITIES FACTOR IN SOVIET POLITICS AND SOCIETY*, edited by Lubomyr Hajda and Mark Beissinger (Boulder, CO: Westview Press, 1990), pp. 204-227.

Motyl, Alexander J. "Russian Hegemony and Non-Russian Insecurity: Foreign Policy Dilemmas of the USSR's Successor States", 5 *HARRIMAN INSTITUTE FORUM* No. 4, 1-11 (December 1991).

Nahaylo, Bohdan. "Baltic Echoes in Ukraine", in *TOWARD INDEPENDENCE: THE BALTIC POPULAR MOVEMENTS*, edited by Jan Arveds Trapans (Boulder, CO; San Francisco; Oxford: Westview Press, 1991), pp. 108-122.

Nahaylo, Bohdan. "Nationalities", in *GORBACHEV AND PERESTROIKA*, edited by Martin McCauley (New York: St. Martin's Press, 1990), pp. 135-153.

Olcott, Martha Brill. "Central Asia: The Reformers Challenge a Traditional Society", in *THE NATIONALITIES FACTOR IN SOVIET POLITICS AND SOCIETY*, edited by Lubomyr Hajda and Mark Beissinger (Boulder, CO: Westview Press, 1990), pp. 253-280.

Olcott, Martha Brill. "The Soviet (Dis)union", 82 *FOREIGN POLICY* 118-136 (Spring 1991).

Pearson, Raymond. "Nationalities: Decolonizing the Last Empire", in *THE IMPACT OF GORBACHEV: THE FIRST PHASE, 1985-1990*, edited by D. W. Spring (London and New York: Pinter Publishers, 1991), pp. 92-115.

Plotnieks, Andris. "The Evolution of the Soviet Federation and the Independence of Latvia", in *SOVIET FEDERALISM: NATIONALISM AND ECONOMIC DECENTRALISATION*, edited by Alastair McAuley (Leicester and London: Leicester University Press, 1991), pp. 134-148.

Rakowska-Harmstone, Teresa. "Chickens Coming Home to Roost: A Perspective on Soviet Ethnic Relations", 45 *JOURNAL OF INTERNATIONAL AFFAIRS* 519-548 (1992).

NATIONALITIES AND NATIONALISM, *continued*

Rakowska-Harmstone, Teresa. "Nationalities and the Soviet Military", in *THE NATIONALITIES FACTOR IN SOVIET POLITICS AND SOCIETY*, edited by Lubomyr Hajda and Mark Beissinger (Boulder, CO: Westview Press, 1990), pp. 72-84.

Samuelian, Thomas J. "Cultural Ecology and Gorbachev's Restructured Union", 32 *HARVARD INTERNATIONAL LAW JOURNAL* 159-200 (1991).

Schroeder, Gertrude E. "Nationalities and the Soviet Economy" in *NATIONALITIES FACTOR IN SOVIET POLITICS AND SOCIETY*, edited by Lubomyr Hajda and Mark Beissinger (Boulder, CO: Westview Press, 1990), pp. 43-71.

Schroeder, Gertrude E. "On the Economic Viability of New Nation-States", 45 *JOURNAL OF INTERNATIONAL AFFAIRS* 549-574 (1992).

Sedaitis, Judith B., and Jim Butterfield, eds. *PERESTROIKA FROM BELOW: SOCIAL MOVEMENTS IN THE SOVIET UNION* (Boulder, CO: Westview Press, Inc., 1991). xii, 220 pp.

Sheehy, Ann. "The Ethnodemographic Dimension", in *SOVIET FEDERALISM: NATIONALISM AND ECONOMIC DECENTRALISATION*, edited by Alastair McAuley (Leicester and London: Leicester University Press, 1991), pp. 56-88.

Simon, Gerhard. *NATIONALISM AND POLICY TOWARD THE NATIONALITIES IN THE SOVIET UNION*. Boulder, CO: Westview, 1991. 483 pp.

Smith, Graham. *THE NATIONALITIES QUESTION IN THE SOVIET UNION*. London and New York: Longman, 1990. ix, 389 pp.

Solchanyk, Roman. "Ukraine, Belorussia, and Moldavia: Imperial Integration, Russification, and the Struggle for National Survival", in *THE NATIONALITIES FACTOR IN SOVIET POLITICS AND SOCIETY*, edited by Lubomyr Hajda and Mark Beissinger (Boulder, CO: Westview Press, 1990), pp. 175-203.

Sunstein, Cass R. "Constitutionalism and Secession", 58 *UNIVERSITY OF CHICAGO LAW REVIEW* 633-670 (1991).

Suny, Ronald G. "Transcaucasia: Cultural Cohesion and Ethnic Revival in a Multinational Society", in *THE NATIONALITIES FACTOR IN SOVIET POLITICS AND SOCIETY*, edited by Lubomyr Hajda and Mark Beissinger. Boulder, CO: Westview Press, 1990, pp. 228-252.

Natural Resources

See Environmental Law and Policy

Negotiating Behavior

See International Law—Negotiating Behavior

Nomenklatura

Nuclear Energy

☆Shcherbak, Iurii. *CHERNOBYL: A DOCUMENTARY STORY*. New York: St. Martin's Press, 1989. xvi, 168 pp.

Official Documents

See Laws and Official Documents in English Translation

Pacific Ocean

Atkinson, Scott. "The USSR and the Pacific Century", 30 *ASIAN SURVEY* 629-642 (1990).

Patents and Trademarks

Frenkel, William G., and Jeffrey Sperber. "From Borscht to Bits: Transfer of Technology and Industrial Property in the Soviet Union", 4 *DE PAUL BUSINESS LAW JOURNAL* 3-48 (1991).

Litman, Gary V. "Reinventing a Law on Inventions: International Aspects of the New Russian Patent Law" (Note), 25 *GEORGE WASHINGTON JOURNAL OF INTERNATIONAL LAW AND ECONOMICS* 171-226 (1991).

☆Mamiofa, Iosif E. "Industrial Property Rights of Joint Ventures in the Soviet Union", 2 *INTERNATIONAL COMPANY AND COMMERCIAL LAW REVIEW* 242-246 (1991).

☆Mamiofa, Iosif E., and Corien Prins. "Protecting Computer Programs—The Soviet Perspective", 22 *INTERNATIONAL REVIEW OF INDUSTRIAL PROPERTY AND COPYRIGHT LAW* (IIC) 605-628 (1991).

Phillips, Jeremy. "Patents and Licensing in the USSR in Light of New Legislation", 3 *INTELLECTUAL PROPERTY IN BUSINESS* 26-28 (1991).

Penology

See Criminal Law and Procedure *and* Prison System

Perestroika

Editorial Note: Perestroika has become a much-used "catchword" in popular writing, and is included in the titles of many works which have only a vague connection with the concept of perestroika. Such publications have been omitted from the following list.

☆Alexeyev, Sergei. *LAW AND LEGAL CULTURE IN SOVIET SOCIETY.* Moscow: Progress Publishers, 1991. 214 pp.

Aurbach, Laurence J., ed. *BEYOND PERESTROIKA: OPTIONS FOR A NEW SOVIET UNION.* Chicago: American Bar Association, Section of Urban, State, and Local Government Law, 1991. iv, 40 pp.

Bazyler, Michael J. "The Gorbachev Revolution", 12 *WHITTIER LAW REVIEW* 147-150 (1991).

Belkindas, Misha. *PRIVATIZATION OF THE SOVIET ECONOMY UNDER GORBACHEV II: 1. THE CAMPAIGN AGAINST UNEARNED INCOME. 2. THE DEVELOPMENT OF PRIVATE COOPERATIVES.* Durham, NC: Department of Economics, Duke University, 1989. ii, 97 pp. (Berkeley-Duke Occasional Papers on the Second Economy in the USSR, 14).

Black, J.L., ed. *USSR DOCUMENTS ANNUAL 1989. THE GORBACHEV REFORMS CONTINUE. THE END OF THE EMPIRE?* Gulf Breeze, FL: Academic International Press, 1990. xii, 435 pp.

Black, J.L., ed. *USSR DOCUMENTS ANNUAL 1990. RESTRUCTURING PERESTROIKA.* Gulf Breeze, FL: Academic International Press, 1991. 2 Vols. (ix, 335 and vii, 379 pp. respectively).

Breslauer, George W., ed. *CAN GORBACHEV'S REFORMS SUCCEED?* Berkeley, CA: Center for Slavic and East European Studies and the Berkeley-Stanford Program in Soviet Studies, University of California at Berkeley, 1990. vii, 135 pp.

Goldman, Marshall I. *WHAT WENT WRONG WITH PERESTROIKA.* New York: W.W. Norton & Company, 1991. 258 pp.

PERESTROIKA, *continued*

☆*THE HEARTBEAT OF REFORM: SOVIET JURISTS AND POLITICAL SCIENTISTS DISCUSS THE PROGRESS OF PERESTROIKA.* Compiled by Juri Baturin. Moscow: Progress Publishers, 1990. 368 pp.

☆Kvint, Vladimir. "Political, Economic and Legal Reform in the Soviet Union", 12 *WHITTIER LAW REVIEW* 143-146 (1991).

Sedaitis, Judith B., and Jim Butterfield, eds. *PERESTROIKA FROM BELOW: SOCIAL MOVEMENTS IN THE SOVIET UNION* (Boulder, CO: Westview Press, Inc., 1991). xii, 220 pp.

Spring, D.W., ed. *THE IMPACT OF GORBACHEV: THE FIRST PHASE, 1985-1990.* London and New York: Pinter Publishers, 1991. ix, 244 pp.

Stephan, Paul B., III. *SOVIET ECONOMIC LAW: THE PARADOX OF PERESTROYKA.* Pittsburgh, PA: University of Pittsburgh Center for Russian and East European Studies, 1990. 90 pp. (The Carl Beck Papers in Russian and East European Studies, No. 805).

Vause, W. Gary. "The Coming End of Perestroika's Golden Age of Law Reform?", 20 *STETSON LAW REVIEW* 201-209 (1990).

Persecution

See Jews,
Psychiatric Abuse,
Religion,
and Stalinist Terror

Philosophy of Law

Butler, William E. ed. *PERESTROIKA AND THE RULE OF LAW: ANGLO-AMERICAN AND SOVIET PERSPECTIVES.* London: I.B. Tauris & Co., Ltd., 1991. 199 pp.

Freeman, M.D.A. "The Rule of Law—Conservative, Liberal, Marxist and Neo-Marxist: Wherein Lies the Attraction?", in *PERESTROIKA AND THE RULE OF LAW: ANGLO-AMERICAN AND SOVIET PERSPECTIVES,* edited by William E. Butler (London: I.B. Tauris & Co., Ltd., 1991), pp. 37-59.

PHILOSOPHY OF LAW, *continued*

Huskey, Eugene. "A Framework for the Analysis of Soviet Law", 50 *RUSSIAN REVIEW* 53-70 (1991).

☆Kumanin, E.V. "Political Pluralism and Law", in *PERESTROIKA AND THE RULE OF LAW: ANGLO-AMERICAN AND SOVIET PERSPECTIVES*, edited by William E. Butler (London: I.B. Tauris & Co., Ltd., 1991), pp. 77-87.

☆Livshits, R.Z. "Jus and Lex: Evolution of Views", in *PERESTROIKA AND THE RULE OF LAW: ANGLO-AMERICAN AND SOVIET PERSPECTIVES*, edited by William E. Butler (London: I.B. Tauris & Co., Ltd., 1991), pp. 22-36.

Police

Andrew, Christopher, and Oleg Gordievsky. *KGB: THE INSIDE STORY OF ITS FOREIGN OPERATIONS FROM LENIN TO GORBACHEV*. London: Hodder & Stoughton, 1990. xxxii, 704 pp.

Borcke, Astrid von. "The KGB and Perestroika", in *THE SOVIET UNION, 1988-1989: PERESTROIKA IN CRISIS?*, edited by The Federal Institute for Soviet and International Studies (Boulder, CO: Westview Press, 1990), pp. 61-66.

Deriabin, Peter, and T.M. Bagley. *KGB: MASTERS OF THE SOVIET UNION*. New York: Hippocrane Books, Inc., 1990. xxiv, 466 pp.

☆"Fear: Confessions of a Well-Known Legal Expert Who Has Criticized the Draft Law on the KGB", 30 *SOVIET LAW AND GOVERNMENT* No. 2, 88-96 (Fall 1991).

☆Gamaiunov, Igor. "Without Hypnosis: Supervising the KGB—Myth or Reality?", 30 *SOVIET LAW AND GOVERNMENT* No. 2, 76-87 (Fall 1991).

Knight, Amy W. "The Future of the KGB", 39 *PROBLEMS OF COMMUNISM* No. 6, 20-39 (November-December 1990).

Oda, Hiroshi. "Law Enforcement Agencies", in *THE SOVIET SOBRANIE OF LAWS*, edited by Richard M. Buxbaum and Kathryn Hendley (Berkeley, CA: University of California, 1991), pp. 127-139.

Political Parties

See also Communist Party

☆Balkina, M.A., ed. *NEW POLITICAL PARTIES AND MOVEMENTS IN THE SOVIET UNION.* Commack, N.Y.: Nova Science Publishers, Inc., 1991. 156 pp.

Bonnell, Victoria E. "Voluntary Associations in Gorbachev's Reform Program", in *CAN GORBACHEV'S REFORMS SUCCEED?*, edited by George W. Breslauer (Berkeley, CA: Center for Slavic and East European Studies and the Berkeley-Stanford Program in Soviet Studies, University of California at Berkeley, 1990), pp. 63-76.

Gardner, Richard N. "The Triple Crisis of the Soviet Union Today", 11 *NEW YORK LAW SCHOOL JOURNAL OF INTERNATIONAL AND COMPARATIVE LAW* 435-437 (1990).

Goble, Paul A. "Nationalism, Movement Groups, and Party Formation", in *PERESTROIKA FROM BELOW: SOCIAL MOVEMENTS IN THE SOVIET UNION*, edited by Judith Sedaitis and Jim Butterfield (Boulder, CO: Westview Press, 1991), pp. 165-174.

Potichnyi, Peter J. *THE MULTI-PARTY SYSTEM IN UKRAINE.* Cologne: Bundesinstitut für ostwissenschaftliche und internationale Studien, 1992. iii, 39 pp. (Report 3-1992).

Sedaitis, Judith B., and Jim Butterfield, eds. *PERESTROIKA FROM BELOW: SOCIAL MOVEMENTS IN THE SOVIET UNION* (Boulder, CO: Westview Press, Inc., 1991). xii, 220 pp.

Starr, S. Frederick. "Voluntary Groups and Initiatives", in *SOVIET UPDATE, 1989-1990,* edited by Anthony Jones and David E. Powell (Boulder, CO: Westview Press, 1991), pp. 97-116.

Tolz, Vera. *THE USSR'S EMERGING MULTIPARTY SYSTEM.* New York: Praeger, 1990. xvi, 123 pp. (The Center for Strategic and International Studies, Washington Papers No. 148).

Political System
See also Political Parties

Commission on Security and Cooperation in Europe. *REFERENDUM IN THE SOVIET UNION. A COMPENDIUM OF REPORTS ON THE MARCH 17, 1991 REFERENDUM ON THE FUTURE OF THE USSR.* Compiled by the Staff of the Commission on Security and Cooperation in Europe. Washington: U.S. Government Printing Office, 1991. viii, 46 pp.

Commission on Security and Cooperation in Europe. *THE USSR IN CRISIS: STATE OF THE UNION.* Hearing before the Commission on Security, Feb. 6, 1991. Washington: U.S. Government Printing Office, 1991. iii, 77 pp. (Sudoc No. Y4.Sc.2:102-1-3.)

Goldberg, Stephanie B. "The Soviet Union Retreats from Reform: Danger on the Right", 77 *ABA JOURNAL* No. 5, 71-73 (May 1991).

☆Gorbachev, Mikhail. *THE AUGUST COUP: THE TRUTH AND THE LESSONS.* New York: Harper Collins, 1991. 127 pp.

☆*THE HEARTBEAT OF REFORM: SOVIET JURISTS AND POLITICAL SCIENTISTS DISCUSS THE PROGRESS OF PERESTROIKA.* Compiled by Juri Baturin. Moscow: Progress Publishers, 1990. 368 pp.

Hosking, Geoffrey. *THE AWAKENING OF THE SOVIET UNION.* Cambridge: Harvard University Press, 1990. ix, 182 pp.

Huber, Robert T., and Donald R. Kelley. *PERESTROIKA-ERA POLITICS: THE NEW SOVIET LEGISLATURE AND GORBACHEV'S POLITICAL REFORMS.* Armonk, NY: M.E. Sharpe, Inc., 1991. viii, 246 pp.

Kux, Stephan. *SOVIET FEDERALISM: A COMPARATIVE PERSPECTIVE.* New York: Institute for East-West Security Studies, 1990. vi, 117 pp.

Millar, James R., ed. *POLITICS, WORK, AND DAILY LIFE IN THE USSR: A SURVEY OF FORMER SOVIET CITIZENS.* Cambridge: Cambridge University Press, 1987. xiv, 423 pp.

Motyl, Alexander J. "Russian Hegemony and Non-Russian Insecurity: Foreign Policy Dilemmas of the USSR's Successor States", 5 *HARRIMAN INSTITUTE FORUM* No. 4, 1-11 (December 1991).

Morrison, John. *BORIS YELTSIN: FROM BOLSHEVIK TO DEMOCRAT.* New York: Dutton, 1991. 303 pp.

POLITICAL SYSTEM, *continued*

Remington, Thomas F. "Parliamentary Government in the USSR", in *PERESTROIKA-ERA POLITICS: THE NEW SOVIET LEGISLATURE AND GORBACHEV'S POLITICAL REFORMS,* edited by Robert T. Huber and Donald R. Kelley (Armonk, NY: M.E. Sharpe, Inc., 1991), pp. 175-204.

Rigby, T.H. *POLITICAL ELITES IN THE USSR: CENTRAL LEADERS AND LOCAL CADRES FROM LENIN TO GORBACHEV.* Aldershot, Hants, England: Edward Elgar Publishing Ltd., 1990. vii, 301 pp.

Schneider, Eberhard. "The Nineteenth Party Conference: Reform of the Political System", in *THE SOVIET UNION 1988-1989: PERESTROIKA IN CRISIS?,* compiled by The Federal Institute for Soviet and International Studies (Boulder, CO: Westview Press, 1990), pp. 30-39.

☆Shevardnadze, Eduard. "Consolidation of the CPSU in a Multiparty System", 29 *SOVIET LAW AND GOVERNMENT* No. 4, 5-20 (Spring 1991).

☆Shevardnadze, Eduard. *THE FUTURE BELONGS TO FREEDOM.* New York: The Free Press, 1991. xx, 237 pp.

Simes, Dimitry. "Gorbachev's Time of Troubles", 82 *FOREIGN POLICY* 97-117 (Spring 1991).

Smith, Gordon B. *SOVIET POLITICS: STRUGGLING WITH CHANGE.* 2d ed. New York: St. Martin's Press; London: The MacMillan Press, 1992. xx, 396 pp.

☆Sobchak, Anatoly A. *FOR A NEW RUSSIA: THE MAYOR OF ST. PETERSBURG'S OWN STORY OF THE STRUGGLE FOR JUSTICE AND DEMOCRACY.* New York: The Free Press, 1991. 191 pp.

☆Sobchak, Anatoly A. "The New Soviet Union—Challenges in the Development of a Law-Abiding State", 20 *STETSON LAW REVIEW* 211-216 (1990).

Swaford, Michael. "Perceptions of Social Stations in the USSR", in *POLITICS, WORK, AND DAILY LIFE IN THE USSR: A SURVEY OF FORMER SOVIET CITIZENS*, edited by James R. Millar (Cambridge: Cambridge University Press, 1987), pp. 279-300.

Tatu, Michel. *MIKHAIL GORBACHEV: THE ORIGINS OF PERESTROIKA.* Boulder, CO: East European Monographs, 1981 (distributed by Columbia University Press). xi, 155 pp.

POLITICAL SYSTEM, *continued*

Tucker, Robert C. *STALIN IN POWER: THE REVOLUTION FROM ABOVE, 1928-1941.* New York: Norton, 1990. xix, 707 pp.

☆Volkogonov, Dmitri. *STALIN: TRIUMPH AND TRAGEDY.* New York; London: Weidenfeld, 1991.

White, Stephen, Alex Pravda, and Zvi Gitelman, eds. *DEVELOPMENTS IN SOVIET POLITICS.* Durham, NC: Duke University Press, 1990. 310 pp.

President

See Government System *and* Political System

Press

See Censorship *and* Glasnost

Prison System

Rossi, Jacques. *THE GULAG HANDBOOK: AN ENCYCLOPEDIA DICTIONARY OF SOVIET PENITENTIARY INSTITUTIONS AND TERMS RELATED TO THE FORCED LABOR CAMPS.* New York: Paragon House, 1989. 610 pp.

Private Economic Activity

Belkindas, Misha. *PRIVATIZATION OF THE SOVIET ECONOMY UNDER GORBACHEV II: 1. THE CAMPAIGN AGAINST UNEARNED INCOME. 2. THE DEVELOPMENT OF PRIVATE COOPERATIVES.* Durham, NC: Department of Economics, Duke University, 1989. ii, 97 pp. (Berkeley-Duke Occasional Papers on the Second Economy in the USSR, 14).

Griffin, Andrew T., and Larry D. Soderquist. "Private Companies in the Soviet Union: Cooperatives in the Era of Perestroika", 32 *HARVARD INTERNATIONAL LAW JOURNAL* 201-225 (1991).

Privatization

Belkindas, Misha. *PRIVATIZATION OF THE SOVIET ECONOMY UNDER GORBACHEV II: 1. THE CAMPAIGN AGAINST UNEARNED INCOME. 2. THE DEVELOPMENT OF PRIVATE COOPERATIVES*. Durham, NC: Department of Economics, Duke University, 1989. ii, 97 pp. (Berkeley-Duke Occasional Papers on the Second Economy in the USSR, 14).

Brada, Josef C., and Michael P. Claudon, eds. *THE EMERGING RUSSIAN BEAR: INTEGRATING THE SOVIET UNION INTO THE WORLD ECONOMY*. New York: New York University Press, 1991. xiii, 228 pp. (Geonomics Institute for International Economic Advancement Series).

English, Richard D. "Privatization by General Fund: Economic Empowerment for Central and Eastern Europe", 24 *GEORGE WASHINGTON JOURNAL OF INTERNATIONAL LAW AND ECONOMICS* 527-586 (1991).

Floroff, Olga, and Susan W. Tiefenbrun. "A Legal Framework for Soviet Privatization", 18 *PEPPERDINE LAW REVIEW* No. 4, 849-892 (1991).

Hanson, Philip. "Property Rights in the New Phase of Reforms", 6 *SOVIET ECONOMY* 95-124 (1990).

Palmer, Matthew S.R. "Privatization in Ukraine: Economics, Law, and Politics", 16 *YALE JOURNAL OF INTERNATIONAL LAW* 453-517 (1991).

Pettibone, Peter J. "Privatization: Opportunities, Risks, Prognosis", in *LEGAL AND PRACTICAL ASPECTS OF DOING BUSINESS IN THE SOVIET REPUBLICS* (New York: Practising Law Institute, 1991), pp. 105-114.

Stephan, Paul B., III. "*Perestroyka* and Property: The Law of Ownership in the Post-Socialist Soviet Union", 39 *AMERICAN JOURNAL OF COMPARATIVE LAW* 35-65 (1991).

Winiecki, Jan. "Buying Out Property Rights to the Economy from the Ruling Stratum: The Case of Soviet-Type States", 9 *INTERNATIONAL REVIEW OF LAW AND ECONOMICS* 79-85 (1989).

Procuracy

Oda, Hiroshi. "Law Enforcement Agencies", in *THE SOVIET SOBRANIE OF LAWS,* edited by Richard M. Buxbaum and Kathryn Hendley (Berkeley, CA: University of California, 1991), pp. 127-139.

Property Law

See Civil Law and Procedure—Property Law

Prostitution

Sanjian, Andrea Stevenson. "Prostitution, the Press, and Agenda-Building in the Soviet Policy Process", in *SOVIET SOCIAL PROBLEMS*, edited by Anthony Jones, et al. (Boulder, CO; San Francisco: Oxford: Westview Press, 1991), pp. 270-295.

Psychiatric Abuse

Bonnie, Richard J. "Coercive Psychiatry and Human Rights: An Assessment of Recent Changes in the Soviet Union", 1 *CRIMINAL LAW FORUM* 319-346 (1990).

Thompson, Lorri M. "Soviet Straitjacket Psychiatry: New Legislation to End the Reign of Terror in the USSR" (Note), 16 *SYRACUSE JOURNAL OF INTERNATIONAL LAW AND COMMERCE,* 271-91 (1990).

Public International Law

See International Law

Reference

See Bibliographies, Bibliographic Studies, and Reference Works

Religion
See also Jews

Bociurkiw, Bohdan R. "Nationalities and Soviet Religious Policies", in *THE NATIONALITIES FACTOR IN SOVIET POLITICS AND SOCIETY*, edited by Lubomyr Hajda and Mark Beissinger (Boulder, CO: Westview Press, 1990), pp. 148-174.

Bociurkiw, R. Bohdan. "The Ukrainian Catholic Church in the USSR under Gorbachev", 39 *PROBLEMS OF COMMUNISM* No. 6, 1-19 (November-December, 1990).

Critchlow, James. "Islam in Soviet Central Asia: Renaissance or Revolution?", 18 *RELIGION IN COMMUNIST LANDS* 196-211 (1990).

Davis, Nathaniel. "The Number of Churches before and after the Khrushchev Antireligious Drive", 50 *SLAVIC REVIEW* 612-620 (1991).

"The Law of the Union of Soviet Socialist Republics on Freedom of Conscience and Religious Organizations", 8 *JOURNAL OF LAW AND RELIGION* 385-395 (1990).

Pospielovsky, Dimitry V. "Church-State Relations in the USSR in 1988: The Local Sobor of the Russian Orthodox Church", in *THE SOVIET UNION, 1988-1989: PERESTROIKA IN CRISIS?*, compiled by The Federal Institute for Soviet and International Studies (Boulder, CO: Westview Press, 1990), pp. 83-90.

Powell, David E. "Soviet Society", in *SOVIET UPDATE, 1989-1990*, edited by Anthony Jones and David E. Powell (Boulder, CO: Westview Press, 1991), pp. 54-74.

Roth, Stephan J. "The New Soviet Law on Religion", 20 *SOVIET JEWISH AFFAIRS* No. 2-3, 27-37 (Autumn-Winter 1990).

Republics

See also Government System
and the individual republics by name

Blaustein, Albert P., ed. *CONSTITUTIONS OF DEPENDENCIES AND SPECIAL SOVEREIGNTIES.* Dobbs Ferry, NY: Oceana Publications, 1977- .

Commission on Security and Cooperation in Europe. *ELECTIONS IN THE BALTIC STATES AND SOVIET REPUBLICS: A COMPENDIUM OF REPORTS ON PARLIAMENTARY ELECTIONS HELD IN 1990.* Compiled by the Staff of the Commission on Security and Cooperation in Europe. Washington: U.S. Government Printing Office, 1990. x, 188 pp.

Motyl, Alexander J. "Russian Hegemony and Non-Russian Insecurity: Foreign Policy Dilemmas of the USSR's Successor States", 5 *HARRIMAN INSTITUTE FORUM* No. 4, 1-11 (December 1991).

Schroeder, Gertrude E. "Economic Relations among the Soviet Republics". A Paper presented at the Geonomics Institute Seminar, Middleburg, Vermont, May 10-13, 1991. 23 ll.

Schroeder, Gertrude E. "On the Economic Viability of New Nation-States", 45 *JOURNAL OF INTERNATIONAL AFFAIRS* 549-574 (1992).

Research on Soviet Law

See General Studies—Research on Soviet Law

Ruble

See Currency

Rule of Law

See Constitution

Russia

Blaustein, Albert P., and Gisbert H. Flanz, eds. *CONSTITUTIONS OF THE COUNTRIES OF THE WORLD*. Dobbs Ferry, NY: Oceana Publications, 1970- .

Carter, Stephen K. *RUSSIAN NATIONALISM: YESTERDAY, TODAY, TOMORROW*. London: Pinter Publishers, 1990. 175 pp.

Cole Corette & Arbutyn. "Legal and Practical Aspects of Doing Business in the Soviet Republics", in *LEGAL AND PRACTICAL ASPECTS OF DOING BUSINESS IN THE SOVIET REPUBLICS* (New York: Practising Law Institute, 1992), pp. 71-102.

Commission on Security and Cooperation in Europe. *ELECTIONS IN THE BALTIC STATES AND SOVIET REPUBLICS: A COMPENDIUM OF REPORTS ON PARLIAMENTARY ELECTIONS HELD IN 1990*. Compiled by the Staff of the Commission on Security and Cooperation in Europe. Washington: U.S. Government Printing Office, 1990. x, 188 pp.

D'Zurilla, William T. "Farewell to Lenin: The Story of Russia's New, Non-Communist Constitution", 38 *FEDERAL BAR NEWS AND JOURNAL* 410-412 (1991).

Furtado, Charles F., Jr., and Andrea Chandler. *PERESTROIKA IN THE SOVIET REPUBLICS: DOCUMENTS ON THE NATIONAL QUESTION*. Boulder, CO: Westview Press, 1992. xxvi, 646 pp.

George, Arthur L., and Thomas A. O'Donnell. "Russian Republic Joint-Stock Decree: Tidings of Great Joy?", 18 *TAX PLANNING INTERNATIONAL REVIEW* No. 8, 14-16 (August, 1991).

LEGAL AND PRACTICAL ASPECTS OF DOING BUSINESS IN THE SOVIET REPUBLICS. Commercial Law and Practice Course Handbook Series No. 604. New York: Practising Law Institute, 1992. 500 pp.

☆Kartashkin, Vladimir A. "Human Rights and the Emergence of the State of the Rule of Law in the USSR", 40 *EMORY LAW JOURNAL* 889-902 (1991).

McLure, Charles E., Jr. *INCOME TAX POLICY FOR THE RUSSIAN REPUBLIC*. Stanford, CA: Hoover Institution on War, Revolution and Peace, 1991. 17 pp.

Secession

Secrecy

☆Kondrashov, Stanislav. "Out of the Darkness of Ignorance: Glimmers of *Glasnost'* in the Kingdom of Military Secrets", 29 *SOVIET LAW AND GOVERNMENT* No. 4, 21-77 (Spring 1991).

Secret Police

Self-Determination

Shipping

Social Conditions

Jones, Anthony, Walter D. Connor, and David E. Powell, eds. *SOVIET SOCIAL PROBLEMS*. Boulder, CO; San Franciso; Oxford: Westview Press, 1991. ix, 337 pp.

Social Justice

Mason, David S., and Svetlana Sydorenko. "Perestroyka, Social Justice, and Soviet Public Opinion", 39 *PROBLEMS OF COMMUNISM* No. 6, 34-43 (November-December 1990).

☆Piasheva, Larissa. *IN PURSUIT OF SOCIAL JUSTICE*. Moscow: Progress Publishers, 1991. 303 pp.

Social Security

☆Yakushev, L.P. "New Approaches to Social Security Provision in the USSR", 130 *INTERNATIONAL LABOUR REVIEW* 329-337 (1991).

Sovereignty

See Baltic,
Nationalities and Nationalism, *and*
Space Law

Soviet Union (in general)

See General Studies

Space Law

Goldstein, Gordon. "Anti-Satellite Weapons and U.S. National Security", 22 *NEW YORK UNIVERSITY JOURNAL OF INTERNATIONAL LAW AND POLITICS* 519-555 (1990).

☆Kamenetskaya, Elena P. "International Space Law: New Institutional Opportunities", in *PERESTROIKA AND INTERNATIONAL LAW: CURRENT ANGLO-SOVIET APPROACHES TO INTERNATIONAL LAW,* edited by Anthony Carty and Gennady Danilenko (Edinburgh: Edinburg University Press, 1990), pp. 172-183.

"Symposium on U.S.-Soviet Military and Economic Relations", 22 *NEW YORK UNIVERSITY JOURNAL OF INTERNATIONAL LAW AND POLITICS* 373-595 (1990).

☆Vereshchetin, Vladlen S. "International Control and the Concept of 'Open Skies'", in *FROM COEXISTENCE TO COOPERATION: INTERNATIONAL LAW AND ORGANIZATION IN THE POST-COLD WAR ERA,* edited by Edward McWhinney, et al. (Dordrecht, The Netherlands: Martinus Nijhoff Publishers, 1991), pp. 31-43.

☆Vereshchetin, Vladlen S. "'Open Skies'—The Metamorphoses of One Concept", in *CONTROL OVER COMPLIANCE WITH INTERNATIONAL LAW,* edited by William E. Butler (Dordrecht, The Netherlands: Martinus Nijhoff Publishers, 1991), pp. 41-50.

Stalinist Terror

Berliner, Rochelle S. "The Disappearance of Raoul Wallenberg: A Resolution Is Possible" (Note), 11 *NEW YORK LAW SCHOOL JOURNAL OF INTERNATIONAL AND COMPARATIVE LAW* 381-432 (1990).

Conquest, Robert. *STALIN: BREAKER OF NATIONS*. New York: Viking, 1991. 346 pp.

Kuromiya, Hiroaki. "Stalinist Terror in the Donbas: A Note", 50 *Slavic Review* 157-162 (1991).

Paul, Allen. *KATYN: THE UNTOLD STORY OF STALIN'S POLISH MASSACRE*. New York: Charles Scribner's Sons, 1991. 380 pp.

Tucker, Robert C. *STALIN IN POWER: THE REVOLUTION FROM ABOVE, 1928-1941*. New York: Norton, 1990. xix, 707 pp.

Vaksberg, Arkadii. *STALIN'S PROSECUTOR: THE LIFE OF ANDRE VYSHINSKY*. New York; London: Weidenfeld, 1990. xi, 374 pp.

☆Volkogonov, Dmitri. *STALIN: TRIUMPH AND TRAGEDY*. New York; London: Weidenfeld, 1991.

State Control

See Internal Control

Statistics

Pockney, B.P. *SOVIET STATISTICS SINCE 1950*. New York: St. Martin's Press, 1991. xviii, 333 pp.

Surveillance

See Internal Control

Survey of Soviet Law

See General Studies

Taxation

Augustyn, Francene M. "Foreign Investment in the Soviet Union: The Dawning of a New Era", 2 *TAX NOTES INTERNATIONAL* 1115-1120 (November 1990).

George, Arthur L., and Thomas A. O'Donnell. *BUSINESS OPERATIONS IN THE U.S.S.R.* Washington, DC: Tax Management, Inc., 1991 (Tax Management, Foreign Income Portfolios, 990).

George, Arthur L., and Thomas A. O'Donnell. "The New Soviet Tax System: Moving into the Modern Age, with Growing Pains", 3 *TAX NOTES INTERNATIONAL* 499-502 (May 1991).

George, Arthur L., and Thomas A. O'Donnell. "United States-Soviet Joint Ventures", 20 *TAX MANAGEMENT INTERNATIONAL JOURNAL* 73-85 and 99-114 (1991).

Hogan, James E. "New Tax and Companies Legislation in the USSR", 16 *REVIEW OF SOCIALIST LAW* 351-362 (1990).

International Chamber of Commerce. *FOREIGN INVESTMENT IN THE USSR. KEY 1990 LEGISLATION.* Paris: ICC Publications, 1991.

Kuiper, W.G. "New Corporate Tax System Introduced", 30 *EUROPEAN TAXATION* 275-286 (1990).

Maisto, G. "Double Taxation Treaty Italy-USSR with Particular Reference to Joint Ventures", 29 *EUROPEAN TAXATION* 113-119 (1989).

McLure, Charles E., Jr. *INCOME TAX POLICY FOR THE RUSSIAN REPUBLIC.* Stanford, CA: Hoover Institution on War, Revolution and Peace, 1991. 17 pp.

☆Milchakova, Natalia G. "An Examination of the New Soviet Income Tax on Individuals", 3 *TAX NOTES INTERNATIONAL* 237-243 (March 1991).

Newcity, Michael. *SOVIET TAXATION: STATUTES, REGULATIONS, AND TREATIES.* Ardsley-on-Hudson, NY: Transnational Juris Publications, Inc., 1991. Looseleaf.

Newcity, Michael. "Tax Considerations in Foreign Trade and Investment in the USSR", 24 *VANDERBILT JOURNAL OF TRANSNATIONAL LAW* 235-267 (1991).

TAXATION, *continued*

Newcity, Michael. "Tax Issues in Soviet Joint Ventures", 25 *TEXAS INTERNATIONAL LAW JOURNAL* 163-207 (1990).

Schneider, Richard C., Jr. "Tax, Investment, and Financing Issues in Projects in the USSR and Eastern Europe", in *LEGAL ASPECTS OF TRADE AND INVESTMENT IN THE SOVIET UNION AND EASTERN EUROPE* (New York: Practising Law Institute, 1990), pp. 235-295.

Turro, John. "Soviet Union Adopts New Tax System", 2 *TAX NOTES INTERNATIONAL* 793-796 (August 1990).

Technology

See Computerization, *and*
Foreign Trade—Technology Transfer

Telecommunications and Television

Bazyler, Michael J., and Eugene Sadovoy. "Television and the Law in the Soviet Union", 11 *LOYOLA ENTERTAINMENT JOURNAL* 293-351 (1991).

Goldstein, Irving. "Telecommunications in the Soviet Union", 5 *JOURNAL OF LAW AND TECHNOLOGY* 21-23 (Winter 1990).

Television

See Telecommunications and Television

Terror

See Stalinist Terror

Trade Unions

See Labor and Labor Law

Trademarks

See Patents and Trademarks

Translations

See Laws and Official Documents in English Translation

Ukraine

☆Balkina, M.A., ed. *NEW POLITICAL PARTIES AND MOVEMENTS IN THE SOVIET UNION*. Commack, N.Y.: Nova Science Publishers, Inc., 1991. 156 pp.

Blaustein, Albert P., ed. *CONSTITUTIONS OF DEPENDENCIES AND SPECIAL SOVEREIGNTIES*. Dobbs Ferry, NY: Oceana Publications, 1977- .

Bociurkiw, R. Bohdan. "The Ukrainian Catholic Church in the USSR under Gorbachev", 39 *PROBLEMS OF COMMUNISM* No. 6, 1-19 (November-December, 1990).

Commission on Security and Cooperation in Europe. *ELECTIONS IN THE BALTIC STATES AND SOVIET REPUBLICS: A COMPENDIUM OF REPORTS ON PARLIAMENTARY ELECTIONS HELD IN 1990*. Compiled by the Staff of the Commission on Security and Cooperation in Europe. Washington: U.S. Government Printing Office, 1990. x, 188 pp.

Davis, Nathaniel. "The Number of Churches before and after the Khrushchev Antireligious Drive", 50 *SLAVIC REVIEW* 612-620 (1991).

Furtado, Charles F., Jr., and Andrea Chandler. *PERESTROIKA IN THE SOVIET REPUBLICS: DOCUMENTS ON THE NATIONAL QUESTION*. Boulder, CO: Westview Press, 1992. xxvi, 646 pp.

LEGAL AND PRACTICAL ASPECTS OF DOING BUSINESS IN THE SOVIET REPUBLICS. Commercial Law and Practice Course Handbook Series No. 604. New York: Practising Law Institute, 1992. 500 pp.

Marples, David R. "The Greening of Ukraine: Ecology and the Emergence of *Zelenyi svit*, 1986-1990", in *PERESTROIKA FROM BELOW: SOCIAL MOVEMENTS IN THE SOVIET UNION*, edited by Judith B. Sedaitis and Jim Butterfield (Boulder, CO: Westview Press, 1991), pp. 133-144.

UKRAINE, *continued*

Nahaylo, Bohdan. "Baltic Echoes in Ukraine", in *TOWARD INDEPENDENCE: THE BALTIC POPULAR MOVEMENTS,* edited by Jan Arveds Trapans (Boulder, CO; San Francisco; Oxford: Westview Press, 1991), pp. 108-122.

Palmer, Matthew S.R. "Privatization in Ukraine: Economics, Law, and Politics", 16 *YALE JOURNAL OF INTERNATIONAL LAW* 453-517 (1991).

Potichnyi, Peter J. *THE MULTI-PARTY SYSTEM IN UKRAINE.* Cologne: Bundesinstitut für ostwissenschaftliche und internationale Studien, 1992. iii, 39 pp. (Report 3-1992).

Solchanyk, Roman. "Ukraine, Belorussia, and Moldavia: Imperial Integration, Russification, and the Struggle for National Survival", in *THE NATIONALITIES FACTOR IN SOVIET POLITICS AND SOCIETY,* edited by Lubomyr Hajda and Mark Beissinger (Boulder, CO: Westview Press, 1990), pp. 175-203.

Uzbekistan

Carlisle, Donald S. "Uzbekistan and the Uzbeks", 40 *PROBLEMS OF COMMUNISM* No. 5, 23-44 (Sept.-Oct. 1991).

Critchlow, James. "'Corruption', Nationalism, and the Native Elites in Soviet Central Asia", 4 *JOURNAL OF COMMUNIST STUDIES* 142-159 (1988).

LEGAL AND PRACTICAL ASPECTS OF DOING BUSINESS IN THE SOVIET REPUBLICS. Commercial Law and Practice Course Handbook Series No. 604. New York: Practising Law Institute, 1992. 500 pp.

Vyshinsky

Vaksberg, Arkadii. *STALIN'S PROSECUTOR: THE LIFE OF ANDRE VYSHINSKY.* New York; London: Weidenfeld, 1990. xi, 374 pp.

War Crimes

Ginsburgs, George, and Vladimir Kudryavtsev, eds. *THE NUREMBERG TRIAL AND INTERNATIONAL LAW.* Dordrecht, The Netherlands: Martinus Nijhoff, 1990. xvi, 288 pp. (Law in Eastern Europe No. 42).

Water

See Environmental Law and Policy